DATE DUE

RIVERSIDE COMMUNITY COLLEGE
LIBRARY
Riverside, California

EXERCISE TIGER

THE DRAMATIC TRUE STORY OF A HIDDEN TRAGEDY OF WORLD WAR II

Nigel Lewis

PRENTICE
HALL
PRESS

New York   London   Toronto   Sydney   Tokyo   Singapore

"Oh, What a Beautiful Morning"
Author: Oscar Hammerstein II
Composer: Richard Rodgers
© 1943 Williamson Music Inc.
Reproduced by permission of Williamson Music Inc.
and Chappel Music Ltd

PRENTICE HALL PRESS
15 Columbus Circle
New York, NY 10023

Originally published in Great Britain by Viking Penguin Inc.

PRENTICE HALL PRESS and colophons are registered trademarks
of Simon & Schuster, Inc.

LC No. 90–7422

ISBN 0-13-127796-0

Designed by Richard Oriolo

Manufactured in the United States of America

10 9 8 7 6 5 4 3 2 1

First Prentice Hall Press Edition

*For all who suffered in and because
of Exercise Tiger. Then and since.
And now.*

ACKNOWLEDGMENTS

When I first started on this book I was for some reason under the impression that the survivors of Convoy T-4 had done little or nothing to trace one another and pool their memories. I had the idea that it wasn't only the United States that had unaccountably forgotten this episode in its history, but that the individual Americans involved in it had also contrived, somehow, collectively to forget. How mistaken I was. Before long I would be echoing Jeanne Porado, sister of a sailor who died on T-4, who wrote to Dale Rodman (March 28, 1988): "What a wonderful network of communication you survivors must have."

For a writer this network reaching out across the United States was invaluable, providing the makings of a vivid and vital history as told by the men themselves. It was almost as though, in the absence of a recorded history, they had been waiting for someone to come along and had been holding their stories in their minds for forty years in readiness for just that purpose. But that is, of course, fanciful: How could they have forgotten? Their individual stories had survived well enough, and survived, usually, with a haunting detail and intensity of vision. That intensity was not, however, without its drawbacks. As survivor Tom Clark has written to me (April 8, 1988): "Participants have such a limited view. Their impressions are responsive only to that very limited area—the finite point of space and time in which they existed." The intensity was a function of the "limited view"; it still remained to master and to tell "the whole story."

Out of the network of individual stories grew the story as a whole. There was something a little miraculous about this. The distance in time seemed to melt away in the intense concentration upon two days in April 1944, as the lens of memory zoomed in on a missing shoe, a tetanus shot, a prayer. Distances in space, too—the wide open spaces of the United States—seemed to melt against the shared memory of that "finite point of space" in the English Channel and upon its shore. For example, someone in Illinois would have one half of a particular memory; the other half, like the torn-off half of a telegram, might be in the mind of someone in Texas or New York or California. The story as a whole was scattered throughout the United States and England, awaiting reconstruction. But without the network of survivors, reconstruction would have been impossible. The tale—which more than anyone else's is their tale—could not have been told.

The cooperation and active help of the survivors lies behind this book, and as its author most of my thanks are due equally to them. It has been an honor to have dealt with these men, whose generosity has been the sign of an unbroken spirit. I will long remember their dignity and good humor, their stoical acceptance of experience. As someone who was not so much as born in 1944 (and an Englishman at that), I am proud that they entrusted me with their memories, and hope that I in return have honored their trust.

Most of all, perhaps, I will remember their sense of undying comradeship with both the living and dead. Arthur Victor, for example, wrote to me (in a letter of October 19, 1988): "I can hardly wait till my buddies and I are reunited and we can be kids again, somewhere in God's world, wherever it takes us." He had, I think, more than a veterans' reunion in mind.

So many people helped me so generously that I cannot list them all here. They are listed in a separate appendix (see p. 287) or among the footnotes. But some I must single out as having helped me not only with their corner of the story, but with the story as a whole.

First among them must be Dr. Eugene Eckstam of Wisconsin and Dale Rodman of California. Dr. Eckstam unstintingly opened his archive to me and, in the form of computer printouts, gave me access to the entire network of survivors—a network of which he, with Floyd Hicks (formerly of *LST 515*), was one of the chief architects. Dale Rodman passed on to me numerous papers and pieces of information, as well as his own research into the question of fatalities, without which Chapter Seventeen could not have been written in its present form.

From them and all the survivors I learned about the psychology of survival and memory, and in particular how, for survival in the fullest sense, it is necessary to grasp what exactly it is that has been survived. Their stories were backed up by documents from archives and documents of their own. Tom Clark sent me a letter he had written to his father in July 1944 and pages of a novel he had started about Exercise Tiger; Arthur Victor, under the danger of court martial, had written down his memories while still a teenager; Joseph McCann's memories of war were like something out of Homer; Angelo Crapanzano showed me that physical courage and great sensitivity are not incompatible. Closer to home, my home anyway, Manny Rubin told me much about Exercise Tiger and took me to see Plymouth Argyle play Manchester City. He was also kind enough to correct some of my misapprehensions about the *LST*. He and many other veterans and survivors provided photographs. Walter Trombold, skipper of *LST 55*, provided photographs of Exercise Tiger taken at the time with his own camera.

Alma Taft in Plymouth, Harry Unsworth in Newton Abbot, and Pat Nettleton of the South Hams District Council in Totnes were helpful in answering my inquiries, as were John Hockaday and J. R. Cranny in Dorset. Patrick Culley of the U.S. Embassy in London patiently passed on my inquiries to the United States. Thanks are due also to reporters on the newspapers of the West Country press, which remain among the best in England. Pierre Verniquet of East Allington gave me invaluable help in the South Hams. Billy V. Balch of the American Legion, and Winston and Gordon Ramsay of *After the Battle,* helped with military inquiries.

My first investigations into Exercise Tiger came from a commission by the Canadian Broadcasting Corporation's radio network editor in London, Judith Melby, who happily thought of the same program idea at the same time as I did. That was in September 1987. That November I did a program for BBC Radio 4 called *Large Slow Target,* produced by Gaynor Shutte and narrated by Leslie Thomas. My first archival research was in the Ministry of Defense archives in the Empress State Building, Fulham. There Arnold Hague was most helpful as, later, were numerous archivists in the United States and Mr. Culley of the U.S. Embassy in London. Other corners of the American archives were explored by Howard DeVoe of New York, who also occasionally provided refreshing blasts of common sense and military know-how. Perhaps this book will aid him in his mission to alter the wording of the memorial plaque at Torcross.

Thank you to my exemplary editors at Penguin, Marilyn Warnick and Jonathan Riley, and my text editor, Barbara Horn. Thanks, too, for their encouragement and enthusiasm, to my friends Kit Wright, Stephen Beard, and Felix Pryor; and, of course, to Susan, for living with me through what was at times an exhausting experience.

I should add a note on ranks. I decided early on that I would not automatically give the rank of every soldier and sailor who appears in this story. The American forces list their ranks in a complicated and, to my mind, rather ugly way. There are already numbers and initials enough in the story and a comprehensive giving of ranks would have made my pages bristle forbiddingly. I therefore confined myself to giving a man's rank and station where it seemed to me relevant in the story to do so.

Likewise I have not gone into slavish detail about the potentially sensitive matter of military decorations. There would have been too many of them and, anyway, the man whom all the survivors say should have got a medal that night, John Doyle, didn't. I would wish rather to draw attention on their behalf to that omission than to the many cases where gallantry was recognized.

I hope that others who helped me will understand why, for reasons of space, I have omitted them here; if there are any I have inadvertently omitted, I apologize, although I think they will probably find their names elsewhere in this text. I should conclude by saying that despite my indebtedness to so many people I remain as sole author solely responsible for the final text.

I have not, however, studied the primary source material given in Appendix II. This is additional material provided by Dr. Ralph Greene of Chicago. Dr. Greene has played a special role in this story—a role deserving of special recognition and acknowledgment. In April 1944 he was one of the doctors who in a "weird vacuum" worked on the wounded of Convoy T-4. In December 1982, in the course of other research, he accidentally again found himself in another version of that vacuum—the inexplicable neglect of the Tiger story since the war. He thus became, in 1983, the first person who had in some way been involved in the incident to start to research it in some depth.

Without these researches by Ralph Greene the TVS documentary of January 1984 would not have been possible in the form that it took; the TVS documentary, in turn, lay behind the ABC *20/20* special, in which Dr. Greene also participated; and without *20/20,* the sophisticated "network" of survivors would not have evolved as rapidly as it did. (The story is told in Chapters Fourteen and Fifteen.) There is a very real sense in which Dr. Greene's solitary initiative and persistence brought the story to light. He deserves the gratitude of the survivors and, more widely, the respect of historians for his work in unearthing and bringing to popular attention this hitherto hidden and neglected episode of the wartime history of the United States.

—NIGEL LEWIS
London, 1988

Contents

I

BOLERO   1

II

TIGER   39

III

THE BURIAL GROUND   151

IV

"THE FIELD WHERE THE
SOLDIERS ARE . . ."   217

Postscript   251

Notes and References   263

Bibliography   283

Appendix I   289

Appendix II   293

Index   295

I

BOLERO

CHAPTER
1

There will be no needless loss of life in the American Army in World War II if the orders and plans of our High Command are carried out. No postwar poet will sing a new "Charge of the Light Brigade," paying tribute to some sentimentally heroic but foolishly sacrificial exploit. No "noble six hundred" will charge unprotected from the guns.[1]

That confident prediction was made in an April 1944 issue of the magazine *Liberty,* and it fairly reflects both a deep American anxiety of the time and the confidence, or hope, that it would prove to be unfounded. In 1939 the United States had a regular army of only 190,000 men; by the end of the war it would be 8.5 million. Over the second half of 1943 and first half of 1944, the D Day buildup period in which this story opens, new American soldiers, sailors, and airmen were pouring into Britain in the thousands every week, to make a total of some 1.6 million British-based American troops by the eve of the Normandy invasion. A vast quantity of American life was being committed to the crucible of the war in northwest Europe and the Second Front, which Russia, to relieve the pressure upon itself, had asked the western Allies to open against Germany. Every one of those hundreds of thousands of men had family, friends, or sweethearts back home; naturally there was unease, and some reassurance was in order.

Thus there were articles like the one in *Liberty,* which went on to be reassuring about the American Army's chief of staff, General George C. Marshall. He took the view, the article said, that "soldiers should live, and avoiding losses to personnel is a most important rule of combat." In the first half of 1944 *Time*,[2] *Life*,[3] and *Newsweek*[4] carried profiles of "the Doughboy's General," Omar Bradley, commander of the U.S. Army in northwest Europe. "Most of them," Bradley noted, "stressed that I valued the lives of my soldiers and would not spend them recklessly."[5] In December 1943 General Dwight D. Eisenhower had been appointed Supreme Commander of the Allied Expeditionary Force—American public opinion would not have countenanced a non-American appointment. Eisenhower's attitude was that his relationship with the American soldier was "sacred."[6]

In the United States there was patriotism and even enthusiasm for the war. There was scarcely a house that did not display the flag of one of the services, meaning a husband, brother, father or, most commonly, son was serving in it. But there were houses, too, in whose windows gold stars and the words "Gold Star Mother" were displayed, meaning a life lost, perhaps in the Pacific Ocean campaign against Japan, or in the North African or Italian campaigns of 1942–43. More gold stars—many more—could be expected from the opening of the Second Front; but America had the word of its military leaders that deaths would be kept to the minimum possible in war.

There would be no unnecessary, wasteful, superficially glorious heroics of the kind that seemed to abound in the military histories of the European countries. No "noble six hundred" would ride, as in Tennyson's poem about the charge of the Light Brigade, "into the valley of death." The war would be won by an overwhelming preponderance of hardware and manpower; scientifically, as in a surgical operation, Nazism would be cut from Europe like a cancer, with as little blood loss as possible.

So strong was this antiheroic impulse that George S. Patton, for one, considered America to have erred in the opposite direction. He would write that it was to him a tragic fact "that in our attempts to prevent war, we have taught our people to belittle the heroic qualities of the soldier."[7] The burden of the *Liberty* article was that there would be no need to remember sentimental heroics or foolish sacrifices after the war because there weren't going to *be* any.

But at the end of the same month as *Liberty*'s prediction, there would be arguably the most needless large-scale loss of American life in the Second World War. It would be an episode of foolish, if unintentional, sacrifice and not a little sentimental heroism. It is hard to assess the relative needlessness of lives lost, but if poignancy and futility are factors, then they weigh heavily here. In a few hours of one April night hundreds of men would die in what was not even a real military engagement, but a *practice,* a dress rehearsal for D Day. They would die carrying out ''the orders and plans'' of their High Command, and many would die because they were carrying out those orders in deadly detail. They would die ''unprotected from the guns'' in what General Bradley, when he first heard the story—five years later— would call ''one of the major tragedies of the European war.''[8]

Liberty's prediction—and its timing—could not have been more wrong. In one thing, however, it was exactly right: no postwar poet *would* sing of the victims of Exercise Tiger. More than that, America would almost utterly forget them for forty years.

CHAPTER
2

Rarely can a Member of Parliament have had to represent his constituents in circumstances as bizarre, distressing, and constricting as those that were first outlined to Colonel Ralph Rayner in "a most secret letter" of September 1943.[1]

Colonel Rayner, a serving army officer, was also the wartime member for the town of Totnes, South Devon. On both banks of the River Dart, Totnes was the point nearest to the estuary and sea at which the Dart was bridged. Its biggest employer in those war years was Curtis Shipbuilders, whose yards were then assembling landing craft for the invasion. The letter was not directly about Totnes, however, but about part of another, and in English terms fairly remote, region within the Totnes constituency, called the South Hams.

The South Hams was a sleepy, deeply rural collection of parishes to the west and south of the Dart, most of them on the horn of land that juts southward from South Devon into the English Channel. Its geographical placing was the clue to its relative remoteness. From the east, the only direct routes to it were by ferry across the Dart from Kingswear or, further north, by the Totnes bridge; the railway ran along its northern edge, with a single branch line to Kingsbridge on another estuary to the west. If South Devon was a backwater of England, then the South Hams was, in turn, a backwater of Devon, touched lightly by modern life and barely at all by the war.

Until at least the end of the First World War people would say of the area that it was a hundred years behind the times. Then many of the narrow, winding lanes flanked by high hedgerows were paved over, and cars and vans started to replace horses and the horse-drawn carriages of the tradesmen, or "carriers," who took produce, passengers, and news to and from the farms and villages. Even in 1943 many of the cob cottages—so called from the "cob" mixture of clay, straw, and granite from which they were built—had no electricity, running

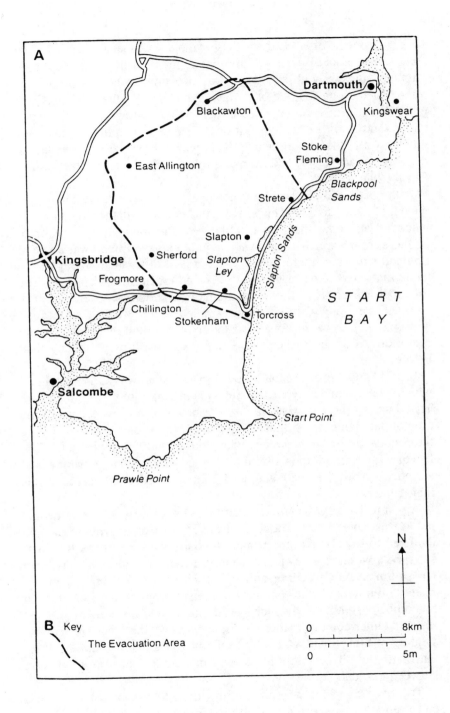

A

Dartmouth

Kingswear

Blackawton

Stoke
Fleming

East Allington

*Blackpool
Sands*

Strete

*Slapton
Sands*

Slapton

Sherford

*Slapton
Ley*

Kingsbridge

Frogmore

S T A R T

Chillington

B A Y

Stokenham

Torcross

Salcombe

Start Point

Prawle Point

N

B Key

The Evacuation Area

0   8km

0   5m

7

water, or flush toilet. Life in these villages was a mixture of rural backwardness and rural idyll. In winter, fires burning in the cottages wreathed the air with wood smoke. In summer there were village fêtes like the one that Colonel Rayner had visited that June. "Great trees," he later recalled, "cast their vast shadows upon little tea tables, and from the branches of one of them an amplifier relayed the music of a hidden gramophone. This was almost the only indication that the year was 1943, for the church had stood there since Elizabethan days."[2]

If the pace of life was slow, however, it was not lazy. There was plenty of work to do. The sea off the coastal villages was rich in mackerel and other fish; on the Skerries, the sandbank a mile or so offshore from Torcross, were ancient mussel beds. Inland was some of England's most fertile farmland, and herds of the reddish South Devon cattle that gave some of the best milk and cream in the country. The principal war effort of the South Hams in a period of severe shortage and strict rationing was to produce as much, and to waste as little, food as possible. The war meant an escalation of the usual rural industry and parsimony. For the farmers, the war also meant more money than before.

In 1943 about every second food ship to Britain was carrying wheat, which grew abundantly in the South Hams as elsewhere in Devon. That January the *Kingsbridge Gazette* had said that wheat was "the crop of paramount importance, and great credit is due to the farmers in the county for the large acreage which has already been planted." The Devon War Agricultural Committee had concluded that "spring wheat varieties—April Bearded and Red Marvel—produced larger yields than winter."[3]

Again in January the *Gazette* carried a leading article urging people not to waste bread.[4] This double refrain of the need to grow wheat and the need to save bread ran through the daily wartime life of the area. In April a woman, an evacuee from elsewhere in England, was fined ten shillings after pleading guilty to a charge of wasting "approximately four and a half pounds of bread scraps which she left in Salcombe post office and which she admitted she was taking to feed her pigs."[5] Other country matters in the local news that year were rabbit stealing in Stokenham,[6] "flabby beef" in Blackawton,[7] and a calf let out of its field by careless blackberry pickers and hurt in a collision between two cars.[8]

The war was a long way off. In the village fête month of June there had been what the *Gazette* called a "temporary excitement" when a German aircraft was shot down and crashed in the South Hams.[9] In

August the paper reported that the Devon regiment was engaged in "some of the most fierce and bitter fighting of the Sicilian campaign."[10] Most inhabitants of the South Hams had never been anywhere as near as the Scilly Isles, let alone the island of Sicily.

Then in late September the sea gave up a specific omen of the devastating change and violence waiting in the wings; compared to what would come the image seems almost peaceful. West of Start Bay the body of a man was washed up on Bantham Beach, where it lay on the sand just below the high-water mark. It must have been in terrible shape. The police surgeon, Dr. Verniquet, examined it in Kingsbridge Mortuary and concluded it to be the body of a man of about thirty, who had been in the sea from three to six months. Dr. Verniquet found a flesh wound in the arm and a bullet wound in the head, "which had been the cause of death."[11] One assumes—although no opinion was offered—that he had died in the war.

Within a week of that macabre discovery Colonel Rayner had received his "most secret" letter from the First Lord of the Admiralty. It told him that some twenty-five square miles of the South Hams, or 30,000 farming acres, were being requisitioned under the 1939 War Powers Act for the training of American troops. The 3,000 people in this lightly populated area were to be moved before Christmas, taking with them their movable possessions, their pets, and their livestock and equipment if they were farmers, to make way for the Americans. Eight villages of the South Hams and their surrounding farmland were to become the setting for what the *Gazette* would call "the American Army Battle School."

After his first shock, the M.P.'s reaction was incredulity that the government could think of surrendering so much rich farmland for war games. There were 180 farms in the area. What about the "paramount" wheat crop? And what about the area's inhabitants, his constituents? Many were old people who had lived all their lives in the same cottage. Others were tenant farmers who had worked through the bad years to build up their farms. All were deeply rooted country people who would find uprooting an especially brutal experience to bear. And where would they go?

Rayner went at once to London, where he "interviewed all the ministers and authorities concerned and lodged the strongest protest." In ordinary circumstances the practice would have been for him to lobby other M.P.s in nearby West Country constituencies, and to gain their backing. But in this period of war "the question was so secret" that he was forbidden to do that. He had to content himself with a promise that his protest would be put to the War Cabinet, which would decide. In the meantime only Rayner knew of the letter from the Admiralty, whose contents he could not divulge.

The decision had been made, however; there could be no question of the War Cabinet reversing it. That autumn was a rainy one. One damp day in late October a deputation of men in suits turned up in the village of Blackawton near the northern corner of the proposed evacuation area. They went around the village school, taking notes, and looked into the fourteenth-century church. Then they drove to Stokenham for a look at the village hall there. Someone recognized among them an official of the Kingsbridge Rural District Council. Rumors began circulating. One suggested that more soldiers were to be drafted into the area. A man remembered 1938, when Montgomery had held a landing exercise on the South Hams beach of Slapton Sands, and wondered whether soldiers were coming "to practice landings again."[12]

On November 4 Sir John Daw, chairman of the Devon County Council, was telephoned by the War Cabinet. The area was to be evacuated totally by December 20—in just over six weeks. Now the machinery of the evacuation was put into gear. On November 8 the Regional Commissioner, Sir Hugh Elles, held two meetings at Exeter Castle. The first was with local councils and groups of helpers like the Women's Voluntary Service (WVS),* the Royal Society for the Prevention of Cruelty to Animals (RSPCA), and the Red Cross. At this meeting Sir John Daw objected that there was insufficient transport and—a theme that would be taken up by Ralph Rayner—that the terms of compensation of the 1939 War Powers Act didn't match the scale of the sacrifice that this South Hams area was being asked to make. At the second meeting that day the area's clergy were given the news and asked to use their discretion as to which, if any, parishioners they chose to tell before the official announcement.

That came four days later, on the bitterly cold morning of November 12, when hastily convened meetings were held in the villages of East Allington and Stokenham. The East Allington meeting was chaired by the Lord Lieutenant of Devon, Lord Fortescue, whose family name had for centuries been identified with the village and with the area's history. A Fortescue had fought on the Royalist side in the Civil War, and the family lived in Falkpit House near East Ellington, where there was, and still is, a pub called The Fortescue Arms. The previous June, Lord Fortescue had learned of the death in battle of his only son and

---

*There would be 156 WVS helpers, the most important of the people and groups involved in the evacuation.

heir, Viscount Ebrington. The day before the meetings there had been the annual Armistice service for the war dead.

Now he had to tell the villagers and farmers of the mass eviction, "the greatest upheaval," as local historian Grace Bradbeer would call it: "the biggest disturbance that this part of the South Hams had ever known."[13] It was an edict as starkly cruel and seemingly arbitrary as one handed down by a wicked king in a fairy or folk tale. At the same time, 9:30 A.M., Sir Hugh Elles was delivering the same astounding message in Victory Hall, the village hall of Stokenham on the southern edge of the designated area.

Mrs. Nancy Hare was one of thirty WVS members at that Stokenham meeting, which was to be followed by similar meetings in Blackawton and Slapton. From Stokenham, she remembered,

> We drove through a maze of narrow lanes to reach Blackawton's school, a stone's throw from a lovely old Norman church, with a glorious view of Slapton valley to the sea. It seemed almost impossible to believe that within a few weeks the land would be barren and not a living soul, man or beast, would exist there. The Admiralty Lands' Officer had fixed his big map on the wall at the far end of the room. Representatives of the Ministries of Food and Power, Health, Labor and Transport soon arrived.[14]

Presumably the earlier deputation had reported back that Blackawton school would make a suitable local command post for the evacuation.

Mrs. Hare's account continues:

> A parish meeting was arranged to be held in the church at 11:30 A.M. the next day. The biggest congregation it had ever contained filled the old church to capacity. Seated with their backs to the magnificent screen were the Bishop of Exeter, the Regional Commissioner, an American general, the chairman of the Devon County Council, a high-ranking Royal Navy officer, the WVS county organizer, and many others. The Bishop opened the meeting with a prayer, and the Regional Commissioner spoke sympathetically of what was going to happen, of the greatness of the sacrifice and the amount of help to be given to everyone. The general and the Admiralty explained their needs . . .

The news came as a tremendous shock. Thirty years later one man told Grace Bradbeer of his wife's reaction, that "she did cry and grieved terrible about it, but 'twas no use grieving."[15] This was the general response: shock followed by a numbed, philosophical acceptance. A man told his son, "If it'll help our chaps out there fighting for us, then us 'ave got to go."[16] Eddie Bowles, then a schoolboy of eleven, said that before the announcement his sister Margaret had come home one day with the groceries and a report of rumors that there was going to be an evacuation: "My mum said 'Don't be so stupid.' We thought it would be impossible to move a village like this." But then, when the news came out: "We had to get out—it was just accepted. . . . Everyone just got on with it."[17] Much the same reaction came forty years later at a 1984 reunion of evacuees organized by the South Hams District Council. One of them recalled, "We knew we had to do it. Everybody mucked in."[18] Godfrey Wills, a thirty-five-year-old farmer in 1943, recalled:

> We just took things as they came then. There was a war on and we expected anything to happen. Everyone just got down to it and tried to put their own house in order. We didn't know about any plans for the evacuation until they told us. It was a surprise. It was difficult leaving because we had to get somewhere to live. And the trouble was that everyone was looking for a place.[19]

For some, though, the shock and desolation of the move were more than a matter of massive inconvenience or mental scarring. That was extensive enough; young children were traumatized by the sudden uprooting, and other people were upset to know in their bones that a time of their lives was over, they would not return to the South Hams.* But for the elderly it was particularly hard. Bradbeer records an old man who committed suicide, a woman who had a heart attack on her own doorstep and died, and an old married couple who would fall ill, fade away, and die within a fortnight of moving.[20]

Formal requisition of the area was on November 16; the countdown had begun to the evacuation deadline only thirty-five days away. An army of voluntary helpers descended upon the eight villages and their outlying farms. Their work was complicated by shortage of transport, gasoline, rationing, and the blackout. There were thousands of tasks to be done and queries large and small to be answered. Information centers were set up in Stokenham and Blackawton. Some families didn't know where they were going to go; a woman had no idea what to do about her twelve pet cats. (The RSPCA had to put many animals to sleep.)

Gradually the contents of whole houses were packed away in thousands of crates, boxes, and barrels provided by the WVS. At the same time the land was rapidly denuded, as farmers sold or moved their herds and took away their equipment and implements and even

---

*A list of surviving evacuees includes addresses in Bermuda and Zimbabwe.

the iron hurdle gates to their fields. Shops and pubs were closed down and—as in a transit camp—emergency kitchens in tents and vans dispensing hot meals took the place of the usual food supplies. An undated Ministry of Food pamphlet stated: ''Arrangements have been made with local Bakers for the supply of Bread to continue after Bakers in the Evacuation Area have closed down or removed elsewhere.''[21] Bread for villages inside the area was to be distributed by bakers from villages outside it, entering the area in clearly marked ''Ministry of Food bread vans.'' In the light of a much later, postwar development in this story, one of those vans should be singled out: the pamphlet specified that Blackawton's bread would be supplied by Mr. Trowt, a baker in Stoke Fleming just outside the area. The baker's daughter, Dorothy, who helped her father with his deliveries, would forty years later come forward with a story that one might construe as another and grisly variation upon the local preoccupation with wheat and bread.

But that story belongs further on. In the meantime the uprooting of the evacuation area continued. ''The spirit of these people,'' said Nancy Hare, ''was wonderful. They were so brave and cheerful. By the second week we had got into our stride. Gradually the smoke from the chimneys grew less and less, and driving through the villages was an eerie experience. Furniture vans loaded to capacity and farm lorries stacked with hay filled the lanes, and these, added to the American traffic which was beginning to filter into the area, made driving a dangerous business.''

By the close of the fourth week the voluntary workers were dealing largely with farmers, who had more goods and chattels to be moved and who wanted every available day for clearing their land of crops. One of them was Godfrey Wills: ''We were one of the last to leave because we had so much stuff to get rid of. It was pretty grim. There was no one about. Everything was deathly quiet. We had to use boxes to sit on because all the furniture had gone.''[22]

One ticklish problem of the evacuation concerned the local churches, which in five of the six parishes were pre-Restoration;* the Admiralty had said that their safety couldn't be guaranteed. A church sculptor was called in from Exeter, and with his foreman and an American officer he visited the churches in turn. He recommended that movable items like candlesticks and chalices be put in storage, and that pulpits, fonts, monuments, and so on be heavily sandbagged. The biggest

---

*Six parishes as against eight villages because the Stokenham church served also the villages of Torcross and Chillington. The church at Strete, on the coast, was nineteenth century.

worry was the wooden chancel screens, which are found in a number of Devon churches—"brittle as gingerbread, some of them," said the sculptor's foreman.[23] These were to be dismantled and packed in straw.

American soldiers arrived to help when two of the churches had already been emptied, sandbagged, locked, and surrounded with barbed wire, and when work on the third, Blackawton, had begun. The Blackawton church, consecrated in 1333, stood on a site where there was thought to have been Christian worship since Saxon times; thus, according to the church guidebook, the "black," meaning "holy," in the village's name. To the back of the church was a Norman font in red Torbay sandstone, carved with a honeysuckle decoration. It had been damaged in the seventeenth century by Puritan zealots, who had broken away the font's lid and lock to prevent superstitions about holy water.

The delicate and somewhat worm-eaten wooden chancel screen before the altar had also been imperiled in its history. On it were carved the initials of Henry VIII and his first wife, Catherine of Aragon; there were small paintings of Catherine's personal emblem, the pomegranate. It was thought originally to have been in a church at Plymouth, where Catherine landed from Spain, moved inland to Blackawton when Henry VIII dissolved the monasteries, and thereby, according to the guidebook, "saved from destruction by a bit of local cunning."

Now, in this new time of danger, an American sergeant noted the delicacy of the wood and remarked ruefully that he didn't think his men could be of much help: "They've been trained to do rougher work." According to Bradbeer, another sergeant strode purposefully into the church, chewing gum, and asked, "Where's Norman's font we hear so much about?"[24]

The Americans were coming to the South Hams; from the first week of December American officers anxious to see the evacuation deadline met were installed in Manor House at Dittisham. Soon, as Colonel Rayner would remark, the evacuation area would become, if only for the time being, as effectively "an American possession" as the U.S. Embassy in London.[25]

The uneasy sense of an ancient continuity precariously on loan to a fundamentally foreign soldiery emerges from the proclamation that, when each church had been evacuated, was pinned to its principal gate. It is worth giving in full:

To our Allies of the USA.
This church has stood here for several hundred years. Around it has grown

a community, which has lived in these houses and tilled these fields ever since there was a church. This church, this churchyard in which their loved ones lie at rest, these homes, these fields are as dear to those who have left them as are the homes and graves and fields which you, our Allies, have left behind you. They hope to return one day, as you hope to return to yours, to find them waiting to welcome them home. They entrust them to your care meanwhile, and pray that God's blessing may rest upon us all.

Charles,

Bishop of Exeter

Temporarily the churches—spiritual centers of Old World wheat fields—were at the mercy of men from the cornfields of the New. The Bishop's impassioned appeal suggests a precious thread of history, as delicate as gossamer or a chancel screen, which it was the semisacred trust of the Americans not to break. But as the American sergeant had remarked, his men had been "trained to do rougher work," and in the evacuation area the work they would be trained for would be rougher still.

Repeatedly during the evacuation, the minds of the evacuees were put at rest with assurances that their houses would be kept under lock and key and would not be entered by the Americans. Repeatedly, too, they were told how necessary their sacrifice was: Untried troops could not land in occupied Europe without some training at the "American Army Battle School" in what to expect. It would be "shameful to badger the authorities." Understandably, however, doubts remained, not least in the mind of Colonel Rayner, who, although the evacuation was now an established fact, had not given up fighting for his constituents.

The Colonel's view was that their sacrifice was harder in that it hadn't been enjoined upon them directly by the enemy, but by their Allies. "We require," he told the House of Commons on November 25, "that those unfortunate West Country folk who are being forced to hand over their hearths and homes at the stark call of duty . . . shall be most generously recompensed. It is hard enough to be hunted from one's farm by the enemy or blasted from one's home by his bombs, but it is a great deal harder to have to cut the ties of a lifetime in order to provide Allied Arms with a stage for the dress rehearsal."[26]

In December Colonel Rayner visited an old lady who had lived in the same South Hams cottage for sixty-three years. Her house was empty of belongings save for the rocking chair she sat on. She told him in a trembling voice that if she could save the lives of some of those American boys by moving she was glad to go.

The evacuation, with all its human turmoil, would have been the biggest local story in the *Kingsbridge Gazette*'s history, but the sacrifice of what would be referred to only anonymously as "an area of the southwest" was a secret to be played down.* The paper could print only a small and veiled reference to the evacuation on page 5 of its November 19 issue. The next piece of local publicity was a poster of December 11, which, again, has the unreal finality of a fairy tale proclamation: On December 21, the day after the deadline's expiry, the Admiralty could "at any time and without notice enforce their right to immediate possession." On that day the electricity would be turned off and "the present measures of supplying food will not be continued."

In that week the police stations were closed and their civil authority was supplanted by military sentries; all tradesmen were forbidden entry. On December 19 the *Gazette* reported (on page 3):

> This weekend should see the completion of the trek of the farmers and villagers in the southwest. It has been a terribly busy week for everyone on the move, but by Monday they are all expected to be in their new quarters. Some of their difficulties they will have to leave behind unsolved. . . .

The winter wheat was threshed and the threshing machines were hauled away. The wheat was put into sacks and taken, too, together with hastily baled hay. Before leaving, evacuees picked vegetables from their garden; those left behind were picked by the WVS. One curious detail: the rats, seeming to sense that man was on his way, had crept from their usual hiding places and come boldly out into the open. They added to the "unreal, slightly fantastic air"[27] of the evacuation area.

A sense of unreal fantasy was by no means uncommon in Britain at that period, when the old way of life was heavily dislocated by the vast and growing American presence. The buildup to D Day was awesome, but it was also very weird and alien, itself a sort of cultural invasion. The code name for this time of accumulation of men and stockpiling of equipment—Bolero, a flamboyant Spanish dance—was not as inappropriate as might at first appear. If there was nothing flamboyant about the ubiquitous olive drab of American uniforms, trucks, and other hardware, there was amazement at the sheer strangeness and

---

*The paper could continue to carry under its title the words "Circulating in Kingsbridge, Salcombe, Modbury and the whole of the South Hams District" after the evacuation had rendered them inaccurate.

scale of the thing as, in Eisenhower's words, "the southern portion of England became one vast camp, dump and airfield."[28]

The first significant American presence in Britain had begun as a relative trickle of men back in 1942, when the idea of opening a realistic second front was not much more than a gleam in the eye. It was in 1942, for example, that the Americans had come to the small South Devon town of Chudleigh Knighton. They were a detachment of engineers, part of the vast logistical "tail" that Montgomery told Churchill was so vital an element in modern warfare. Chudleigh Knighton, slightly inland but with easy access to the coast, was an ideal location for one of these backup supply units.

Among the engineers were the first black men that most of the local townspeople had ever set eyes on. They began putting up Nissen huts to store gasoline—each hut filled with a thousand or so four-gallon jerry cans. The men drank in the local pub, The Claycutter's Arms, whose landlord, Frank Coles, would later remember his astonishment on the night that the boxers Joe Louis and Jack Dempsey both walked in to drink there; Joe Louis, a sergeant in the American Army, gave wartime exhibition bouts in the nearby town of Bovey Tracy. Multiplied by their thousands, small encounters like those in The Claycutter's Arms would amount to a culture shock felt everywhere in Britain, but especially in the south and southwest.

Some encounters were more decisive. At the end of May 1943 U.S. soldiers in Britain still amounted to only a division—about 15,000 men, 30,000 with its "divisional slice" of backup troops. Soon after that, as the trickle of Americans into Britain began to become a flood, the 893d Tank Destroyer Battalion arrived in the South Devon town of Chudleigh. One of the battalion's tank drivers was Herbert Cannon, a twenty-five-year-old from Wisconsin. His unit was based in a camp in Holman's Woods on the slopes of Haldon Hill. Within months he had met and married a local girl, and in months after that, less than a year together, he was in Normandy. He survived the invasion but died in the Battle of the Bulge in December 1944. In 1948, at his widow's request, his remains were brought from a U.S. military cemetery in Belgium to Chudleigh, where they lie today in a grave facing Holman's Woods, where he trained. Local people still recall him as the young man who once crashed his tank into the side of a barn. More lastingly, his name is carved on the war memorial in Chudleigh town center.

Also in 1943 a massive American supply dump was set up near Bovey Tracey, and other American units pitched camp in woods and spinneys throughout the area. A black sergeant in the Engineers,

Charles Carpenter, befriended a local boy called Clifford Paddon. Carpenter had worked in show business in the States, as lyricist of the songs "You Can Depend on Me" and "You Taught Me to Love Again." After the war, as an impresario, he would manage Bobby Darin's first English tour. After the war, too, he would write regularly to Clifford Paddon and visit Bovey Tracey whenever he was in England, until his death in 1980.[29]

There are many similar vignettes, but perhaps a few statistics will give an overall picture. By the beginning of 1944 there were some 840,000 American troops in Britain, the great majority of them in the south. The men were billeted in private homes or in requisitioned country houses, packed into camps of Nissen or Quonset huts, and tents. Every week thousands more arrived by troopship. Every week, too, ships docked in Britain with more of the vast quantity of equipment necessary to support an army. Much of it was war *matériel*. To Normandy with the American army would travel 137,000 wheeled vehicles and half-tracks, 4,217 tanks and other full-tracks, and 3,500 artillery pieces. In England the civilian population and the troops were awed to see the Sherman tanks, jeeps, trucks, and artillery parked in the fields in lines seeming to reach to the crack of doom. Tons of supplies were necessary to keep up the American way of life and standard of living: chewing gum, candy, hot dogs, cheese from Wisconsin, dental fillings. The total tonnage of American supplies by D Day would be sixteen million. A joke of the time that captures its unreality, even surrealism, was that if it weren't for the barrage balloons, England would have sunk under the weight of the American war equipment.

If the sense of unreality was general, however, it was nowhere more potent than in the evacuation area of the South Hams. Nancy Hare's account suggests that application of the evacuation deadline was not quite as strict as the prepublicity had intimated. "December 20th, the fateful day, came at last," she said.

A few farms were still occupied owing to transport difficulties. We had to go and see for ourselves that some people had really gone.

We walked many miles in gum boots in mud almost up to our knees, usually with a local policeman as guide. A few irate farmers arrived at the information center to say they had been packed up for two days and the lorry hadn't turned up. It was difficult to persuade a very old couple, both eighty-five, who just couldn't understand why they had to move out of the cottage in which they had lived all their lives. The old lady had never been in a car before.

There was another old lady who lived on a farm unapproachable except by horse and cart. She was ill and had to be moved by ambulance. A tractor took her across the fields to the road where the ambulance was waiting. She arrived smiling. Two other old ladies had made their own arrangements and were somehow forgotten. They were the last inhabitants of a deserted village with an uncanny feeling of emptiness. The only clue to their whereabouts was a smoking chimney.

Grace Bradbeer, too, conveys the ghostly feeling that pervaded the once thriving community.

One WVS helper sent to check a coastal village found that on this particular morning the sun was shining brightly, the blue sea was calm and sparkling. . . . But in spite of the lovely crisp morning there was something unreal and creepy about it. She looked in all the windows and tried all the doors and not a soul was in sight. "It was very sad and eerie," she said. "Just one black cat walked across the road—that was the only sign of life there was in the whole village."[30]

Nancy Hare meanwhile was one of the WVS helpers doing the final checkup in the inland village of Blackawton. "We left Blackawton to the Americans on December 24. Someone suddenly remembered—'Tomorrow is Christmas Day!' "

The stage was empty and ready for the new play to be performed upon it. The old cast had gone; the old properties and furniture had been struck. Tanks would replace the threshing machines and American soldiers in their olive drab would replace the threshers. It was exactly as Colonel Rayner had described it, "a stage for the dress rehearsal," a 30,000-acre theater of war in an unusually literal sense, soon to be costumed in camouflage. But neither the colonel nor his evacuee-constituents knew just how accurate a theater it was. Perhaps that is why the inhabitants were given so little time to go, in order to cut down the opportunity for shared speculation as to why *their* area, and not some other, had been chosen for the battle school. Certainly a German spy would have been interested in the local man's guess that the army was coming "to practice landings again." In a sense, simply by being told to leave, the 3,000 people of the South Hams had each been given a fragment of military intelligence.

They had been told, for example, that the evacuation might be expected to last about six months—a piece of information that could have helped to narrow down the date of D Day. That—the timing of the invasion—was half of what was then the biggest secret in the world. The other half was where the invasion would take place. The

Allies were engaged in an intense campaign of deception, called "Fortitude," to try to convince the Germans that the invasion would be mounted from southeast England on the Pas de Calais, when in fact, as the military planners knew, it would be largely from the southwest and on Normandy. The countryside of the American battle school so closely resembled the *bocage* country of Normandy that it might have been guessed by extrapolation that Normandy was the place.

Normandy, like Britain, had not been a battleground for many centuries; generations of undisturbed labor had created an intensively cultivated and crowded landscape. The *bocage* to the west and south of Caen was hundreds of little fields measuring about 150 yards by 100, separated by earth banks encrusted with bushes and trees and dense hedgerow. One person involved in the invasion compared the *bocage*— it means coppice or grove—to a gigantic shrubbery. This would be hard country to take, but, once taken, it would be difficult to dislodge the invader. The British had at least seen or known similar country. Many British soldiers in Normandy would be struck by the similarity— apart from the poplar trees, the châteaus, and the Norman peasant women. Normandy particularly resembled the west of England. There were cider-apple orchards, as in the West Country, and solid stone farmhouses that might have been transplanted from Devon. The people of Normandy, too, would seem familiar. "The male inhabitants," wrote an observer of the time, "on the whole might have been imported *en masse* from Cornwall; they were bluff, red-faced-looking specimens, who gave you the impression that they had spent many years in small fishing smacks off the coast. . . . " Even the poor weather of June, the invasion month, would strike a familiar note to the English troops, as if "Normandy had laid on a typical English summer for the invaders."[31]

If this was familiar enough ground to the British, however, it was not to the Americans, and at least one purpose of the battle school was to accustom them to this strange terrain. To American eyes attuned to the vanishing perspectives of the prairies, the *bocage,* or for that matter the South Hams, seemed almost fantastically chock-full and over-grown. Bradley called the *bocage* a "checkerboard,"[32] which suggests the impersonal grid system of a city like Washington; but it was a grid whose web of lines was formed of bushes as densely tangled as barbed wire. The *bocage* extended fifty miles inland, and many American lives would depend on the ability to push rapidly through such country. What might in peacetime have seemed the friendliest of terrains took on a most hostile aspect in war. The Americans would devise a system, called "rhino," whereby steel tusks mounted to tanks would gouge and tear a way through the undergrowth.

The most important and impressively accurate part of the invasion stage was its coastal apron, the gently curving beach of Slapton Sands, which ran for three miles from Torcross, the village at the southernmost corner of the evacuation area, towards Strete at its easternmost corner. The eight villages and their surrounding acreage were just the convenient hinterland of this beach, which was why this part of the South Hams had been chosen for the "American Army Battle School."

But why Slapton Sands? The quickest answer to that question is another: Where else in southwest England would have been more suitable for landing exercises? The military usefulness of the beach had been recognized with Montgomery's exercise of 1938. It was recognized again in 1940, when, with the nearby beach of Blackpool Sands, it was mined, surrounded with barbed wire, and put out of bounds to the local people. If Montgomery could see the landing potential of Slapton Sands, so too could the Germans, and in 1940 a German invasion of England was considered a real possibility.

Slapton Sands would have to be swept for the British landmines, but then its length, the absence of a heavily built-up area behind it, and its ease of access from the West Country embarkation ports would make it probably the best candidate for the landing "stage," independent of other considerations. But there was another consideration. Slapton Sands possessed a feature that, while it made much of the beach less than ideal for an armed amphibious landing, happened to correspond almost exactly to actual conditions on the ground that the Americans would have to master in one theater of the real D Day "show."

"At an early date," according to Eisenhower, the invasion planners had approved an idea strongly supported by himself and General Bradley for an assault on the east coast of Normandy's Cotentin peninsula. Both Eisenhower and Bradley believed that this assault was necessary for the early capture of Cherbourg, and thereby the success of the entire invasion. One of Eisenhower's worries about it, however, was that the only available beach on the Cotentin peninsula—the beach code-named Utah—was "miserable." Eisenhower meant miserable in a military sense:

Just back of it was a wide lagoon,* passable only on a few narrow causeways that led from the beaches to the interior of the peninsula. If the

*The Germans had flooded the fields.

exits of these causeways should be held by the enemy, our landing troops would be caught in a trap and eventually slaughtered by artillery and other fire to which they would be able to make little reply.[33]

Like Utah, Slapton Sands had water just behind it—the brackish mile-and-a-half long lake known locally as the Slapton Ley. Like Utah, there were narrow exit points on this half of the beach, from which invading troops could have been caught in a deadly cross-fire. Eisenhower's idea of a causeway applies exactly to this stretch: Driving down the narrow strip of land, the lake on the one hand, the beach and sea on the other, it seems that the ribbon of road must be laid on man-made foundations. But it is all natural.

Slapton Sands is a long beach and resembles Utah only over about half of its length. One cannot really believe the usual inference that it was chosen for that reason. The earliness of Eisenhower's "early date" for the Cotentin peninsula assault is somewhat qualified by the testimony of General James Lawton Collins, commander of the U.S. Seventh Corps, elements of which would make the Utah assault. He states that Utah was not included in the invasion plans of early 1943 drawn up by the Anglo-American staff under the British Lieutenant General Frederick Morgan. Those plans had been seen by Eisenhower, before his appointment as Supreme Allied Commander, Europe. He had thought the assault front too narrow, but it wasn't until his appointment, in December 1943, when the South Hams evacuation was already well under way, that he had told his deputy, Montgomery, to represent that view. "But so far as can be determined," commented Collins, "Montgomery was given no instruction with respect to landing a corps on the Cotentin [Cherbourg] peninsula."[34]

The half-resemblance of Slapton Sands to Utah was almost certainly an accidental bonus rather than the decisive factor when it came to choosing the evacuation area. Slapton Sands also acted as a stand-in for Omaha Beach, and the "early" approval of Utah in the invasion plan would continue to be beset with doubt and worry. A week before D Day Eisenhower would be agonizing over it, questioning its wisdom and wondering whether to call it off. It was only at the last moment that Utah became solidly part of the invasion plan.

That crisis came later, however. At this period—November and December, as the South Hams evacuation drew to its painful close—the Allied command had another crisis on their hands, which preoccupied them all from Eisenhower and Winston Churchill downwards. That crisis can be summed up in three simple initials: LST.

CHAPTER

3

  "The destinies of two great empires," said Churchill, "seem to be tied up in some goddamned things called LSTs."[1] The punchy colorfulness of Churchill's complaint depends upon its colorless conclusion and the lack of color in that watery acronym. LST has an importance in the history of those ships both during the war and since. According to a sailor who served on them: "We were the forgotten men of the fleet partly because we had initials and numbers, not names."[2] But Churchill was right: For several months of 1943 and early 1944 the destinies of empires hung upon those now almost forgotten ships crewed by forgotten men. Not that Churchill himself would easily forget them. "The letters LST (Landing Ship, Tanks)," he would write, "are burnt in upon the minds of all those who dealt with military affairs in this period."[3] They were burned also in the minds of their sailors, but with a slightly different meaning. They had sailed the LST in the Pacific, North African, and Mediterranean campaigns, and with the black humor of war they would joke that what the initials really stood for was Large Slow Target.*

The joke was not inexact. An LST was large enough, an ocean-going ship displacing 5,000 tons; but it was also slow. Its two twelve-cylinder General Motors Model 567 engines† were reliable, but moved the ship at a maximum of only twelve knots through the water. As for its aspect as a target—an LST's vulnerability didn't lie only in its slowness and size. It was armed—some LSTs had up to eighteen guns, but most of them were 20 mm, with some 40-mm cannon in gun tubs forward and astern. This was not heavy armament if an LST

---

*The sailors also called the ships simply a "T," a "Large Stranded Target" or, in the Pacific, "Last Ship to Tokyo."
†On the American LST.

should come up against a proper warship: "We had guns but we depended on others to defend us."[4]

An LST was not a proper warship. It was a war horse, or war mule, the country cousin of the navy. It was a strictly functional ship, its function (which it fulfilled admirably) being to transport as many men and machines as practically feasible between two points. This functionalism, as well as a certain expendability, was reflected in its naming by initials and numbers. But it dictated, too, radical differences in design from the capital ships of the navy. The concept of the LST had (according to Churchill) come originally from Britain in the early period of the war, to be refined and modified in the United States. By 1944 the ship had been around for some five years, but was still, like the very idea of an amphibious force, something of a naval novelty, with teething problems yet to be sorted out.

Some of the problems were inherent. The LST was the wartime forerunner of the modern roll-on, roll-off ferry—which still doesn't inspire total design confidence. At its bow were doors and a ramp that could be lowered to let out men and vehicles. Inside, the ship was built to contain as much as possible, and so its 322 feet from bow to stern lacked a proper reinforcing system of bulkheads and ribs. It was almost all hold, "just a big welded box," and the hull was like "a thin piece of fabric between you and the fish."[5] (The smaller LCTs—Landing Craft, Tanks—were nicknamed "herring boxes.")* Perhaps the biggest design difference was not immediately apparent. So that it might easily beach itself—for this ship was all about beaches—an LST had no keel. When a new LST was launched, it was sideways, an ignominious breech birth, not the proud head first of the capital ships.

It wasn't a ship that inspired tremendous confidence in the men who traveled on it. A soldier remembers boarding an LST: "I could see that *289* was shoddily constructed. It constantly creaked even at its mooring. I unrolled my bedding on the top deck. I thought the shallow-draft LST might capsize if the sea became rough, or if we were attacked."[6] On the plus side, the complement of an LST could console itself with the belief that the draft was considered too shallow for a submarine's torpedoes.

The shoulder patch of the U.S. amphibious forces was a yellow eagle on a red ground, its talons grasping an anchor and submachine gun. Stirring stuff, but the patch was worn on what wasn't a uniform so much as a wartime version of workmen's clothing, an antiheroic getup of dungarees over a heavy blue work shirt, high-top shoes, and

---

*Also "Noah's arks" and "tin cans."

a watchman's cap. In warm weather out at sea some crew members would wear swimming trunks. "We didn't pay much attention to our uniforms and many of us looked civilian," was one explanation.[7] The crews of the LSTs had little contact with the regular navy and, on the whole, didn't really feel themselves to be part of it.

Then there were the shipboard living conditions. The crew's quarters were in the stern in three layers of bunks behind a bulkhead separating them from the tank deck. The port and starboard bulkheads had folding bunks for army passengers, and brackets for stretchers (on their return from the landing beaches the LSTs would run up a flag called Mike, a diagonal white cross on a blue ground, signifying a hospital ship). The quality of the quarters differed slightly from ship to ship, but as a rule they, too, were dictated by the LST's function. "They were cramped, crowded," said one crewman, Emanuel Rubin:

> You lived on top of one another. When there were soldiers aboard, you couldn't move. It smelled always of people. I used to dream of being on an aircraft carrier, like a city, instead of on this ship where we were all packed in like sardines, working around the clock like haulage contractors.

If the LSTs were regarded, individually, as disposable war horses they were, collectively, indispensable. In the Bolero run-up period to D Day they were not simply one of many high matters of state; they were at the top of the agenda. "In this period of the war," wrote Churchill, "all the great strategic combinations of the Western Powers were restricted and distorted by the shortage of tank landing-craft."[8]

The history of these distortions is immensely involved; Churchill himself suggested they might make the subject of a separate military study. They need not detain us too long here. Essentially the problem was that there weren't enough LSTs for D Day. A great deal of number crunching went on—almost to the last minute. How could the shortfall be made up in time? Could LSTs in the Pacific theater be transferred to the European? The most vexing and divisive question: How many LSTs should remain in the Mediterranean for the Italian campaign, and for how long? How many more new ones were needed, and to which theater of war should they be sent? This last question mattered in their construction. For example, an LST serving in the rougher, tidal seas of northwest Europe required different davits—shipboard cranes—from an LST serving in the almost tideless Mediterranean.

At the same time the nerves of the high command were stretched, and strains were put upon the alliance as the problem exposed differences of strategic approach between the Americans and the British. The problem at root was one of production. "I often wondered," wrote Bradley, "why, with our seemingly unlimited industrial production, someone in Washington had not thought to give LSTs a higher shipbuilding priority." But it was also political. "It was indeed scandalous," Bradley continued, "that the major decisions of history's mightiest military endeavor were determined in large part by a shortage of LSTs."[9] In the end, D Day would have to be postponed from May to June to permit a month's more production of the ships.

In early November 1943, as Churchill and Roosevelt were corresponding about the shortage, USS *LST 496* was launched sideways into the Ohio River at Evansville, Indiana, one of the makeshift "cornfield shipyards" of the American Midwest. The banks of the Ohio, "down beside where the waters flow," were the setting for several of these yards, with others at Jeffersonville, Indiana, and Pittsburgh, Pennsylvania. They perhaps explain why names of men from the state of Ohio, so deep inland and far from the sea, crop up time and time again in the records of the American wartime navy. If the sea was not in their blood, shipbuilding was, and at that period the yards of the Ohio River and elsewhere were working a crash program. An LST was not considered to have a long life expectancy, and despite the high production rate, the meeting of the D Day deadline was still felt to be touch and go.

LST 496 would live as a ship only for some eight months, until D Day plus five. By then it would have acquired its own history along with the sweat-smell of the hundreds of men it had carried. But its early life after its launch, when it smelled still of fresh paint, can be considered fairly typical of the LSTs of the sprawling "cornfield shipyards."

At Evansville it took on its "nucleus crew," or "plank owners," under its captain, Stanley Koch, a rancher from Missoula, Montana. "The only reason I'm in the bloody navy," he would say, "is that I did a little sailing."[10] His lead signalman, also in that first nucleus, was perhaps more committed to the navy. Emanuel, or "Manny," Rubin had studied at Danville Military Academy in Virginia and enlisted at nineteen. At signal school in Samston, New York, he was trained in the use of flags, the Morse code and the Aldis lamp. "We also used flares to indicate what to do. Red, blue, green, yellow all meant different things—scatter, hit the beach, bunch up." He had made some transatlantic crossings before being assigned to the nucleus of *496*; that nucleus would be expanded with men picked up at ports of call en route to make a full crew. Some of them would be regular navy "mustangs," or "strikers,"* with at least some experience; most of the officers would be "ninety-day wonders," fresh-faced young men newly turned out from cram courses at the navy schools.

A motor machinist's mate on another LST recalls:

> Most of the crew had never seen a ship or the ocean until put on the LST. The officers had college degrees or credits but knew little of ships. Our first executive officer was a schoolteacher who knew nothing. We had no one on the ship who knew how to operate a sextant, and almost never found Panama City, Florida. We just ran up and down the coast of Florida until it was sighted. We were as green as grass and so were the other ships. It was a wonder that more ships were not lost to blunders.[11]

That—with the exception, at least, of its trained signalman—was pretty much the situation on the *496* in the early winter of 1943. At roughly the same time as the peaceable citizens of the South Hams had begun to face up to the forthcoming fact of their mass eviction, it started the long journey from the Midwest that would take it to the Second World War. The new ship, helped by the river's current, cruised slowly down the Ohio into the broader expanse of the Mississippi:

> The river was flooding, and it was very desolate, foggy, and a little scary. There was no sign of life, just the stumps of trees sticking from the water. We took on two Mississippi pilots, salty old sea dogs who dated back almost to Mark Twain days. The captain expected them to speak like sailors, but they said things like "Hey, Jesse, line her up with that stump over there."†

The first stop was New Orleans, at the Mississippi's mouth. There the ship's mast was raised—it had been kept flat because of the many bridges. Then the *496* broke its umbilical cord with the United States with its first blue water on the Gulf of Mexico. It was evening. "Off Louisiana there were flames hundreds of feet high as they burned off the gas from uncapped oil wells. It was like hell." On the first day at sea a boat davit broke away. It was replaced at the next port of call, Mobile, Alabama, where a shipyard worker told Manny Rubin that a weakness of the LST was often its welding. Pieceworkers on tight deadlines would skimp by doing spot welding instead of welding to make a stronger, continuous seam. In the Gulf defectively welded

---

*"Striker" was a seaman learning a specific skill en route, to become a petty officer on that specific ship.
†This account of the journey of *496,* and the quotations in it, are Manny Rubin's.

davits would cause the loss overboard of a generator and several LCVPs (Landing Craft, Vehicles and Personnel) carried aboard the LST.

From Evansville, the *496* had had a three-inch cannon at its stern—"it gave inner confidence" —but at Mobile it was removed and replaced with an antiaircraft gun. Training was given in 40- and 20-mm gunnery prior to firing the guns for the first time for real on the ship's trials, or "shakedown cruise," in the Gulf of Mexico. There the new sailors "learned the ropes" of their new ship. Manny Rubin remembers a surreal Aldis lamp "conversation" between himself and the signalman of an antisubmarine blimp floating over the Gulf. The blimp signaled that it was lost: "Where are we?" The *496* signaled back: "Middle of the Gulf of Mexico." The blimp replied "Ha ha." The *496* guided the blimp home by pointing its bows in the right direction. Often, however, it didn't know what the right direction was; among the ship's teething problems was a defective radar.

That was put right in New York, where the *496* docked after rounding the Florida peninsula. Now the ship's crew knew where they were bound. In New Orleans and Mobile they had tried to guess from the nature of the stores taken aboard whether their destination was the Pacific or the Atlantic. Now, as they picked their way north along the ports of the eastern seaboard, it was clear they were going to Europe. In Providence, Rhode Island, the *496* took on its load: gigantic steel pontoons and, on the upper deck, the LCT that all the new LSTs piggybacked across the Atlantic. Then to sea again. The ship's last North American port was Halifax, Nova Scotia, where, in a pattern common to the LSTs, it would join the convoy taking it to Europe.

Meanwhile, in the cornfield shipyard of Seneca, Illinois, the most productive of the yards, construction work had finished on USS *LST 515*. Just after Christmas 1943 the new ship's nucleus crew gathered together for the first time in Seneca. One of them was Quartermaster Wendell Hoppler: "I had never learned to swim."[12] Another was the ship's communications officer, Elwin Hendrick: "Feather merchants. Nobody on anything larger than a rowboat in their life. We didn't know our ass from our elbow, a capstan from a cathead."[13]

The new crew took some confidence in their commanding officer, John Doyle. Of Irish and Norwegian ancestry, Doyle was in his late twenties, an experienced sailor who had been in the navy since 1936. He was a "mustang," a man of previously noncommissioned rank suddenly promoted because of the war. In December 1941 he had been in Pearl Harbor when the Japanese attacked. In 1943 he had been commissioned ensign and posted to Solomon Island, Maryland, for amphibious training on Chesapeake Bay; then, just after Christmas leave 1943, to Seneca to take over his first command.

The scaffolding was removed from *LST 515,* and early on the morning of December 31 she was slid sideways into the Illinois River. Even the not very graceful LST was called "she," like other ships of the navy. Wendell Hoppler recalled that the sponsor of the ship's commissioning ceremony was "a pretty, young local lady called Rebecca Brown." Now the *515* was afloat. "We loaded our supplies," said Hoppler, "six LCVPs, which doubled as lifeboats, food, fuel, bedding, radios, charts, codebooks. As quartermaster, I was in charge of the charts. Captain Doyle asked me, 'Hopler, where are we going?' I told him it looked like Europe."

It took about four months to throw together a wartime LST. Tom Clark, ensign and gunnery officer, was part of the nucleus crew for *LST 507,* which he saw for the first time before its launch in Jeffersonville, Indiana. It was swarming with workmen and women putting the finishing touches to it and teams of inspectors checking the work already done. Thirteen years later, in 1957–58, Tom Clark would draft part of a novel about his war experience, and Chapter 2 would begin with the *507* still on land. "It seemed impossible," he wrote, "that the thing could ever be cleaned up in time to fight the war. . . . From the side it looked like a naval architect's gravest mistake. There was no proportion to her. . . . Her superstructure rose like some kind of a weird hut, or squatter's shack which had preempted the deck space. . . . I felt that the whole thing, the whole outline of the ship, was like a small boy sitting on the end of an unbalanced seesaw. . . . Could anybody love the *507?* . . . Who could take pride in her?"[14]

Tom Clark's lightly fictionalized account provides more insights into how it felt to serve on an LST.

Where was her backbone? I realized . . . that the "T" didn't have a backbone, for the LST was designed to push herself on the sands like a stranded whale, and pull herself off by her stern anchor, as if she had some kind of tail. . . . This iron mess that I saw before me was designed ambivalently. . . . A ship that can go on land is not a ship. . . . [She] was intended to push her belly on the beach, and pull herself off rump first. The LST was illegitimate. And so they hadn't bothered to give her a name. She had a number. . . . We amphib LST sailors would sail iron masses with numbers, clumsy-looking hulls which would breaststroke the waves while others cleaved, waddle while others glided. . . . We would get there last after having left first.[15]

On January 1, 1944, the day after the *515* was launched in Seneca, the *507* started down the Ohio to the Mississippi and New Orleans, where it would be commissioned with its initials and number. "We didn't even rate a bottle of champagne across our nose. Our commissioning officer was only a three-striper."[16] In New Orleans more crew came aboard. Among them was Lieutenant Jim Clark, who would be the ship's flotilla supply officer. He would also be Tom Clark's roommate; on an LST, two officers shared a cabin. The two Clarks would become "dear friends" for a time. Jim would loan Tom a hundred dollars, and tell him to be sure to be married by a priest; Tom would bet Jim that he would become a priest after the war. Jim Clark was of a religious disposition: "He had a way of saying 'God' which made God seem real."[17] In his fiction Tom Clark has him as the character Bechak saying on their first meeting:

> God does know. He knows right now what's going to happen to this ship. He knows how much time you've got. I've got. And he knows how long the *507* will be on top of the water, how many lives the "T" will take or how many lives will be taken in it.[18]

Then Bechak, or Jim Clark, calls the attention of Hayes, or Tom Clark, to a message penciled on the fresh gray paint of the bulkhead by his bunk. It is there in Tom Clark's novel and it was there in reality, a message from one of the women who had worked on the *507*: "Dec. 6th, '43, Dear Sailor, God bless and keep you and may this ship guard and protect you and bring you home safely. Judy."[19]

By the end of 1943 the transformation of the six South Hams parishes into the Slapton Assault Training Area, as the Americans officially called it, was complete. The evacuation over, American soldiers had poured into the area in large numbers, sealing it off with barbed wire, road barriers, and gates guarded by American sentries. The villages and their nearby fields were turned into concentrations of troop encampments, motor pools, signal stations, and ammunition and other dumps. Children found the sentries friendly; over the gates they handed out the American novelty of chewing gum.

In mid-January the *Kingsbridge Gazette* carried a little informative piece about the Dukw,* or duck, the "curious amphibious transport

---

*U.S. Army conventional vehicle description code. The "D" was for 1942, the date of the "duck's" invention; the "U" was for amphibian; the "K" meant all-wheel drive; the "W," dual rear axles.

vehicle'' that had been puzzling some of its readers. (Below the piece was an advertisement for ''rabbit skins and moles. Tame rabbit skins stretched and dried.'') Duck was also the name of the Slapton Sands dress rehearsal exercise scheduled for the end of that month, the first in a series of exercises that would gradually increase in scope and realism, and would end about a month before D Day. The big Slapton Sands exercises, in chronological order, would be Duck I, II, and III, Fox, Beaver, Tiger, and Fabius. Some, like Duck, would be rehearsals for the landing on Omaha Beach, when the naval force carrying the troops would be Force O; others, like Beaver and Tiger, would be for Utah (Force U).

They unfolded in an atmosphere of dread and foreboding, which deepened as the early winter of 1944 turned into the spring. Ralph Ingersoll, a former journalist who was then an American liaison officer on General Montgomery's staff, wrote:

> The cards were about to be laid on the table in one of the greatest military showdowns in history. . . . Everything across the Channel was mysterious. . . . What we were doing had no precedent. The veterans of Africa and Sicily—and even they were a small minority—had no comfort to offer. The more they knew, in fact, the less reassuring they were—for they seemed only to remember the confusion and the wreckage and the terrific dependence of the amphibious operation on chance, on the luck of weather and the enemy's mistakes after the landing.[20]

One purpose of the exercises was to try to bring as great a degree of scientific exactitude as possible to these haphazard circumstances. Another very important purpose was to train the untried and inexperienced troops. An infantry private, although he required the least training of any serviceman, had still to be competent in a bewilderingly wide variety of areas. Here is a list of them: the use of a dozen different weapons; camouflage; concealment; mine removal; the detection of booby traps; patrolling; map reading; combat intelligence; recognition of American, Allied, and enemy aircraft and armor; use and disposal of captured equipment; processing of prisoners of war; first aid; field sanitation; and maintenance of health out of doors and in improvised shelters over long periods. The South Hams evacuation area really was what the *Kingsbridge Gazette* had called it, a battle school.

More nebulous, but equally important, was the need to battle-harden the men. The physical reality, and unreality, of this process was well expressed by Lieutenant General Frederick Morgan in his personification of the British soldier (who also underwent it) as Private Snodgrass. By early 1944, he says:

We had got to the stage of submitting Private Snodgrass to a pretty grueling course of so-called "Battle Inoculation." He was marched insensible, deprived of rest or sleep, starved, frozen, soaked, and shot over before he was pronounced fit to adventure into the comparative luxury of the battlefield. But strive as we may after realism in training, we can never quite simulate that moment of shock when the first bullet arrives that is aimed to kill rather than to miss.[21]

"Battle inoculation" was a euphemism for brutalizing young sensibilities; but the survival of these men whom Eisenhower's naval aide, in a celebrated description, would call "as green as growing corn," might depend on a degree of brutalization. There were a thousand and one new things to be learned, and quickly; and things already taught to be relearned in conditions approximating those of actual combat. They had to shed their civilian selves. They had to be habituated to the murderous noise level of actual warfare. They had to learn, first, fear, then the denial of fear. Of death, too. In one exercise an officer would bawl out some novice soldiers staring at a dead body on the coastline, "Haven't you seen a dead man before?" They had to learn to function in the unnatural, and terrifying, environment of the battlefield. Military success and their own lives would depend on it.

The perceived purposes of the exercises varied according to standpoint and seniority. At the highest level of command the concern was with the big picture; overall strategy; cooperation and synchronization of activity between the various arms of the forces; and ease of cooperation between the various Allied elements. Eisenhower had personally decided on a new landing idea. The landings would not be at night, by high tide (eighteen feet in the Channel), but by dawn light as the tide was starting to flood. This would provide surprise and enable the landing craft to negotiate obstacles laid down by the Germans between high and low water. Exercises would allow the high command to judge the practicability of this idea.

Lower down in the chain of command the individual commander would be concerned with the performance of his unit; lower still, the individual soldier would be worried about zeroing his rifle or about the weight of his pack. There were numerous problems to be sorted out through experiment, and other, as yet unknown, problems that only experiment would bring to light. The soldiers, especially ones with some experience, tended to despise exercises; the dividing line between fantasy and reality was shifting and finely drawn, and a military operation could not really be rehearsed with the precision of a play. It all looked fine on the charts, where Slapton Sands, all tourism gone, had been divided into Red Beach and White Beach; but the charts could not accurately reflect the difficulties of the actual terrain, which, in turn, could not reflect those that would be encountered on the beach in France.

There was still uncertainty as to what the French beaches would actually be like. For a time there was a scare when a scientist suggested that one of them at least was essentially peat with only a thin covering of sand; peat would not support the heavy armor to be landed. Commandos with earth augers were sent clandestinely across the Channel to test the subsoil, and the peat story was discovered to be untrue.[22] Still, however, conditions on the English test beaches were new and challenging. The amphibious Dukws, for example, had been used to effect in the Mediterranean, but the experienced Dukw-drivers found that the former approach to an amphibious landing no longer applied. Selby Hardenbergh of the 46th Amphibian (DUKW) Truck Company recorded in his diary for March 11, 1944:

> Weather cool and clear for Exercise Fox. . . . Operation successful except that all Dukws stuck on hitting the beach. Fifteen-pound tire pressure was used, but due to the loose gravel and gradient of one in five and less, the tires could not catch hold. . . . This was the poorest beach for Dukw operations anyone in the Company had ever seen. It was too steep and there was no footing in it for the Dukws. It is a far better beach for landing craft than Dukws.[23]

Hardenbergh was right, and in an early stage of Exercise Tiger the commander of Force U, Rear Admiral Don P. Moon, would experiment by using landing craft alone. But that meant the transferral of supplies on the beach, under fire, to other vehicles. There was really no substitute for the Dukw, which could travel right up the beach, and problems like Selby Hardenbergh's simply had to be overcome.

The LST, likewise, had seen service in the Mediterranean; many would be transferred to northwest Europe for the invasion. In a pre–D Day paper presented by a Royal Navy captain it was suggested that these experienced crews would require a week's special training if they were to master the tide fluctuations and other conditions of the English Channel.[24] How much more training would the "green as grass" crew of a brand new LST need, in tides and in almost every aspect of seamanship under fire and in war conditions? This training could be acquired in the "series of exercises . . . each larger than the last, each involving more men and more ships."[25]

The Normandy landings would be immediately preceded by bombardment of the coast from ships stationed offshore. For these, too, rehearsals were necessary. What types of gun would open fire, from what ranges? One target for the naval gunnery exercises was the ruin of the Royal Sands Hotel, slap-bang on Slapton Sands. Before the war it had put up fishermen and wildfowlers. In 1940, after the beach was mined, a local dog called Pincher had got under the barbed wire and set off a mine. Sympathetic explosions—six mines altogether—had half-demolished the hotel. Now it lay on the dividing line between Red and White beaches. For the Utah rehearsal, Exercise Beaver, late in March, the Royal Sands ruin served as enemy headquarters, and would be further demolished by naval gunfire. Meanwhile, the American 101st Airborne Division, simulating the real role it would play on D Day, had "parachuted" behind the beach—the men had jumped, not from planes, but from the tailgates of trucks.* Following the naval bombardment, troops of the Fourth Infantry Division would land and advance inland to "capture" Okehampton, which was doubling, although, of course, the soldiers didn't know it, for Cherbourg.

The series of exercises also enabled new and secret weaponry to be tried out: flamethrowers, sea- and airborne rocket launchers, and tanks adapted for special purposes. These tanks, nicknamed "funnies," were put to imaginative use. One, for example, was equipped with a flail to explode mines in its path. The "funny" that the Americans most took to, however, was the DD, or so-called "swimming" tank. In its American model this was a converted M4 or M4AI Sherman. Around the upper body of a conventional Sherman was fitted a collapsible, rubberized canvas collar. Bottles of compressed air were used to inflate the collar upwards into a screen, turning the tank into a makeshift, if unwieldy, boat. The tank's engine, as in Dukw, could turn either its tracks or two brass propellers—hence the DD, for Duplex Drive.

On January 27, 1944, Eisenhower and Bradley had seen trials of this "funny" and been much impressed by its potential as self-propelled "instant artillery" for the beaches. They had ordered some 300 new Shermans converted to DDs; within six weeks, the phenomenal war production rate had delivered the first hundred of them from the United States to Liverpool Docks, ready for trials in the final exercises preceding D Day. These amphibious Shermans would be used both at the Utah landing, where they were a success, and at Omaha, where they weren't. According to Bradley, they were " 'secret weapons' on

*It was called "the GMC drop."

which we were counting heavily.''[26] To keep the secret, the DDs were always kept under black shrouds, even when they traveled in a convoy.

In a sense all the invasion vehicles were "funnies." They had to be able, if necessary, to be driven for short distances through water reaching up to the driver's waist, and to this end the British had come up with a waterproofing compound of grease, asbestos fibers, and lime, which was smeared over the vehicles' engines and moving parts. From the hood of each rose the temporary stovepipe that would enable the engine to "breathe" while underwater, but because of the waterproofing they overheated rapidly and had difficulty "breathing" even on land. One of the delights to come on Normandy's Far Shore was the half an hour under enemy fire that would be needed for dewaterproofing. This, too, was to be tried out in the rehearsal exercises.

There were many purposes, large and small; it would be fruitless to try to list them all. One more purpose, however—highly important if essentially incidental—deserves mention here. The exercises also fulfilled an intelligence function[27] and were organized with it in mind. They were designed for an English beach, but the course was so constructed as to give German shore radar operators across the Channel many anxious moments. The ships of an exercise might start, for example, by heading in the direction of Cherbourg. Seeing the radar blips of hundreds of ships, the Germans would wonder whether this was the invasion at last, the real thing, or just another exercise. They would start to relax again when the ships turned away, to follow the English coastline. The radar operator would perhaps start to doze off, only to be rudely awakened when the ships made a wide, sweeping turn in the direction of Cherbourg again. This was unsettling, a war of nerves. But it was also crying wolf. If the Germans could be brought often enough to believe that exercises like Duck, Beaver, and Tiger might be the invasion, then perhaps they would believe that Neptune,* the first amphibious phase preceding Overlord, might be an exercise. The trick was to flummox them so that they wouldn't know *what* to think. A specific example of this technique can be found in a note of March 18, 1944: "In order to assist plan 'FORTITUDE'† you should endeavor, paying due regard to security, to make the large-scale exercise (Exercise 'FABIUS') appear similar in character to the

---

*For security reasons, after September 1943 Neptune was the code-name used on all Overlord tactical planning papers.
†The plan to deceive the Germans that the cross-Channel attack would come from southeast England on the Pas de Calais.

mounting of 'NEPTUNE.' '' So the ships of Tiger and the other big exercises were also in a sense decoy ducks, disinformative radar blips. The idea was to make the Germans complacent and careless; but that kind of trick can turn against itself.

On January 16 the *515* set off down the Illinois River for the Mississippi. On the Illinois, through a signal misunderstanding, it rammed a barge and damaged its bow doors. "Doyle," said Wendell Hoppler, "was furious but kept his cool."

Doyle was a highly controlled man, who had quickly won both the respect and the liking of his crew. He seemed, they had noticed, to be a different man depending on whether he was on ship or on shore. At sea he appeared distant, even dour, in his devotion to duty. He insisted on discipline without being a disciplinarian. "Very strict but fair," was one crewman's opinion of him. "He didn't say much but meant business."[28] Every day after leaving Seneca there were "drills *ad infinitum*—abandon ship, gunnery, man overboard, manual steering, General Quarters,* etc."[29] Ashore, he was gregarious with his men, companionably one of them. In his cabin he kept a large collection of records, one of which became perhaps too well known to his crew. Every morning the ship's intercom system would belt out the song "Oh, What a Beautiful Morning" from the Broadway hit musical of 1943, *Oklahoma,* then as young as the *515* was.

On January 26 the ship arrived at New Orleans before heading to Florida and its Gulf of Mexico shakedown cruise. In New Orleans the bow doors were mended and the rest of the crew came aboard. Among them was Hermann Grosse, then nineteen, who recalled that on the cruise, "Our bows were often swamped. We rolled a lot and the deck was awash. I was real scared but got used to the motion. Many got seasick. Some guys broke down mentally and were transferred off."

Its trials over, the *515* followed much the same northbound route as the *496*. At Red Bank, New Jersey, it took on thirty-three freight-car loads of cargo, among them heavy artillery shells. "For the first time we were scared. We knew that if we were torpedoed, the whole ship would blow up."[30] In freezing weather, its bows encrusted with ice, the *515* then negotiated the Cape Cod Canal to Boston. There it picked up its LCT and a new and unusual crew member.

It was thought that "he must have been smuggled aboard after midnight, when the ship's crew was asleep and the officer of the day

---

*The U.S. equivalent of the British "Action Stations."

was off somewhere having a cup of coffee." It was a dog, a terrier whose barking gave his presence away to everyone on the first day out of Boston bound for Halifax. "The crew wondered, 'What's Captain Doyle going to do?' The captain did absolutely nothing." The dog was adopted as the *515*'s mascot. They called him Beachhead.[31]

In England in late March Bolero moved into higher gear to become the immediate, high-tension prelude to Neptune and Overlord, the invasion of occupied Europe. The south coast began to burst at the seams as the troops moved into their staging areas. These were extended ovals, each circling five miles or so of road, banked one upon another from the slopes of the southern hills almost to the coast. From their shapes on the maps the staging areas were called "sausages"; for the same reason the round, clustered encampments of tents where the soldiers were bivouacked inside the "sausages" were called "eggs."

Convoys roared through the countryside day and night moving men and supplies into these areas, from which, in indeterminate stages, they would move to the embarkation ports and thence into the loading zones. All the traffic in them was one way. Special maps picked out the circular route in red and blue—to the loading areas and back from them. When the invasion had happened, the roads back would be needed mainly for ambulances bringing the wounded and trucks bringing the dead. The field hospitals and graves registration units were based just behind the staging areas, and behind them, in turn, were the railhead companies pouring in supplies, the huge ammunition dumps, the field bakeries, the signal battalions with their coils of copper wire.

"It was all there," wrote Ralph Ingersoll, "the whole great army of invasion, packed in as tight as the little wheels and cogs in a Swiss watch."[32] It was all there, crouched down in the soft green of the Devonshire hills, as neat and orderly and peaceful in preparation as it would be untidy, confused, and violent when it was dashed against the hostile shore in combat.

Ingersoll echoes Eisenhower's observation that on the eve of the invasion "the whole mighty host was tense as a coiled spring."[33] In the months of the big exercises the mighty host was mobilized and the coiled spring's flexibility was tested. In Ingersoll's bizarre image, "the eggs and sausages filled, bulged, emptied again through successive maneuvers."[34] But Ingersoll adds that "with every amphibious exercise, through the winter and early spring, we seemed to get worse at it instead of better. . . . Vital equipment got lost, plans seemed forgotten, and all sense of coherence disappeared."[35] The exercises, in fact, deepened the mood of gloom and pessimism in advance of the invasion: "Demonstrably it could not be done."[36] But resolve had to be kept up at all costs. Whatever mistakes were made, finally it was "to hell with everything except getting on the beaches."[37] Which was not too different from the adage that actors use when rehearsals go wrong: "It will be all right on opening night."

LST 515 started out from Halifax on March 28, as Exercise Beaver was being enacted on the beach at Slapton Sands 3,000 miles away. At Halifax it had joined a large convoy, mostly LSTs with an escort of six destroyers. "Now," said Wendell Hoppler, "we felt that we were really getting close to the war."

The menace of submarine attack had eased by early 1944, but the Atlantic crossing was still fraught with danger. The convoy in which the *496* had traveled had been attacked an hour out of Halifax; a food supply ship had been sunk and the crew of the *496* had had to traverse the Atlantic on a diet of Spam. On April 6, just south of Iceland, the *515*'s convoy, too, was attacked. "We saw the distant flames of two torpedoed freighters on the edge of our convoy," said Wendell Hoppler. "This was getting too real!" Up until then, he said, "it had been sort of fun and games." But now "we began to realize we were in a very serious and possibly fatal business."[38]

On April 17 the *515* put in at Milford Haven, South Wales. "There," Wendell Hoppler recalled, "we heard 'Roll Me Over' for the first time, a new experience for an Illinois farm boy. . . ."

> Roll me over, lay me down and do it again
> Roll me over, in the clover. . . .

A change, too, from the daily reveille record played on the *515*:

> The corn is as high as an elephant's eye
> And it looks like it's climbing clear up to the sky
> Oh, what a beautiful morning, oh, what a beautiful day
> I've got a beautiful feeling
> Everything's going my way.

From its Midwest cornfield shipyard, the *515*, its novice crew and its pet dog, Beachhead, had made it across the Atlantic to the European Theater of Operations. From Milford Haven it was a short haul around Land's End to Plymouth. The *515* was just in time for Tiger.

II

TIGER

CHAPTER

4

One of the first priorities of General James Lawton Collins, on being called from the Pacific theater to England to take command of the U.S. Seventh Corps, was to visit his opposite number in the U.S. Navy, Rear Admiral Don P. Moon. The Seventh Corps had been chosen for the risky Utah Beach landing that both Eisenhower and Bradley considered vital for the Normandy invasion's success, and Moon was commander of the naval Force U (for Utah), which would be responsible for carrying elements of the Seventh Corps safely to the beach and landing them there.

In February 1944 Collins went to Plymouth to visit Moon. The two men got on at once. "I liked him right off," wrote Collins later. The headquarters of the Seventh Corps was then in Braemore, a small village south of Salisbury, but many men of the Corps were billeted in Devon and the West Country, and Plymouth was the base of the navy that would take them to France. Moon's offices were in a badly bombed part of the city near the waterfront, where Moon was in easy reach of his LSTs, his support ships, and his command ship, the USS *Bayfield*.

Collins told Moon that he wanted to move his command post to Plymouth, and Moon said he would have extra corrugated-iron Quonset huts added to the small huddle in a bomb-out site across the street, in an area well guarded and ringed with barbed wire. In mid-March Collins had the operational part of his Seventh Corps headquarters moved to Plymouth, where he joined Moon in detailed planning for the amphibious landing on Utah Beach.

Collins had left Plymouth "assured that we had made a good start towards sound and friendly relations."[1] Later, however, after his headquarters move, Collins liked Moon no less but began to know him a little better. Moon was still "an attractive friendly man . . . pleasant to do business with . . . genuinely cooperative,"[2] but Collins had also spotted what looked to him disturbingly like weaknesses in a naval commander required to make life-or-death decisions.

He thought that Moon was anxiously overdiligent and not good at delegating responsibility. "I became a bit concerned," he would write, "about Don Moon's working overtime and his tendency to do too much himself instead of giving some of his responsibilities to his staff. Occasionally I tried to get him to leave his office early and join me in a walk or a game of tennis, but was never able to do so. I thought also that I detected a certain lack of firmness and a tendency to be overly cautious, which worried me."[3] Collins also noticed a "small thing" that, however, struck him enough to mention it in a letter to his wife: "He is the only Admiral I've ever met who wears galoshes on a mere rainy day. . . ."[4]

The two men got down to planning the Utah landing. Collins had some amphibious experience from the Pacific, where he had distinguished himself at Guadalacanal. Moon's experience had been more peripheral, as commander of a destroyer squadron that in November 1942 had helped to cover the landings in French Morocco. By 1944, according to one man who worked under him, he was "a respected officer," but "some of us wondered about his lack of previous experience in amphibious operation."[5]

It has to be stressed that nothing on the scale of the Normandy invasion had ever been seriously contemplated, let alone attempted, before. Everyone was, to an extent, working in the dark, whether experienced in amphibious warfare or not. It wasn't just the Americans and the British who were unused to working together in such close detail; so were the American army and navy. According to the American Fleet Admiral Ernest King, "Joint army-navy training began in September 1943," and the 1944 rehearsals "were conducted in order to perfect our technique and to achieve effective coordination between the troops and the vessels of the expeditionary force."[6] But King was writing in hindsight; that wasn't, as we have seen, how it appeared before the event. It wasn't a matter of perfecting the thing, but of making it work at all. America's aggregate experience of amphibious warfare was one thing; but for Collins and Moon the Utah landing was still a venture into the unknown, and they had still to weld an effective cooperation between themselves and their two forces.

The first opportunity they had to test-drive their plans was in Exercise Beaver, March 27–31. That exercise was "far from successful: coordination between units broke down and the men who took part remember it mainly for the confusion."[7] The biggest test would be

Exercise Tiger at the end of April; if Beaver had been a washout, perhaps Tiger would bring the precombat confidence they needed.

Tiger was to be the most realistic of the D Day exercises thus far, a full-scale dress rehearsal for the Utah landing. Martial "makeup" had already been applied to Slapton Sands so that conditions there resembled those on the Far Shore: two lines of concrete mine-encrusted tetrahedras had been laid with tide levels in mind, just as in France; steel piles had been driven into the seabed; barbed wire and minefields had been put down; and roads from the beach had been blocked. Americans pretending to be Germans would "defend" the beach against Americans pretending to invade it. Live ammunition would be used, the men firing over one another's heads. The invaders would bring interpreters, and "prisoners" would be "interrogated" for specially planted, realistic "intelligence." There would even be simulated casualties, burials, and field cemeteries so that the medics and graves registration units could do their stuff. "Umpires" would report on the performances of the various units.

A total of some 25,000 men would be landed after spending as long at sea, traveling through specially extended, mine-swept channels, as they would on D Day itself. Three hundred and thirty-seven ships would take part. Like the Utah landing, the exercise would be in two main phases. The first would be an assault wave of beach engineers to blow up and otherwise eliminate obstacles to make way for the "instant artillery" of the amphibious tanks and shock troops of the thus far "unblooded" Fourth Infantry Division; in the second, follow-up wave, other LSTs would bring reinforcements and units to strengthen and consolidate the beachhead. The British Royal Navy would provide the bulk of the shore bombardment force and all the close escorts for the various convoys.

Anglo-American naval coordination was one of the things that U.S. Rear Admiral Arthur Struble wanted to discuss when, on April 3, as the failings of Exercise Beaver were being analyzed, he journeyed to Plymouth from U.S. Navy headquarters in Grosvenor Square, London. Struble was chief of staff to Rear Admiral Alan Kirk, commander of the Western, or American, Naval Task Force. Both Moon, of Force U (or TF—for Task Force—125), and Rear Admiral John L. Hall, Jr. (Force O, for Omaha, TF 122) came under Kirk, which gave Struble, as his chief of staff, a certain clout. With Moon, Struble seems to have exercised his clout when he could. The two men had known one another a long time, since at least 1916, when Moon, a class behind Struble, had graduated fourth in that year at the U.S. Naval Academy.

In early 1944, according to someone who knew both men, "Struble was jealous of Moon because Moon had the assignment Struble wanted very badly. Anyone would prefer to be in command rather than chief of staff. They should have been close friends—and were not."[8] Now, however, they found themselves thrown together in the planning for Utah and for Tiger.

If it is unclear exactly what lines of command were laid down between the British and American navies, that is perhaps because, at least until and including Tiger, those lines themselves remained unclear. The temporary merging into a Neptune force of parts of two different fleets presented, with the best will in the world, operational, practical problems. The British commander in chief, Plymouth, Rear Admiral Sir Ralph Leatham, had foreseen that they might arise. On January 1, in the buildup to the Omaha exrcise Duck I, he had sent to Rear Admiral Hall, Force O, a memorandum whose patient, stiff politeness incidentally captures the artificiality—as it perhaps seemed to the British admiral—of such close cooperation with another navy. "Broadly speaking," Rear Admiral Leatham wrote, "I apply the customs and traditions of the British service, which I believe accord closely with yours. I regard you in exactly the same light as any British flag officer in command of a British force operating within my command. It is my conception, therefore, that from the time of leaving Falmouth [the base port for Duck I] you are in tactical control of your forces, including the British vessels forming the close escort."[9]

Here was the accepted, closely cooperative Allied line, as well as the operationally practical one: Utah and Omaha were American shows—the Americans should run them. Rear Admiral Leatham's memo was passed on to Hall's superior, Rear Admiral Alan Kirk, and after further discussion in Grosvenor Square and elsewhere Leatham's proposals were substantially agreed to in Plymouth War Order No. 138 of February 28. By its terms, the Western Task Force was to be under the control of Rear Admiral Kirk, and the American naval commanders were to work out between themselves "a special chain of command . . . in order to exercise that which would ultimately be used in Overlord."[10]

There was, then, to be no British interference in the American command structure, even when American ships were closely escorted by British ones. The chain of command was yet another of the myriad questions to be settled in the season of exercises. That did not mean, however, that there should be no British input whatsoever into the operations, or exercises, of the Americans' Western Task Force. Rear Admiral Leatham's "Duck I" memo again: "Should I have any information of enemy attack'' [which indicates that the possibility of German attack on an exercise was envisaged even before the first one], ''it will be passed to you to take such action as you may think fit. I regard myself free to suggest action if necessary.'' This is close to the Americans having responsibility without power. They were to have control over, and so responsibility for, the Western Task Force, while the British would be free, but not obliged, to ''suggest action.''

That latter proviso was enshrined in paragraphs 3 and 6 of the subsequent Plymouth War Order. There were good reasons for the proviso. The Americans were exercising in British coastal waters, which were Rear Admiral Leatham's ''patch.'' While the British close escorts would be under American command, the distant covering forces (of British ships) would remain under the Admiral; nor would the Americans control shore radar, nor RAF aircraft sighting potential attackers.

Tiger's schedule, drawn up at Allied Supreme Headquarters on April 19, would specify ''a short movement by sea *under the control of the U.S. Navy*'' [my italics]. But in his January 1 memo Rear Admiral Leatham had retained for himself ''an overriding control, should there arise circumstances which render it strategically necessary for me to cancel or curtail the exercise.''[11] That is, Rear Admiral Leatham could not unnecessarily interfere in an exercise, but he could call it off. The Americans had tactical, but not strategic ''overriding,'' control, a classic recipe for military disaster. There was a potentially fatal loophole here. The hazy chain of command confirmed in February gave the Americans paper control over what, in later April, would become a paper Tiger.

If anyone might have been expected to be aware of the potential dangers of a mixed command and responsibility, British and American, strategic and on-the-spot, it was Rear Admiral Don P. Moon. Almost two years before, as a captain aged fifty-two, he had witnessed the destruction, in circumstances that the Tiger disaster would echo, of Convoy PQ 17, the most costly convoy loss of the Second World War. And PQ 17 had been destroyed as a direct result of what might politely be called—although sailors have other, less polite names for these things—a confusion of responsibility.

The convoy had been made up of thirty-seven merchantmen, more than half of them American, with a close convoy of nineteen, mostly British, warships and a distant covering force of American and British ships. Moon had been Senior Officer, Destroyers, on one of the ships of the covering force.

In late June 1942 PQ 17 had started out from the Icelandic harbor of

Hvalfiord loaded with enough war *matériel* to have "supplied a complete army and air force of, say, a small Baltic country."[12] In fact, its destination was at first the port of Murmansk in the beleaguered Soviet Union, later changed to Archangel. Russian war supplies were being carried mainly in American freighters escorted chiefly by the Royal Navy. For the first time on this grand scale, American ships were under British command, in a showpiece of inter-Allied cooperation that was about to turn turtle and become a spectacular example of Allied disarray.

On the Fourth of July, American Independence Day, PQ 17 was attacked by German aircraft and submarines. Its close escort moved at full speed to the counterattack, cheered on by seamen on the decks of the merchantmen. Meanwhile, however, the Admiralty in London had been tracking the German battleships *Tirpitz* and *Admiral Hipper*. Just after nine that evening it sent three messages to the convoy in rapid succession, the last ordering it to scatter. The captain of one of the British close escort destroyers, Roger Hill, said that because the signals were from the Admiralty "we never doubted that the *Tirpitz, Hipper,* and large destroyers were just below the horizon."[13]

These powerful, if still mind's-eye, adversaries now became the escort's chief concern. But soon, with a sinking feeling, "the whole ship's company . . . cast into bitter despondence," Hill realized that they weren't there, that no surface action was to take place, and that "we were leaving the convoy, scattered and defenseless, to be slaughtered."[14] Terrible messages began reaching his radio office on the merchantman's wavelength: "Am being bombed by a large number of planes," "On fire in the ice," "Abandoning ship." Twenty-three ships of PQ 17 were sunk, with a loss of 153 lives.

Hill remarked that "the Admiralty had made a complete balzup. They knew the *Tirpitz*, etc. were at sea, had lost them by reconnaissance, assumed they were about to fall on the convoy, and ordered 'Scatter.' "[15] He added that he would "never forget how they cheered us . . . and it has haunted me ever since that we left them to be destroyed. I had little faith ever after in the shore staff who directed operations at sea."[16]

This was the fellow feeling of a sailor for others at the mercy not just of the sea and of the enemy, but of the shore-bound brass hats as well. Brass hats, however, have their gut reactions, too, and it was all too easy to construe the PQ 17 debacle in a political sense. In the longer term, Hill asserts that the American Fleet Admiral Ernest King "hated the guts of the English," and that after PQ 17 he swore "Never U.S.

ships under the Limeys again."[17] Moon, whose ship had shot down one of the German attackers, might well have shared both Hill's and King's sentiments, but, in any event, his and all the Americans' faith in British shore staff and in "Limey" worthiness to escort their ships was to be tested again almost two years later—and to the limit—in Exercise Tiger.

Moon, if he tried to contend with the mixed-command question at all, would have had to contend with a wartime spirit of the age much more powerful than himself or any individual. Vital to an understanding both of the Tiger disaster and its postwar aftermath of deafening silence is a grasp of the fact that in the prelude to D Day nothing—*nothing*—was to be allowed to weaken the Anglo-American alliance.

This had been so for some time, if never more strongly than in the tense period preceding invasion. Admiral King's reported attitude of 1942, for example, would not have pleased the powerfully "coalition-minded" General Eisenhower.[18] In the North African, Sicilian, and Italian mainland campaigns of 1942 and 1943 he had made it clear that he would tolerate no actions or behavior that drove a self-destructive wedge between the Allies. According to one writer on Eisenhower, "He had no objection to an American officer calling a British officer a 'bastard,' but . . . if he called him 'a British bastard' he would go back to the U.S. by slow freight."[19]

Another writer says that in the 1942–43 campaigns:

> British and American troops, ships, and planes were intermingled in action so intimately as to be indistinguishable on the war maps. . . . Africa and Sicily were cleared and Italy invaded by this strange host of differently uniformed, differently fed, differently mannered but single-destined men.[20]

The same writer quotes Eisenhower on the eve of one of the 1943 actions:

> This is an Allied battle. I will clamp down on anyone who tries to start any trouble between Americans and British under my command. There will be neither praise nor blame for the British as British or the Americans as Americans. . . . We will fight it shoulder to shoulder.[21]

The stress on unity at all costs was essential to the eventual success of the Allied cause, and its upkeep was perhaps Eisenhower's outstanding diplomatic achievement as Supreme Commander. But it was also a unity that was willed against the reality of the situation that often actually obtained in joint American and British operations, in which rivalry could shade into contempt, hostility, and even hatred. It could be very vulgar indeed.

American censors in Britain were frequently obliged to excise from letters home obscene references to British plumbing, the British soldier, and British women, who were often described as dirty and perverted.[22] As for the British attitude, the witty, late-Bolero-period joke about the Americans that they were "overpaid, oversexed, and over here" could conceal something much darker and not at all funny. There were British servicemen who would actually exult at the large loss of American life in Tiger. A former Royal Navy destroyer gunner said that

> it was common knowledge among Royal Navy crews that a disaster had befallen an American convoy in April. Most of my pals had such hatred of the Americans that we felt that, if not a good thing, it was a well-deserved humiliation. . . . These officers and men were the most disorderly and irresponsible rabble I ever encountered. They were filthy, foulmouthed, undisciplined, and full of VD.[23]

That is in the tradition of Wolfe's comment on the New England Rangers who fought under him in Quebec in 1758: "The Americans are in general the dirtiest, most contemptible, cowardly dogs you can conceive, rather an encumbrance than any real strength to an army."[24]

One sees the wisdom from both sides of Eisenhower's intransigent position on inter-Allied relations. "Anglo-American cooperation," as his chief of staff, Lieutenant General Frederick Morgan, delicately stated it, "is dignified into an international problem of unexampled complexity, needing constant discussion, attention, and argumentation. . . . It is regarded as a delicate hothouse growth that must be carefully tended lest it wither away. Or it is a noxious weed that needs extirpation, for of course its existence contaminates many a cherished plot."[25] To elaborate Morgan's latter point: Not even a world war could eliminate the national and departmental pecking orders, and the alliance infinitely complicated it. The British and Americans were on the same side, but were also rivals and semistrangers to one another.

One morning in mid-April Captain James Arnold of the U.S. Navy was called into the office of Rear Admiral John Wilkes, in charge of American shore bases and of amassing landing craft for the invasion. Captain Arnold was privy to some of the D Day secrets and so possessed the highest Allied security rating of Bigot, an ungainly reversal of the TO GIB (for Gibraltar) that had been stamped on papers relating to the 1942 North African "torch" landings.

Now Arnold was told about the upcoming Utah Beach rehearsal,

Tiger, and told, too, that he was to be Naval Officer in Command (NOIC) for the Utah landing. He would be responsible for the orderly movement of ships and landing craft onto the beach, and his commander suggested that he might benefit from liaison with the officer who would be his counterpart on the British beach code-named Gold.

Captain Arnold set off on an all-night jeep drive down winding blacked-out lanes to a shale beach near Bognor Regis. He recalled that British officers were "sauntering along the beach," whose shore was densely packed with landing craft, "smoking pipes and chatting amiably." A sign led him to a low stone building where he found "several officers wearing Royal Navy uniforms, drinking tea from pannikins."

He introduced himself, whereupon "a four-striper with a bristly black beard" said that he was the NOIC for Gold Beach and told Arnold (in a stage English that had perhaps passed through the American's prism):

> I've been wanting to have a talk with you American blokes. You see, we don't know a damned thing about this NOIC setup. . . . I've made no plans myself. Seems to me it will be an on-the-spot decision sort of mess. Any plan you make can't work anyway. . . . And don't forget Jerry will jolly well see that any carefully formulated plan will be knocked into the King's whiskers.

Captain Arnold left feeling slightly bemused, his tea barely tasted, uncertain whether his overwhelming impression was of the British "muddling through" or simply muddle.[26] This mutual Anglo-American incomprehension was to bedevil Exercise Tiger. Someone on Rear Admiral Moon's staff would comment that there was very poor communication between British and American naval commanders.[27]

Tiger had another fatal weakness, contingent upon its being an exercise, essentially a peacetime affair, in time of war. To set the scene: Britain was on Daylight Saving, Double Summer, or "Baker" Time; the long, light evenings were ideal for the tennis that Collins had tried to get the diligent Rear Admiral Moon to play, but in their joint headquarters in Plymouth's Fore Street the two men and their staffs were planning their part in history's mightiest military endeavor. "As D Day approached," wrote Collins, "preparations for our takeoff gradually increased in intensity, and tensions began to build. Our relations . . . grew closer as we worked out the final details of loading and landing tables, signal communication, naval gunfire support and the many other joint arrangements involved in an amphibious operation."[28]

Tiger had been fixed for the week of April 22–29. But before that date, what were Moon and Collins *really* planning? It was still Utah, of course, not Tiger, still the operation not the exercise; or rather the planning of Tiger concerned them, as it had to, only insofar as it would prefigure Utah. They wanted a realistic model of what the real thing would be; they wanted, among other things, proof or disproof of the rightness of their "joint arrangements." This is a subtle but important point. The escalating realism of the exercises could not fully compete for the mind's attention with the forthcoming reality of D Day. The dress rehearsal was not the show; however realistic Tiger might be, it could not be real.

But Tiger *was* real. It was not to take place in friendly, peacetime waters, after all, but in the English Channel in 1944. Even so, the Channel was dangerous perhaps, but whatever danger Tiger might face could not—could it?—be more than a foretaste of the danger awaiting on the Far Shore. It was only an exercise. And who would face the lion's share of the real, the D Day, danger? Why, the first assault wave, the shock troops, the amphibious cutting edge of Utah. So concentrate the heavy firepower in that first force. The backup convoys would have an easier time of it, bringing up the rear once the assault and the big naval guns had softened the resistance. The enemy would be too busy trying to repel the troops already on land. This was how Utah was thought of, and therefore how Exercise Tiger, Utah's maquette, or architect's model, was thought of, too. The thing was a *dry run*.

But in Tiger the roles would be reversed. The first, heavily protected assault wave would not be facing a real enemy; the second, follow-up wave, which on the day itself would be sailing into the rear of an already established front and which would therefore require less sea protection, would on the exercise be correspondingly less protected and so more exposed to the dangers of the Channel. Had the concentration been on planning and on protecting this vulnerable second wave, rather than on planning it as a mock-up of the D Day reality, Tiger might never have met with disaster. But then, of course, the exercise would have lost its *raison d'être*. In the end, Part Two of Tiger would turn out to be more "real" than Part One precisely because it had previously been viewed as less so.

Exercise Tiger's "battle orders" were issued on April 18:

> . . . the force will firmly establish Seventh Corps in position north of Start Point in order (1) to ensure the capture of Okehampton with minimum

delay and (2) to assist in securing a lodgment area as a base for further operations leading to capture of the Devonshire southern coast ports.[29]

You are a veteran of Operation Torch in North Africa, and Husky in Sicily. Perhaps Anzio, too. You've lost friends in battle. Or you are a rookie. You wear the uniform of the Fourth Infantry Division with the ivy-leaf-green patch on your sleeve. You have never heard guns fired in anger. Six months ago you were in the States, in training. A couple of months before that you were a civilian. You are eighteen or twenty years of age, and ten years ago you were playing make-believe war games with your buddies in the yard.

Veteran or rookie, your reaction to this exercise-speak isn't all that different. You're reading, or your commander is telling you, that you've got to go out there and capture the Devonshire coast. But you *live* in Devonshire, or somewhere in the West Country. For now anyhow. In the Queen Anne Barracks, or QAB, a bunch of Quonset huts in Falmouth. Or billeted with a pub landlady. Or in a 16'x16' eight-man tent pitched under an oak tree at a field's edge. This is a *game*. Then you read or are told the next bit:

> Attack by enemy aircraft, submarines, and E-boats may be expected *en route* to and in exercise area.

Now you knit your brow. Is this part of the game, too? Crying wolf maybe. But hell, there *is* a war on. And the doubt sticks, even though you tell yourself this is an exercise, and you ask someone else: This thing about expecting enemy attack now—is that realism or is it real? But he doesn't know either. He shrugs. And you don't know. You're eighteen or twenty and death is only a word. You spit out your gum and think about something else.

Exercise Tiger would be all about this wrong-footing of realism and reality.

CHAPTER
5

The danger was real. It took the form of nine torpedo boats then moored in the French Channel port of Cherbourg, which would be the Utah Beach objective. The occupied city that Eisenhower and Bradley wanted so much to capture was for the time being the base port for the Fifth and Ninth *Schnellboote* flotillas of the German navy.

Schnell means "fast," and these boats were indeed as speedy and gracefully maneuverable in the water as an LST was lumbering and slow. Their Daimler Benz engines, totalling 6,000 horsepower, drove them at a maximum of thirty-seven to forty knots as against an LST's best of twelve. They were slim craft more than a hundred feet long; their hulls, three skins of teak over a light metal frame, were designed to cut through waves and to plane at high speed. They were vulnerable to aircraft and to the long-range guns of destroyers, and marauded the English Channel—or *der Kanal*—only after dark. Their camouflage was the black of the night, not the battleship gray of the sea. It gave them a sinister appearance even by day.

Each *Schnellboot* carried two torpedoes. The earlier models had a light machine gun on deck for their own protection; later ones had two 20 mm cannon, firing green tracer. Their bullets lit up green only when well away from the boats so their exact source in the night couldn't be pinpointed. The boats had no radar of their own and depended for their targets upon guidance or visual sightings. They were designed for coastal work and had a range of 700 miles. With the decline of the German U-boat fleet, and particularly that of the *Luftwaffe,* the importance of the *Schnellboote* had grown. The Germans thought of them as the U-boats of the coastal waters. The Allies called them E-boats, an abbreviation of "enemy war boats."

The E-boats had had, and would have, a successful war, although their own losses were high. Operating in the Mediterranean, the Baltic, Black, and North seas as well as the Channel, their tally by the war's end would be more than a hundred naval ships and a quarter of a million tons of merchantmen.

Probably the E-boats' most successful area of operations was the Channel, where by the time of Tiger they had sunk at least eighteen vessels. Ten of them had gone down in Lyme Bay, the wide crescent of water between Start Point in South Devon and Portland Bill in Dorset, which was their favored hunting area. On the night of February 26, 1943, the Fifth Flotilla, then operating out of Guernsey, sank four ships in a convoy of fourteen crossing Lyme Bay. In July that year they sank six merchantmen, again in Lyme Bay. And it was in the waters off Start Bay, a southern indentation of Lyme Bay, that Exercise Tiger would maneuver into position for its "assault" upon Slapton Sands.

The enormous increase in English coastal traffic occasioned by the season of American exercises had not gone unnoticed by the Germans. Nor, as already noted, had it been intended or hoped that they wouldn't notice. The exercises helped to "cry wolf" over D Day. As noted also, Admiral Leatham had pondered the possibility of a German attack on an exercise even before the first one unfolded. On January 6, only five days after his memorandum, seven E-boats in the Channel attacked a Bristol-Portsmouth convoy, sinking three ships and an escorting antisubmarine trawler.

So far, however, fears of an attack upon an exercise had not materialized. In the Americans' favor had been poor weather, which had largely confined the E-boats to port and prevented sorties. The E-boats were made for speed, and were less stable on rough water; they had also to slow down to a maximum of about ten knots to launch their torpedoes. This made them more vulnerable in the really rough weather, which the big ships could plough through without bother. So Exercises Duck I, II, and III, Fox, and Beaver had all, in a sense, been under the protection of bad weather.

Especially Beaver. It had unfolded over the last few days of the equinoctial month of March, when, traditionally, in the Channel the high tides are highest, the low lowest, and the twenty-foot or so tidal rise and fall of the Channel are at their most fickle. (The highest tidal variations in the U.K. are in the Channel Islands, not far from Cherbourg.) One remembers Masefield's lines in "Sea Fever" about the "Dirty British coaster . . . Butting down the Channel in the mad March days." A ship at sea operates within its own chosen time frame; the Falklands War, for example, was fought on Zulu, or Greenwich Mean Time. But a ship cannot ignore the weather or the tides, and thereby the phases of the moon; perhaps that is another reason why a ship is always feminine (but, like the moon, not in Germany). Tide tables were a tremendous consideration in the Normandy invasion; tide tables and the prevailing southwesterly winds, and so seas, were considerations in Tiger, too.

Now the "mad March days" were over. It was April, traditionally a month when the Channel weather settles down and turns for the better. Here was another wrong-footing. If the bad weather had protected the earlier exercises, it had also created an illusory two-month lull in E-boat activity before Tiger. Had the weather been worse over the last week of April, it seems reasonable to speculate that the E-boats would not have attacked.

But the E-boats were waiting. All they needed was a window in the weather.

Eisenhower's master plan for the Utah landing involved a large paratroop drop behind the beach before the arrival of the first seaborne assault wave. The 82d and 101st Airborne Divisions were to prevent or slow down the arrival of enemy reinforcements and to take the potentially lethal "causeways" that led inland between the beach and the flooded area behind it. The idea had been tried out in Exercise Beaver; it was to be tested in Tiger, too. The "battle orders" of April 18 specified that "Friendly aircraft will fly over exercise area in operational flights. Units from 101st Airborne Division will participate by simulating landing west of Slapton Sands range area at about H—4 [i.e., minus 4] hours. . . . The 9th Air Support Command will provide direct air support. . . ."[1]

Here was yet another complexity of the Tiger/Utah plan. During April 21 to 24, final briefings for the exercise were held at the Royal Marine Barracks in Plymouth and one person attending them was General Elwood Quesada of the Ninth Air Support Command. The planes, ships, tanks, and soldiers all had to be in the right place at the right time, with the Slapton Sands "D Day" scheduled for the morning of April 27 and "H Hour" for 7:30 A.M. By then the paratroops should have been landed and "fighting" for four hours. Then the first "assault" wave would land; later would come convoys carrying backup troops and equipment.

But the lull in E-boat activity had not induced complacency among the Allied planners of Exercise Tiger. The warning about "expected" E-boat attack in the exercise's "battle orders" has already been mentioned. The planners may have been staging a "pretend" exercise, but they knew that the danger was real. Allied Naval Commander, Expeditionary Force (ANCXF), the British Rear Admiral Sir Bertram Ramsay, who had been appointed in October, said after Tiger: "It had always been felt that the enemy might react when large-scale exercises were carried out in the Channel. . . ."[2] It was a danger, too, to which Rear Admiral Moon appears to have been alive. On the last day of the formal briefings, April 24, two days before the "assault wave" sailed, he apparently called a conference of commanding officers at which they were warned about the E-boats. A British naval officer from Plymouth went "into considerable detail" about their hit-and-run tactics.[3] He would have explained how it was the E-boats' usual practice to split up into two formations at ten to fifteen miles from their target; how at the appointed *Stichzeit,* or "stab time," they would form wedges to penetrate the close escort; how they would fire their torpedoes simultaneously (at 7,000 to 8,000 yards) to improve their chances of a hit.

Thomas Glennon, a "ninety-day wonder" who commanded a unit of Landing Craft Control (LCC), recalled a pre-Tiger Plymouth briefing on "procedures and communication" at which several British officers were present. One of them, he remembered, said: *"If Jerry doesn't have a go at us this time, he's absolutely crackers"* (my italics).[4] Subsequent developments are all the more mysterious in light of this apparent awareness of, and stress upon, the danger of E-boat attack.

In the Americans' "special chain of command" the commodore of the Tiger backup convoy T-4 was to be Commander Bernard Joseph Skahill, an Irish-American about fifty years of age for whom a navy career had meant escape from his childhood in the "Hell's Kitchen" area of New York City. His executive and communications officer was Lieutenant Moses D. Hallett, twenty-six, who remembers himself in the wartime navy as having been "green with a capital G—trying desperately to make sense out of an insane situation—doing my best to do my job competently."[5]

Neither Skahill nor Hallett at any time liaised with commanders of the Royal Navy ships that had been detailed as their close escort. Nor was there any established agreement on signal procedures to be used on the exercise. According to Lieutenant Glennon, a "session with the British escort officers . . . was standard procedure," and one can only echo his incomprehension that it failed to take place. The evidence for this and other fatal omissions is quite clear; as to exactly why and how they occurred, one can only speculate.

In 1983 Moses Hallett could not recall that while in British waters "we were assigned or were given an operational U.S. Navy or Royal Navy radio frequency. . . . I did not know what the proper frequencies were. . . ." Before Tiger he had found Rear Admiral Moon's staff "with few exceptions, inclined to be arbitrary and unhelpful. . . . Almost every question at a pre-Tiger briefing with some of [them] was answered with 'That's in your Ops order' [but] we didn't receive an Ops order." And Hallett added: "I can't explain why we weren't given the right radio frequencies to monitor. At the time and after the fact I assumed Admiral Moon's staff had goofed."

Hallett's point about absent Ops orders is backed up by the fourth and last in a list of contributory causes of the Tiger disaster later diagnosed by Rear Admiral Leatham: "the late distribution of the exercise orders and incompleteness of some of the sets supplied which gave very little time for their study and digestion by the many officers concerned."[6] Moses Hallett again:

> When we sailed for Tiger, neither the commodore nor I had been able to get copies of the escort orders, the communications plan, or the task force operations plan. We were told that we were to use the [ship's] Tiger operation orders and that we didn't need to know any more.

Rear Admiral Leatham didn't specify whether distribution of exercise orders was the responsibility of Rear Admiral Moon and his staff. One imagines that it was. His other contributory causes, however, clearly fell within the responsibility of the British shore staff in Plymouth. But the Plymouth staff was overworked. On the night of April 25–26 there had been an action against enemy destroyers, and plans were under way for another action on the 28th. Real Channel operations, that is, were to clog the workings of the "realistic" Channel exercise. And so would another exercise, "Fabius, following closely on its [i.e., Tiger's] heels." Fabius, an Omaha Beach exercise, was scheduled for Slapton Sands in the early days in May. Leatham explained that its last-minute planning, entailing "many urgent movements," overlapped with the execution of Exercise Tiger.

Leatham's letter was dated May 5. But more than two months later the British Rear Admiral Llewellyn V. Morgan, Director of Signal Division, wrote that the "unhappy encounter" of Tiger occurred "at a time when a revised W/T [wireless/telegraph] Organization was being 'worked up' in preparation for Overlord but when certain W/T services needed for Overlord were not yet in existence."[7] Here is an elaboration upon Admiral Leatham's third contributory cause, namely that the

Channel actions and the last-minute planning for Fabius had brought about an "immense recent increase in communications . . . which caused abnormal delays in the distribution of signals." But Rear Admiral Morgan specified, as well as delays, that a "revised" signal system was being "worked up." This is not the same as oversights or delays under pressure of overwork. It suggests that the Plymouth shore staff and Convoy T-4 were on different wavelengths.

On April 24, two days into Tiger's running schedule, Rear Admiral Ramsay had issued his naval operational orders—"the most detailed ever issued by a commander in chief"—for Overlord. His staff had been working on them throughout April. "Things have reached the intense stage," Ramsay wrote in his diary, "of getting orders into print and all the staff are stretched to the limit. . . ."[8] In his letter of May 5 Admiral Leatham would echo Ramsay and say of his Plymouth staff, which was also closely involved in drawing up the orders, that they had been "severely stretched."

The operational orders amounted to almost 1,000 pages of foolscap, which, when bound, made a volume three inches thick. So detailed were they (American commanders would object that they were *too* detailed) that in them was "a diagram for every hour . . . giving the effect, when turned over quickly, of a moving picture."[9] This was the massive book that landed on the desks of the Plymouth High Command, to be "opened forthwith,"[10] just as Tiger was getting under way.

Two days later, on the 26th, before any of Tiger's convoys had put to sea, Rear Admiral Ramsay moved into "battle headquarters"[11] at Southwick Park, a Georgian house in the Forest of Bere seven miles north of Portsmouth dockyard, which would thenceforth be the "nerve center"[12] of Neptune/Overlord. Stopping in Plymouth only to visit Rear Admiral Moon, Ramsay flew on to Southwick Park and there at once continued the planning for Neptune/Overlord, and for Exercise Fabius in the first week of May.

Fabius was to simulate Neptune "as closely as possible without actually crossing the Channel and landing in Normandy."[13] Here was an exercise both more realistic than Tiger and three times bigger in terms of ships involved. Fabius would also involve British as well as American troops (although the British would practice landing on beaches other than Slapton Sands). Crucially, Fabius would be the exercise on which Bertram Ramsay, possessing "complete operational control,"[14] would "try out the arrangements whereby [he] would assume control of operations in the Channel."[15]

Here, for Tiger, was an appalling accident of bad timing. If D Day was to be the real thing, Fabius, with its thousand ships, was to be the real "dry run," thus demoting Tiger, in this period of suspense and high tension, doubly in importance. One has to ask whether Tiger might not have passed off safely, or at least more so, had it not been scheduled so few days before Fabius, and whether it would have ended in disaster had not the operational orders for Neptune/Overlord been issued on the 24th while it was actually in progress.

According to a document of 1944, from April 26 and the move to Southwick Park:

> ANCXF [Rear Admiral Ramsay] and his staff were working at high pressure preparing additions and amendments to the Naval Orders as required by existing circumstances, coordinating the activities of all authorities involved, making necessary arrangements to fit naval activities with Army and Air Force intentions, dealing with major new proposals, and generally perfecting details for implementing the Naval Plan.[16]

Having met the deadline of getting the Neptune operations orders into print, therefore, Rear Admiral Ramsay and his staff were now feverishly rushing to meet the deadline for Fabius only a week away.

Among these frantic additions, amendments, coordinations, etc., were the "many urgent movements" to be handled by Admiral Leatham and his overworked staff in Plymouth. Among them, too, was Rear Admiral Morgan's "working up" of a new communications organization for Neptune/Overlord. The realistic exercise Tiger unfolded over exactly the few days when the reality of the forthcoming invasion of France had suddenly, dramatically, been enhanced, "but when certain W/T services needed for Overlord were not yet in existence."

Commander Skahill's medical officer, Lieutenant George Hawley, believed that T-4's sailing orders contained a typographical error whereby the ships were given "the wrong radio frequency to guard" (i.e., to monitor).[17] Hallett, who was in charge of the convoy command's communications, confirms the wrong frequency, but not the typographical error—"I can't explain why," he said—and in the absence of surviving copies of the sailing orders it cannot be proved. It does not seem impossible, though, in the light of Rear Admiral Morgan's observation, that under pressure of planning the Fabius and D Day signal schedules, frequencies were abruptly altered before T-4—the last of Tiger's convoys—put to sea or while it was at sea. T-4 could have been given a radio frequency that was right *at the time* only for it to turn *in effect* into a typographical error as signal schedules were switched.

This is speculation, but as an explanation it does at least have the advantage that it would have been less gross a blunder than a simple clerical error. But that is possible, too. A wartime British communications officer states that "at the time there were many changes in signaling procedure, especially when Americans were involved. Many were written incorrectly and therefore misunderstood."[18] So the question has to be left open as to whether clerical error or an abrupt wavelength change was to blame. What does emerge with clarity is that Tiger's T-4 convoy had everything going against it, absolutely everything.

CHAPTER

6

Whilst on the Italian campaign, the men of the First Engineer Special Brigade had won the unusual distinction of being allowed to tuck their trouser legs into the tops of their eight-inch jump boots, paratroop style. They were the one nonairborne unit in the U.S. Army able to dress like that, an individual touch that marked them out a little in the sea of olive drab. It was also a mark of experience, a sort of battle honor.[1] Now the First Engineers were preparing to go into battle again, having been shipped over from Italy for the invasion of France.

They were, as the "special" in their name indicated, an *ad hoc* brigade: a variety of units specializing in different skills pertaining to modern, amphibious warfare. As engineers they were required to exercise these skills, in which they were trained or semitrained, but also, as General Bradley pointed out, to perform "as longshoreman, trucker, traffic cop, and warehouseman."[2] By the time of Tiger the Brigade numbered some three to four thousand; by the Normandy invasion its hard core of experienced veterans was due to be replenished and enlarged upon to give it a strength of just over 16,000, or a "divisional slice."

Since arriving in England the First Engineers had gone through a punishing program of exercises. On beaches in Cornish coves they had repeatedly practiced the handling and dumping of cargoes. The Brigade had been in the first Slapton Sands exercise, Duck I, and in later ones, to make a total of fourteen exercises after Beaver in late March. Its men were sick of exercising. Its nucleus had seen the real thing in Italy and knew that for engineers the reality on the beach under fire tended to be markedly different from what they told you back at base camp that it would be. By April, and Tiger, a sense of boredom with the constant exercising extended even to the Brigade's commander, Colonel Eugene Caffey. According to a memorandum, "In spite of the time consumed by the exercises the Brigade was able to carry on intensive training of its units in their basic missions. . . ."[3] The exercises, that is, were fundamentally seen as a distraction.

For the distraction of Exercise Tiger the First Engineers had drawn the lot of being in the backup support group; the first, "assault wave" engineers were to be drawn from the Sixth Special Brigade. But it wasn't quite as straightforward as that. Allocation to this or that wave seems at least sometimes to have been on the basis of the special skills of a brigade unit.

One unit that was divided between the two waves, for example, was the Thirty-third Chemical Decontamination Company, part of the First Engineers. The Thirty-third had participated in all the brigade's fourteen exercises before Tiger. Its responsibilities had been loading and unloading landing craft, the operation of machines for making smoke (for cover), location and removal of land mines, and decontamination of mustard gas and training the soldiers in its perils. (After a German attack on the Italian port of Bari in December 1943, there had been a scare among the Allies that mustard gas might be used to repel the cross-Channel attack.)

The Thirty-third was composed of 160 men in five platoons of thirty-two. But for Tiger it was to be broken into four groups of forty, three to go in on the assault wave, and the fourth to follow in the backup. Former corporal in the Thirty-third, E. Dale Rodman, recalled that on April 22, the first day of Tiger's schedule, his company "arrived at a marshaling area, somewhere in South Devon, along with thousands of other troops from the First Brigade, infantry, and tank companies."[4] The infantrymen whom Rodman saw were from the Fourth Infantry Division, elements of which had been inspected the week before by Montgomery; their commander, Major General Raymond O. Barton; and their deputy commander, General Theodore Roosevelt. They had been told they would "play a big part in D Day."[5] Men of the Fourth Infantry Division had been exercising on a hill overlooking Exeter when they were rushed to the coast for Tiger.

Not that they, or any of the ordinary soldiers and sailors involved in the exercise, were actually told its name; or, at first, whether or not it was even an exercise. Being an enlisted man has a lot in common with being an extra in a film. Both soldiers and extras grow accustomed to being herded about like cattle for purposes of which they are at best dimly aware. Both are used to hours of pointless hanging around punctuated by sudden, adrenalin-pumping calls to action, which then often turn out to be false alarms preceding more waiting. A film extra would have no difficuty in understanding the U.S. infantryman's standard gripe that his life was a long routine of "hurry up and wait." And when the soldier is on an exercise, the resemblance is more marked; then all the soldier's preparation and ability, all the care he might have taken to be, or to appear to be, the real thing is like the extra's at the service of make-believe. On an exercise, as on a film lot, the sense of reality is subtly subverted.

To have been a soldier on Convoy T-4 of Exercise Tiger must have felt not unlike being an extra on the set of a war movie that all of a sudden turns into real war. But, for the moment, the First Engineers and the infantry kicked their heels in their marshaling areas, where, Dale Rodman recalled, "troops from different units were formed into boatload groups."

To take the film analogy a final step further, if Tiger's soldiers and sailors were its extras, then the stars were its spectators, the commanders and planners who would assess it and for whom, in a sense, the whole show was being mounted. On the evening of the 25th, in London, General Eisenhower boarded his private train, *Bayonet, en route* via Salisbury for Slapton Sands and Tiger. With him were General Bradley, General Leonard T. Gerow (Commander, Fifth Corps, which would make the Omaha landing), and the Deputy Supreme Commander, British Air Chief Marshal Sir Arthur Tedder. The following day Rear Admiral Ramsay would open his battle headquarters in Portsmouth, and Eisenhower and Montgomery would not be long in following him there, with battle commands of their own in the woods adjoining Southwick Park. Eisenhower's trip to Slapton Sands for Tiger was part of the process whereby the entire invasion machinery was being moved into a new gear, out of London and operational theory and discussion, and into Portsmouth and South Devon and the published fact of the Neptune/Overlord Operations Orders.

Meanwhile the Palace, Sattra, and Tembani hotels in Paignton were preparing for a large influx of other observers, American and British, navy, army, and air. Some would observe from landing craft, which were waiting for them in Dartmouth. Others would observe from the land. All were advised to wrap up well in warm clothing and to bring with them canteen cups and field glasses.

Balloons were flown over Brixham and Torquay to protect ships that would be on the exercise (until the last moment before D Day the Allied commanders would worry that the Germans would bomb the invasion fleet packing the south-coast harbors). In Plymouth Rear

Admiral Leatham issued orders for the exercise's distant covering force, or defensive "screen," of Royal Navy warships. Lyme Bay would be sealed off from German attack by four of the fast, new "O" class fleet destroyers and a further covering force of motor torpedo boats (MTBs) and motor gunboats (MGBs). Other MTBs and MGBs were to lurk off Cherbourg to stop the Fifth and Ninth *Schnellboot* flotillas based there: a clear proof that the danger of E-boat attack was anticipated.

Having been hurried to their marshaling areas, and kept waiting in them, Tiger's soldiers were now to have to hurry up and wait all over again. Dale Rodman recalled that "we boarded the ships on the morning of the 26th." Martin "Chicago Mac" McMahon, who was in an underwater demolition team (UDT), said that "At about midday, April 26, we were ordered 'Grab all your gear,' and were trucked to Brixham, Devon."[6] At Brixham and in Plymouth Harbor the eight LSTs that would make up Convoy T-4 of Tiger waited to take on their boatloads of troops.

In Plymouth were LSTs *515* and *496*, whose progress from the American Midwest across the Atlantic has already been charted. With them were the *511* and the *58,* built respectively in Seneca, Illinois, and Pittsburgh, Pennsylvania, and both in England since February. For the *58,* which would tow two steel pontoons to bridge the lake behind Slapton Sands, this would be her first trip from Plymouth Sound in the two months she had been in England. The fifth ship in the Plymouth section of Convoy T-4, *LST 531,* had docked in England in the first week of April. Wendell Hoppler of the *515* recalled seeing the *531* anchored nearby in Plymouth. He was encouraged to practice semaphore and blinker, and "talked for a while on blinker light" to a friend, John Shea, aboard the *531.* They agreed to "pull a liberty" next time their ships met.[7]

In Brixham Harbor were T-4's remaining three ships: the *499* (built, like the *496,* in Evansville, Indiana), the *289,* and the *507.* In her few months' history the *507* had acquired a few sea experiences of her own; small things, but she had known nothing larger. In an abortive beaching exercise on her shakedown in the Gulf of Mexico she had broken her anchor chain (the LST would steam toward a beach, and drop the anchor as a brake; its chain was colored to indicate how much had been run out). And rounding Land's End for Brixham, one of her propellers had been badly bent: "an intoxicated British Pilot guided our ships directly over a buoy."[8] Just before Tiger the *507* had been in dry dock having the propeller repaired. Now she was again as good as new, which she practically was; almost brand new, the *507* and all of Convoy T-4.

Now, a day or more before they were due to put to sea, their first ever boatloads of soldiers came aboard. The shipboard wait was intentional. It was conscious policy "to marry the LSTs and the troops concerned."[9] Angelo Crapanzano, who worked in *507*'s engine room, recalled that they were "taking the army aboard to acquaint them with the layout of the ship, where to eat, where the heads [i.e., lavatories] were, and how to secure the vehicles and equipment."[10] He might have added that the soldiers had also to acquire a grasp of naval jargon and to learn to obey naval as well as military orders. It was all part of the process of getting the soldiers to think amphibian.

As he stepped aboard, each soldier was issued with a carbon dioxide inflatable lifebelt. In perhaps the cruelest of Tiger's reversals of roles this belt, which was issued with an eye to saving life, would be the cause of many, perhaps most, of the deaths. It was an army belt, different from the bulky kapok- (or silk-cotton-) filled jacket that was worn in the navy. It resembled two bicycle inner tubes about two inches each in diameter. The tubes were pleated so that the wearer might take out as much slack as he needed. Two handles, when squeezed, punctured two CO_2 cartridges, inflating the tubes.

But quality control of the lifebelts had not been very thorough. Some were found to have defective CO_2 cartridges, and others no cartridges at all. Evidently, while in their marshaling areas, the soldiers had been told not to discharge the capsules prematurely. But Dale Rodman recalled that "no instructions were given regarding their proper use." Most signficantly, because the soldiers had cumbersome packs on their backs, with barracks bags and weapons slung over their shoulders, there was nowhere else to wear the lifebelt but around the waist.

Angelo Crapanzano said that "no one knew where [the *507* was] heading except Captain Swarts, who had sealed orders." Tom Clark of the *507* wrote to his father on the Fourth of July, 1944 (nine weeks later), that as the soldiers boarded there were "rumors flying, gossip, scuttlebutt."[11] The rumors were fueled both by the days of bored inaction and by ignorance of what was going on. The sailors, if they did not know exactly where they were to sail to, seem (some at least) to have known they were on a "dry run," but the soldiers didn't know even that. Douglas Harlander, Assistant Executive Officer of the *531* (in Plymouth) believed that "most of the men thought they were embarked on the actual invasion of France."[12] According to a crewman on the same ship, Henry Schrawder, "the scuttlebutt was

Poland.''[13] Quartermaster Eugene Carney of the Fourth Infantry Division (boarding the *515*) wasn't sure what to think: ''Rumors—soldiers live on them—began flying.'' His strongest feeling on arriving in Plymouth had been ''Not another dry run!'' But when he saw that the ship's tank deck ''was loaded with small planes and trucks filled with machine guns'' he knew that this was ''no routine practice.''[14]

When each ship had been fully loaded with her assigned complement of men, vehicles, and equipment, she was ''sealed'': no one aboard could leave. Now, surely, there was no reason to keep the soldiers in suspense any longer. Angelo Crapanzano remembered that his captain's sealed orders weren't opened until the *507* was under way. But perhaps the procedure differed from ship to ship. Douglas Harlander of the *531* said that it was after his ship had been sealed, but while it was still in Plymouth Harbor, that ''we were informed that we were on a combined army-navy rehearsal for the cross-Channel assault.'' As already noted, the rehearsal's name was not given.

Now the soldiers had to do their best to get their rocky ''marriage'' to their LSTs off to a good start. Navy medical corpsman Arthur Victor recalled that the *507* was ''packed with about 500 soldiers . . . amphibious Dukws, jeeps, trucks . . . loaded from one end of the ship to the other, top deck and tank deck. We were a floating arsenal.''[15] Lieutenant Eugene Eckstam (a medical officer on the same ship) remembered that the soldiers ''consumed their canned 'C' rations on deck, where they rambled around in a large cicle.''[16] Tom Clark wrote to his father that the *507* had been ''anchored in a beautiful cove'' (he meant Brixham Harbor):

> Time passed slowly then. The army with their lifebelts and helmets swarmed about the ship. In the wardroom the Vic [i.e., the Victrola record player] played constantly. We took the little loudspeaker that [we] had purchased for our room and hooked it up on the main deck so that the troops could listen to music while we lay sealed. The weather was ideal, hot sun, blue water. . . .

Sealed off from the outside world in Plymouth and Brixham harbors the eight LSTs lay idle in the ''ideal'' weather, their shipbound army passengers killing time like film extras waiting for the next big crowd scene. On the surface everything was proceeding in a calm and orderly fashion; the swelling undercurrent of chaos was invisible to the men themselves. But to turn T-4 into Bradley's ''major tragedy,'' one more flaw was needed and, incredibly, that flaw would be forthcoming. The confused sequence that would produce it, in yet another misunderstanding, was set in motion by an apparently trivial incident outside Plymouth Harbor while the soldiers and sailors tried to snatch some sleep aboard their sealed and crowded LSTs.

The incident involved a First World War vintage "S" class destroyer called HMS *Scimitar*. She had had an eventful war. In 1940 she had evacuated almost 3,000 soldiers in six trips to Dunkirk; battle honors in the Atlantic and Arctic had followed. In 1942 she had been in British destroyer squadrons escorting the liners *Queen Mary* and *Queen Elizabeth,* laden with American troops; towards the close of that year she had taken part in the invasion of French North Africa. At the end of January 1944 she had been transferred with her sister ships *Saladin* and *Skate* to the Plymouth Command under Admiral Leatham for duties in the Channel. On April 19 Admiral Leatham had detailed the three "Esses" among sixteen ships of his command scheduled to escort the convoys of Exercise Tiger.

There had been signs that the *Scimitar* was beginning to show her age (twenty-six in 1944; she would be scrapped in 1947). In December 1943 she had "developed defects," and in January 1944 was under repair for a short period. Perhaps this was why she was transferred from the Atlantic to the nearer waters of the Channel. But the *Scimitar* was certainly not so old or unseaworthy as to be crippled when, at 4:45 on the morning of April 27, "whilst laying stopped as marker vessel," she was rammed by an American landing craft.

The damage was slight: "plating distorted and holed at forecastle plate at 22 station."[17] It was not a very large hole, only about two feet square; nor was it in a very dangerous position—forward on her port side, twelve feet above the waterline. This hole in *Scimitar*'s side would, however, be the last of several—in communication, organization, command, timing, and sheer common sense . . . *holes* through which Convoy T-4 would slip to disaster.

CHAPTER
7

The LST chosen for the command ship of Convoy T-4 was the *515* under its experienced captain, Pearl Harbor veteran and regular navy "mustang" Lieutenant John Doyle. The convoy's command structure, under Bernard Skahill, was independent of that of the ship under Doyle, yet another separation of powers that would figure large in the story of T-4 and produce a strong clash of personality between the two Irish-Americans. The *515* was the flagship—Skahill was the convoy's Flag Commodore; but it was also Doyle's ship, and at one point on the convoy's journey Doyle would be overheard to remark that there wasn't "room enough for both of them on the bridge."[1]

They might have got on if things had not gone wrong. But they did go wrong, and perhaps judgments of Skahill tend therefore to be a little retrospective. To Hermann Grosse, a sailor on the *515,* he "came aboard looking old and feeble," and certainly at about forty-eight years of age—thin, slightly stooped, and with thinning hair—Skahill must have been easily the oldest man aboard T-4. He was a trained navy man of long standing—the U.S. Naval Academy, Class of 1921—but to Grosse, "he seemed to lack leadership."[2] His judgment was echoed by Wendell Hoppler: "Skahill was a pipsqueak. He seemed to be dreaming and lacked leadership."[3]

Lieutenant George Hawley, however, the convoy's Chief Medical Officer, knew Skahill in more depth. Hawley said he was "the kindest, most gentle man I have ever known, completely unsuited for the competitive aspects of a naval career. . . . He and I played dominoes hour after hour, day in and day out."[4] Commander Skahill seems to have retained his fondness for the game of dominoes: In a photograph of him taken in 1958 there are dominoes in the foreground.

His Communications Officer, Moses Hallett, said of him that he was a "colorless personality," but that " 'cordial personal relations' were not the order of the day."[5] In other words, it mattered more, then, to get things right than to get along, and, in fact, an easygoing tolerance would not be possible or in place in the extreme situation in which T-4 was to find itself. The strong-minded Lieutenant Doyle would feel compelled to challenge the bases of Skahill's authority and personality, as even *this* corner of Tiger's command structure went wrong.

The Plymouth section of Convoy T-4 put to sea at 9:45 on the morning of April 27. The *515* would lead the line of LSTs, and as the ship slipped its mooring in Plymouth Harbor, the loudspeaker system crackled into life with Doyle's voice saying, "This is a drill, but we're going into enemy waters." The ships "cleared the harbor easterly" and then, in Plymouth Sound, formed themselves into a convoy of five, the *515* at its head, followed by the *496, 511, 531,* and the *58* towing its two pontoons. Also waiting in the Sound was the Royal Navy flower-class corvette *Azalea,* which would precede the *515* as escort.

The *Azalea* had been built at Beverley in Yorkshire and "adopted" by Beverley womenfolk, who from time to time would send parcels of knitwear to keep her crew warm. She was, at 205 feet, shorter than an LST and, at 925 tons, much lighter. She was a litter faster, though: a maximum speed of fifteen knots to the LST's twelve. Her captain was Lieutenant Commander George C. Geddes of the Royal Naval Reserve, a Scotsman from the Glasgow area. Before the war he had sailed on the ocean liners of the Canadian Pacific Company; before *Azalea* he had captained the HMS *Northern Reward,* an Atlantic trawler on contraband duties in the Scottish islands. The *Northern Reward* under Geddes had evacuated troops from Dunkirk, but with his transfer to the *Azalea* his duties had become more specialized. The Yorkshire shipyard had built the corvette specifically as an antisubmarine escort vessel, and by April 1944 George Geddes was well used to escorting ships—in the western approaches, from Gibraltar, and on the West African route. His experience as an escort officer had perhaps taught him to think of the biggest threat as coming from submarines. Later he would tell Rear Admiral Moon: "I was a mile ahead at the actual time of the attack":

REAR ADMIRAL MOON: Is that a normal distance to keep?

LIEUTENANT COMMANDER GEDDES: I consider it is from the point of view of an attack from a U-boat.

REAR ADMIRAL MOON: I infer that you consider your main menace was the U-boat rather than the E-boat?

LIEUTENANT COMMANDER GEDDES: No, sir, because around there the E-boat is really expected, sir.[6]

With U-boats in mind, the *Azalea* was equipped with hedgehog and depth charges. But she had other armament, too; fewer guns than the average LST, but of heavier caliber. Perhaps, as with Commander Skahill, the experience of T-4 would later color how those on the convoy perceived *Azalea*. A number of survivors have said that they thought the corvette was an antisubmarine trawler. For example, Elwin Hendrick, Doyle's communications officer on the *515:* "As convoy T-4 was forming up off Plymouth I got a look at our escort through binoculars. She loked more like a converted trawler to me than a corvette." (In what must be a slightly mistaken memory, Hendrick recalled that "as we were forming up outside Plymouth I took a blinker message from her: 'My best speed ten knots.' ")[7] Likewise, someone on another LST would recall that "we were reported to have more firepower than the trawler,"[8] when, in fact, the *Azalea* was armed with four-inch cannon forward and a two-pounder on the bridge, with two antiaircraft Oerlikons and a two-pounder about the bridge and funnel.

But the *Azalea* was not intended as T-4's only or chief escort. The bulk of the convoy's firepower protection was to be provided by the 26-knot destroyer *Scimitar;* in a common British escort pattern of the time, it would steam along T-4's flank while *Azalea* took the bow position. *Scimitar,* however, had the small hole in her side and at 7:52 that morning had signaled Plymouth to that effect; also that in the seven hours since she had been rammed the hole had been covered over from the inside to stop water coming in, and that her captain considered her "fit for sea providing there is no deterioration of weather."[9]

There is a confusion here that will probably never be cleared up in complete detail. Rear Admiral Leatham, in his later apology to the Americans, maintained that the *Scimitar*'s signal "should have been addressed to Com Force U," Rear Admiral Moon, who would later ask the *Scimitar*'s commanding officer, Lieutenant Shee, RNR, whether he had sent him "any dispatch about your damage." Shee's reply would be: "I didn't consider it serious enough to warrant a dispatch. My signal to Plymouth of the damage was routine. . . ."

Setting aside any difference between a dispatch and a signal, here is another case of apparent misunderstanding, as Leatham acknowledged when he wrote that even though Shee's signal had been wrongly "addressed," it was "I regret, not repeated to Com Force U." This is the more mystifying in the light of Shee's statement to Moon that when he was signaled to have the damage repaired, "I questioned the order and told C-in-C Plymouth that I was supposed to be rendezvousing with a convoy outside."[10]

Questioning of orders, or the lack of them, was just what T-4 needed, and it is hard to reconcile Shee's statement with Leatham's that "the Staff Officer principally concerned . . . was, in fact, under the impression that Com Force U and Senior Officer Escorts [captain of the 'hunt' destroyer *Tanatside,* which appears a little later in this story] were aware of the damage and had ordered *Scimitar* to return to Plymouth."[11]

The *Scimitar* was ordered into port for dockyard repairs, which could not begin until April 28. At some point after 10 A.M., as the first five ships of T-4 were lining up in Plymouth Sound, the *Scimitar,* their second escort ship, steamed past them in the opposite direction. Here followed another extraordinary communications failure. Lieutenant Geddes on the *Azalea* told Moon that he "saw the *Scimitar* going into Plymouth and assumed that was in order, and reported to the convoy commander." Skahill's failure to question this is incomprehensible; but, as Geddes continued, "throughout the whole time we never had any signals by wireless from the LSTs. We could have got them by changing to another wavelength, but that would have meant dropping one of our own lines." The first five ships of T-4 were about to sail out into "enemy waters" deaf, dumb, virtually blind (few of the LSTs had radar), and defenseless.

So were the three LSTs in Brixham, but perhaps because they had less far to go before meeting up with the Plymouth section off Berry Head, the eastern tip of Start Bay, they left harbor later, on the afternoon of the 27th. The first of them in line was the *499,* followed by the *289* and *507,* the last ship from Brixham, as it would be the last of T-4 when it was complete. Tom Clark of the *507* wrote to his father that July:

> . . . the word came through to get under way. I had the deck at that time. For the soldiers it was quite a thrill. I did my best to look important, standing on the bridge, impassively, glasses in hand, taking bearings and in general putting on a very good show. Some soldiers did not bother to get excited.

The latter were probably the soldiers with some experience of amphibious warfare, like Martin McMahon, the underwater demolition man on the *289.* Among the *289*'s 395 soldiers, according to records, were some 250 of McMahon's own 1048 UDT Company. When he had boarded the boat, McMahon had philosophically unrolled his bedding on the top deck, mistrusting the shallow-draft LST in a rough sea or under attack. He hadn't been briefed about E-boats, but "the poop was that they were lurking in the Channel.'' He had been on LSTs in the Mediterranean, where he had seen action in Algeria and Sicily. Now, although ''no one had any idea of where we were going,'' McMahon at least knew that they were only on a dry run.

Other soldiers were less experienced. The picture of one on the *507* stuck in Tom Clark's mind:

> The little army barber, a private, was back there on the fantail, still cutting hair as we got under way. I saw him there and remembered the haircut he had given me earlier—not a very good one—remembered, too, that he was of Polish or German extraction, and he talked with an accent. On seeing him I had said to myself: ''Here's a fellow who looks out of place in a uniform.''

The *507* had no barber's pole, but on its top deck were a number of field ambulances, with their red crosses on white backgrounds; standing on the fantail, the ''little army barber'' was the very last man at the back of the last ship in line.

Angelo Crapanzano of the *507*'s engine room remembers—a fact that would be significant for him—that they had been given tetanus booster shots that day; he was feeling feverish. He said that as the Brixham section left the harbor ''we had two corvettes as escorts, but after about an hour they both turned about and left.'' This probably overlaps with the vaguer memory of McMahon on the *289* that when they left Brixham ''we were cleared to sail as we had proper escort, and then we heard later that we had none.'' The purpose of the two corvettes would seem to have been to put the inexperienced Brixham LSTs on course for their rendezvous and wish them Godspeed.

Now all the ships are at sea, sailing into the dusk of British Double Summer Time, and at 8:30 P.M. meeting off Berry Head to form T-4. In the same order as before the Brixham section attaches itself to the ships from Plymouth, *Azalea* a mile ahead, 600 yards between the LSTs—although their station keeping would prove shaky. It is still quite light, and the mood of the men aboard the ships is, by and large, lighthearted. On the *515*, although alcohol was forbidden on all ships, they have even built up a secret store of drink for a planned ''post dry run'' party. But that is for afterwards; on the journey itself the *515* is to maintain the strong discipline that Doyle had built up on its transatlantic crossing, with its daily diet not only of *Oklahoma!* but of ''GQ [General Quarters], collision, and abandon-ship drills.'' The same discipline would be extended through the evening and night to soldiers newly aboard, and if they had been overexercised already, like

Eugene Carney of the Fourth Infantry Division, they didn't take to it much: "We were repeatedly given instructions on procedures in case of attack. We were getting damn tired and disgusted." Carney felt that there were more important jobs to be done on shore.[12]

These drills, or the absence of them, were to matter, however, if not to Carney, then to other men. Another ship that seems to have followed the same rigorous routine while on T-4 was the *511* from Brixham. The *511* went through "fire drills, battle-station drills, life-raft drills and, for army personnel, the use of inflatable life belts in case of abandoning ship."

The men of T-4 would need to be able to "think" deeply amphibian before the night was out, but on other ships the discipline was more lax. On the deck of the *289*, for example, Martin McMahon and other

> soldiers made ourselves as comfortable as possible, lined up with our mess kits for chow from the galley, and bitched about the lack of liquor. The intercom was constantly blaring but we paid no attention. We had no drill of any kind. We did nothing, just got out of the way of the LST's crew.

And the *507*, apparently, had had nothing of the *515*'s training in emergencies. Arthur Victor said that "we never had any drills to abandon ship," for example, and although he did remember some battle drills while on T-4, "they didn't amount to much because we didn't really take them seriously. We went through the motions, but never felt threatened. It was like being on a cruise."

Angelo Crapanzano confirmed the cruiselike feeling. "The crowded army men," he said, "had the usual pastimes of card and crap games, writing letters, guys with guitars singing, joking, etc." At chow that evening Arthur Victor had an argument with someone and high-spiritedly threw mashed potato in his face, and later:

> We were partying. Crewmen and soldiers had banjos and guitars, and I seem to remember clarinets. There were harmonicas and flutes and drumming on jeep and truck fenders. Some guys tied their shirts around their waists and rolled up their pants legs and tied hankies around their heads like babushkas, and played females. No booze, but we formed a conga line of soldiers and sailors and danced around the vehicles on deck, and we did the hanky dance, and we sang as we danced. We just had a hi-old time.
>
> After the party I was standing at the rail with another good buddy, who was totally depressed. He kept saying "I've a feeling of doom and I know I'm going to die." I told him it was nonsense and as long as we were

together we'd get through the war OK but no amount of talking could dissuade him from his feelings. I told him I'd see him in the morning and went to my compartment. That's the last time I saw him.

Back in his compartment, Arthur Victor and his friend Kenneth Scott (''Scotty'') had a pillow-fight and soaked one another with water before hitting the sack.

Other men on other ships of the convoy also had premonitions of doom. Joseph Griffin, a crewman on the *289,* had said on leaving the United States that he would never see home again: ''I'll be killed on this ship.'' Joseph Kennedy, of Columbus, Ohio, a 27-year-old in the First Engineers, had fought in North Africa, Sicily, and mainland Italy with a friend he'd known since March 1941. They had both been promoted to staff sergeant on April 17, and Kennedy's friend had said: ''Joe, I'll never live to receive my first full pay.'' For Tiger, they were to have been on the same LST, but Kennedy was switched to the *289* boatload while his friend stayed in the *531.*[13]

It would vitally matter that night which unit you were in, which ship you were on, and where you were on your ship. But that would be later. Now it is between 9 and 10 P.M. The sky is dark, with a setting quarter moon. Visibility is good. The air is chilly, and the ships' intake valves are registering a sea temperature of 42° Fahrenheit. Led by their solitary escort, the eight Large Slow Targets are about to embark on another of that night's ''endless maneuverings.'' The idea is that the ships should stay at sea for as long as they will on D Day. Off Torquay and the promontory called Hope's Nose they start a long, slow turn to starboard. From here their course to the transport area twelve miles off Slapton Sands is shaped like a perfect question mark.

The transport area is full of ships, as T-4 starts its turn. Rear Admiral Moon would report that at the close of April 27 his Force U had 221 ships and boats of all shapes and sizes under its protection in Lyme Bay, ''awaiting unloading and sailing empty at daylight.''[14] There were 21 LSTs, 28 LCIs, 65 LCTs, and ''14 miscellaneous and 92 small landing craft'' (probably LCVPs, lowered from the LSTs). Moon also referred to an APA, or attack transport: the USS *Bayfield,* command ship for Tiger, as it would be for Utah. On board the *Bayfield* with Moon were General Collins of the Seventh Corps, and Major General Raymond O. Barton, commander of the Fourth Infantry Division, which that morning had made the assault on Slapton Sands.

It had been a day of mixed fortunes. It had begun chaotically, when at 6:25 A.M. Moon, prompted by his second-in-command, Captain M. T. Richardson, decided to postpone H Hour by one hour. This had sown confusion in the early stages of the amphibious landing, throwing out the immaculately synchronized operations of navy, army, and air; with only an hour's notice, all the complex, interlocking schedules had had to be revised, with the result that "bombers, Navy vessels, aeroplanes and special units fouled up in everything from timing to orders."[15] Because of "early" landings at the previous H Hour by units that had not heard of its postponement, the "softening-up" fire of Typhoon aircraft armed with rockets and of Rear Admiral Leatham's naval "gunfire support" group had had to be canceled or interrupted. (One British naval officer involved in Tiger's gunfire support was First Lieutenant Terence Lewin, of the tribal-class destroyer HMS *Ashanti*, later Admiral of the Fleet Lord Lewin, naval architect of the Falklands War. He recalled that *Ashanti*'s target "was the upper left-hand window of a house behind the beach.")[16]

Meanwhile, the LCTs in Lyme Bay, with their precious cargo of DD amphibian tanks, had been kept waiting, bobbing about like sitting ducks, while the beach engineers—too slowly, as it seemed to observers—destroyed obstacles. However, the tanks had gone in successfully enough—although two of them had sunk—followed by the infantrymen. The landing had been achieved.

In postponing H Hour Moon had not been adhering to the convention that the realism of the exercise would rigidly imitate the forthcoming D Day reality. He would say that he had learned from his mistake. His subsequent actions would show this not to be so; that a tendency to postponement was, on the contrary, a built-in bias of his personality. Here, off Slapton Sands, was the first open manifestation of that potential weakness, that "certain lack of firmness and a tendency to be overly cautious" that had worried General Collins.

Moon doubtless regretted his postponement of H Hour at that evening's conference with Collins and Major General Barton aboard the *Bayfield*. But Tiger was an exercise. One of its purposes was to expose exactly such weaknesses, in an admiral as well as in the ordinary fighting man. Tomorrow everyone would put up a better show.

That night on the *Bayfield* the 8 P.M. to midnight watch as Command Duty Officer was held by Commander John Moreno, a 35-year-old who was Air and Assistant Plans Officer on Rear Admiral Moon's staff. Shortly after 10 P.M. Moreno received a mysterious dispatch concerning E-boat activity in the Channel. The dispatch was, he later recalled, in plain language, but was "vague as to origin and exact meaning"; it was, he said, "a warning rather than a contract report," and it was "clearly addressed to other activities in addition to CTF* 125" (i.e., Rear Admiral Moon). Moreno didn't know what to make of the dispatch; he considered later that it might have been interpreted "if we had had a British liaison officer on our staff," but in any event, "all I could do was pass it on to my relief with the comment that 'we couldn't make much sense out of it.' "

No other record exists of this dispatch. It was perhaps from an aircraft that made a visual sighting of the E-boats as, at 10 P.M. (British time), they slipped out of Cherbourg. Shore radar first picked up their presence, according to Plymouth records, "at about midnight." Seven minutes after midnight, at 0007, on the morning of the 28th Plymouth signaled "ships on port wave" that radar contact had been made with the enemy traveling due north off Portland Bill. Four minutes later, at 0011, the lookout of the destroyer JMS *Onslow,* patrolling off Portland Bill, sighted the slim silhouette of an E-boat darting to the north. Then, at 0020, *Onslow*'s radar picked up three groups of E-boats heading northwest. By this time the operations room in Plymouth was plotting the boats on its charts; by this time, too, Plymouth had woken up to the blunder that had kept HMS *Scimitar* in port.

It had done so well before the E-boats had put to sea. According to Rear Admiral Leatham's subsequent report, it was at 7:30 P.M. on the 27th that "the Staff Officer concerned realized that something was amiss." At 7:38 the Staff Officer sent a message inquiring as to the "names of escorts of convoy T-4." He had sent for Lieutenant Shee, captain of the *Scimitar;* but it must have taken a time to find him, because it was not until 11:06 that the unnamed officer, at last "fully realizing the true situation," asked the captain of HMS *Tanatside,* the Senior Officer, Escorts, to "detail another ship as escort to convoy T-4."

As yet, however, Plymouth apparently knew nothing of the E-boats; the absence of a second escort for T-4 was not yet perceived as an emergency. Nor was the naval message of 11:06 instantaneously understood by *Tanatside.* It had first to be decoded, and it was a further hour and forty minutes before *Tanatside*'s captain was able to take "immediate action to detail HMS *Saladin* as relief escort." Almost an hour after that, *Saladin* left Start Bay. The Naval Officer In Charge (NOIC), Portland, signaled "Expect to meet friendly patrol."

The friendly patrol, however, was too little and much too late. The

*Commander, Task Force.

E-boats had already exposed "the system of patrol lines which looks so solid and comforting on a chart" as "an ensnaring myth of security."[18] Now, having penetrated the patrol lines, they were at loose in a sea crowded with ships, including the eight barely defended and uninformed LSTs of T-4. And, extraordinarily, although her head escort, *Azalea,* had known of the presence of E-boats since Plymouth's "port wave" message just after midnight, she continued, apparently obliviously, to "steam right into the enemy."[19] In Plymouth's later postmortem of the affair, it was this that would arouse the most incredulity and censure. One of the naval chiefs would wonder whether Lieutenant Commander Geddes, Commander of the *Azalea,* had been waiting for orders according to the terms of the Plymouth War Orders. It was noted, too, that his sailing orders were to close the shore only in the event of an attack. But the naval chief added that this "seems little excuse for steaming . . . in line ahead at 3½ knots towards an enemy for nearly two hours after the initial enemy reports."[20] Geddes was severely criticized, on paper, if not, apparently, to his face, for "lack of initiative."[21]

In communications between themselves as part of the postmortem Plymouth's naval chiefs also disagreed as to whether or not the absence of *Scimitar* had been a deciding factor in the disaster. The majority view was that "an extra ship might have made all the difference."[22] The role of that extra ship was now, early on the morning of the 28th, to be taken by *Saladin.* But *Saladin*'s number one boiler was unreliable, and her top speed was limited to twenty-three knots. T-4 was thirty miles away, and in fewer than forty minutes the E-boats would set upon it. *Saladin* would not arrive in time to repel the attack, only to pick up survivors.

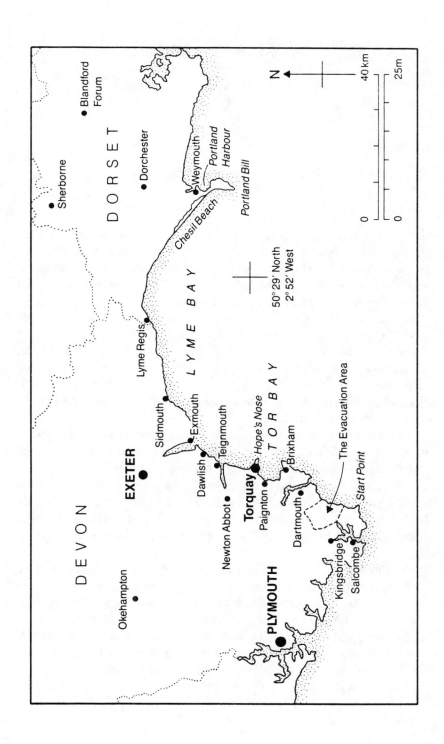

CHAPTER

8*

It is midnight aboard Convoy T-4. On the LST first in line, the *515*, sharecropper's son Wendell Hoppler has just taken over the quartermaster's watch, 0000 to 0400. He keeps a log and records barometer levels. He notes that the sea is "very dark," the weather "clear and calm," with "a faint slip" of setting moon.

Aboard the *507*, last in line, Angelo Crapanzano has drawn the 0000 to 0400 engine room watch. This evening he feels feverish and goes down to the main engine room feeling quite ill. His engineering officer, Lieutenant Smith, feels his forehead and tells him to report to the sick bay, where the pharmacist's mate finds his temperature to be 104° Fahrenheit. He knows this is from his tetanus booster shot; he had the same reaction in boot camp.

The main engine room turns the ship's propellers. Just forward of it, a thin bulkhead away, is the auxiliary engine room, providing the ship's on-board electrical and hydraulic power. In there are a group of sailors, including two called Watson and Carrol. Watson is feeling good because in a five-handed poker game that has just ended he has won ten dollars from his shipmate, Albert Nickson. Nickson has gone up to his quarters for a shower prior to turning in for the night.

On the same ship, E. Dale Rodman of the Thirty-third Chemical Decontamination Company has checked the bulletin board on the tank deck. Like all army corporals aboard, he is liable for guard duty. The night before, he had held the midnight to 4 A.M. tank deck duty. In that night's long watches, the deck so thickly crowded with Dukws, trucks, and half-tracks that he couldn't walk between them, he had learned for the first time in his young life to enjoy a good cup of coffee.

Tonight on the bulletin board he had seen the name E. Redman—not

---

* For notes on this chapter, see page 269.

Rodman—assigned to the same watch. This typographical error and the fact that he is known as Dale to his friends will save his life.

Assuming it is someone else, Dale Rodman turns in for the night, in one of the three separate sleeping areas designated for the forty men of the Thirty-third aboard the *507*. He is asleep when the officer of the day comes looking for E. Redman. He is told the Thirty-third has no such person. The officer then assigns Corporal Joseph Rosiek from the Thirty-third to that shift.

Navy officer Tom Clark is also fast asleep on the *507*. It has been a long day for him. After his watch on deck when the *507* left Brixham Harbor, he had gone for a briefing in the officers' wardroom ''and found out what we were supposed to do.'' Then he had sat and talked with other officers about their dry run, before relaxing with games of poker and bridge, the telling of jokes and riddles. Clark had hit the sack early, read for a while, switched off his light and said his rosary.

Now he is being awakened by his friend, Lieutenant Franklin ''Scotty'' Gill, to be told that he has the 0000 to 0400 watch. ''Ho ho,'' he says, ''not this boy.'' After discussion, the matter is settled in Clark's favor by the captain, and another officer is assigned. Clark soon falls asleep. . . .

By the time he has done so, the radio room of the *Azalea*, miles ahead at the front of the convoy, has received Plymouth's seven minutes past midnight ''port wave'' warning of E-boats on the loose off Portland Bill. Tom Clark is still fast asleep when at about a quarter to one the captain of *Tanatside* takes ''immediate action'' to detail *Saladin* as his convoy's relief escort.

At 1 A.M. in the *507*'s sick bay Angelo Crapanzano is relieved of his overnight engine room watch and told to go to his bunk and sleep off his fever. He has ''a weird gut feeling'' as of somebody telling him, ''Find your life jacket.'' He finds his on top of his sea chest, labeled ''Crappy.'' Then, he thinks, he must have fallen asleep. . . .

It is a while later that a number of people aboard the *507* hear a strange grinding under the ship's hull. Soldier Leslie Morse hears it, ''a scraping and dragging noise from under us that seemed to follow across the ship and then stopped.'' Dale Rodman hears it, and so does soldier John Menzies—''something rumbling across the bottom of the ship,'' which he, like Rodman, will later surmise to have been a torpedo that did not explode.

Angelo Crapanzano, feverish and fast asleep, does not hear it; as a sailor, he is also perhaps more used to the sounds of a ship. The next thing he knows is that the General Quarters horn is blasting:

I jumped out of my bunk, put on my Mae West,* ran to the ladder and climbed down to the main engine room. There was the sound of 40-mm guns blasting. I asked Lieutenant Smith, who had been relieving me, "What's going on?" He shook his head and said, "I guess they're trying to make it as real as possible."

Albert Nickson is also up by now. He has thrown some clothes on and hurried to the main engine room, his post in General Quarters. A "motor mac" (motor machinist) called Koski is at the throttles "acting very excited. Being the same myself, I asked him to quiet down a bit because he was only making it worse all around." Lieutenant Smith comes over to Nickson and tells him that he's going topside to see what's going on.

Ensign Tom Clark is slower to leave his bunk. Hearing the gunfire he at first says "phooey" and turns over on his side. "You see," he told his father in his letter nine weeks later, "I was really tired."

He still doesn't want to get up when GQ sounds, but his training wins over his weariness. He is gunnery officer, and in General Quarters has to be at his station to man the battle phones. He gets up from his bunk, and over his pajamas puts on trousers and a sweater. He puts shoes on his bare feet, and remembers, too, his navy life belt and a hat.

In the companionway outside, a bit of commotion is going on. Ensign Fred Beattie, roused by the GQ warning, is yelling at Lieutenant Gill that his gang is always making off with the life jackets of his men on the bridge. "Hot exchange. Frank turned and headed off, presenting his chubby lil' old arse too invitingly, and I found myself planting a well-aimed foot right on target. We didn't have time to really square off."

Tom Clark is dressed now. He climbs to the boat deck, where he sees "a figure huddling against the bulkhead." Soon he knows why, for the "incredible" is happening—they are being fired upon.

He climbs another ladder, collects his battle helmet, then climbs to the super conn (a canvas shelter at the ship's highest point, atop the bridge), where he sees "the graceful parabola of tracer shells arcing across the stern." Lieutenant Bruce Hoffmann has the deck, and Clark asks him what's up. Hoffmann isn't sure, but thinks their escort vessel is firing on them by mistake. . . . Tom Clark's rude awakening coincides with the first anniversary of his joining the U.S. Navy on April 28, 1943.

---

* Kapok inflatable flotation jacket.

It is just past 1:35 A.M. Navy medical corpsman Arthur Victor, an 18-year-old from Pittsburgh, asleep below on the *507*, has been awakened by a sound of pounding above his head, guys running excitedly in all directions. He sits up and yells, "What the hell is going on?" Someone hollers, "We're being shelled!"

Victor jumps out of his bunk and wastes no time getting dressed. He rushes from the compartment up the ladder to the top deck. When he opens the hatch, instead of seeing gunfire, to his relief he finds guys standing around, quietly waiting. All seems quiet and serene.

Another member of the *507*'s medical team, Lieutenant Eugene Eckstam, had "hit the sack early to get a good sleep before the practice landing." Awakened by the alarm, he goes to the wardroom, where there is excited talk of "a trigger-happy gunner on the next ship firing at questionable shadows, the bullets coming close to us." Corporal Dale Rodman is also up by now. He has to wake up several buddies around him on the port side. Some do not want to go to their forward deck stations for a "dry run."

The other LSTs, seeing the tracer off the *507*'s port beam, are also puzzled by it. Lieutenant Harry Mettler, captain of the *289*, thinks it is perhaps from 40-mm guns, but he can't quite pinpoint where the firing is coming from. This is consistent with the "flashless powder" and late ignition of the E-boats' tracer.

The Germans on the E-boats are, as it happens, a little puzzled themselves as to whose tracer fire is whose. One of their flotillas is using red tracer all but indistinguishable from the American tracer; the other is using tracer of a color variously described as yellow, green, and greenish-yellow. Later, in a German report on the attack, it will be recommended that "it seems imperative that all our ships be uniformly equipped with yellow tracer ammunition."

On the *515*, meanwhile, far at the head of the line of LSTs, it is Moses Hallett's recollection that convoy commander Bernard Skahill is still in his bunk. The arrangement between him and Skahill is that he, Hallett,

> should be "on duty" whenever he [Skahill] was not—when we were at sea—which in fact meant that I was up and about in the wardroom or on the bridge from sunset to 0800 when we were under way. I was expected to inform the commander whenever anything "unusual" occurred.

Evidently things aren't yet thought to be sufficiently "unusual" to wake Skahill. They soon will be, but for the moment the *515* is as puzzled as everyone else. The tracer fire is thought to emanate from the

511, two ships behind it in line. On the *511*, "Firing was seen astern, believed to be part of the exercise." The *58*, fifth in line, has seen other tracer fire off her starboard beam, the shells passing overhead and hitting the water some 400 yards to port.

The picture is confusing, but consistent overall with the habitual E-boat tactics of firing tracer shells or flares to illuminate a ship from one beam while E-boats take aim with torpedoes on the other. A complicating factor here, however, is that they are on an exercise: No one is yet sure whether the fire is real or not; or if it is real, whether it is friend or foe; and if it is friend, whether it is part of the "rehearsal realism" or a case of mistaken identity.

On all the LSTs, General Quarters are sounded in response to the tracer fire. The captain of the *496*, Stanley Koch, wakes up and shouts "Why the hell are we on GQ? We must all be up at 2:30 anyway."

On the *515*, following a practice General Quarters soon after midnight, part of the dry run, GQ is being sounded as a precaution all over again, with the rider now, "This is *not* a drill!" Infantryman Eugene Carney aboard the *515* grumbles that they are no more settled in their sacks than they are aroused by alert bells.

The *515* switches on her radar but can pick up no rogue blips. After some twenty minutes Lieutenant Doyle apparently decides that whatever the tracer's origin, it is a false alarm. In the navy phrase he "secures," or relaxes, from General Quarters at 1:53 A.M. At much the same moment so do the *496*, the *531* in midconvoy, and the *499*.

It is sixteen minutes since *Saladin* has put out from Start Bay on her "friendly patrol" to join T-4 as its relief escort. On the convoy itself, if the sense of being on something of a cruise has passed, so for the moment has the fear of imminent danger. For a few more minutes most of T-4 will relax in the false impression that it is, after all, secure.

Arthur Victor and three fellow medical corpsmen have taken up their General Quarters stations on the port stern of the *507*, near the very tail end of T-4. From this post they are expected to attend to any possible wounded—"unlikely on a 'dry run.' " But for some twenty minutes it had seemed a possibility. Now, though, they can relax in a sense of relieved anticlimax. Arthur Victor

> looked into the night. The heavens were blanketed with stars. All in all it seemed to be a very beautiful morning. I crouched at my post whispering to my buddies and was told that the pounding I heard had been the pounding of shells thrown from an unknown source in order to knock out the watch, but with no success.

With Victor were Carl Dailey, Willard Rutherford—"my buddy that night, but not usually"—and Raban Lewis, "a big bear of a boy from the Deep South." After a few minutes of "silently waiting and staring out to sea," Victor walks to the portside railing and stands beside the raft, "caught up in the beauty of the night." Rutherford joins him there. "Feeling nostalgic, we started talking about love and stuff."

In this period of apparent lull the crew of the *58* are surprised to see the *499*, just behind them in line, pick up speed and pull out of station to aft of the *58*'s port beam. It appears that the *499* is taking evasive action from a torpedo, at 2:03 A.M. If so, it is the first of T-4's ships to come under torpedo attack.

Vincent Dunn, a first loader on one of *499*'s stern guns, recalled that "we had a fish coming at our ship at about 265 degrees. I told our gun captain. He informed the bridge. We made a slight turn and the fish went by us."

On the *507*'s bridge and super conn a nervous edginess persists. What the *515* far ahead has seen is a burst of tracer fire lasting about a minute; the *507* has seen several bursts from her port quarter. "Source of firing," said her subsequent after-action report, "could not be determined."

Now Ensign Beattie is up in the ship's control area, and Lieutenant Hoffmann is free to go to his GQ station. Before he goes he and Tom Clark try to figure out what is going on. Clark later wrote to his father:

> Finally we determined to be careful even if it were friendly action. There was a bright moon out. . . . Now I had the phones and we followed the ship with radar. Getting a bearing from radar, I had the number one and number three batteries follow the ship in accordance with reports. I was a little nervous. We were the last ship in the formation and we were traveling very slowly at the time. Soon the radar reports became a little ominous. Three more ships were picked up off our starboard quarter. By now we were pretty sure something was amiss. *All our conclusions prior to this time had been tempered by the knowledge that we were on a dry run, and that there would be other friendly craft in the area* [my italics]. The ship that had fired continued out. Radar suggested then "one mile, mile and a quarter—coming in now, one mile."
>
> By this time Hoffmann had left, and Beattie, the captain, and I were on the super conn.

At this point Lieutenant Swarts, the captain, gets angry with Beattie because he feels he has not closed up sufficiently on the next LST in line. (LST *507* has become, in British navy parlance, a "tail-end

Charlie''; on the convoy, Rear Admiral Moon will conclude, there has been ''considerable straggling.'') ''We argued, and I asked him if he wanted to relieve me as conn officer. He did.'' Then:

> ''Look for him in the loom* of the moon, Clark,'' said the captain. I remember that well because it seemed illogical, for the loom would outline them. Yet I turned my glasses off our starboard quarter, for the moon made a ribbon of silver towards us from that direction. I peered and could see nothing. I had my glasses to my eyes when the torpedo hit us. . . .

Down in the *507*'s main engine room Angelo Crapanzano is logging the changes of speed being sent down from the wheelhouse. The last thing he records is at 0203, when there is a deafening roar and everything goes black:

> I felt myself going up, then down, hitting my head on something. I must have blacked out for a few seconds but then I felt cold water around my legs. I scrambled up the ladder. The six guys in the auxiliary engine room never knew what hit them. The torpedo struck there, the heart of the ship. . . .

On the port stern Arthur Victor, admiring the starry sky, now sees stars as a tremendous explosion rocks the ship:

> I was lifted from my feet and hurled back against a bulkhead. Although my head hit so hard I almost passed out, my helmet absorbed most of the shock and I was only dazed, with nothing worse than a split upper lip. I staggered to my feet. . . .

Below, Eugene Eckstam has just left the wardroom to go topside to see what is going on. He is passing the door to the captain's quarters *en route* to the starboard hatch when ''BOOM!!!'' and the ''quaking crunch of metal'' drops him painfully to his knees on the steel deck, covering him with ''falling dust and rust—then darkness and silence.'' Eckstam stands up despite his aching knees, wondering, ''My God, what happened?''

Eckstam already has on his helmet, foul-weather gear and gas mask. In the darkness, as the auxiliary engineer room goes out of action and electrical power is lost, he looks for a battery-powered battle lantern. He finds one where he knows it will be, just across the corridor from the captain's door. Lighting it, he locates others. The explosion, he sees, has ''popped the first-aid cabinet.'' It is leaning over, its doors

* The indistinct, rippling line of reflection of the moon on the sea.

wide open. Its supplies are all over the wardroom. A few casualties come in now, "some ambulant and some on litters but most carried by buddies. . . . " Eckstam and his fellow medic Ed Panter attend to them.

On the upper conn Tom Clark, Fred Beattie, and Lieutenant Swarts have been "tossed about like corks" by the explosion. Tom Clark, festooned with the wiring of the battle phones, has lost his helmet and his right shoe. The three men climb down, Clark taking the phones with him. He feels the deck plates "so very cold against my bare foot." Soon the metal deck will be too hot to touch, but for the moment the flames do not seem bad, although "a nasty orange flame, looming brightly against the blackness of the night" is, in Clark's words, "nonchalantly crackling its path through the army vehicles topside."

From the main engine room Albert Nickson has run up to the bridge, where Swarts asks him "if all the boys had got out." Nickson reports that everyone is safely out of the main engine room but not the auxiliary. He meets a badly burned man from the auxiliary engine room called Sturivant. "It was a miracle how he ever got out. He said Watson and Carrol and the other boys didn't have a chance."

Beattie and Swarts go below, and Clark finds himself alone on the boat deck. He plugs the battle phones into a number of sockets, trying to contact the bow, but the torpedo has knocked out the ship's communications.

Her power, too. At the stern Victor sees fire fighters drag their hoses to the by-now blazing hole amidship, then fall back gasping at the intense heat. But the hoses don't work anyway. At the ship's bow end Dale Rodman witnesses the helpless navy men trying "to fight the giant flames with no pressure in their hoses."

The flames make a wall of fire and dense smoke across the ship. The stern is "wild with confusion," men yelling, "We're gonna die!" Victor and Rutherford try to grab hold of "guys running crazily about the deck" to calm them down, but they break away, panic-stricken.

Calmness in the crisis seems to derive from an intense concentration upon detail. For Tom Clark it is a fixation upon his shoes. On the boat deck, trying to get the phones to work, he feels his shoeless right foot "getting colder and colder," until at last he is determined to go back to the super conn for his shoe. He climbs the ladder again and finds one, but it's too small. It is Fred Beattie's. "By a queer coincidence both of us lost our right shoe."

Clark yells to the gun crew to keep their eyes peeled for a target, then starts down the ladder intending to find a shoe below. But the captain yells up to him to stay on the super conn. He goes up again and realizes that his ship is lost. The flames are tremendous, "a dull roar punctuated by the crackling and sputtering of small arms ammunition."

It is almost time to abandon ship, but there are still established procedures to be gone through. One of them is destruction of the ship's codebooks. With just this eventuality in mind the ship has a weighted bag in which to throw the codebooks overboard. A signalman gives a codebook to Fred Beattie: "I sailed it into the flames on the main deck, remarking that destruction would surely result. . . . Time to get the hell out."

Tom Clark turns to the stern, where lines of men lit up by the flames are heaving ammunition overboard. Beattie and Jerry Brown are down there. So are Albert Nickson and Angelo Crapanzano, who now sees the wake of another torpedo flashing towards his ship. Up on the conn Tom Clark hears the cry, "Torpedo dead astern!"

"Gosh," he will write to his father, "I never want to relive the few seconds I spent waiting for the torpedo to hit. I waited and waited until I realized it had passed. Then again the same cry, the same waiting, again the enemy missed. Thank God."

At the stern, men with fire axes are trying to chop steel cables in a hopeless effort to launch two LCVPs, the small landing craft that double as an LST's lifeboats. The force of the torpedo blast has jammed their lowering mechanisms. Most of the oval life rafts are likewise rusted immovably in position, although Victor and Rutherford are trying to get one free. Most of the men at the stern will have to try to survive immersed in the bitterly cold sea.

The captain, Lieutenant Swarts, yells to Clark to come down from the conn and to pass word to abandon ship. Clark comes down. He doesn't trust his life belt, so decides at this late juncture to take the risk of returning to his cabin for his Mae West. Uppermost in his mind is the knowledge that because of water pressure failure they have been unable to flood the *507*'s magazine full of shells: The ship could blow sky-high at any moment.

He goes to the wardroom and tells Eckstam and Panter, tending the injured there, to abandon ship. A red-haired medic is tending to a soldier with a broken leg. Clark tells them to abandon ship, too, then leaves the wardroom, forgetting—that persistent shoe again—that his right foot is bare. All of a sudden the deck underfoot burns him "like heck" and he has to hop to his stateroom on one foot. Once there, he feels about in the dark for his Mae West, a wallet with photos of his mother and father and his wife, Mary Ellen, and a shoe, which he carefully puts on.

At the stern Rutherford and Victor have freed their life raft and kicked and shoved it overboard. To their dismay, it lands upside down, its survival kits submerged. Jerry Brown asks for a volunteer to go into the water and look after it, and a medical corpsman called Arlan Star at once jumps over and swims to the raft.

He is perhaps the first man off the *507*. It is a terrifying jump to make, in the night from the high side of a ship into a sea that is at once cold and burning, dark and lit up by leaping flames, because by now much of the sea around the ship is a burning sheet of oil. James Murdoch later told the Pentagon about this:

> All of the army vehicles naturally were loaded with gasoline, and it was the gasoline which caught fire first. As the gasoline spread on the deck and poured into the fuel oil which was seeping out of the side of the ship, it caused fire on the water around the ship.

Few of the men are as quick to jump as Star. "We have rehearsed this many times in boot camp," said Raymond Bartholomay of the *507*, "but there were a few new wrinkles here. In boot camp we were always sure to be 'rescued' in a hurry as our 'ocean' was a 75′ × 100′ swimming pool." The jump holds fewer fears for Pharmacist's Mate William Reckord: "I used to dive off a bridge at Lake Delhi [Iowa] and also swim across the Mississippi River at Dubuque, so the jump and swim was no problem."

One of those afraid to jump is Arthur Victor's buddy Carl Dailey. His life belt is already inflated. Victor leads him to the railing and helps him climb over. "Wait till we're ordered to abandon ship," Victor says, "and then jump. You're going to be OK." But this is the last time that Victor ever sees him.

It is all happening very quickly, above decks and below. Men are running everywhere, preparing themselves for the sea. Below, Eugene Eckstam is making the most difficult decision of his life—it will still give him nightmares forty years later. Wearing his gas mask, he is looking into the inferno of the *507*'s tank deck, where Dale Rodman was due to have been on guard. It is "a high roaring furnace fire." Cans of gasoline on the crowded, canvas-covered trucks are exploding in balls of flame, small arms ammunition is exploding, but "the greatest horror" is the agonizing screams for help of the trapped army men.

The danger is that the fire will spread to the stern, and Eckstam knows that the men in there on the tank deck are beyond his or anyone's help and that smoke inhalation will soon end their suffering. So he takes the hard decision to dog—or close—the hatches. This, too, is standard procedure, and the hatches can be dogged shut or opened from either side. Corporal Joseph Rosiek of the Thirty-third, Rodman's substitute, is in there as Eckstam dogs them. Then Eckstam makes his way up the stern deck.

On the stern Jerry Brown now shouts, "Abandon ship!" Rutherford says to Victor, "See you later," and over he goes. Victor throws down his helmet and starts over the side, but then sees a fellow corpsman, who he knows can't swim, at the rail shaking with fear.

Victor goes to him. The nonswimmer begs, "Don't leave me," and throws his arms around Victor. "I won't," says Victor, "so long as you do what I tell you. Your life belt will hold you up." Victor tells him to take his hand and they'll jump together. "When we hit the water, keep away. Don't grab me. Your lift belt and my swimming will support us both." He says, "I'll do anything you say, but don't leave me to die."

On the stern, Brown, Beattie, and—by now—Clark are telling the men to jump overboard and avoid the burning oil. There is a story that some men as they jump shout "Dry run!"—evidence, if true, of an almost superhuman stupidity or sense of humor. This can't be a dry run any more. The flames are leaping and the sea is on fire. The ship is listing to starboard, and men as they jump are landing on top of others in the water.

Angelo Crapanzano makes his own terrifying jump into the sea. The ship's engines, which he tended, have been out of action since the torpedo hit, and under the stern he sees "soldiers and navy men hanging on by the screws."

On the ship's fantail Victor and the nonswimmer climb over the rail, hold hands and jump. They hit the icy water together, but the impact breaks their grasp, and to Victor it seems an eternity before they resurface and can breathe. Then:

> in terror he grabbed me and pushed me under. I fought to the top as he tried to climb on my shoulders. I screamed "You're drowning me!," but he was so wild with fear he clutched me around my neck in a stranglehold. I struggled. Broke his grasp and kept him at arm's length. I had to hit him to slow him down.

The nonswimmer grabs hold of the ship's fender and climbs on. In the water, Victor tries to talk him into leaving the fender for the raft, but the man refuses, even when Victor tells him that if he stays, the ship's suction as it sinks will drown him.

Victor makes "one last fruitless effort" to save him, then gives up and turns to swim for the raft. The corpsman screams at Victor to come back, and Victor stops and says that if he will work his way to him, he'll get him to the raft. But again the nonswimmer refuses point-blank to give up the false security of the ship, so Victor wishes him luck, turns and swims for the raft, "never looking back but feeling sick inside."

Elsewhere in the water, Angelo Crapanzano is supporting his wounded shipmate John McGarigal, who has a deep gash in his head, which is bleeding badly. Then a raft comes drifting towards him, a ghostly, smoking raft that has floated through the flames of burning oil. Its inner section has burned away, but its outer oval frame is still buoyant. Crapanzano, supporting McGarigal, wraps an arm around the oval for support. Nine army men quickly join them. Crapanzano can see men still running around the stern deck of the sinking *507*.

Among them is Tom Clark, who is trying to persuade some twenty terrified soldiers to enter the water. They cling to the rail and refuse to jump. Clark threatens to shoot them, although he has no gun and is laughing as he says it. He and Fred Beattie try to pry the men's hands loose from the rails. Clark pries off one soldier's, who turns to Clark and says, in a slight foreign accent, "Please don't!"

Clark looks at the man and recognizes "the little army barber" who had been cutting hair on the *507*'s fantail as the ship pulled out of Brixham Harbor. Clark pauses a moment, then tells him, "All right then, but you better get off." He will be dead the next time Clark sees him.

Eugene Eckstam meanwhile has climbed down the sinking *507*'s cargo net and gingerly entered the cold sea. As a medical man, he values ease of movement when treating someone, so doesn't wear the bulky naval kapok jacket but the potentially lethal army-style CO_2 inflatable belt. It rises to his armpits and as it does so, pulls his jacket and shirt up, exposing him to the icy water. He manages to pull his clothes down and feels a bit warmer. Then he swims. He realizes that something is impeding his swimming, but not that it is the gas mask, which he still has on. Ed Panter, in the water nearby, shouts to him "Toss it!" Eckstam, conditioned by his navy routine, calls back, "But I have to check it in!"

Having abandoned the nonswimmer, Victor has swum for the raft launched by himself and Rutherford. Rutherford is clinging to the side of the raft when Victor gets there. Inside the raft is Star, and the redheaded corpsman guarding the soldier with the broken leg, whom he had lowered into the raft on a rope. It isn't long before a dense swarm of men surrounds the raft. Those who don't find a space for themselves on the sides have to hang on to one another for support, in five or six concentric rings of desperate men.

This is the raft that Eckstam sees as, having ditched his gas mask, he swims farther from the *507*. He joins the outer ring of men. The raft is now almost an arm's length underwater because of its weight of men and submerged survival gear. The survivors have to hold their heads up higher so as not to inhale water as they bob up and down with the waves. On the other side of the raft Victor sees Eckstam and five more of his buddies. They shout encouragement to one another. He looks for Dailey, the friend who'd been frightened to jump. He isn't there. Neither is Raban Lewis.

On the stern deck of the *507* it is time for Tom Clark to think of saving his own skin. He told his father the story:

> I don't know why I did the next thing, but I knew I'd have to go in very soon, so I urinated. We could do very little for the remaining soldiers. At this time the ship gave a pronounced lurch and we felt sure she did not have much longer. Fred Beattie looked at me and said, "C'mon Tom, it's time we got out of here." We looked about the stern and threw over anything which would float. All you could hear was the wail and moan of men in the water.
>
> Fred jumped first, and caught a board. I asked him how the water was and he said fine. I jumped and what a terrible moment. I never felt water so cold in my life. The jacket was good and it held me up. I had shoes on but I had them fixed so that I could kick them off if they got too heavy.
>
> Strangely enough, Dad, I didn't lose my head or get excited. I can say now that I never had the slightest doubt that I would come through it. I thought of the grief it would cause you all, but I thought mostly of Mary E. and what right had I to marry, leave her with my child, and get killed. I'd have ruined her life. I kept thinking, too, of the thirty days' survivor's leave, of getting home and taking her in my arms and staying that way the rest of my life.

But for the moment Tom Clark's survival by no means seems assured, and Fred Beattie, beside him in the water, is thinking, "You cannot stay alive in this water without something to hold on to." Then he sees a raft that is overboard but still tethered to the *507*. Beattie wonders if he can reach it before it is burned up. He says to Clark, "I see a raft. I'm going to get it. You wait for me here.'' He thrusts his flimsy wooden board into Clark's hands and swims toward the ship. But already Clark is being swept away by the current, and will be nowhere in sight by the time Beattie returns with the raft.

It is probably Fred Beattie's raft that Arthur Victor sees at about this time. In his rush to get up on deck during the tracer fire Victor has made the ''almost fatal error'' of forgetting his life belt. Now he compounds the error by removing his waterlogged jacket, with the intention of lightening the load on his own raft by swimming to the other one.

But soon the other raft is overloaded, too, so Victor decides to stay put, his jacket having drifted away, leaving him clad only in jeans and his olive drab T-shirt, small defense against the penetrating cold of the English Channel.

Then Victor feels ''a sharp heat'' strike the back of his neck. Someone screams. He turns and sees giant flames and billowing black smoke as a burning slick of oil rolls toward them. They kick to outstrip the flames; but the flames creep closer. Men abandon the raft in panic. Victor thinks of swimming off, too, when the fire stops and dies out not more than twenty feet away ''as though the hand of God reached down'':

> I was shocked into disbelief, then started shaking and sobbing quietly to myself with relief. Then I vowed that no matter what happened, from here on out I was not to become that fearful again. If I stayed patient and calm and took it as it came, I knew I could make it. A lot of guys who had left returned—some didn't. There were about fifty to seventy-five of us now as we drifted on.

Tom Clark told his father that ''cries, screams, and moans filled the night.'' From the *496*, signalman Manny Rubin sees far behind the lurid glow of burning oil on the water, the burning ship, and smaller, sharper pinpoints of red—the life belt lights of men in the water ''snapping,'' in one soldier's rural image of a harvest of death, ''on and off like lightning bugs.''

David Moore, senior army officer aboard LST *289* ''had just entered the LST amidship when there was an explosion heard, and Lieutenant Logan entered and stated very calmly that the LST directly astern had just blown up and that the screams of the men were terrible.'' Harry Mettler, the *289*'s skipper, realizes all right that it is the *507* burning behind him. He considers stopping to pick up survivors, but rejects the idea as too dangerous.

On the *289* they know what's happened, but the reality still hasn't dawned upon the rest of the convoy. On the *515* it is only now, with the explosion of the *507*, that something sufficiently "unusual" has occurred for Moses Hallett to get convoy commander Bernard Skahill out of his bunk. And Commander Skahill can't be sure whether the burning ship far to the rear is one of "his."

Both the *515* and the *496* have picked up unidentified radar blips. But they are on an exercise, not far off the English coast, and Lyme Bay is covered by a protective screen of ships: might those blips not be more of the many friendly craft known to be in the area? The convoy stays on course and continues to keep radio silence.

Still no one is quite sure exactly what is going on, but if there is a lingering doubt as to whether the burning ship to the rear is perhaps a prop in an elaborate war game, if the bursts of panicky tracer fire from most of the LSTs after the hit on the *507* could still be part of the "dry run," there is no doubting the reality of the next development.

It is the sinking of the *531*. Ensign Douglas Harlander is in the *531*'s chart house "fearfully watching the flames" of the burning *507* when the first torpedo strikes his ship. The blast hurls him up and backwards. He lands heavily but isn't badly hurt. His first thought is to alert the army officers below, and he staggers from the chart room. An army captain sharing Harlander's cabin is still in the sack. "What's going on?" he asks. Harlander throws him a life jacket and tells him to hurry to the main deck.

Gunner's Mate Henry Schrawder is with two other men in one of the *531*'s forward gun tubs. They are firing their 40-mm cannon, in the words of Schrawder's commendation for sticking to his post, "at the retreating E-boats until the list of the ship renders it useless."

That can't have taken long. Harlander is returning from below and going to the dressing station when the second torpedo strikes, a minute after the first. It strikes in the same area, blowing a hole in the officers' toilet just aft of Harlander's quarters and widely ripping the ship's seams. Harlander goes out to the portside main deck and finds the ship to be "completely engulfed in flames except portside aft."

That description is prosaic compared to what the other ships witness. Manny Rubin sees "a gigantic orange ball explosion, like something from the movies, a flame like it had come from hell, with little black specks round the edges which we knew were jeeps or boat stanchions, or men." Now tons more burning diesel oil spill on to the sea so that, in Manny Rubin's words, there is "a red-hot glow on the water." To Tom Clark the scene is "like the movies."

On the *496* now everybody is "petrified." All Manny Rubin can hear is "the men in the half-tracks and trucks crying hysterically." Hysteria is also felt among the men around Arthur Victor's raft, floundering helplessly in the water. Victor and all of them see the ammunition explode from the *531*'s bow "like a Fourth of July celebration" and "bodies flung in all directions like rag dolls":

> We were in a state of unbelieving shock, as we knew that there were hundreds of guys on board whose losses were even greater than ours. More men became hysterical, screaming that the Germans were going to kill us all. Most were convinced that the entire convoy would be destroyed. Others cried that the Germans would come back and shoot us in the water. I kept screaming, "Don't panic! Stay put!"

With the second torpedo hit, the *531* quickly lists 45 degrees, too much for Schrawder's gun. From the *511* Thomas Holcombe sees it firing "red streaks straight up" and assumes that the gunner has been killed. To all who have seen the huge explosion the idea that anyone could have survived it is incredible.

But Schrawder has, and is abandoning ship. So is Douglas Harlander. In his Mae West he climbs overboard as the *531* starts to capsize and sink, which it will do six minutes after the first torpedo strike. Harlander actually walks down the ship's side as she rolls over, and by the time he reaches the waterline his feet are splashing in the sea:

> The chill of the water was almost paralyzing. Despite my heavy clothing, I swam away as fast as possible, knowing there would be suction. I realized I had lost a shoe. I untied and kicked off my other shoe after negotiating around some surface burning oil. Diesel oil covered my entire body, slowing my progress toward a small life raft. To this day I have a fearful feeling when I smell burning oil.
>
> While swimming away I saw in the glare of the flames a life beltless soldier hanging onto a wooden board. He shouted to a nearby soldier, "Do you want to trade my board for your life jacket?" The sailor immediately replied "Yes" and made the swap. I have often recalled this bargaining under such adverse conditions.

Harlander reaches the "small life raft." Made to hold two men, fifteen survivors of *531* cling to its sides.

William Holland of the *531*'s main engine room has survived:

> I jumped overboard and went down until I stopped, then, much to my relief, compressed my life belt (it sure was) and it brought me to the

surface of burning water. I was able to get a hand on a life raft. There were so few around at the time. What there was in the area were overcrowded, and I was not too welcome.

John Perry, a soldier aboard the *531*, has survived. Asleep in the front seat of his Dukw when the first torpedo struck, he had grabbed a gas mask and made it through an escape hatch onto the deck. There he had got hit in the legs and fallen overboard, but had managed to swim to the *531*'s bow, still sticking out of the water, and had clung there with a few other men. There he would last the night.

By now it is clear to all the ships that the E-boats have them, in Manny Rubin's words, "trapped and hemmed in like a bunch of wolves circling a wounded dog." The attack is developing rapidly to landward and seaward along the entire line of ships.

On the bridge of the *515* all has been frantic activity since the torpedo hit on the *507*. Wendell Hoppler, at his GQ post at the *515*'s helm, staring straight ahead from the enclosed bridge, has not seen the *507* hit. But officer of the deck Brent Wahlberg has ordered, "Sound GQ again," and Hoppler has jumped from the helm to shout down the intercom, "Man your battle stations. This is *not* a drill!"

Hoppler has taken the wheel again when someone yells, "Torpedo astern!" Lieutenant Doyle orders "Hard to starboard," and Hoppler is battling to turn the ship's twin rudders when the shock wave from the explosion of the *531* reaches the *515*, lifting its stern from the water so that the rudders respond easily.

Eugene Carney goes to the *515*'s deck rail and a sailor rushes by. "You're damn lucky to be alive," he says; "a torpedo just missed us by an inch." Carney wonders who is in the water measuring this. At his gun station high on the *515*'s stern Floyd Hicks sees "the silhouette of an E-boat flashing behind us, outlined by the glare from the burning LSTs."

The *515* identifies the E-boats by radar and opens up with its 40-mm guns, hoping to keep the attackers at a distance. But it is "like shooting at a ghost." Moses Hallett, on watch, and officer of the deck Wahlberg both see the fleeting shadows of E-boats astern, low on the water, fore and aft of the burning wreck of the *531*. On the table drawn up later by Commodore Skahill, only the *496* and the *58* will positively register as having seen the E-boats. The boats are easier to hear, their Daimler-Benz engines reverberating "like the roar of an express train in a tunnel."

They are first heard by the *58* at 2:17 A.M., a minute or so before the explosion of the *531* just ahead of it in line. Deep in the ship's engine room, Engineering Officer Howard Irwin hears the explosion and picks up the sound-powered telephone to ask the bridge what's going on.

Up on the bridge the concern is to steer clear of the burning wreck of the *531* and, if possible, to put attacking E-boats between herself and the *531*, using the *531*'s flames to highlight the boats as targets. The *58* pulls to port, a maneuver complicated by the *499* already off her port beam and by the two pontoons she is towing (for the bridging of the Slapton lake). The bridge calls the engine room and asks for flank speed, maximum power. The men in the engine room hear the *58*'s 40-mm guns open up above them.

Later the commander of the *58*, Lieutenant John Wachter, will draw a series of diagrams to illustrate the development of the attack of T-4 and evasive actions taken by his and other ships. They show that as his ship pulls to port, so, just behind him, does the *289* under Harry Mettler. Roughly as the *531* is hit, the *289* sights the wake of a torpedo moving at fifteen to twenty knots off her starboard quarter. Mettler tells his engine room to assume flank speed and his helmsman to steer a zigzag course easterly towards Portland Bill. The same evasive "scattering" tactics have by now been adopted by the *58* and all the LSTs.

At 2:28 A.M. the *289* opens fire on an E-boat overtaking her to port. Gerald Frederick of the ship's small-boat crew is at his GQ station near one of the aft LCVPs. He shouts to Coxswain Russell Keyes, "Hell, I think this is an invasion!" and then runs below to fetch something. At the stern the 40-mm gun captain sights a "surface runner" torpedo cutting a broad wake toward his ship. Below, Frederick hears the gun captain yell over the PA system, "Here comes a torpedo!" The stern gun crew aims and fires at it, while the gun captain uses his battle phone to give the torpedo's direction and speed to the bridge for evasive action. Mettler orders "Full right rudder!" and for a transfixed few moments observers at the stern think the torpedo might miss.

It strikes, mangling the stern and wounding twenty-one men, including Frederick and Keyes. The wound to the ship is above the waterline. It puts her rudders out of action but not her propellers. Now she can only turn in useless circles to port. The blast, without surrounding seawater to help deaden it, is literally deafening for some. The whole ship shudders and reverberates. Men toward the bow, like Joseph Kennedy, wonder if they have run aground or even beached themselves as a prelude to landing. Martin McMahon on the deck above hears "a jarring like an earthquake." Eighteen-year-old sailor

William Kuntz, below, has no idea what has happened, but is "sweating blood."

At the stern, thirteen men are killed at once, including most officers on the bridge, but not Mettler, who falls to the deck below but is unhurt. Among the dead is Joseph Griffin, who had prophesied on sailing from the States that he would be killed aboard the *289*. The previous night he'd been put on the sick list and confined to his bunk in the after-crew's quarters, exactly where the torpedo struck. (Today he is buried in grave E1 15 of the Cambridge military cemetery in England.)

Also killed is the gun captain, who stayed at his post. His body will not be recovered—at least, not in one piece. "We never found him," said William Kuntz. "The only thing found was his battle helmet with the right side cracked from the crown to the edge near the ear." The *289* doesn't sink. She will lower LCVPs and deploy them alongside as makeshift rudders to steer her, limping, back to port, as, in the words of David Moore's report, "A course was set by the North Star and we headed for the British Isles."

William Kuntz credits the gun captain with the *289*'s survival. "That man lost his life saving the rest of us. We were hit, but if it had been anywhere else on the ship's hull I'm positive we would have suffered the same fate as the other ships."

Hoses are brought from amidship to fight fires that have broken out in the crew's quarters and on the bridge. Gunner's Mate Charles Garton, one of the wounded, gathers up spilled 40-mm shells in danger of detonation, and gathers weapons and ammunition from the ship's armory for the LCVPs that are to be lowered. Only then does he go to the wardroom, which has been turned into a hospital for the treatment of burns, minor wounds, and a major groin injury to an army captain.

There will be more men wounded aboard the *511*. The third LST in line, she has, like other ships, peeled away to port, toward Portland Bill. Louis Deniero, of Elmira, New York, is on watch duty at the bow.

He had heard the torpedoing of the *507*, far behind him. Then the *511* had shaken from stem to stern as the *531* just behind her exploded. Deniero at the time was going down a ladder to his battle station. He slipped and trapped his legs in the iron rungs. Freed by some soldiers, he went to his gun and started firing at what looked like a fast small boat charging by. "I could hear screams on all sides. I still often think of it in my sleep, and hear the man yelling for help in the cold water."

At about 2:30 A.M., as the *289* is torpedoed, the men of the *511* feel a severe jolt and hear the "frightening scrape" of metal against metal at their ship's bow. Deniero and others are convinced it is a torpedo that has failed to explode. "That," said Deniero, "was God's help."

The *496* to the starboard has just been under attack from an E-boat whose tracer, the boat lifted by a swell, goes high. Manny Rubin on the super conn, protected only by its canvas windbreak, "scared to death," breathes the word "Momma" as he sees the tracer streaking toward him. The bullets hit the bridge and the smokestack from the galley, and a piece of shrapnel shears through Rubin's steel helmet, gashing his forehead.

Hastily patched up by a medical corpsman, Rubin returns to his post on the super conn. His captain yells up from below, "Can you see anything?" Through his night glasses he scans the surrounding sea and spots what might be whitecaps or the bow wave of a ship a couple of thousand yards to port. Now he is sure—it's a bow wave, coming closer. Everyone hears him yell that information down to his captain, and others on deck look fearfully out over the darkened sea. Now the bow wave can be seen with the naked eye, and an army man on a half-track on the deck, without instructions, opens up with his heavy-caliber machine gun. Following his cue, the ship's own guns open up on the same shadowy target.

They are firing mistakenly on the *511*. From his battle station in a gun tub on the *511*'s starboard quarter, Thomas Holcombe sees a life raft ten feet from him cut in half by red tracer. It isn't a long burst of fire and no one is killed, but eighteen Americans have injuries ranging from the loss of an eye to severe wounds of the abdomen and groin. The firing ceases when the men on the *496* realize they are hitting a hull too high for that of an E-boat, and that it's one of their own ships.

On the *515*, convoy Commander Bernard Skahill has told his communications officer, Moses Hallett, to flash a radio report of the attack to Portland Bill. It is acknowledged at 2:32 A.M. The scattered ships zigzag separately for the safety of land, Chesil Cove and Chesil Beach on the western shore of Portland Bill. The attack is not yet over. At 2:37 A.M. the bow lookout of the *58* sees a torpedo pass the bow close to the surface. The *58* uses full rudder to maneuver so that motor noise is either dead ahead or dead astern, thus presenting the smallest target surface.

But her maneuverability is still hampered by the pontoons she has in tow, and at 2:39, seeing there are no craft to her stern, Lieutenant Wachter gives the order to cast them off. Bright magnesium flares are sighted "in various directions." It's thought that the E-boats are sending up the flares to prevent the *58* and other ships from making directly for the nearest shore, by breaking the cover of darkness.

At three o'clock the *58* casts off her pontoon tow, and two minutes later an E-boat is sighted "in the light of a bright flare." The intermittent flares will continue to be sighted until about four o'clock.

The remaining ships of the convoy are now far from the slowly sinking wreck of the *507*. Arthur Victor's life raft with the fifty to seventy-five men clinging to it has drifted away, but is still within sight of the ship. The enemies now are not E-boats but water and the cold. Hypothermia will claim many more victims among those who have survived thus far. It is about now that the first man around the raft dies. He is one of Victor's medical group, a nineteen-year-old called Saxton, married and with a four-month-old baby.

"He had lost hold of the raft," said Victor, "was floundering in the water, screaming for help. He called to Rutherford, who was supporting another corpsman on his back and could only manage to extend a leg. The boy was able to grab a foot, but slid off, sank from view, and never came up. We couldn't believe he went so fast. In a twinkling. No going down for the third time."

This was perhaps between 3 and 4 A.M. It is hard for the men in the water to judge. "Time," said Raymond Bartholomay, "was being measured in a different way now." In the darkness Bartholomay feels something brush by him in the water. "It felt coarse and all I could think of was sharks. It wasn't moving, so I touched it and tried to identify it. It resembled the other shapes. I suddenly realized that what I had felt was clothing and the shapes were bodies."

Bartholomay sees some people and swims over to join them:

> These were the first live persons I had seen in a while. We were holding onto a small piece of wreckage that wasn't too stable and one fellow was trying to sit up on it. Every time he tried, the object turned over and spilled us all underwater. It seemed almost like a game. That is when I started to pray the Lord's Prayer over and over. I was beginning to get drowsy, a bad sign in cold water, and praying supplied some hope.

On his raft, too, Arthur Victor was praying, "Please, dear Lord, if not for my sake, at least for the sake of those I love, please see me safely through this. My life is in your hands. Our Father, who art in heaven . . ." Victor wasn't alone. "Everybody was praying now. The name of God rang through the night. Others cried out 'Jesus Christ!' which sounded like cursing. But I called it praying."

Next to go on Victor's raft was the boy hanging onto Rutherford.

Gently his grip relaxed and he slid beneath the water. "He never said a word. Just quietly disappeared beneath the surface and never came up. It happened to be his nineteenth birthday. We could only pray for him, too."

As men began to die, those still alive around the raft faced a new enemy—their own mutinous fear. Victor remembered:

A few soldiers banded together and worked their way closer. They threatened to get on the raft and take it over. They said that because we were sailors we were fishlike and better in the water than they were. They complained that they didn't have life belts and should be allowed on the raft. I showed them I didn't have a life belt either and they could see I was half-naked. I assured them that getting torpedoed wasn't a daily occurrence for us. I finally told them that if anyone tried to mount the raft, we'd do whatever it took to keep the raft from being swamped.

My heart was pumping, but to my relief the leader never made a move and the others backed off. But the soldier with the broken leg, weighing 200 pounds or more, lost his senses and lay across the raft, pushing it quite a way under the water. Being as big as he was, he couldn't be made to get off the raft and hang on to the side. He sprawled out and the raft went under.

The mutiny wasn't over yet. The *507* had one black crewman, Steward's Mate Second Class Clarence Ellis, who had served steaks in the officers' wardroom. He, too, clung to Arthur Victor's raft:

He had snuggled up to me and held on tightly. Up to now he was OK, but suddenly someone shouted to "get that nigger off there!" I felt him stiffen and move even closer. I put my arm round him and shouted back that he had as much right as anyone to be there, and anyone who tried to pull him off would have to deal with me. I felt sorry for the guy and told him to stay close and not to worry.

I waited for an answer and for someone to make a move, but no one did. The mess steward never said a word and never left my side.

I had become almost unbearably cold by now. I had also been swallowing oily tasting salt water that made me nauseous, and I started puking. I pissed my pants to feel the warm. I remember how good it felt pouring over my thighs. But I kept puking my guts. The memory of that oily smell has bothered me ever since.

I wanted so very much to plant my feet and feel solid ground beneath me. It was maddening just to dangle and feel nothing but a bottomless pit.

I yearned to be on that raft for just a little bit of time. But it was never to be, and I knew it.

Across the raft from me my good buddy Scotty [Kenneth Scott] had been having a hard time hanging in. From the start he was in a state of frenzy and kept begging and pleading to get on the raft, asking me over and over again to help him. Star and I kept up a steady chatter to try and calm him down. But it did no good. He didn't seem to hear. He kept pleading and even tried to get on, but we had to keep him off. I kept yelling at him to hold on. Then someone hollered over that he thought he was dead.

I looked over and saw that he wasn't moving. He was bobbing in his belt head down. The corpsman next to him said he wasn't breathing. I told him to feel his neck for a pulse. There was none. I told him to place his head under water and look for bubbles. There were none. We had seen enough dead already. I said there was no choice but to let him drift away. Someone else moved into his spot.

I was sick to my stomach, sick at heart. Only a few hours before he had led our pillow fight. I wanted to rage when I saw him go. It was such a waste.

Then I wondered, and I still wonder, was he really dead? How could he be when he was so vibrant and full of life? How could he die like that? A part of me died that night. Most of all I feel guilty about Scotty. His death haunts me.

To go on. The *507* was still in sight but fading from view. Fog was beginning to surround us. We could still hear cries for help. We called out and signaled with our only working flashlight to give our position, but only a few managed to make it to us. Rutherford had stomach cramps and was doubled over in great pain. I wasn't sure he could make it. Another corpsman, I think it was Paul Ragusa, asked me to take his hand and hold him up so he could lay his head down. We held hands off and on for most of the night. (While the mess cook cuddled closer; I'm happy he made it.)

Tom Clark was going through his own, separate struggle for survival. Fearful of getting too near to the men fighting to climb onto rafts he had decided ''to play a lone wolf hand.'' ''It must have been comical,'' he told his father. Using the flimsy piece of wooden board that Beattie had given him as a psychological rather than physical prop, Clark treaded water and told himself to keep calm. He encouraged himself with the thought that when he'd come through he would have the statutory thirty days' survivor's leave in the United States. ''Take it easy, Clark, take it easy.''

Then, about a half-mile off, he saw a life raft outlined by the fire from the ship and decided to swim for it after all. Sometimes he lost sight of the raft in the swell and was scared, but he kept on kicking toward it until, about a hundred yards off, something told him his shipmate Jerry Brown was aboard, and he called out "very nonchalantly": "That you, Brownie?"

"Yes."

"Have you got the captain?"

"Yes, he's here, Tommy."

"Got room for one more?"

"Damn tootin', come on over."

Brown and an enlisted navy man were atop the raft, paddling it. Fred Beattie, who had found the raft, was inside it with Albert Nickson. Bruce Hoffmann and Lieutenant Swarts, the captain, were in the water, holding on with three army men. Clark joined them. Tracers and flares at that time were still exploding far over the sea. The *507*, burned through amidship, was like "a fiery jackknife, bow and stern obliquely pointed."

"I shan't tell you," Tom Clark wrote to his father, "all the despair and hopes that I lived through. The captain went out of his head and kept seeing imaginary rescue craft. We finally had him in the raft, and Beattie went out."

Fred Beattie was none too happy about this development. After awhile in the water he realized that he

was going off, too. I thought to myself, "Hell, this raft might not be here for them if I hadn't gone back for it. So why should I die?" So I pushed up to sit on the edge with my legs in the water. I remember the cold, the wet, and it seemed to be growing ever more quiet. I looked up and saw a black sky, brilliant with stars. I thought of home and family, and thought, "I don't want to die." Strength seemed to come back.

A soldier died and, said Tom Clark, "we tried to bring his body with us, but finally had to let him go." Clark twined his fingers in the ropes running round the raft. The captain hung on to Brown, who in turn hung on to Clark, who was trying to keep the captain's head out of the water. Brown shifted his grip to the collar of Clark's Mae West. Clark found it unpleasant, and said, "Brownie, let go my neck. Try hanging on my hair."

Brown tried, but after a while said, "Hell's bells, Tommy, you got a bum head." At which, Clark told his father, "we had a little laugh."

Clark's account of the survival of the fittest around his raft independently paralleled the experiences of Arthur Victor around his. Clark spoke of the men surrounding the raft in a

> formation of rings: the first ring hanging on to the raft, the second ring holding on to the first ring of men, the third ring holding on to the second ring and so on. Inside the raft will be the wounded or the person who had "taken charge." And the rings will compress on each other as the men weaken and attempt to make physical contact with the precious raft. The raft will tilt or turn over and there will be fewer rings.

Tom Clark described, too, the symptoms of his own incipient hypothermia in the icy water of the English Channel.

> There were periods when I went into a gentle sleep. It was as if I were looking down from the sky and seeing myself in the water—I was a spectator watching myself. When I awoke I would realize I was not kicking my legs. Gradually my legs froze. So in my time in the water I would "fall asleep," then waken. I remember that it didn't seem long until the cries of the stricken were no more. I awakened from one of these "sleeps" to a dead quiet, then the sounds of voices.

On Angelo Crapanzano's raft, too, it is "dead quiet." All around him at first had been the sounds of men "yelling—screaming—praying—dying." Gradually, the sounds of distress had "tapered off" as people drifted apart and died.

Some, really, died as a result of their own panic. Around the shell of Crapanzano's raft, for example,

> three soldiers said they were going to make a swim for it. I tried to talk them out of it, as they had no way of knowing in what direction they should go, but they went anyway. An army captain went completely berserk. Yelling and screaming, he let go and disappeared.

Crapanzano believed that his 104-degree fever from his tetanus booster shot helped him to "fight the numbing cold." But he also had a dogged will to survive, helped by his concern for his badly wounded shipmate, John McGarigal. He was driven, too, by something more personal. Much as Tom Clark thought that he owed it to his wife to survive, so through Angelo Crapanzano's mind that night ran the repetitious thought "that I had never had a woman and couldn't leave the world as a virgin."

During his "lone wolf game" Tom Clark had seen two LCVPs, which survivors at the bow end of the ship had succeeded in cutting free. For hours of that night these boats would tantalize the men in the water with their engine noise. "The unfortunates," wrote Tom Clark, "would hear the motor of the boat and scream for aid." Among the "unfortunates" were the men around Arthur Victor's raft. "Several times," said Victor, "we heard the drone of an LCVP nearby. We shouted hoarsely to it and signaled with our flashlight, but it never came."

The LCVPs, however, had been having problems of their own—a slightly less stark version of horror, but horror nonetheless.

Adelbert Sickley was in one of the boats:

> I was a strong kid and could pull myself over the side and was able to help get others aboard. Then I heard a kid in the water hollering "Adelbert!" I grabbed him by the hair and pulled him into the boat, which was now overloaded with thirty to forty men, and many others were clinging to its sides. It was tough to have to keep them from trying to get aboard and capsizing us. We had so little freeboard that we almost sank.

Army man Dale Rodman was on the other LCVP, which had been launched thanks to his initiative. He had climbed down the *507*'s cargo net to find that its rear cable was too short and was holding the boat out of the water. A sailor was unable to release the grappling hook and said they would all have to go into the water.

Rodman had turned to a soldier nearby and asked for his rifle, with the idea of using the live ammunition intended for the Tiger exercise to shoot the cable in two. The soldier said he would do it himself. He had fired, the cable parting after only the one shot, and the LCVP had successfully settled into the water.

Another soldier, Stanley Stout, may or may not have been aboard the same LCVP, on which, said Rodman, "there were about fifteen people" as the navy pilot accelerated and pulled away from the burning LST. Stout said that "we stopped to pick up men for the next thirty minutes or so."

So as not to imperil their own survival, the men in the LCVPs had to stay away from the large concentric circles of men around the rafts. The two LCVPs confined themselves to rescuing solitary swimmers.

Dale Rodman, for example, heard "the familiar voice of Corporal Marvin Koen in the darkness. Corporal Koen and I had been together from our first days in the army. I directed the LCVP towards him and helped pull him aboard as he came alongside."

Rodman and Stout independently agreed that the LCVP each was in was filled with some sixty men, well beyond capacity, when, in Stout's words:

We pulled out about a half to three-quarters of a mile from the three burning LSTs and sat there. This was the hardest part: to watch 750 to 1,000 men die and not be able to do anything to help them.

The night cries gradually became quieter until the only sounds left were the few explosions still coming from the burning LSTs. All the men in the water were now dead.

An understandable assumption, but a mistaken one. One man in particular was still very much alive. At some point while it was still dark Arthur Victor's buddy Raban Lewis, the "big bear" of a southern boy, "came swimming out of the darkness. I couldn't believe it," said Victor. "He acted like it was nothing, like a Sunday afternoon in the lake."

Soldier Leslie Morse had also seen Lewis: "a sailor swimming with no preserver and in his underwear. Someone said he was a long-distance swimmer as a civilian." Arthur Victor asked Lewis where he had come from:

He just said, "Out there." He said he gave up his spot on the raft and swam around, keeping the rafts within shouting distance. He said he could hear us, so he wasn't afraid. I wanted him to stay, but after he rested he said "Bye!" and took off.

It is still dark, but now the very first light of April 28 is beginning to streak the sky. William Holland of the *531* is sharing a raft with a dead man. He hears floating over the water the sound of men on two nearby rafts singing "Oh, What a Beautiful Morning"—"Typical of we U.S. people," he wrote later. "I almost cried," he said, "and then joined in."

On Tom Clark's raft, too, Clark suggests that they sing a song " but Fred Beattie started "Anchors Aweigh" in too high a key and we abandoned singing." Clark's comment to his father was, "I guess we were at the dangerous stage."

The assumption that the men in the water were dead was certainly not one shared by Lieutenant John Doyle, skipper of LST *515*. On the bridge Doyle and the convoy commander, Bernard Skahill, have been arguing about whether or not to turn back to try to find survivors. On this at least the convoy's orders were clear: In the event of attack each ship was to make at once for the shore. It was also folly to expose the vitally necessary LSTs to the risk of a daylight air attack, with more loss of life. And the E-boats might still be in the vicinity.

We do not have Skahill's personal testimony here, but this was doubtless the case he put. At all events, Skahill and Doyle "got into it," with Doyle putting the instinctive navy man's case that it was his duty if possible to save fellow sailors and soldiers shipwrecked in the sea.

At some point shortly before 4 A.M., according to what may be the somewhat melodramatic recollection of infantryman Eugene Carney, Doyle's voice came over the loudspeaker:

Now hear this! Hear this! We're having a disagreement on what to do. Some want to go back to our base to save the ship and our lives. But my navy men and I agree that you don't win wars by running. I have no authority over army soldiers and I won't risk your lives without voluntary consent from you. The E-boats might return and we could still be sunk.

At which point, according to Carney, "immediately, as though rehearsed, we all cried in unison, 'Let's stay and fight!' We were so angry that we would have fought the Germans with pocket knives."

And that is how the battle of wills on the bridge seems to have been decided. Shortly before 4 A.M.—at 3:58 according to Ensign Brent Wahlberg's meticulous entry in the *515*'s log—the ship turned 60 degrees. Seventeen minutes later she turned another 64 degrees, and the log for that time (4:15) records "proceeding to scene to pick up survivors."

By now the belated "relief escort" *Saladin* was on the scene. The *Saladin*'s medical officer, J. B. Wilson, later a family doctor in Scotland, recalled that "as we neared the disaster area we passed through a sea of hundreds of corpses, clad in life jackets but face down in the water."

Saladin's chief role in the rescue was to pluck off survivors still clinging to the wreck of the half-submerged *507*. Wilson's recollection is that they came directly on to the *Saladin*'s forecastle and that there were about 120 of them. (Another, more likely, estimate is "about fifty.") They were taken at once to the wardroom, but Dr. Wilson remembered that "they did not require medical attention."

The evidence suggests that the *Saladin* then went to pick up Adelbert Sickley and his fellow survivors from *507* in their LCVP. Sickley recalled that the ship came alongside and lowered rope ladders, down which the British crewman climbed to help them up. "One Limey

said, 'Now you know what it's like to be sunk,' and another, 'I bet you
Yanks are glad to see us damn Limeys now.' "

But Sickley also recalled that they were "treated kindly" and given
a breakfast of hot coffee, beans, bread, and grog. "It don't sound like
much but it was sure delicious." Meanwhile, over the *Saladin*'s
loudspeaker came a warning that the ship was to fire her four-inch gun.
This was to sink the wreck of the *507*, which would otherwise have
been a danger to shipping. The *515* seems to have arrived soon after
the sinking and was, apparently, sighted by the *Saladin*, although the
515's records make no mention of the British ship.

At 4:35 the *515* was "approaching burning wreckage at various
courses and speeds." By this time there remained only some twenty
men out of the fifty-plus who had clung around Arthur Victor's raft,
and Victor himself was close to the end of his strength—although he
still clung to the hand of the fellow medical corpsman who'd asked for
his help.

"The raft was almost arm's-length under," and Victor was exhausted "from the maddening effort of just relying on my arms for
support." He had given up hope of rescue:

> I was freezing, growing weaker, and had only the desire to sleep. I even
> thought about the easiest ways to die—to lay my head down and inhale
> water, or to push off and give up. But I quickly got those thoughts out of
> my mind. I pulled myself up, took a good hold and a deep breath and said,
> "To hell with it!" I made up my mind that if there was only one survivor,
> it would be me. I was more afraid of being a quitter than of dying.

Victor was still leaning over the raft when the corpsman whose hand
he was holding suddenly pulled away and yelled that he could hear a
ship's motors. Then he yelled, "I can see it!" Victor thought he might
be having delusions, "but there it loomed up as though it rose from the
water. We couldn't tell if it was friend or foe and we didn't much
care."

"There looming up in the blackness," wrote Tom Clark, "was the
bow of the most beautiful LST in the world"—the *515*. Now the
survivors had to cross their last hurdle; it was when they were within
inches of safety that the will to live seems finally to have collapsed in
many of them.

Bruce Hoffmann, for example, with whom, hours before, Clark had
speculated about the tracer fire in the night: "With rescue in sight
Hoffmann simply petered out and started to drift along from the raft.
I grabbed him and told him to buck up. He said OK."

The *515* was very close to the raft on its starboard side. As its gangway hove into view, a soldier on Clark's raft made a grab for a rope dangling from the ship while, on the decks above, Carney and other soldiers rooted for him to make it. At the same time they threw down another line, which Clark tried to make fast to the raft while still holding Hoffmann. But the soldier who had grabbed the line was too weak to hold it. He fell back onto the raft and "in his frenzy," said Clark, "grabbed me by the head and pushed me under. I yelled to Brown, 'Jerry, get this guy the hell off me!' but in the struggle I lost hold of the raft and also Hoffmann." Clark managed to grab and to get his leg around the bottom rung of the *515*'s Jacob's ladder, but Hoffmann was swept underwater and drowned. (The men, their legs and arms paralyzed by the cold, were unable to swim.) Tom Clark might have been the first person rescued by the *515*.

His rescue, or a very similar scene, was observed by Floyd Hicks from his viewpoint aboard the *515*:

> We were in the midst of men bobbing in the water. We came to a dead stop and could hear them begging to be picked up. Some were swearing because they thought we were going to leave them. I could see a life raft with a few people in it and many in the water, some holding on and others bobbing nearby.

But Floyd Hicks didn't only observe:

> We immediately threw a rope ladder over the side and I climbed down into the raft. One real young fellow wearing only underclothes was dead. But I was able to help the others, secured with lines, up the ladder to the deck. I had to drop into the icy water—brr, it took my breath away—several times.

At the fantail a crewman everyone knew as "Swede" Jensen made several dives into the water to pull floundering survivors to the rope ladders.

By now Angelo Crapanzano was almost alone on his raft with his wounded friend McGarigal. "I couldn't feel my legs any more. From my waist down I was paralyzed from the penetrating coldness of the water. I was very concerned about my legs having to be amputated." Then Crapanzano saw the light of an LCVP—one of three lowered by the *515*—approaching his raft. At that point he passed out.

On the LCVP approaching the burned-out shell of Angelo Crapanzano's raft was Coxswain Joseph McCann of the *515*. Before the war he had been a fisherman in Everett, Washington; he knew the sea and, from his experience of the nighttime invasions on the North African and Sicilian campaigns, he knew about seamanship at night.

McCann felt that he was "given a gift from God to sense things in the water at night, such as obstacles, and to always have a complete sense of direction, as well as the ability mentally to calculate tide, currents, and wind drift."

On being told aboard the *515* to get his small-boat crew ready, McCann had gone to the ship's "officer's country" and removed a battle lantern from the bulkhead:

> Normally, I would never have allowed a light of any kind to be turned on in an LCVP that I was running at night. But I knew, on this occasion, I would have to, in order to work my way through the men I anticipated would be in the water.

The light that Angelo Crapanzano saw just before he lost consciousness was McCann's battle lantern.

It was tied to the end of a bow hook on the LCVP, whose ramp was lowered. With the light in this position McCann's crew could get a good view without affecting the night-wise McCann at the boat's helm. So as not to mangle bodies, the living and the numerous dead, McCann kept the boat's engines off, using the current to drift away from the *515*. They came upon the charred oval frame of Crapanzano's raft. It supported Crapanzano, McGarigal, and a soldier.

"I actually started to pull away," said McCann, "because it appeared as if [they] were dead. But my motormac, Fraley, thought he had seen some slight movement. Upon checking, we found they were unconscious. I felt they should be taken directly back to the *515*."

Lights and cargo nets had been lowered down the sides of the *515*, but when McCann returned to the ship, the unconscious men could not be taken up the nets, so the *515* opened her bow door and lowered her ramp. "This," said McCann, "made it much easier."

But it also immobilized the *515* in the event of an emergency—like the return of the E-boats. At this time, said Chief Engineer Ensign David Roop, "LST *515* was a sitting duck."

"From this point on," said McCann, "my boat crew stayed busy. We did not have time to keep track of how many men we picked out of the water."

One man, however, McCann did keep track of, in a personal experience of horror that stood out in his mind among all the horrors that night. It came just after daybreak, when McCann was "shocked back to full reality'' by his discovery in the water of the body of naval Lieutenant Henry Q. Saucier, his head ''split wide open.''

Saucier was, like McCann, a veteran. ''I had started out,'' said McCann, ''in North Africa with Lieutenant Saucier'':

> He was an ensign at that time. We had gone through Tunisia, Sicily, and Salerno together, and he had bailed me out of several scrapes. He was what I called ''an enlisted man's officer.''
>
> I was to find out later that he was on board the *507* because of the flip of a coin with Lieutenant Kent Larson. Lieutenant Saucier lost the flip and his life. I wouldn't have wanted to lose either of them.
>
> My impulse was to bring Lieutenant Saucier's body on board. But Fraley reminded me of my orders. We were only to bring the living back to the ship. If, then, I had known what I have come to know now, I would have disobeyed orders and brought his body on board. The biggest regret I have today is leaving his body in that damn cold, oily water, not knowing if he received a proper burial.
>
> While I was contemplating this, Fraley said, ''Look, there's a ship's safe floating in the water.'' He and the bow hookman were attempting to reach the safe with a bow hook. I told them to leave it. If I couldn't bring Lieutenant Saucier's body back, I damn sure wasn't going to save a ship's safe.

Arthur Victor was pulled from the water by one of the two other LCVPs launched by the *515* in addition to McCann's. On his raft two more sailors died at the psychologically crucial point of rescue: the boy whose hand he had held all night and another corpsman.

''After hours of clinging to the raft,'' said Victor, ''with rescue in sight, in an instant they were gone. I was so mad that the ludicrous thought came to my mind that I could have killed them.''

Victor and the few remaining living of his raft were hauled into the LCVP, where Victor ''snuggled up to another guy.'' The coxswain, seeing that he wore only a T-shirt, put his jacket over him. ''I never knew anything could feel so deliciously warm,'' recalled Victor.

Clark and others from his raft are by now aboard the *515*. In the ship's wardroom their oil-soaked clothing is cut from them. Wrapped in blankets, they are plied with brandy and whisky, which the *515*'s crew (liquor was not allowed on board) had set aside for the planned ''post dry run'' party.

It is there in the wardroom that Lieutenant Swarts, skipper of the *507*, has died after his ordeal in the water. ''Went to the wardroom,'' wrote Fred Beattie:

met Skahill and Doyle—saw Clark—found the skipper laid out on the fantail with other corpses—felt for a pulse—thought I found a faint one—asked a nearby sailor to do something. He said something to the effect that it was hopeless but I should try if I felt there was something to be done—felt too exhausted and helpless—I left.

Wound up on the port rail amidship with Nickson staring at the bodies floating below like dead fish after an underwater explosion. Nickson remarked, "Jeez, Mr. Beattie, the Jerries play for keeps."

Etched in Tom Clark's memory from the *515*'s wardroom is the sight of Bernard Skahill, "under great stress, understandably nervous and on edge, justifying his order not to return to the scene of the torpedoing." Skahill has told his communications officer, Moses Hallett, about his disagreement with Doyle, and Hallett has "piped right up with my opinion that I thought Doyle had been right, and got told that I would never make a good naval officer—subject closed." Nevertheless, "Did I do the right thing?" Tom Clark hears Bernard Skahill muttering to a number of officers in the wardroom. "I did what I had to do."

Carried to the wardroom after his rescue, Arthur Victor is amazed to see the nonswimmer he had tried to save at the risk of his own life. He has survived, too. "He never opened his mouth to speak to me again, even after I told him how glad I was that he made it."

The survivors were taken to "officers' country" and the crew's quarters and were placed in bunks where, like Tom Clark, they "shivered and trembled." The medically qualified Eugene Eckstam fell asleep, to be awakened after a while by a pharmacist's mate, "who offered me a double shot of whisky and some coffee and asked if I "could help take care of some wounded." Angelo Crapanzano came to "blanketed in a bunk," and the first question he put to the pharmacist's mate was "How are my legs?" Eugene Carney offered one of the rescued soldiers whisky as he was being wrapped in a blanket. He looked unusually young. "No," he said, "I've never tasted whisky and I promised my mother I never would." (He was, if inadvertently, medically wise: Liquor hinders treatment of hypothermia.)

"A lot of men," said Carney, "died that night and piled up on us. I asked some soldiers to move them onto litters so we would take them below. We were hampered by the railing on the stairs and removed it with a hacksaw. Most of the younger men had never handled a corpse and hesitated to take hold of the dead. My uncle had owned a funeral home and I had helped him. I would take hold of a body under the armpits, and tell a squeamish soldier to grab him by his shoes. From then on the men lost their fear of the dead and we did this detail all night, over and over until we were exhausted.'' They stacked the dead like cordwood, according to crewman Elwin Hendrick.

Joseph McCann was still out in his LCVP looking for the living:

> By now the sun was coming up very bright. We observed three British motor torpedo boats moving very fast from the north to the south. I felt sure they would move out and around all of the bodies and debris in the water, but they did not. Instead they cut right through and were churning up bodies in their screws. I said, ''My God, they are going to go right through about a hundred or more bodies that I haven't checked for life.'' I moved directly to that area and found no life. I then returned to the *515*. I was confident that all of the living had been picked up by us and the other boats which had been put into the water.

By this time—the hours from British Double Summer Time daybreak to 8 A.M. or so—the rescue area has begun to fill up with ships. Floyd Hicks of the *515* remembers the ''O'' class destroyer HMS *Obedient*—one of Admiral Leatham's covering force—coming into the area before the *515*'s departure from it. ''I saw her graze a lifeboat with people in it. She hailed, 'Take good care of the wounded you have aboard.' We were very unhappy with the British navy and that feeling still persists.''

Devon farmer Julian Perkin was then a warrant officer candidate aboard the *Obedient*:

> We arrived in the area at daybreak and the sight was appalling. There were hundreds of bodies of American servicemen, in full battle gear, floating in the sea. Many had their limbs and even their heads blown off. We took aboard all those we could find still living and applied first aid and resuscitation. One American I was attending in the wardroom collapsed and died, obviously through the terrible shock of the ordeal. They were all such young men—it was tragic. Of all those we took on board, there were only nine survivors.

Perkin added that ''those the doctor pronounced dead were pushed back into the sea,'' perhaps not as callous as it sounds, because by this time ''small American landing craft with their ramps down were literally scooping up bodies. It was a ghastly sight!''

What Perkin saw may have been the LCVPs of the *515*; perhaps, though, a separate operation to retrieve the bodies of the dead had already begun. This, too, is unclear, but a story similar to Perkin's is told by Charles Breher, now a retired roofer in Clare, Michigan. On a convoy of landing vessels that morning he saw

> hundreds of floating bodies less than ten miles from shore. We picked up one body of a navy man wearing a Mae West and a wristwatch that was still running. We were about to pick up other bodies but an unknown officer in another boat pulled alongside and [in an action similar to that of the *Obedient's* crew] told us to drop them back in and not to pick up any more.

What exactly was happening over these hours, exactly where and when, it is impossible to say. The area was too large, there were too many ships in it, and April 28, 1944, is too long ago for absolute clarity and certainty.

Floyd Hicks of the *515* said that after *Obedient*'s arrival, but before the *515*'s departure, "other American and British ships now appeared." Among them was the *Obedient*'s sister ship, *Onslow,* which rescued Douglas Harlander of the *531*:

> Its crew lowered a line and secured it under by useless, paralyzed arms to lift me aboard. Then I learned that the raft's remaining occupants were dead. As they laid me on the deck, a British sailor said, "I know how you feel. I've been sunk six times myself." I never thought a hard cold deck could have such a welcome feeling.

One of these ships, *Obedient* or *Onslow,* rescued Dale Rodman and his companions in their dangerously overloaded LCVP. In the ship's wardroom Rodman saw his company commander (the Thirty-third Chemical Decontamination Company), Ralph A. Suesse, "lying dead on a table, naked except for his olive drab T-shirt, his skin bluish-red. I heard a medic say he might have survived hypothermia if he had not removed his clothing." Today Suesse is buried in the Cambridge military cemetery, where Joseph Rosiek, who took Rodman's place on the *507*'s tank deck, but whose remains were never recovered, is also commemorated on the Wall of the Missing.

Among the American ships to go to the scene was the high-speed, heavily armed minesweeper USS *Tide-AM-125.* An escort vessel for Tiger, *Tide* was one of the ships dispatched as soon as word was received that there had been a disaster. She set off soon afterward from Plymouth, and encountered *en route* the *289* limping toward Dartmouth.

Tide offered to tow the crippled ship, but Harry Mettler, her captain, refused, saying he still had power. (Later, he also refused assistance from a variety of other craft, until being taken in tow at 11 A.M. by a French tug. Signaled to go into Brixham, Mettler successfully protested that there were better medical facilities in Dartmouth, where he arrived at 2:45 that afternoon.) *Tide* then arrived at the scene of the disaster. From on board the ship Charles E. Modeste saw grotesquely floating in the sea "parts of bodies, legs torn from torsos, one body without a head." The ship slowed and zigzagged in an attempt not to hit the bodies, "but there were too many of them, so finally we just allowed the bow wave to push them aside." To Modeste's recollection, his ship found and picked up no survivors.

"It is odd," he later wrote, "how some things stick in one's memory. In mine, a crate of oranges floating and a jeep with enormous mud tires, floating serenely upright." Perhaps *Tide* arrived a little later than other ships. The chronology of their various comings and goings is hard to pinpoint.

The *515*'s movements can be followed more surely. Her log records that by 7:35 A.M. McCann's and the other small boats were back in the mother ship. It was reveille time, but on this occasion, said Wendell Hoppler, "there was no 'Oh, What a Beautiful Morning.' "

"Underway various courses and speeds *en route* to Portland, England," says the *515*'s log, "with approximately one hundred and eighteen (118) walking survivors, fourteen (14) litter cases, forty-five (45) dead." Ensign Brent Wahlberg's figures, from his diary of the time, differ from the log's. "We picked up," he wrote, "46 dead, 16 hospital cases, and about 200 that were OK after a hot shower." Wahlberg said that the *515* left the area when relieved by a British destroyer, which continued the search.

But the *515*'s rescue mission wasn't quite over yet. One more man would be saved from the water in an image that would stick in a number of crewmen's minds.

He was spotted around 8 A.M., a naked man, very fat indeed, perhaps 250 pounds, "a mesomorphic, Tony Galento–like build," said Elwin Hendrick. The *515*'s crewmen—"buttoned up and heading for port"—saw him and wondered whether he was dead—he must, after all, have been in the sea for more than five hours. Or perhaps he was clinging to the piece of wreckage with him—a crate, Wendell Hoppler remembered, of grapefruit. Then someone saw him move an arm, and an LCVP was lowered to pick him up. He survived; perhaps his fat gave him buoyancy and helped protect him from the cold.

To the men of the *515* the fat man's survival seemed a near-miraculous exception to the general sea of death around them. And it is that, not survival, which is the central image of the T-4 disaster: a young American soldier, a pack on his back and life belt round his waist, dead and face down in the waters of the English Channel. Multiply that image by hundreds and one has an idea of the legacy of horror, bitterness, and anger that the disaster has left. And perplexity, too: *Why* did they die?

It has been suggested that they did not die in vain. That lessons were learned, valuable lessons that helped to make the Normandy invasion the historic success it was. But it is at the least absurd to suggest that hundreds of men should die to demonstrate such Archimedean truths as that a life belt should not be worn around the waist and (recommendation L among conclusions drawn after the disaster) that heavy shoes weigh down a man who is trying to float.

Nor were even these simple "lessons" at once acted upon. Soldiers making the D Day landings still wore the CO_2 inflatable belt. It was only several weeks later that the navy-style kapok jacket was substituted (recommendation K).

The truth is that the victims of Exercise Tiger died about as much in vain as it is possible to die in. That is one reason why their deaths continue to haunt. Another is the mystery attaching to the fundamental question: How *many* died? More than forty years later that would still be a matter of dispute, speculation, and investigation. It will be looked at later on, but here perhaps is the place to examine the question of *how* they died, the physical causes of their deaths.

Many died in the violence of the torpedo explosions, others in the fire on the *507*'s tank deck. Blown to pieces, burned to a crisp, their bodies went down with their ships. But what of those who made it alive into the water and died later?

Tom Clark had had forty-four years to ponder that question when in 1988 he concluded that the majority of them died from hypothermia and exhaustion. Writing as if the disaster happened yesterday, he wondered

> why no attempts were made to give timely rescue. I mean within the hour.
> All the men had to be in the water for over two hours. So many were unable
> to endure. It is a very distinct possibility that many lives would have been
> saved if rescue efforts had been made one hour earlier.

He added that the men's own panic and their frantic cries for help "expended great energy" and furthered their exhaustion.

But many also drowned. Clark himself noted when day broke upon the disaster's aftermath a "white froth" around the mouths of dead men in the water. A standard textbook of medical jurisprudence states that a very nearly precise diagnostic sign of drowning "is the presence of fine foam at the mouth and nostrils. The foam is composed of fine bubbles and results from the churning together of air, mucus, and water."

How, though, did they drown? The misplaced buoyancy of a CO_2 belt around the waist does not appear sufficient to upend and drown a soldier bent on his own survival. It could, however, have given the *coup de grace* to a soldier who was not "thinking amphibian."

Men were knocked unconscious as other men jumped and fell on top of them in the water. Some, as they jumped, retained their battle helmets, whose extra surface area, hitting the water hard from a height, gave the impact the force of a knockout blow. The misplaced life belts then upended these unconscious, helpless soldiers in the water, packs on their backs, in the attitude later noted by many people on the scene.

One of them was former Leading Seaman Leslie Johnson, today in retirement in Grimsby. In April 1944 his ship was HMS *Sutton,* a coal-burning minesweeper, or "Smoky Joe," of First World War vintage.

At daybreak on April 28 the *Sutton* was moored among others of her minesweeping flotilla in Portland Harbor. Her manhole covers had been removed for refueling and coal was noisily "chuting" into the bunker below, where stokers "trimmed" the coal as it fell. Soon afterward the order came for the *Sutton* to put to sea.

Leslie Johnson has never forgotten that day. The sea was glassy calm. The sun climbed into a near cloudless sky as the *Sutton* steamed west, and Johnson was puzzled that no order had yet been given to prepare for minesweeping. Soon, though, the ship's crew was mustered together and told of the disaster a few hours before.

Johnson was leading seaman of the forenoon watch. At midday he was relieved by the afternoon watch. Soon afterward the pounding of the engines subsided and the ship decreased speed. From the upper deck, looking to the bow, Johnson saw what looked like "bundles" floating on the calm sea. The order came: "Seaboat's crew—man the seaboat!"

The seaboat was one of the whaler type, pointed at bow and stern. It was a row boat, with a crew of five under the orders of a coxswain. Johnson was summoned and told that the leading seaman of the afternoon watch, who was also an electrician, had been called away to mend a fault in the *Sutton*'s dynamo and that Johnson would take his place as coxswain of the seaboat.

Johnson and his crew were issued circular rope strops. They climbed into the seaboat. The *Sutton* was still in motion as the boat was lowered from its davits to hang just above the water. When the ship lost momentum, the order was given to "slip the seaboat." The fore and aft pulley hooks were disengaged and the seaboat fell with a splash into the water.

With Johnson at the tiller, the crew dipped their oars and rowed toward the floating bundles dotting the sea. Brilliant sunshine and the quiet splashing of the oars. Now the Englishmen in the seaboat could see that the "bundles" were the bodies of American army personnel, most of them face downward in the water.

Johnson ordered "Oars" and his crew stopped rowing. He ordered "Boat your oars" and they removed the oars from their rowlocks and stowed them inboard. Gently, the crewmen pulled the first body close to the seaboat's side.

Johnson took one of the circular rope strops and left the tiller. With some difficulty, he slipped the strop over the legs of the corpse, then over the pack on its back, until it was under the armpits. Then the slack in the strop was placed over a rowlock, thus securing the corpse to the seaboat's gunwhale.

Close by were two more bodies. Johnson noticed that they were linked by a cord "tied from one body to the other." He wondered whether the bodies were those of two friends who had not wanted to be parted as they plunged into the sea from their stricken LST. It is more likely that the two men had been in one of the concentric circles around a raft and had used the cord to keep one or both of them from slipping away.

When five bodies had been attached to the seaboat by rope strops, Johnson gave the order to "Pull away," and the five crewmen gently rowed the five dead American soldiers to the stern of the *Sutton*. The stern davits were turned outboard and hoisting tackles were lowered to the seaboat. The men in the boat attached the tackles to the rope strops, and one by one the bodies were hoisted aboard the *Sutton*.

When the seaboat had gathered all the bodies in the immediate area, it was towed by the *Sutton* to the next group of floating bodies, where the same grim duty was repeated, and so on, five bodies by five, five by five, until no more could be seen and the *Sutton*'s deck was stacked with the dead.

What made the duty especially haunting was that as the men were lifted aboard the ship, their heads hung down and their faces seemed to stare into the faces of the men in the seaboat below. Johnson and his men were attaching one body to the hoisting tackle when a couple of postcards with writing on them fell from the pockets and drifted away in the water.

Johnson recalled that the seaboat went out perhaps ten times, making a total of some fifty bodies. Over each stack of them on the *Sutton*'s decks a canvas sheet was "reverently" placed. A seaman was posted to stand guard over each group of bodies.

Meanwhile, the *515* had put into Portland Harbor. Another LST signaled to her "PVT-INT," meaning "What happened?" Wendell Hoppler was about to reply when an officer shouted at him to stop. Hoppler was allowed to signal only NEG. Then his light was turned off. "All communication was stopped."

The curiosity of the other LST was perhaps prompted by the long line of ambulances, bumper to bumper, which both Hoppler and Eugene Carney saw stretching along a long, sloping road leading down to the water.

Joseph McCann noticed something else as they docked in Portland. The harbor was full of American LSTs, which all had their flags at half-mast. McCann commented to someone near him, "They must be mourning all of the deaths this morning." Later he found out that the flags at half-mast were for the Secretary of the U.S. Navy, William Franklin Knox. He, too, had died that morning, peacefully, at the age of 70.

CHAPTER

9

The convoy's instructions in the event of attack were to proceed to the nearest stretch of coastline. Obedient to those instructions, the surviving ships of T-4 had made for Chesil Beach, running for some eight miles north to south on the Lyme Bay side of Portland Bill, on the South Dorset coast.

Reputedly thrown up on a single night of storm in the early nineteenth century, Chesil Beach was known locally, from the memory of maritime calamities over the years, as "Dead Man's Bay." It is one of the most dangerous beaches in Britain, a place of freak waves and strong, conflicting tides; but in the wake of the E-boat attack it seemed a safe landfall to the men of LSTs *511, 496, 499* and *58*. All had taken shelter at some point either along the beach, in Chesil Cove, or on Portland Isle, which is not an island at all but a peninsula joined to the mainland by a narrow causeway.

Tecwyn Morgan was the NCO of an antiaircraft gun mounted on the ridge of Chesil Bank. At first light that morning he was up on the ridge to inspect the gun. A sentry was on duty. He handed Morgan his binoculars, pointed north toward Chesil Cove, and asked, "What do you make of that lot?"

Through the binoculars Morgan saw at the foot of the cliff two American LSTs. From one of them—the *511*—a group of "dinghies" (probably LCVPs) was ferrying men from the boat to the beach. At about the same time a man was on his way down the coast road to his work in Portland:

> I could see that something or other was being ferried ashore and this was so unusual on that side of the island* that I made a detour to take a look. It was a real shambles. Wounded young American soldiers were being

---

* Portland Harbor was on the other, eastern side.

brought up the beach on stretchers. It was an awful sight, their bodies torn and mutilated.

Evidently other people had gathered, too, because this man's account continued: "A lot of the watching women were openly crying."[1]

At his antiaircraft gun, Tecwyn Morgan trained his binoculars down the coastal road and saw a line of vehicles approaching: ambulances, come to take the wounded men to the hospital. Then the stretcher parties appeared, climbing from Chesil Beach, "going past us," said Morgan, "with their silent human burdens, and then on down to the road and the ambulances. When all casualties had been landed, the dinghies returned to the ships, leaving the sentry, myself, and, standing motionless, some distance away, a Royal Navy chief petty officer. When all the dinghies were seen to have returned safely to the LSTs, the CP officer turned on his heel and made his way off the beach."

Within the hour, said Morgan, he was back. He told the NCO to assemble the gun crew, which, in Morgan's words, "he then proceeded to address thus: 'What you have seen this morning must be blotted from your mind. You haven't seen it. You can't talk about it because you know nothing of it. It's something that never happened.' "[2]

Meanwhile at Portland, on the other side of the peninsula, the same oblivion was being imposed upon the Americans. The *515* had moored and its own complement of soldiers had disembarked. Now it was the turn of the survivors. In Fred Beattie's words: "Landed at British base—everything cold, wet, and gray—we were a dismal line of survivors staggering out of the tank deck."

On the gangway Joseph McCann was somehow telling how at first light that morning he had seen the British MTBs speeding across the disaster area and probably mangling bodies in their propellers. He was not very complimentary. Feeling against the Royal Navy ran high. There had been, and would be, talk of their "yellow" escort turning tail and fleeing. There was resentment, too, against Bernard Skahill, and against the entire high command. "It seemed obvious," said Wendell Hoppler, "that they had goofed."

An officer of the *515* walked over to McCann and told him to shut up. Not only were no flags to be put out for the victims of T-4, they were not even to be talked about. He was "forbidden to ever speak of the incident or anything related to what had happened that morning in the Channel."

"We were ordered to keep absolutely quiet about the tragedy,"

Floyd Hicks recalled. "We were told by Captain Doyle to say nothing of our horrible experience," said Wendell Hoppler, who a few days later, in Brixham, met a WREN at a dance. She was a radar operator who had followed the action on her screen that night. "She saw my rating and asked if I was in the Channel on the 28th. Neither of us said any more about it. We were too afraid to talk about it."

It was standard wartime practice that details of naval or military engagements, air raids, ship movements, and so on should not be discussed openly or with unauthorized people. The evidence is that the habitual "code of silence" was more strongly enforced in the aftermath of the T-4 disaster. Already its implications for morale, security, and Allied solidarity had been realized. The story was quickly battened down so that the men who had experienced it would not disperse it among the forces at large. An army that hoped in a few weeks' time to take an enemy-held, heavily fortified coastline did not wish it to be known that it had suffered heavy losses in an exercise in "friendly" coastal waters.

Under the accepted conditions of service in the U.S. Navy, all the men who had lived through the sinking of their ships could now expect thirty days at home in the United States. "Survivor's leave," it was called, the cherished right that had helped to keep Tom Clark's spirits up in the sea. But they weren't going to get it. Not yet, anyway. The Normandy invasion was too close and the planners of the high command didn't want hot news of the disaster spreading in the United States at such a sensitive time. What most of the men were now about to experience was not survivor's leave, but something more like house arrest.

First of all, though, they experienced the exhilaration of survival. Quite soon, and for the rest of their lives, they would feel the strange guilt of the survivor—"Why, when so many died, did I live?"—but for the time being it was enough to find, as Fred Beattie did in the center of Portland base, "a circular bed of marigolds to stimulate my amazement that there was still something of beauty in the midst of all the horror."[3]

One of the survivors staggering to the ambulances—his legs were all right after all—was Angelo Crapanzano. He recalled that, with some others, he was driven to a hospital and checked by army doctors under "tight security." Arthur Victor was taken to the hospital, then, a few hours later, to "a Red Cross, where we were given army fatigues and shoes, toilet articles and beds. We slept there overnight." This was perhaps the red-brick Red Cross building where, Eugene Eckstam recalled, he was given a bagful of basic equipment. "The included toothbrush and comb," he said, "were the most valuable possessions I owned at the time." In the *507* at the bottom of Lyme Bay was a tailor-made navy full-dress uniform that his father had bought for him; later, Eckstam would weep at its loss.

"The next day," said Arthur Victor, "we were taken to an army base and counted in. Then the army boys went one way and we went the other. We were taken to another area and housed in a dilapidated barracks, *under guard,* for three days, and ordered, under threat of court martial, not to discuss the incident with anyone outside of our immediate group."

Albert Nickson and John Fedyszyn of the *507* were taken to the same or a similar camp. Both men, at any rate, independently remember being taken from it late one night to unload an ammunition ship. At about 2:30 A.M., Nickson remembered, there was an air raid warning. It turned out to be an alert, but "you should have seen us all take off. The least little noise made us jump and it still does."

John Fedyszyn was jumpy, too. In his camp, he said, "the biggest scare" was the rattle of stones thrown by the English children on the Quonset huts' tin roofs: "It sounded like we were getting hit again." Albert Nickson remembered that there was a big bomber base nearby. "At night you would think some of the planes were going to crawl into bed with you, they came in so low. A very ideal place to recuperate, you can imagine!"

Nickson remembered that during his time at the base "they were busy trying to get us clothes, get our records squared away. An investigation was being conducted, for what reason I will never know." Leslie Morse of the 557th Railhead Company remembered that "we were kept in a sort of isolation and told not to talk to anyone."

Other survivors were in other places. HMS *Onslow,* with Douglas Harlander of the *531* aboard, had docked in Portsmouth. Harlander had been kitted out in clothes donated by the Royal Navy—a black, high-necked sweater, trousers, loafers (see photo 17). He limped off *Onslow*—he had minor leg wounds—to a waiting ambulance, while nearby dockers stopped work and stood to attention. He was taken to "a U.S. Army Quonset hut hospital," where he and Ensign Eugene Hoch, another surviving officer of the *531*, were given a hut to themselves. Hoch, "very upset," was kept in when Harlander was discharged the next day.

The British destroyer that had rescued Adelbert Sickley took him to

Weymouth, where he was given a bunk in a barracks. The American Red Cross presented him with a shaving kit, for which he was charged. That was another problem. According to Wendell Hoppler and others, the sailors of T-4 "were late in getting paid, as the sunken *507* had the payroll aboard." Their paychecks were at the bottom of Lyme Bay, or perhaps in the ship's safe that Joseph McCann had seen floating but refused to bring on board.

Later Sickley was taken to Portland, where, he recalled, "there was a lot of confusion about identifying the survivors." One night he was awakened and asked his name. He had his dog tag to prove it, but for a time he had been identified as dead: A drowned sailor had been picked up wearing one of Sickley's shirts, with his name on the label.

The *289* had been towed into Dartmouth. Gerald Frederick, wounded and on a stretcher on the upper deck, remembered that as she arrived, a radio or ship's record player was playing a comical song of 1944:

> Mairzy dotes an dozey dotes
> An liddle lamsy divey
> A kiddle ee divey too
> Wooden U?*

The ship docked, and the dead and wounded were taken off on stretchers. The wounded were taken to the Britannia Royal Naval Hospital (its presence in Dartmouth was why Harry Mettler had insisted his ship should go there). Gerald Frederick would later be left with the impression that their stay in hospital was prolonged on purpose "to keep us out of circulation."

His and other survivors' impressions are backed up by a message of April 29 from Southern Base Section to SHAEF† in London. "Walking patients," it said, "being interrogated, segregated and will be returned to home stations."[4] The notion of any "interrogation" of survivors was, however, directly contradicted in a letter of the following day, the 30th, from Lieutenant Colonel Grundborg: "Practically all persons were suffering from shock and exposure. It was not deemed advisable

---

* This is a phonetic transcription of the song; research has failed to turn up a printed version. It "translates":

> Mares eat oats and does eat oats
> And little lambs eat ivy
> A kid'll eat ivy too
> Wouldn't you?

† Supreme Headquarters Allied Expeditionary Force.

to secure statements from survivors, as medical attention, feeding, and resting of survivors was given priority."[5]

Survivors' accounts of these days likewise contradict one another. Some, like Arthur Victor's, certainly suggest a degree of "segregation." A still harsher experience would appear to have been that of infantryman Eugene Carney:

> We were told to keep our mouths shut and taken to a camp where we were quarantined. When we went through the mess line we weren't even allowed to talk to the cooks. If, for example, we wanted two potatoes, we were told to hold up two fingers. If three, three fingers. We could have all we wanted but could say nothing. It seems that we were in that camp a long time, although it may only have been a few days. . . .

Elwin Hendrick of the *515*, however, said that "we were never quarantined nor sworn to secrecy." Martin McMahon, a soldier aboard the *289*, although he could recall being warned to say nothing, had no memory of being quarantined. Naval officer Tom Clark recalled that "a group of us were taken to a commandeered country estate, given army fatigues, and restricted to the area for several days." Survivors' experiences of segregation and secrecy probably differed according to their rank, their arm of the forces, which ship they had been on, and the port where they landed. "We all went to different places," said Arthur Victor, "army, navy, medics, small-boat crews."

The Southern Base Section message of the 29th also broadly gave the whereabouts of the wounded and "walking" survivors: "253 walking patients being accommodated at Blandford, and 63 hospitalized in vicinity of Dorchester." Another document gives more precisely the Vicarage Base, near Plymouth; the Navy 814 Hospital at Netley, near Southampton; and the U.S. Navy Base Hospital at Milford Haven in Wales.[6] Wounded men were apparently moved between hospitals as their condition improved, perhaps to be nearer their "home stations."

Oddly, however, and perhaps significantly, no survivors were admitted to the 316th Station Hospital at Stover, near Newton Abbott; the American hospital nearest to the scene of the disaster, it had at that time only seven patients, and the fact that it had a week previously been designated a prisoner-of-war hospital seems a callously bureaucratic excuse for denying its use in an emergency of this size. The obvious inference is that it was, for security purposes, a little too close for comfort.

Security was a prime consideration, as is clear from the experience of the 228th Station Hospital in Sherborne, which might reasonably be described as "in vicinity of Dorchester." Ralph Greene was then a captain in the U.S. Army Medical Corps based there. In late 1943 the 228th's 800 beds had been full of American servicemen suffering from malaria and hepatitis brought back from the Mediterranean campaigns. Since then, however, there had been little but routine medical care to occupy its forty medical officers and eighty nurses.

Now, early on the afternoon of April 28, Greene's phone was ringing and an adjutant was telling him "Colonel Kendall* wants all officers in the rec room at once." In the rec room, Greene remembered, Colonel Kendall told his officers that in less than an hour the hospital would be admitting a great many emergency cases. "SHAEF demands that we treat these soldiers as though we're veterinarians. You will ask no questions and take no histories. There will be no discussion. Follow standard procedures. Anyone who talks about these casualties, regardless of their severity, will be subject to court martial."

The hospital's officers were told that no one would be allowed to cross its perimeter until further orders, and as they hurried to their stations a cordon of counterintelligence men carrying bayoneted rifles was surrounding the compound of hospital huts. The officers wondered what emergency had occurred, and Greene thought, "They really mean business."

Half an hour later a stream of ambulances and trucks poured through the hospital gates, filled with "still wet, shivering, blue-skinned, blanketed, and bandaged young army and navy men." Most of them, in Ralph Greene's recollection, responded quickly to treatment, but some of the more severely wounded died, while the doctors worked on them in a weird vacuum. . . . Groans and sighs were all that marred the silence."[7]

Among the wounded received by the Sherborne hospital were the eighteen aboard the *511* who had been shot up by their sister ship, the *496*. Marvin Wohlbach was one of the *511*'s wounded. He said that their first stop after being landed in Chesil Cove was the 50th Field Hospital, where their dressings were changed, "and then we were moved on by ambulance to the 228th Station Hospital, where my wound was cleaned and stitched up. We stayed there a few days, and then were sent to a U.S. Navy hospital in Southampton,† where my stitches were removed."

After unloading her wounded, the *511* had joined the other LSTs

---

* The hospital's commander.
† Probably Netley.

anchored about half a mile off Chesil Cove. On the *496* sailor Joseph Sandor saw what looked like masses of seaweed floating on the water; when the sun came up, he saw that they were bodies.[8] Manny Rubin, on the same ship, saw them too: "After we had raised the anchor we proceeded at just two knots, barely moving, because we were pushing bodies away with boat hooks."

It was between 6 and 7 A.M., less than an hour to go to the convoy's deadline on Slapton Sands, when the four LSTs reunited to make half of what had been Convoy T-4. The ships would not make the deadline (they would arrive shortly before four in the afternoon).

At Slapton Sands General Omar Bradley, commander of the U.S. First Army, observing the exercise, noted the nonappearance of Convoy T-4. He was displeased by this "breakdown" in the beach engineer organization. In the real thing it "might not only jeopardize the assault but . . . most certainly delay our buildup [and] a mismanaged beach could imperil the invasion."[9]

In the afternoon Bradley was told by General James Lawton Collins, commander of the Seventh Corps, that there had been an attack on T-4: "A ship—or ships—it was reported, had been hit. I asked if there were any losses. Some, I was told, but no one yet knew how many. Not until the troops were reformed at the completion of the exercise could a thorough count be made."[10] Bradley apparently formed the impression that there had been a "minor brush" with the enemy, with slight losses, nothing on a scale to justify the nonappearance of Convoy T-4. Later that day he "suggested to Collins that he assign a new commander to the Utah Beach engineer brigade."[11]

That evening, the 28th, British Signals Intelligence (SIGINT), at last decoded a German naval message sent at 10:00 P.M. British time the night before: It disclosed that nine E-boats were to leave Cherbourg for operations to the west.[12] Advance warning of the attack on Tiger, almost twenty-four hours too late. Eisenhower, however, now back at SHAEF headquarters in London, still didn't know of the disaster. His naval aide, Harry C. Butcher, recorded in his diary:

As the day closed, I was in Ike's office when Beetle [Walter Bedell Smith, Eisenhower's chief of staff] phoned on the intercommunication system to say that by E-boat action last night we had two LSTs sunk and one damaged in the exercise. . . . Casualties are estimated at 300 to 400. Beetle said this reduces our reserves of LSTs for the big show to zero. Ike told Beetle to get a cable off to the Combined Chiefs advising them of the loss.[13]

Bedell Smith sent the cable the next morning. "First report," he said, "is that three LSTs were sunk and one damaged."[14] The figure of three was a misunderstanding based on a report from HMS *Saladin,* which confused the different pieces of wreckage she had sighted. It was corrected by a cable that morning to SHAEF from Rear Admiral Ramsay in Southwick Park "greatly regretting" that present reports suggested 300 to 400 casualties "but until a complete count of survivors can be made any figures should be treated with reserve."[15]

Ramsay was then deep in the planning for Exercise Fabius, and it is interesting to note that Bedell Smith's cable described the E-boat attack as the "German reaction to first phase of Fabius." That suggests that Tiger and Fabius were conceived as *joint* sections of one grand, unfolding design.

That day, the 29th, Eisenhower wrote to General Marshall that the previous evening's news of the disaster "was not a restful thought to take home with me." He told Marshall that "apparently we lost a considerable number of men," and that "we are stretched to the limit in the LST category, while the implications of the attack and the possibility of both raiders and bombers concentrating on some of our major ports make one scratch his head."[16]

It would be a mistake to imagine that Eisenhower was devastated by the disaster. Mention of it crops up only in the third paragraph of his letter to Marshall, which is largely about a piece of misbehavior by Major General Patton and about a meeting in which Churchill had tried to persuade Eisenhower not to bomb French roads and railways. Tiger barely gets a look-in. But, of course, Eisenhower did not yet know the scale of the disaster; nor, had he known, could he, as Supreme Commander, have allowed it at this critical time to rock his confidence in Overlord.

Nor did Rear Admiral Moon yet know in detail what had happened. Aboard his command ship, *Bayfield,* his concern was still with the completion of Exercise Tiger. During the night there were several air alerts as Force U lay off Slapton Sands, but the feared second E-boat attack did not materialize. Moon had told General Collins that the last of the beach unloadings, postponed from the evening before because of the fear of an attack, would be over by noon on the 29th. Just after noon the *Bayfield* signaled to shore that the role of naval Force U was over, and the sailors prepared to put to sea. At five that afternoon the *Bayfield* anchored in Plymouth Sound and Moon at once left his ship to go to the USS *Augusta,* Rear Admiral Kirk's flagship, for a meeting with Kirk, Admiral Wilkes, and Kirk's chief of staff, Moon's old Naval Academy contemporary, Arthur Struble.

Struble, it may be recalled, was said to be "jealous of Moon. . . . They should have been close friends—and were not." That was the opinion of Commander John Moreno, Rear Admiral Moon's air and assistant plans officer, who witnessed a meeting between the two men—a meeting that, in Moreno's view, broke Moon's spirit.

Moon, said Moreno, "was not congenial with his chief of staff [Tompkins] and for some reason he turned to me immediately following the Tiger debacle." Accompanied by Moreno and another member of his staff, John Fletcher, a communications officer, Moon reported to the *Augusta*. Fletcher recalled that Moon gave him a handwritten note to take to Rear Admiral Kirk. He took a look at it and was fascinated to see Moon's comment: "This was a costly egg in our omelet."[17]

Moreno, meanwhile, had headed for the cabin of a friend of his, one of Kirk's staff, on the *Augusta*. He feared that Moon's meeting with Struble would be "a very humiliating hearing for my Admiral, which I didn't want to witness." When he got to his friend's cabin, however, Struble's orderly came and told Moreno that Struble wanted him to be there, too.

Inside Struble's stateroom Moon was waiting at the door while Struble stood at the outboard bulkhead looking out over Plymouth Harbor. A British submarine had just arrived with a broomstick lashed to her periscope—the "sweep the seas" boast. Struble, noting it, muttered, "Well, at least someone did his duty," then turned around and, in Moreno's words, "brutally snarled" at Moon: "All right, Moon, what happened?"

"I think," said Moreno, "that was the instant that Moon's mind snapped." Moreno remembered that the meeting ended with Struble saying that Fleet Admiral King, in Washington, would be greatly concerned about the loss of lives and ships. "I got Moon off the ship as quickly as I could," said Moreno, "and we went back to our deserted shoreside HQ."

It is a strong thing to say of a man that his mind has snapped. Subsequent developments would show, however, that Rear Admiral Moon was under tremendous strain, and evidence of it on the last day of Tiger is provided not only by Moreno but by others whom Moon, on his return to his "deserted shoreside HQ," met in an attempt to answer the questions that Struble had put to him: What happened?

One of them was Douglas Harlander, chief surviving officer of the

531, discharged from the hospital that day and driven to Plymouth. To him, Moon when they met seemed "a kindly man, but under great strain." (Harlander thought how well Moon's name fitted his round, moon face.) Two other men whom Moon talked with after the meeting with Struble were the British commanders of the escort ship *Azalea* and of the escort that failed to turn up, *Scimitar*. What Lieutenant Shee of *Scimitar* thought of Rear Admiral Moon we do not know, but it was the opinion of George Geddes until his death that the Tiger disaster lay behind Moon's later collapse, so one imagines that he, too, noticed "great tension."

One brief exchange between the American Rear Admiral and the Scottish corvette commander encapsulated the command failure that lay behind the Tiger disaster: a failure for which, finally, no single individual would formally be held responsible, not Ramsay, nor Kirk, nor Leatham, nor Moon, nor Bernard Skahill. Moon asked Geddes whether he and Skahill had made arrangements for "radio communication circuits":

> "No, sir."
> "Did the Convoy Commander* make any arrangements with you before departing port as to radio communications?"
> "No, sir, I joined the convoy in position after the convoy came out."
> "Would it have been possible for you to have gotten together before and make arrangements?"
> "Yes, sir, I think we could have contacted at the first conference."[18]

Lieutenant Commander Thayer, another U.S. Navy officer who was there (so was John Moreno), then asked Geddes whether his ship had received "E-boat reports from the shore broadcasting stations." Geddes replied: "We received them and were studying them when it started." By the time Plymouth's seven minutes past midnight "port wave" warning had been decoded, therefore, the attack was about to begin—that, at least, is the best interpretation one can put upon the reply that Geddes gave.

It is contradicted, however, by Captain St. John Cronyn's† subsequent astonishment that *Azalea* had continued to steam "in line ahead at 3½ knots toward an enemy for nearly two hours after the initial enemy reports. That she [*Azalea*] received these signals is stated in

---

* Skahill.
† See note 18, chapter seven.

C-in-c's letter." The censure implies that no precious time had to be deducted for decoding and that if *Azalea*'s bridge was studying the reports when the attack began, it had been studying them for almost two hours.[19]

Geddes, however, was at the sharp end of a command confusion that was none of his making. Whose orders was he expected to attend to and obey? Rear Admiral Leatham's, from Plymouth? Bernard Skahill's, from the *515*? Rear Admiral Moon's, from the *Bayfield*? And why did not Leatham exercise the "overriding control" he had retained for himself and, as in the *PQ 17* affair of 1942, with far more justification, order the convoy to scatter? But, of course, Plymouth could not make direct radio contact with the LSTs.

Geddes, with the discipline learned from his escort duties in the Atlantic, was obeying his orders to the letter. Rear Admiral Leatham remarked in a note of May 23 that "Convoy T-4 had instructions to close the shore in the event of attack and this they apparently did."[20] Yes, but only after the attack had already begun. Henry Cooke, Deputy Director of Operations Department, took up this point:

> The C-in-c says that T-4 had orders to close the shore in the event of *attack*: This was apparently construed as meaning actual contact with the enemy. Had the convoy been routed close inshore at the first warning there would have been a good chance of escaping attack.[21]

Exactly, and that is exactly what did not happen.

George Geddes likewise stuck to his orders after the attack had begun. In the previous chapter's account of the attack *Azalea* is conspicuous by her absence; but so, to the men under attack, had she seemed at the time. Here is what she had done. With the first tracer fire she had turned and come zigzagging down the convoy's starboard side. "I had intended to illuminate* at first," said Geddes, "but there was doubt which side of the convoy was being attacked. Had I lighted up the nonattacking side, I would have lighted up the ships." Geddes told Moon that he had been unable to open fire "because I was alongside of the LSTs and would have hit them." He thought that the LSTs were firing at him "as tracer crossed my bow." He added that he could get no radio contact with the LSTs and that after the two LSTs were hit and on fire, "the flames spreading immediately," he had remained astern of the remaining ships as they scattered "over a wide, three-mile front."

---

* i.e., with starshell or parachute flares.

Moon then asked Geddes, "How many survivors did you pick up?" Geddes replied: "I didn't pick up the survivors. . . . [W]e have had instructions not to pick up survivors until the actual attack is considered to be over. Being the only escort present, I considered my correct action to remain with the convoy while I radioed for assistance."[22]

Rear Admiral Moon had plenty on his mind to preoccupy and disturb him that first evening back in Plymouth. John Moreno said that "dinner that night was a disaster. There were only three or four of us at the flag mess and poor Moon was clearly out of his mind." Again a strong thing to say, but it would have been surprising if Moon's mind had not been on the "costly egg" rather than on his dinner, and no wonder, after T-4, that dinner, too, was a "disaster."

The next day, the 30th, Moreno was ordered to go to the Royal Navy HQ in Plymouth, where he spoke to Rear Admiral Leatham's chief of staff—"a typical ruddy-faced sea dog"—about the mix-up over HMS *Scimitar*. Moreno recalled that the Royal Navy man "apologetically blushed further in his pink cheeks and said, 'This is a bit of a red herring. It can only be handled between my admiral and yours.' "[23]

Lieutenant Commander Geddes was given a week's leave at his home in Southport, near Liverpool. He said nothing, then, to his wife, Jean, about the disaster. He was not, anyway, she said, the kind of man to enlarge much upon things, but as a naval wife in wartime she was used to the "code of silence." After the war, however, until his death in December 1987, he would occasionally let fall to her his feelings about that night. It was "something he couldn't fathom, something that shouldn't have happened," "a fiasco," "a field day for the Germans," "horrendous," "a tragedy." She said that he was "at the court of inquiry or whatever," and that she knew "that my husband's report of events was accepted."[24]

The Tiger disaster did have its repercussions upon personnel, however. "A few days" after the exercise, General Collins called Colonel Eugene Caffey into his office and in a "crushing surprise" relieved him from command of the First Engineer Special Brigade. "He did not say why," according to Caffey's own account; "I did not ask why." But Caffey had "supposed that those in authority knew the major reason for the disappointing showing and that they knew that it had nothing to do with me."[25]

In the immediate shadow of the Tiger disaster Eisenhower's aide, Harry Butcher, was anticipating possibly greater casualties during the next massive Anglo-American rehearsal. "This exercise," he wrote on May 1, the eve of Fabius, "is the one really expected to attract major opposition of the enemy as its convoys move far out into the Channel. A counterpropaganda scheme has already been laid on in the event the Germans undertake to tell the world the invasion is on and that since it has not landed in France, the Allies have been defeated."[26] In Fabius, the disinformative "crying wolf" aspect of the D Day exercises was to be taken further than ever before. "With the sharp E-boat reaction to Tiger," Butcher added, "it looks as if we will see action in Fabius."[27]

The intelligence people, meanwhile, were wondering about the timing of that "sharp reaction." The Allied invasion of continental Europe was widely felt to be imminent. On April 17, only ten days before Tiger, the German Admiral Doenitz had warned that a large-scale landing was to be expected at any moment. Could the E-boats have been sent out with the express intention of picking up intelligence about the invasion?

There had been, on Convoy T-4, several "Bigoted" officers privy to at least some of the secrets of D Day, and some of them were missing (the usual estimate, but it remains an estimate, is ten). Where were they? Had one or more of them—appalling thought—been plucked from the water alive and taken prisoner by the E-boats? In the interests of the living who would land in Normandy it was better that these missing men should be found—which is the same as saying that it was better that they should be dead.

At the instigation of Montgomery, Major Ralph Ingersoll had no sooner returned to London from South Devon than he was required to drive down there again. The representative of the admiralty on Montgomery's staff had assured Montgomery that on the basis of reports received the E-boats could have taken no prisoners; but the still skeptical Montgomery apparently wanted to be sure, and ordered his own investigation.

In Dartmouth, Ingersoll found the badly damaged *289* and two army lieutenants who had witnessed the attack from her deck. The E-boats, they told him, had played searchlights over the heads of men bobbing in the water, and had cruised about the attack area with plenty of time to pick up survivors.

This was, in fact, what the E-boats had hoped to do. At 2:35 A.M. one of them had sent a radio telegraph message stating the intention "to capture swimming sailors" (*"Gefangennahme schwimmender Seeleute"*).[28] No searchlights had been switched on, however, and no survivors had been picked up. The effect of Ingersoll's story, together with other information reaching Montgomery's headquarters, was nevertheless galvanizing. Now the hunt for the bodies in the sea was really on, not just out of a reverent wish to reclaim and bury the dead, but out of the overriding need to preserve the secrets of D Day and to know that they were preserved.

Ingersoll wrote later that "there was a whole day in Montgomery's headquarters when it was seriously contemplated trying to alter the operation because of the knowledge which the enemy must now be presumed to have." But in any event, "by one of those amazing miracles which characterize war, although the bodies of hundreds who went down were never recovered, the remains of every single one of the Bigoted officers was found."[29]

Further reassurance was given by the high-level British intercept and decoding operation, Ultra. Its intercepts of German signals suggested that the E-boats had been on a routine attack mission that had happened to strike particularly lucky. It appeared, Ultra found, that T-4 or earlier Tiger convoys had alarmed the German naval command with the prospect of an imminent invasion; the Allied planners, "crying wolf" again, had this time brought out the wolves, the E-boats. They had been in the area west of Portland Bill since 11 P.M. on the 27th, but had sighted no major formations of Allied ships; also, by 3:47 on the morning of the 28th the senior officer, E-boats, had realized that the ships of T-4 had turned to the north. Not the invasion, then. Ultra had reported the German conclusion: "No major Allied landing attempt need be assumed."[30]

If this was all the intelligence that had been gathered from the E-boat foray, then the planners of Neptune/Overlord could sleep more easily. More reassuring still was what Ultra did *not* pick up: no messages to suggest that the Germans had learned anything of significance from the E-boat attack.[31]

At this time, according to Bernard Skahill's communications officer, Moses Hallett, there was a certain "fuss and feathers" as to whether he and Skahill should be court-martialed. But, he said, "no one . . . ever suggested that we had been given the correct frequencies to guard and had been remiss." And he added:

I do *not* know—and doubt that anyone will ever know—what caused the failures other than the extensive *inexperience* of all concerned. Why T-4 didn't get an Op Order, why there were *no* Task Force frequencies assigned to the LSTs, why that poor signals officer told *Scimitar* to stay in port without arranging for a replacement. Why, why, why??? I do not know.[32]

Skahill himself, in a report of May 3, said that he should have broken radio silence to inquire if the first ship aflame (the *507*) was an LST. He had not even realized at first that it was one of "his" ships! Among his other *mea culpas:* that he should have opened fire on radar pips that appeared just prior to the sinking of the *531*, and that he should have given orders to the remaining ships to scatter instead of relying on visual and radar observation of ships scattering. After other, less interesting, observations, Skahill in his report commended Harry Mettler for bringing the *289* safely to port, and John Doyle of the *515* (whom he had verbally reprimanded on the convoy itself) for rescuing survivors.[33]

Three days later, on May 6, Rear Admiral Moon presented his own summary report on the disaster. By now he was armed not only with Skahill's account, but also with the after-action reports of the commanding officers of the surviving LSTs and of the chief surviving officers of the vessels that had been sunk, Douglas Harlander (the *531*) and James Murdoch (the *507*). In his report Moon expressed the opinion that important but unnecessarily costly lessons had been learned. Again, they are for the most part "lessons" that a child could have anticipated in advance—about the wearing of life belts and the launching of LCVPs—although another lesson is not so self-evident: that vehicles should carry only enough fuel to give a margin of safety.

Moon also recommended that "there should be at least four escorts and probably more, to cover the bows, quarters, and flanks of any convoy,"[34] but in Britain at war, in 1944, stretched on all fronts, that was asking for the impossible. Another of his recommendations was "increased use of planes to attack E-boats . . . and their bases."[35]

Moon's report was presented on the day Exercise Fabius ended. It was not the bloodbath that Harry Butcher had feared. Far from it. The tally was one soldier "hospitalized with pneumonia," and a second lieutenant "shot accidentally in the buttock."[36]

CHAPTER

10

By now, as Exercise Fabius was ending, the military and naval bureaucracies had built up an overall picture of the losses suffered in the T-4 disaster. As already noted, the accuracy and comprehensiveness of this picture would remain in question for many years. It was easier to document the numbers and identities of men killed or missing in action (KIA or MIA) on the navy side. The ships had fixed complements and were, in a sense, the floating homes of the men who crewed them, while the soldiers were on the ships only temporarily, on the amphibious phase before landing. And the soldiers belonged to a variety of units, each of which was separately responsible for documenting its own dead or missing.

Toward the close of the first week in May the authorities were confident enough of their paperwork to send the requisite information, this or that man KIA or MIA, to the United States. Now doorbells rang across the country as the grim telegrams were delivered to next of kin. They rang in Texas, Wisconsin and Tennessee, South Dakota, Kansas and Iowa, Oregon, Pennsylvania, West Virginia, Mississippi, Massachusetts, Ohio, and Illinois, as homesteads in the Midwest and apartments in the big industrial cities qualified for gold stars in their windows. Almost 200 telegrams went to addresses in Missouri—most of the 3206th Quartermaster Service Company had enlisted from there, and the 3206th had been all but wiped out aboard the *531*.

Missouri took more than its fair share of the enormous payload of suffering and grief that the disaster distributed throughout the nation. And, of course, the telegrams made no mention of a disaster; they gave no indication that behind this or that brief billing of name, rank, and serial number, a man killed or missing "in action," lay a long list of hundreds of men. Each small group of family and friends imagined itself to be suffering alone. Again, the conduct of the war, the interests of the living, demanded this playing down of death on such a scale.

But it necessarily added to grief a dimension of mystery. There had been no invasion of the European coastline; naturally, the recipients of the telegrams wondered what sort of ''action'' their men had been involved in. . . .

Give or take a few hours, and allowing for the British Double Summer Time and the transatlantic time difference, it was at about the time that her son Conrad was killed that Mrs. Maria Schwechheimer in faraway New York saw him in a dream. Maria had been born and had grown up in the Saar region of Germany. So had her husband, George. Their two children, Conrad and Helen, had been born in Germany. In the First World War George Schwechheimer had fought for Germany. In the Second World War their German-born but naturalized-American son, Conrad, was fighting for the United States as one of the men of the 557th Quartermaster Railhead Company based in Devon.

In the German economic collapse of the Twenties, George had emigrated to the United States. There, in New York in 1926, he had found himself a job and an apartment big enough for his wife and children. In late 1928 he wrote to Germany telling his family to join him. Maria and the children—Conrad was then only seven—had made the long ocean crossing to the States.

Their ship was nearing New York harbor when her captain, in answer to an SOS, turned to the south. A South American ship, the *Vestris,* was sinking off the Carolinas. They came upon the scene at night. A circle of rescue ships, their lights ablaze, surrounded the sinking *Vestris.* Barrels of oil had been poured on the sea to calm the waves. Conrad climbed to a high point to get a better view of the rescue as their ship brought some thirty survivors on board. One of them was a small boy clutching a cat and crying for his mother and father; Conrad, who would die in a shipwreck, tried to calm him. Because of the rescue operation, Maria and her children would arrive ten days late in New York.

At the time, Maria saw the wreck of the *Vestris* as a bad omen, but told her children, ''God will help us in the new country, because he is showing us not to despair.'' Once in the United States, Conrad had soon begun to justify her optimism. The Schwechheimers were devout Catholics. Conrad served as an altar boy at St. Joseph's, their parish church in Yorkville. He was good at his studies, excelling in French and—his favorite subject—mathematics; by his teens he had formed the ambition to study engineering. He was also an all-rounder at sports: At St. Ann's Academy he was on teams in everything from swimming to punchball. He was good-looking, too; tall, with warm and attractive brown eyes and a "cheerful smile," and popular among his peers, who nicknamed him "Schwech." The magazine of St. Ann's carried a small profile of "this likeable Senior." It commended his "sparkling wit," his cheerfulness, his skill at public speaking, his application to his books, his becoming modesty. "Some day, not far off," it said, Schwech was expected "to be one of the country's outstanding architectural engineers." In 1939 he graduated from St. Ann's with honors, and enrolled for a five-year engineering course. Even then he continued to serve at the altar of St. Joseph's.

Then came the war, and in 1943 Conrad Schwechheimer answered the draft. He joined the army at Fort Kilmer, New Jersey, before being sent southwest for basic training to Camp Breckinridge in Kentucky and a camp in Evansville, Indiana. Then east again, to Camp Shanks in upper New York State, within easy reach of his adoring family. His qualifications in engineering made him a natural choice for the Engineers, and probably by this time, October or November 1943, he had been attached to the 557th, as a private, first class.

From Camp Shanks, he went to visit his family in their apartment at 505 East 84th Street. After dinner, he sat and talked and played records—his family's last evening together with him alone. The next evening he brought home two of his new army friends. It was their first visit to New York City and they marveled at the height of the Empire State Building and the speed of the subways. Later that evening Conrad and his sister, Helen, telephoned some friends and they all went dancing at a New York nightclub called The Glass Hat. Early the next morning Conrad exchanged his dress shoes for his army boots and made it back to Camp Shanks just in time.

After the night of dancing, his family never saw him again. He was expected the next night, too, with six of his new friends, and his mother, sister, and father waited until ten o'clock, the dinner still in the oven. But no one came: Conrad had been shipped out to Europe too suddenly even to telephone home.

They next heard from him in letters from Devon. In some of them, sensitive passages had been cut out by the censor, but in one letter to his best friend, Johnny Walsh, Conrad managed to get past the censor his consternation over what he saw as the disorganization and incompetence of the U.S. Army. He asked his friend not to tell his family about his feelings of worry and apprehension.

On April 26 Conrad Schwechheimer was among the men of his company to file on board *LST 507* in the "beautiful cove" of Brixham

Harbor. Almost certainly, as the *507* set sail on the afternoon of the following day, his place was on the tank deck, amongst the thickly packed vehicles. In his twenty-three years Conrad had undergone a number of changes: from German child to the American teenager "Schwech," from the costume of an altar boy to the dinner jacket and bow tie of his graduation ceremony. Now he wore the uniform of an American soldier: olive drab, his trousers tucked into his jump boots, a pack on his back and a barracks bag and carbine slung over his shoulder.

But that wasn't how his mother, Maria, saw him in her dream. She saw him dressed in black, with the Roman collar of a Catholic priest. He was holding out his hand to her, and in "a strained voice" was saying, "I have to go—I have to go." Then, in the dream, he squeezed his mother's hand, and she awoke and called aloud his name. She ran to the bedroom door. Helen got up and comforted her mother, whom she had never before seen so distressed. She told her mother not to worry, because "nothing was happening on the English coast," but the next day, although there was no news, the heavy sense of doom persisted, and they marked the calendar: April 27–8, 1944.[1]

Two weeks later the doorbell rang and the standard army telegram was delivered:

> The Secretary of War desires me to express his deep regret that your son . . . has been reported missing in action since April twenty-eight in European area if further details or other information are received you will be promptly notified.

On April 17 twenty-four-year-old Corporal Joe Ciccio of the 3206th Quartermaster Service Company had written to his sister Rose, at home in Kansas City, Missouri:

> I want a special favor done for me. Next month comes Mother's Day. Go downtown and get something nice for Mother. I just want her to know that I remember her at all times. Tell her to keep her chin up and not to worry. It won't be long before we will all be home.[2]

Now the telegram arrived, stating that he had been killed in action in the "European area."

The Navy telegrams were sent at the same time:

> The Navy Department deeply regrets to inform you that your son . . . was killed in the performance of his duty and in the service of his country the Department extends to you its sincerest sympathy in your great loss his

remains were interred in allied territory outside the continental limits of the U.S. pending cessation of hostilities. If further details are received you will be informed.

For security reasons, the Navy telegram carried a rider: "To prevent possible aid to our enemies please do not divulge the name of his ship or station."

The forces had carefully thought through the stage management of these hundreds of announcements of death across the country. According to David Moore, chief army officer aboard the *LST 289*, the telegrams were followed up by letters of condolence, but in writing his, "I was not allowed to discuss the circumstances because of security restrictions. As I recall, the particular phraseology used was worked out with Brigade S-2.* And possibly higher command."[3]

The telegrams were sent in the second week of May, two weeks after the disaster. One reason for the delay, as for the blackout on precise information of the disaster, was the insistence before D Day on putting the needs of the living first. A mother in St. Louis, Missouri, say, might know that her son was serving with another mother's son from the same city. Let us imagine that one of these sons had died in the Tiger disaster and the other had lived, to be given whatever medical treatment was necessary and to be taken to his place of "segregation." There, soon after the disaster, he would, like William Reckord of the *507*, have been "required to write a letter home and make sure that April 29, 1944, was clearly shown on the V-Mail letter."[4]

The letter said that he was safe, that he had survived. In the imaginary situation in St. Louis, it insured one of the mothers against worry when she heard the other mother's news.

They arrived in homes throughout the land, the telegrams of death, the letters that meant life. . . .

* Staff-2, the brigade's intelligence officer.

CHAPTER
11

Reports had been prepared by the chief surviving naval officers of the sunken LSTs, and by army officers who had been aboard. There had been investigation by the staffs of Rear Admiral Moon and Admiral Wilkes, and by Moon himself. On May 5 Rear Admiral Leatham had given his explanation of events from the British side. Now, after the naval and indeed military manner, these reports would snowball upward to become a blizzard of paper at the top, ending with Fleet Admiral King in Washington. But, for the moment, the next step was Rear Admiral Kirk. He had all the information gathered so far, and now it was his turn to comment.

To grasp what happened next, and what didn't happen, it is necessary to stress again that in the buildup to D Day the Americans and British could allow no serious rift to open between them. Not even the unnecessarily costly, or downright needless, loss of hundreds of young men of one nationality, in whose deaths negligence by the other nationality was felt to be instrumental, could be allowed to imperil the Allied solidarity.

George Cronin, an American, was at that time a top secret control officer at the U.S. Naval Headquarters in Grosvenor Square, London. He and other ''paper pushers'' in the HQ knew about the T-4 disaster but, he recalled, ''we were very closemouthed about it at the time, because we didn't want to upset the British.'' Cronin elaborated:

> There were a lot of mistakes made. The Americans made them. The British made them. We didn't want a witch hunt. We were getting ready for the invasion and there were more important things going on. In the interests of Allied cooperation and no bickering, the thing was allowed to pass without further investigation.[1]

One strained and ''extremely formal'' relationship that ''might have had very serious effects upon the Anglo-American partnership''[2] was that between Rear Admiral Kirk and his British superior, Rear Admiral Bertram Ramsay. The tension between them had eased a little, according to one of Ramsay's biographers, when Kirk was given his own "seagoing command"[3]: 3 battleships, 3 cruisers, and 40 destroyers. That rather implies that Kirk had been sulking because he hadn't any boats of his own to play with and, in a general way, much of the problem between Ramsay and the Americans seems to have been a matter of style and ego. Ramsay, said another biographer,

> got on well with the Americans and thought highly of their commanders. Discussions round the table usually took place in a friendly atmosphere, but differences of opinion were inevitable. If he felt he was right and a principle was involved, he would not change his view merely to preserve good feeling.[4]

As for the Americans' view of Ramsay, his personality rather than his competence as a commander, there is Eisenhower's remark that "we sometimes laughed among ourselves at the care with which he guarded, in British tradition and practice, the 'senior service' position of the British Navy."[5] That suggests the Americans thought Ramsay was a bit of a stuffed shirt.

Tension had mounted with the issuing of Ramsay's voluminous operations orders on April 24. One surprised American naval officer commented, "With us, the Admiral tells what to do, he doesn't tell us how to do it."[6] Ramsay knew of this reaction. "In their reports," he said, "the U.S. naval commanders have commented that, in their view, my orders extended to too much detail."[7] More generally, he remarked on the problems between himself and the Americans: "I am aware that the United States naval authorities had to exercise considerable restraint in submitting to a degree of control by superior authority higher than that to which they were accustomed."[8]

Ramsay was talking there not only of the usual command structures required by D Day, but also of British naval "tradition and practice" as against those of the U.S. Navy. And, of course, in the distance, he had always to reckon with what the British perceived as the Limey-loathing head of that navy, Fleet Admiral King in Washington, of whom the British Admiral Andrew Cunningham had said, "Not content with fighting the enemy, he was usually fighting someone on his own side as well."[9]

This was potentially explosive territory. The Tiger disaster, with all its possibilities for blame and recrimination, could blow up the carefully laid foundations of Allied solidarity. On May 1, Ramsay was at a meeting with Eisenhower at SHAEF in London. It would have been strange indeed if the disaster had not been mentioned at that meeting—the loss of life aside, the loss of the two LSTs was a matter of paramount importance for Ramsay. But if it was mentioned, Ramsay's own subsequent "Narrative of Events Prior to Operation" does not record it. At the top of that meeting's agenda was "the reported considerable extension of underwater obstacles in the assault area." This, in the context, was a more pressing matter than Moon's "costly egg in our omelet." It was decided that the obstacles had to be dealt with "dry-shod, i.e., when they stood in less than two feet of water." A very weighty matter hung upon this apparently routine decision, involving as it did, "a reconsideration of the time of H Hour, which, being bound up with D Day, involved in its turn the fixing of a target date for D Day."[10]

In an apparent reaction to the Tiger disaster, however, Admiral King in Washington appointed, this first week in May, a naval adviser to the supreme commander, Rear Admiral Bernhard Bieri, who had been on Eisenhower's staff for the 1942 North African landings and whom Ramsay also knew. With "consummate tact,"[11] Eisenhower arranged that Bieri should be attached to Ramsay's staff, where his first task, as recorded on May 9 by Harry Butcher (who called Bieri "the wise Admiral") was to try to obtain three LSTs from the Mediterranean to fill the yawning hole in Ramsay's operations orders left by the loss of the three from Convoy T-4.

The first two weeks of May brought a bigger threat to Rear Admiral Ramsay's authority, however, than the appointment of Bieri. Rear Admiral Kirk had now finished his assessment of the Tiger disaster, and at some point between the finish of Fabius and May 8 he went on record giving his reactions. His chief recommendation, picked up by him from Rear Admiral Moon, was that there should be attacks on the E-boat bases to eliminate, before D Day, the danger of E-boat attack. Ramsay did not like the "tone" of Kirk's letter,[12] but he kept his misgivings to himself until at least the next commanders' meeting, on May 8, when to his dismay he found out that Kirk had apparently gone over his head to Eisenhower.

So the T-4 disaster turned into an administrative wrangle of extreme touchiness. Ramsay wrote in his diary that Eisenhower had asked him at the meeting what he thought of Kirk's proposal. Ramsay replied that it was "under consideration," but then, pressed by Eisenhower, that the E-boats were "certainly a serious menace, but it would be a mistake to overestimate it; that it was impossible to ensure security, but everything would be done to destroy E-boats prior to D Day.'' (It might be noted that on D Day the German navy's one challenge to the invading force, if an ineffectual one, came from the E-boats; also, that if the Allies had bombed the E-boat base, it could conceivably have alerted the Germans to where the invasion was *really* to be.)

Eisenhower then asked Ramsay for his response to the idea of a naval bombardment of Cherbourg. Ramsay replied that he thought it risky and would not order a bombardment unless he received a direct order from Eisenhower to do so. So if the T-4 disaster had not come up at the commanders' meeting of May 1, it was certainly aired at this one a week later, albeit only with a stress upon its implications for what Kirk had called "pending events." Ramsay applied the same stress when, admitting that "naval defensive measures on this occasion were undoubtedly on the weak side," he drew the moral that the "incident" had highlighted "the need for every available warship and craft to take part in the opening phase of Neptune. . . ."[13]

Ramsay continued to brood on what he perceived as Rear Admiral Kirk's insubordination, and on May 11 wrote to his wife from Southwick Park: "I'm just going up to London now to see Eisenhower about rather a delicate subject which I feel must be represented to him. . . ."[14] The delicate subject was Kirk and the vexed question of the inter-Allied chain of command. A biographer of Ramsay wrote that the British admiral regarded the leaking to Eisenhower of Kirk's letter, with its unfortunate tone, "as a violation of the principles of command, and if the complicated machinery was to run smoothly the sequence of authority must be followed rigidly irrespective of nationality."[15] The Tiger disaster had revived the old sensitivity and touchiness in the Ramsay-Kirk relationship.

"Kirk," Ramsay told Eisenhower, "was his subordinate, and if they failed to get agreement it would be Ramsay's duty as commander in chief, and not Kirk's, to represent the matter to the supreme commander." Then Ramsay discovered that there had been some "misunderstanding." Kirk's letter had reached Eisenhower, not directly from Kirk, but "through another American channel." With that, Ramsay, in the words of a biographer, "poured oil on the waters and the whole thing blew over."[16]

Oil on the waters is an unfortunate figure of speech for the Tiger disaster, which had sparked off the trouble between Kirk and Ramsay; "the whole thing blew over" sums up what thereafter, at the highest levels, was to be the attitude to the disaster. Eisenhower, with his usual diplomatic skill, had averted recriminations and closed the rift that had begun to open in the Allied naval command. But a price to be paid for the reaffirmed "solidarity" was the memory of men who had died.

There was simply no time for recriminations or postmortems. D Day was now less than a month away. In the latter part of May Eisenhower and Montgomery moved their headquarters to mobile trailers— Eisenhower called his "a circus wagon"—in the Forest of Bere adjoining Ramsay's HQ in Southwick Park. There they got down to the final planning for Neptune and Overlord.

There was no time for survivor's leave. Most of the men who had been sunk on Convoy T-4 had none. An exception was Henry Schrawder, of the *531*. His ship's chief surviving officer, Douglas Harlander, had written a letter requesting leave for him and fellow survivors. It won him a month's grace before, on June 1, he was reassigned to *LST 345*.[17] But Marvin Wohlbach, who had been wounded in the "attack" of the *496* on the *511*, had no survivor's leave. When he was well again he was returned, on May 17, to the *511*.[18] (A number of survivors of the *507* and the *531* were transferred to the *511*.) Eugene Eckstam, of the *507*, was likewise soon on duty again on a new ship, the *LST 391*.[19] Angelo Crapanzano, of the *507*, recalled that about two weeks after the disaster his chief surviving officer, James Murdoch, came in carrying some official papers:

> I was sure he was going to say "You're all going back to the States." Instead he said, "You men are all skilled petty officers, sent to schools by the Navy Department, experienced, etc., etc. You are all going to be reassigned. . . . " I was stunned and couldn't believe what I heard. How could they? We were still licking our wounds.[20]

Crapanzano was reassigned to *LST 294*, which would land at Utah Beach soon after H Hour.

On May 30, however, a week before D Day, the wisdom of the Utah landing was still a matter for anguished debate in the complex of headquarters surrounding Southwick Park. On that day Eisenhower's (British) tactical air commander, Sir Trafford Leigh-Mallory, urged him to abandon the idea of the airborne landing behind Utah Beach. Leigh-Mallory, according to Eisenhower, told him that it would amount to the " 'futile slaughter' of two fine divisions."[21] To General Bradley, Leigh-Mallory was a Jeremiah, who produced "absurdly alarmist estimates that showed we would suffer 50 percent casualties among paratroopers."[22] Bradley, however, although he pressed at the time for an airborne landing, wrote about Leigh-Mallory's opposing view with hindsight (and Leigh-Mallory, proved wrong, would apologize to Eisenhower). At the same time, Eisenhower found it "difficult to conceive of a more soul-racking problem." If Leigh-Mallory was right, "it appeared that the attack on Utah Beach was probably hopeless, and this meant that the whole operation suddenly acquired a degree of risk, even foolhardiness, that presaged a gigantic failure, possibly Allied defeat in Europe."[23]

We know what Eisenhower's decision about Utah was. On June 6, as part of the overall D Day assault, it went ahead as planned, complete with paratroop landing, and was a resounding success. An ironic factor in that success was a mistake that, unlike the mistakes surrounding T-4, worked in the Allies' favor—a regiment landed on the "wrong" stretch of beach, which turned out to be less well defended than the "right" one. The story of Utah is well known and this isn't the place to recapitulate it, but there as aspects of the story that gain in depth when viewed from the perspective of Tiger and the Tiger disaster.

The first concerns the behavior of Rear Admiral Moon. On the afternoon of D Day, when the first assault wave had gone in but the backup troops were still landing, the Admiral suffered exactly the same crisis of confidence that had made him postpone Exercise Tiger's H Hour.

"It was well that I had remained aboard the *Bayfield*," General Collins of Seventh Corps wrote later, "because that afternoon Admiral Moon became agitated over the loss of a few vessels from mines and gunfire, and by a report from Navy Lieutenant Mark Dalton, who had been sent ashore by Moon's Intelligence Officer, Commander Robert H. Thayer, to check beach conditions. While listening to Dalton's report *Moon suddenly suggested suspension of landing operations* [my italics]. I had to put my foot down hard to persuade the Admiral not to do so. . . . Confident that Admiral Moon would remain steady . . . I decided to go ashore the following morning."[24]

For the duration of the Utah landing Moon did remain steady, and on the night of June 8 Collins went out to the *Bayfield* to thank him and his staff for their "fine cooperation."[25] But Moon clearly had not learned from Exercise Tiger that he who hesitates is lost; perhaps Collins had learned the lesson for him, by proxy, and so had known when to put his foot down (Moon had postponed Tiger's H Hour, after all, on his own initiative when Collins had unluckily *not* been aboard the *Bayfield*). If so—and one wonders how things might have developed if Collins had not been there—it was perhaps the most important lesson taught by Tiger.

Tiger was also in the background of the success of Utah of the DD "swimming" Sherman tanks. Two of them, on Tiger, had sunk off Slapton Sands, but on Tiger and on earlier exercises, Collins had gone off in a small boat to study at close quarters the tanks' behavior in the water. As a result, he had insisted that at Utah the LCTs carrying the tanks (four DDs apiece) should go as close inshore as possible. The decision proved, said Collins, "both a lifesaver and a DD saver."[26] Of the thirty-two DDs deployed at Utah, four went down when their LCT struck a mine, but the other twenty-eight were launched and made it safely ashore.

But Rear Admiral Moon's weakness under stress and the weakness of the DDs when launched too far offshore were both lessons learned from the early, assault phase of Exercise Tiger, not from the T-4 tail-end. It is difficult indeed to construct a plausible argument to show that the many lives lost on the last convoy of the dress rehearsal helped to save lives on the show itself. Certainly, fewer lives were lost at Utah, far fewer.

Estimates vary, but all seem small compared both with T-4 and with the scale and military importance of Utah. The usual figure given is 197, one under the number *of sailors alone* who died on T-4. More than 400 members of the First Engineer Special Brigade died on T-4; by contrast, only fifty-five men of the brigade were killed (with one missing) both on the Utah landing and *in the entire Normandy and northern French campaign.*[27] Bradley said of Utah that it was "a piece of cake."[28] In *The Longest Day,* published in 1960, Cornelius Ryan wrote that men on the Utah assault found it "an anticlimax; the long months of training at Slapton Sands in England had been tougher."[29]

True to the form of Exercise Tiger, one compares the dress rehearsal with the show and finds a reversal of realism and reality.

Among the ships that accompanied the Americans to Utah was the corvette *Azalea* under George Geddes.[30] But Geddes, although he appears not to have known it, was still under a cloud, and it was actually on D Day plus one that St. John Cronyn pressed home his point that in escorting T-4 Geddes had shown "lack of initiative." Normandy had only just been invaded, but the Royal Navy's internal inquiry into its own share of responsibility for the Utah rehearsal disaster continued inexorably.

The following month, on July 17, St. John Cronyn's censure of Geddes was endorsed by Rear Admiral Llewellyn V. Morgan, Director of Signal Division, as "the most pertinent point,"[31] although in light of the signals mix-up (the Rear Admiral's own department), it is hard to see how it can have been.

In late July Rear Admiral Moon was transferred to the Mediterranean to lead the Camel Force, the equivalent of Force U for the Anvil/ Dragoon invasion of southern France. If Moon had had little experience of amphibious landings before, he had plenty now and was, wrote Russell Weighley, "an experienced officer who knew what an amphibious assault force ought to be."[32] That, according to American naval historian Thomas Buell, is why Moon was "precipitately" sent from the Channel and Atlantic to the Mediterranean, where he was to assist Vice-Admiral Kent Hewitt, Commander of the Western Task Force. Fleet Admiral King had spoken to Moon and been "impressed with his amphibious expertise. Disregarding objections . . . King made his decision without fully considering the consequences."[33]

Arriving in the Mediterranean in the midst of hasty planning, the perfectionist Rear Admiral Moon once again found that the reality fell messily short of his ideal, and in an astonishing duplication of his earlier hesitations off Slapton Sands and Utah Beach he *again* asked that the planned landing should be postponed.

Anvil/Dragoon had been scheduled for August 15, but on August 4 Moon protested to Vice-Admiral Hewitt that the men could not possibly be ready in time. Hewitt sought to reassure Moon, as General Collins had sought to do in another theater of war. After several hours of discussion, having promised that a rehearsal would be held to improve the men's combat worthiness, and that he would put up the possibility of a postponement, Hewitt thought that he had succeeded. "Admiral Moon," he wrote, "left my office apparently satisfied and in good spirits."[34]

Rear Admiral Moon's command ship for the Mediterranean was still the *Bayfield,* which was moored in Naples harbor. Back in his stateroom he spent a sleepless night and on the morning of August 5 shot himself with his .45 service revolver. He was found dead in his cabin by his Filipino messboy, and later that morning his chief of staff, Captain Tompkins, called the officers to the wardroom and said simply, "I have to announce that the Admiral is dead."[35]

Rear Admiral Moon was the only high-ranking American forces suicide of the Second World War. "His death," wrote Weighley, "could be attributed to the strain of overwork"—that excessive diligence which General Collins had noticed in Plymouth. Officially it was attributed to combat fatigue; that, too, is plausible, and both overwork and combat fatigue were surely contributory factors in his suicide.[36]

Another analysis, however, would suggest that Moon killed himself as the culmination of a massive crisis, which began with that "snapping" of his mind following the T-4 disaster and his interview with Admiral Struble. That, certainly, was John Moreno's reading of events. "His reaction to the attack on Convoy T-4," he stated flatly, "was to be greatly disturbed. He never got over it and it was the direct cause of his subsequent suicide."[37] This was also the reading of men who were on Convoy T-4. George Geddes was convinced that Moon killed himself out of guilt over the disaster, and Moses Hallett could remember "being told by someone that I could forget about being court-martialed because Moon 'had blown his brains out.' " It was his impression, too, that in killing himself Moon had taken responsibility for the disaster.[38]

By this reading Rear Admiral Moon was yet another, slightly belated victim of Tiger. So, very nearly, was George Geddes. He died much later than Moon, on December 28, 1987, but the documents on file show that in 1944 he came close to being made the Royal Navy's scapegoat for the T-4 disaster. The last word in the Royal Navy's inquiry, however, went to Rear Admiral E. J. P. Brind, Assistant Chief of Naval Staff, Home. On August 7, two days after Moon's suicide and more than three months after the Tiger disaster, he wrote that "the circumstances leading up to the loss of the three LSTs are far from clear. . . ."[39]

After outlining the hazy responsibility that both Rear Admiral Moon and Rear Admiral Leatham had held for the convoy, Brind touched on the similarly hazy situation that had obtained lower in the chain of command between Skahill and Geddes. Drawing no clear conclusion ("We are not aware . . . of the relative responsibilities . . ."), Brind drew the only conclusion he could, which was none at all: "It is not therefore intended to attribute blame to the commanding officer of *Azalea*," he wrote; and more generally, of all concerned, "I recommend therefore that no action should be taken. . . ."[40]

Rear Admiral Brind's letter also mentioned, rather in the spirit of some tiresome proceeding taking place an impossible way away, an inquiry that "the Americans" had carried out into the disaster: "But we have no record of this, and to get to the bottom of the incident it would require considerable extra correspondence."[41] That last, almost throwaway, remark, when one considers the number of lives that had been lost, is staggering. But the war was still being waged—it wasn't the season for witch hunts. Nor on the American side. The writer Edwin P. Hoyt suggested that "ultimately, Commander Skahill bore the onus for the disaster in the Navy's eyes."[42] This is directly contradicted by John Doyle, skipper of the *515*, who while on T-4 saw Skahill at close quarters and had a disagreement with him regarding the rescue. He might have been expected to be the first to condemn Skahill, but, on the contrary, calling him "an officer and a gentleman," he says bluntly that "Commander Skahill was not at fault."[43]

Edwin Hoyt quotes the commander of American naval forces in European waters, Admiral H. R. Stark, to whom the snowballing reports on the disaster went after Kirk. Stark effectively had the U.S. Navy's last word, as Brind had the Royal Navy's, and the spirit of their respective judgments was much the same. On May 19, a week after Rear Admiral Ramsay's sensitive meeting with Eisenhower, and months before Brind's last word, Stark wrote that "no further action is contemplated."[44]

So the lid was screwed down on the Tiger disaster. Itself a triumph of bad timing, it also occurred at a bad time for future remembrance. Before D Day the need for secrecy and security had been paramount; after D Day, when the impact of the disaster had anyway been dulled a little, memory of it was swept away in the riptide of the invasion and history in the making. The disaster had, as it were, missed its historical moment.

It is not surprising that after years of brooding upon the Tiger disaster and its curious omission from the high-profile historical record some survivors would put a sinister gloss upon postwar handling of the affair. But at the time, with the uniformed man's easygoing acceptance of the chaos of war, soldiers and sailors saw it rather as a gigantic snafu. More refreshing than the official inquiries is the concise summing-up by Elwin Hendrick of the *515*: "The Tiger catastrophe was due to command and communications failure. *C'est la guerre!*"[45] And of Bernard Skahill: "Skahill found himself in a situation slathered over with 'the rotten touch of circumstance.' May he rest in peace!"[46]

"No action should be taken. . . ." "No further action is contemplated. . . ." But if there was to be no official memory of the Tiger disaster, it would continue to be remembered, unofficially, in the minds of its survivors. The memory was still fresh in Tom Clark's mind when he wrote to his father on July 4, 1944:

> Like all men who live through something like that, I wonder why my life was spared. I remember seeing them bring boatload after boatload of bodies aboard. My friends, my buddies. Enlisted men I'd talked and worked with. My roommate, fresh out of navy school, Smithy the engineer, the man with the mustache, Jim Clark, who loaned me a hundred

1. The rescue ship *LST 515*. Note, forward of the ship, the gun tubs and the bow doors giving direct entrance to the tank deck. A lift raised vehicles to the main deck. Amidship are the oval life rafts. Stern, the davits, or shipboard cranes, for lowering LCVPs. Just forward of the mast is the "super conn," the highest manned point of the ship.

2. The *515*'s Engine Room Crew. Far left, standing, Engineering Officer David Roop. Fourth from left, standing, Floyd Hicks. Front center, the ship's mascot, Beachhead. For the full story of Beachhead's life see note 31, chapter three.

3. Life below decks aboard an LST. Perhaps "Oh What a Beautiful Morning" is on the gramophone as the sailors write home and leaf through magazines. To the right of the picture are the men's bunks.

4. The officers' mess-room on an LST. In the U.S. wartime Navy black sailors served only as stewards and cooks. *LST 496* had "four guys called Henry." When *LST 507* was sunk there were men who didn't see why the ship's one black steward should be allowed to survive.

5. The Fourth Platoon of the Thirty-third Chemical Decontamination Company, just before Exercise Tiger. Front row, seated, fourth from left, Dale Rodman. Standing just behind him, Joseph Rosiek, who took Rodman's place on the *507*'s tank deck. Standing, far left, the company's commander, Captain Ralph Suesse.

6. Exercise Tiger, soon before setting sail. "Loaded from one end of the ship to the other, we were a floating arsenal." This is the crowded main deck of *LST 55*. Top left, part of the deck of *LST 289*. Photo taken by the *55*'s skipper, Walter Trombold.

7. April 27, 1944: "Time passed slowly then. Hot sun, blue water . . ."
The doomed *LST 507* on her final full day afloat. Photo by Walter Trombold.

8. "D Day" on Slapton Sands, April 27. *LCT* (Landing Craft, Tanks) *954*
and *LST 382*. Between them on the beach a Dukw ("duck"). Photo by
Walter Trombold.

9. The mangled stern of *LST 289* after it had limped in to Dartmouth. Note, just below the mast, the gun tub where James Chandler stayed at his post and died. Photo by Walter Trombold.

10. "She looked more like a converted trawler to me than a corvette . . ."
HMS *Azalea*, Convoy T-4's Royal Navy escort.

11. Lieutenant-Commander George C. Geddes, RNVR, 1942.

12. "A colorless personality . . ." "An officer and a gentleman . . ."
Bernard Skahill, commander of Convoy T-4.

13. " 'Aft through the hawse pipe' right after Pearl . . ." John Doyle,
captain of the *515*.

14. Commander John Moreno, Rear-Admiral Moon's Air and Assistant Plans Officer. "For some reason he turned to me immediately following the Tiger debacle . . . ''

15. "A gift from God to sense things in the water at night . . .'' Former fisherman Joseph McCann, aged 15; photograph taken in November, 1943.

16. Emanuel Rubin and Ken Small on Slapton Sands, 1987. In the background the salvaged "DD" Sherman tank. "Manny" Rubin is wearing an *LST 496* cap made in his own clothing factory. Photograph © *The Times*.

17. Survivors. Back row, left to right: Ensigns Jerry Brown, Tom Clark, Fred Beattie, Dr. Ed Panter, Lieutenant James Murdoch (Executive Officer), Dr. Eugene Eckstam. Front row, left to right: Unknown (possibly a sailor called Bernard Cary), Douglas Harlander of *LST 531*, wearing the clothes given him by the Royal Navy, Lieutenant Scott Gill. Photograph taken early May, 1944, soon after Exercise Tiger.

18. "The medal was thrown in a drawer. I wanted to forget . . . ." Survivors Angelo Crapanzano and Tom Clark, April, 1985.

dollars to bring Pottsie [Tom Clark's nickname for his wife] down to New Orleans. . . . Jim is a saint in heaven this day. . . . Hoffman and Saucier, veterans of three invasions, and the army officers—nine out of eleven lost their lives that night. There were twenty-three officers aboard and eight were saved. An experience like that leaves funny impressions, Dad. . . .

Tom Clark asked his parents to be discreet, which was just as well: He was giving them classified information. In the same month of July David Moore, who had been senior army officer aboard the *289*, was in the United States on rotation, and at the time, he said, "The incident was still classified . . . so I was unable to tell the next of kin of those killed or missing." (In many cases it would be forty years or more before the next of kin first gained an outline of the true circumstance.)

David Moore added that as far as he knew "the security classification was never lifted," and Moore, it should be remembered, was one of the officers who was made responsible for enforcing the security. "Even," he said, "after the need to keep any knowledge of the incident from the enemy was past, higher command was not interested in publicizing the affair. The U.S. and British navies were both embarrassed by the foul-up in providing escort services."

In other words, according to David Moore, the information blackout began as a legitimate concern with security only to be prolonged for essentially political reasons to do with face-saving. And Moore gives us another reason for embarrassment: the same "delay in sending any rescue craft to the scene" that was to puzzle Tom Clark for forty years. The delay occurred, said Moore, "despite the fact that the U.S. naval base at Portland was only a short distance away and that an SOS had been sent in the clear" (*en clair:* decoding could not be held responsible for the hours of delay).[47]

On July 8, just as Tom Clark's letter reached home, the men of T-4 who were officially "missing" were declared to have been killed, and their status was altered from MIA to KIA.[48] In the first two weeks of the following month more telegrams were sent out to kill whatever hope still remained among the next of kin of the MIA men: "The Secretary of War desires that I tender his deep sympathy to you in the loss of your son———who was previously reported missing in action." It had taken, it should be noted, more than a month for the "report" to arrive.

This is not to suggest callousness on the authorities' part. Is there any especially gentle way, in wartime, for a bureaucracy to tell a mother that her son has been killed? There are certainly crasser methods than were employed with one mother of a sailor who died in Tiger. In her case, the telegram of May 12 was followed up eleven days later by a letter offering the Secretary of the Navy's "personal condolence." On June 9 her senator sent her a letter. "I realize," he wrote, "there is not much one can say to alleviate the feelings of parents over the loss of a son"; he nevertheless expressed his "deepest sympathy." Six days later, a letter was sent with practical information on the repatriation, after the war was over, of her son's body.

Then, in October 1944 a letter arrived from her son's executive officer, a fellow sailor who had known him personally. It said that her son had been "respected and admired by all his shipmates . . . a credit to his ship and to the Navy. Our prayers are with yours." The letter said that "during the action" her son had been "at his battle station, in one of the damage control parties, performing his duties with the highest degree of loyalty. . . . He left the ship when it was abandoned and was not seen again until his body was taken from the water later that day."

Eventually, his family was sent the few personal effects that had been retrieved from his body: his dog tag, an identity bracelet with his name on it, a signet ring, and three English coins.[49]

These are not the actions of a heartless bureaucracy, but at the same time these official communications with the dead man's family are significant for what they omit: the precise circumstances of his death and the fact that he was by no means the only man to die. The family still didn't really *know*, and as one of the survivors would remark years later, "There seems to be peace in knowledge."[50] By then, though, memory would have gone to work. For the time being, the long business of forgetting had begun.

III

THE BURIAL GROUND

CHAPTER

12

There is a Spanish proverb that nicely accompanies the Hispanically named Bolero period preceding the invasion of occupied Europe: "Guests and fish smell bad after two days." The Americans had been crowding into southern England for considerably longer than that, but now, with the invasion, the towns and countryside were suddenly, magically, emptied of them.

Not entirely, of course. There were still the soldiers responsible for supplying the army, the administrative staffs, the construction battalions, or CBs, composed largely of black soldiers, the station hospital awaiting their wounded. There were still the sentries on guard around the South Hams evacuation area. But most of the Americans had filed aboard the LSTs for France, to die there, or to fight on across France, Belgium, and Germany to the Battle of the Bulge and Berlin, and then, if they still lived, eventually to the United States and home. Wherever they went, England at least—and at last—was rid of them.

During Bolero, before the invasion, every effort had been made to understand and extend a welcome to the strange "guests" from across the Atlantic. In South Devon the welcoming red carpet had been laid before the evacuation of the South Hams for the American Battle School. In November 1943, for example, Mrs. L. K. Elmhirst had lectured to the Kingsbridge Workers' Educational Association about the United States. Americans had automobiles with radios and lived in houses with central heating and "most attractive kitchens." In those kitchens were such model marvels as "pressing machines for laundry work," and electric stoves with automatic timers to cut the heat off when the roast was cooked. Americans tended "to make something nice of their homes—perhaps not very much of their gardens."[1]

With the invasion successfully launched, however, and the Americans in France, the English hospitality developed an edge as, at last, more of the people's envy and other real feelings began to be aired in public. An article in the *Kingsbridge Gazette* of June 16, ten days after D Day, bursts with a sense of strained politeness. It was by an anonymous "Local Government Officer," and was subtitled "Reflections, on 'Occupation' by our American Ally."

The author stressed that "we have been proud to have been the hosts in a small way to our American friends." Their "charming frankness," he said, and their friendliness "melted most hearts." At the same time, however, the first few months of the "occupation" had been a "nightmare," with "reports pouring in of slight damage to fences, gates, houses, roads, and property, and trivial complaints of action by our visitors which didn't please the residents, or which were contrary to our conservative English customs."

The government officer's chief complaint concerned what he saw as the messiness and wastefulness of the Americans: "the worn-out roads, the accumulation of cigarette packets and rubbish on our footways and open spaces." He added that "chewing gum became the chief diet of the townspeople." Refuse collection and disposal had been, he said, "a headache," with a "colossal" quantity of rubbish piled up every day outside American premises: "Tidiness and wartime economy in food scraps and clothing could not possibly be said to be American virtues." The American example, that is, blatantly contradicted the wartime parsimony that had been urged upon a rural population that hated to see anything go to waste.

The American messiness could be lethal, too. It wasn't only empty cigarette packs and wads of chewing gum that were left lying around. In May three boys were playing in a field at Woolston Farm, outside the evacuation area about four miles northwest of Kingsbridge. In a rabbit hole they found an interesting new toy: an antitank grenade. It exploded, killing two of them. The grenade had been left behind from an exercise at the end of April, probably part of Exercise Tiger. Perhaps the names of two English children should be added to Tiger's death tally.[2]

An incident like that was not calculated to endear local people to the American presence. Certainly the Americans were allies, fighting shoulder to shoulder with the British, but the invasion was still in the future, while the American "occupation" was a daily fact of life. The Americans were not in France with their chewing gum, their hot dogs, and their dangerous weaponry, but in the previously sleepy English countryside, now loud with their accents, their vehicles, their war games. At the fringes of the evacuation area, where the red flags were up to indicate an exercise in progress, people heard the pounding of guns and explosion of shells and wondered what was happening inside the area to the houses, the fields, the roads, the pubs, and churches. Sometimes there were accidents of aiming and shells soared out of the area to explode in populated areas. One shell exploded in a graveyard in Loddiswell, strewing shrapnel among the graves. "It was hardly safe to be dead!" said a local woman.[3]

By May there was acute desperation among many of the evacuees of the South Hams, stripped of their livelihoods along with their homes, farms, and shops. The MP, Ralph Rayner, continued to champion their cause. Astonishingly, given the sensitivity of the matter both socially and in terms of security, he had been permitted to advertise the plight of the evacuees with a broadcast in the United States that spring. His hope was that "that wealthy nation would endeavor to see that no one evacuated was a loser financially by their forced sacrifice"[4]—he was holding out a begging bowl to the American public.

Rayner was himself a little desperate. From the beginning he had regarded the terms of the Defense Regulations and the Compensation Act of 1939 as woefully inadequate to the case of the evacuees. It was not enough that government officials had been "instructed within the four corners of the act"[5] to be as generous as possible; the act itself did not allow sufficient latitude for generosity. Effectively, the evacuees were thrown on others' charity and there was a sense in which, as the *Kingsbridge Gazette* had pointed out in an editorial, their predicament was worse than that of the millions of refugees of continental Europe and Russia:

> The very fact that fear and the instinct of self-preservation will be absent will make the uprooting for them all the harder to endure. The sympathy and consideration which will be extended to them by friend and official alike will in a way add to their difficulties.[6]

Rayner went directly to the American public only when he found that there was to be no revision of the Compensation Act and that there was no provision in American law for compensation in these circumstances. Soon, however, he was ordered "by the highest authority . . . for reasons of high policy,"[7] to stop his charity campaign.

Now the 3,000 evacuees were on their own. In the second week of May articles in the national press advertised their distress. At the same time, though, the U.S. Army had set up a contingency fund to help with the worst cases of hardship. "Individual evacuees," said the *Daily Express,* "have been called for interviews by the Regional Commissioner."[8] On May 12 the local *Gazette* public-mindedly but shortsightedly complained: "All this fuss, bother, uprooting of homes and family life, for the sake of a few months of military maneuvers. For every acre of land which has been acquired in this area for this purpose, there must be a square mile available in the U.S.A." The paper urged Ralph Rayner now to concentrate his best efforts "to prevent more than 30,000 acres of the best agricultural land in England from becoming derelict."

However, D Day and the departure of the Americans was then less than a month away. Whatever damage there was, most had already been done; how much, the residents of the area would find out. But not yet. The departure of the Americans for real battle did not make the Battle School immediately available for peaceful habitation. Although rumors of their imminent return circulated among the evacuees, it would be some three months before they actually did so.

Meanwhile, although the U.S. Army had begun to distribute its £6,000 contingency fund, the evacuees were "getting poorer every week," as the *Gazette* reported on June 23. It was only on July 4, American Independence Day, that the regional engineer of the Ministry of Health wrote in a letter that the American battle-training area had been given up by the services and that it was "proposed to restore it to the civilians."[9] A week later the regional commissioner's office wrote that "the derequisitioning of the area was on the way."[10]

The "derequisitioning" was a long and complicated business, initially entrusted, as the *Gazette* rather curiously remarked, to "over 1,000 American colored troops and other people."[11] The plan was to start at the area's perimeter and coastline, including Slapton Sands, and work inward and inland (although the local historian Grace Bradbeer said that the coastline was left till last). The first priority was the "deshelling" of the area. "There are," said one observer, "infernal machines lying about that are still alive."[12]

Another problem was the electricity supply. Where there had been one in the evacuation area, the cable carrying it ran though "the most heavily shelled part."[13] The idea was to try to shoot a new cable into position "by means of a lifesaving rocket." The main water supply and sewerage system, again where they had previously existed, seemed to be in good enough shape, but after the months of neglect and damage they had to be tested. Food was another problem. "It is going to be difficult," said a local government official, "to get the retailer in before the people, because the retailer says he wants to see the customers before he returns."[14]

Then there were the houses. The condition in which many of them had been left would provoke more ill will and anti-American feeling than any other aspect of the evacuation when the time came for the evacuees to return. For the time being the evacuees were dependent on eyewitness reports filtering out of the evacuation area, and there is evidence here of a little discreet news management in order to ease the considerable shock to come.

Certainly the true situation did not emerge in reports of a July 21 meeting of the Kingsbridge Council, at which the chairman reported on a tour of the area he had made two weeks before. The purpose of his visit had been to inspect the condition of the roads, which, "generally speaking," he had found to be "not too bad." He reported, though, that a good many roadside hedges and walls had been flattened. In an image that echoes the fairy-tale feeling that had preceded the evacuation, he said that "it looks as though a giant with big teeth had come along and taken a bite out here and there."[15]

While inspecting the roads, however, the chairman "could not help looking at other things as they went by." One thing that struck him was the "extraordinary quantity" of rabbits and birds. Pigeons were especially numerous, but, in fact, during the exercises they and all the birds had been frightened away by the noise of gunfire. John Hannaford, a Torcross butcher who ventured into the area after D Day, had been struck by the extraordinary *absence* of birds: Even the soft raspberries (which ripened just too late for the Americans to pick) had been left untouched on their bushes.[16] The birds had returned since D Day and the departure of the Americans, but the rabbits (and the rats) in their underground burrows had been thriving throughout, and the chairman said that "rabbit trappers are going to have the time of their lives when they get back."[17]

Rabbit trappers had, in fact, been making regular illicit visits to the area during its occupation, and from them, the coast watchers, and others, reports of the state it was in had filtered to the people outside. But the trappers did not penetrate the area deeply and the security cordon around it remained by and large unbroken: A local doctor was fined by the police for making a brief visit to his own home.

So most of the reports were really rumor, a plant that, like wheat (and now, weeds) flourished abundantly in the rich agricultural area of the South Hams. It was surprising that the chairman should repeat rumors after his on-the-spot visit, however. He said that "the village of Strete, except for the beautiful building that was used by the Women's Institute, has been burned down." In fact, the reality was almost exactly the opposite: Strete had escaped substantial damage, with all its buildings standing except for the Women's Institute and two adjoining houses. The chairman was nearer the mark when he spoke of "miles and miles of barbed wire"[18] and of village streets throughout the area being littered with broken glass from blown-out windows. He estimated that the repairs would require "about one acre of glass."[19]

"Many things," he went on, "which we have all heard about the conditions of houses in the area have proved to be completely false." In this instance, however, the rumors did have a basis, and the chairman discounted them despite having entered only two houses on his visit to the area. He wasn't therefore really in a position to answer a query put to him by the Reverend H. Stone, about rumors of "a great deal of petty pilfering." Councillor Hedley answered for him:

> There is nothing left to steal now, except fruit.
> THE REVEREND STONE: Take my Vicarage. Someone removed a copper boiler. That is petty pilfering.
> THE CHAIRMAN: Please let us remember that we are all rather talking a bit in the air.[20]

In another exchange, the chairman hoped that the evacuees would feel proud

> that they have played a real and personal part in our recent landings in Normandy. Many of the men who stormed the beaches on D Day carried out their training on the beaches in this area. We, therefore, to a certain extent, share the success that they have so magnificently achieved.
>
> COUNCILLOR HEDLEY: I agree with these remarks, but the fact still remains that much of the financial sacrifice could have been avoided.
> THE CHAIRMAN: The smallness of the casualties in the initial landings were due in great measure to the training the troops received on our beaches.
> THE REVEREND STONE: Then should they not be more generous to the people?
> THE CHAIRMAN: Is sacrifice always to be paid for?[21]

That question, an unusual one to put to a vicar, might have been asked of the American victims of Tiger as well as the English evacuees.

It emerged at the meeting that the evacuation area was expected to be ready to receive people by October 1, although some villages wouldn't be ready until December. A vote was taken on whether to release these dates, which would in fact prove pessimistic, to the public. It was passed, but clearly the condition in which the area had been left and the evacuees' likely reactions to it were considered to be touchy questions. This time the mess that the Americans had left was much more than cigarette packs and chewing gum wrappers.

There was another side to the evacuation, too. If many lives had been turned upside down by it, to others it had been a revelation. Leaving their sleepy South Hams backwater for the first time in their lives, they had caught up on the century and seen how it was possible in 1944 to live much more comfortably. In terms of the conveniences of modern living, the South Hams were about as far behind other parts of England as England was behind the United States.

The American "occupation" triggered in these people a very American ambition to better their material well-being. For the first time, during the months away from the South Hams, some of them had "experienced in other places the amenities of electric light and water laid up." They did not want, according to a South-West Region official, "to revert to a remote country cottage with oil lamps; pumping water from a well in all weathers. They have now found something that they prefer much better."[22] In the words of an American First World War song: "How are you going to keep them down on the farm, now that they've seen Paree?"

In 1984, the fortieth anniversary of the evacuation, the South Hams District Council prepared a list of names and addresses of former evacuees. They are names rich with the West Country: Luscombe, Hannaford, Mitchelmore, Soper. The addresses today are all over England, with a few in Wales and the two most far-flung in Zimbabwe and Bermuda. But most ex-evacuees live still in the West Country, where they originated, and of that majority, most still occupy addresses that lie within the boundary of the old wartime evacuation area. *Plus ça change* . . . Most people, despite the upheaval of the evacuation and the temptations of a more "modern" life elsewhere, itched to return to the homes they had vacated for the Americans.

But they couldn't yet do so. The Americans had gone, but they had not returned. The land where they had lived lay in a curious limbo, as if after a plague that had wiped out the people but left the evidence of their habitation; a no man's land full of rabbits, rats, and pigeons. Overgrown and gone to seed, "the area seemed to lie as if under a spell," wrote Grace Bradbeer, "waiting for the touch of a magic wand.''[23] Really, it was the people who would be the magic wand, and the people who were waiting; as the weeks passed, so their frustration mounted at the delay. It was incomprehensible to them. What was holding up the authorities?

Official policy was to do everything possible to get the farmers back first, so that the land could be cleared, some autumn sowing could be done, and the area could quickly resume its traditional role as a breadbasket of England. The farmers knew what a daunting prospect that was; one of them at least was unable to face it and opted to put down new roots elsewhere. Another farmer, Tom Walters-Symons, painted a picture of the neglected land and the desperate state it was in. Swedes, kale, and rape had gone to seed and couldn't now be cut by machinery. In going to seed, the land had lost its manurial value. Charlock had gone to seed—the stumps would have to be cut and burned. "Billions of seed" would be destroyed. There were hundreds of acres full of docks, couch grass, thistles, and horse-thistles. The clovers were rotting: "It cannot now be cut and cattle will not eat it." Many pastures were rotting: "These lands are spoiled for years."[24] And so on—the farmer's eye saw not only the desolation but its consequences for the future. In the words of another farmer, "You know what they say: 'One year's seeding, seven years weeding.' ''[25]

The turning of the seasons would brook no bureaucratic delay, and yet, inexplicably, the delay lengthened and still nothing happened. The *Gazette* was not being impatient when in an editorial of August 18 it complained that

> the next two weeks . . . are vital in the matter of clearing the ground from weeds and cutting back overgrown hedges. . . . We have been led to believe that England is the land of the free and that it was only a matter of comparatively short time before these people would be able to go back. It is now ten weeks, at least, since the area was used for the purpose for which it was originally taken over.[26]

The *Gazette* noted that police permission was required in order to enter the area, and that "feeling appears to be running somewhat high among many who were evacuated. . . . We have endeavored to ascertain but, so far, unsuccessfully, on what serious grounds permits are denied."[27] By now, apparently, the American army clearance squads had moved out of the area; perhaps it had been their task only to "deshell" it and remove "infernal machines." They had been replaced by civil defense personnel, who had moved into some of the houses. Their owners objected that they had temporarily relinquished them for the Admiralty on behalf of the Americans, not for the civil defense.

Perhaps the *Gazette*'s leader did the trick. At any rate, over the weekend of August 19–20 the first three inhabitants returned to their old homes in the evacuation area. The first village to be "liberated"— as the *Gazette* called it in a popular phrase of the day—was East Allington, a village in the northwest of the area, well inland, which had not suffered too badly from the "occupation."

One of the first three to return was Mr. W. Jones, described by the *Gazette* as "the popular 'mine host' of the Fortescue Arms." Three weeks before, the paper had noted a "brave show" of Union Jacks in the pub's (broken) windows. Now its landlord pulled the pints, and with the village baker-cum-grocer and the local owner of a car leasing service and hardware store drank a toast to the "liberation." Across the road, the hands of the church clock had stuck at five past five. More people returned, and by Tuesday, said the *Gazette,* "all was merry and bright inside the Fortescue Arms. Once again there came the familiar clink of glasses, a cheery greeting from the jovial landlord. . . ." Wisps of smoke had begun to curl from the chimneys of the village houses, and there was "the happy ring of children's laughter as they played outside their homes. So, after a spell of nearly nine months, East Allington has been reborn."[28]

And so, village by village, field by field, the whole evacuation area was gradually "liberated" and "reborn." Sherford was the next village, in early September, followed by Chillington and Blackawton. And so, little by little, the people discovered what had transpired in their absence. Familiar landmarks had vanished—like the semiruin, familiar enough by 1943, of the Royal Sands Hotel. Slapton Church had been badly damaged, it was thought by Royal Navy gunfire. Amazingly, one small stained-glass window had been blown out of the vestry but survived intact in the churchyard. At Stokenham a shell had blown a hole in the Church House Inn, damaging the church roof and smashing all the stained glass on one side. At Blackawton it was the vicar's impression that the church had been the scene of a gigantic disorderly party. The floor was deep in cigarette butts, the hymn and prayer books were strewn everywhere, the organ had been taken to bits and the organ pipes apparently used as "penny whistles." The broken glass of liquor bottles lay on the floor with that of the smashed stained-glass windows.[29] So much for the Bishop of Exeter's eloquent plea: "This church, this churchyard in which their loved ones lie at rest, these homes, these fields are as dear to those who have left them as are the homes and graves and fields which you, our Allies, have left behind you. . . ."

What most enraged returning residents was the condition of their own homes. And their dismay was the more difficult for them in that any expression of it was liable to be interpreted as a churlish, and even unpatriotic, slur upon Allied soldiers who had just risked their lives in one of history's great battles. On August 2 the regional information officer, South-West Region, had told pressmen just before a short guided tour of the evacuation area that he "thought they would agree that where one had an aggregation of troops they would have damage." He had added:

> But, naturally, we do not want in any way to point the finger at our American ally and to say that they have behaved badly. Considering what the area has been used for, and the great debt we owe to the Americans, that kind of criticism and talk can well be left alone.[30]

Against this background, a local churchman's letter to the *Gazette* in response to its editorial of August 18 was written under a cloak of anonymity. Signing himself Clericus Rotundus, the churchman recalled the *Gazette*'s puzzlement over the continuing delay in the evacuation area's rehabilitation and said that one explanation of it was "not far to seek." He pointed out that there was no evidence of shells having fallen in the villages on the southern boundary of the area and yet "practically all" the houses in them had been "defiled, looted, and despoiled." Clericus Rotundus did not find it surprising that

> the people most affected should not be encouraged by those in authority to make an inspection of their devastated homes, more especially when they were given to understand before their eviction that their houses would not be occupied by troops. . . . That was a gross and stupid deception, and it would appear that this policy is still being maintained.[31]

Under another Latinate alias, Intra Muros, an aggrieved householder wrote that he had found "wantonly damaged doors, walls, and ceiling, and the bedrooms used as public conveniences . . . not an apple left on the trees."[32]

Another householder gave his name, C. L. G. Moore. He wrote of "electric switches, baths, basins smashed, woodwork burnt or taken away, and in my case even lawn mowers have disappeared; I presume to be used on the beaches of Cherbourg peninsula." He, too, felt deceived by the authorities:

> Many times when I could hear the guns from here [Chudleigh, just outside the area] I had ideas of what was happening and the serious damages which

would be caused, but I had no idea that after the definite promise made to us that no troops would be allowed in our houses that this promise was broken in every respect.

Often Mr. Moore had been reassured that "all was lovely in the garden," but now he knew why "no limelight was to be thrown upon the evacuation" and why "it was shameful to badger the authorities."[33]

Grace Bradbeer argued in 1973 that most of the damage should be laid at the door not of the Americans, but of vagabonds and thieves and "naughty boys" who had entered the area.[34] But if it is hard to imagine why young American soldiers might have wanted to appropriate the vicar's copper boiler or Mr. Moore's lawn mowers, it is also difficult to imagine a congregation of vagabonds and thieves holding a party of the Hogarthian proportions of the one apparently held in Blackawton church. That scene is reminiscent of the behavior of any "aggregation of troops" of any nationality, anywhere. And it was unmistakably Americans who had daubed and scrawled the inside walls of many houses with pornographic pictures and graffiti, who chopped up doors, floors, and banisters for firewood and used some houses as latrines.

Another messy problem that the Americans left behind them in the evacuation area was dumps of old food, especially the enormous tin "logs" containing the government-issue Spam. On these the rats had thrived, but it wasn't until the food dumps were removed, and the rats had to find another food source, that "an army of rats began moving from farm to farm"[35] to feed on the seed corn newly brought in by farmers. Yet again one finds—in the image of a desperate "army" of rats—the local and rural life of the South Hams mirroring as in a fairy tale the wider history of the time: In January 1945 it was the Nazis who had been driven from their fortresses, and on the 12th of that month the *Kingsbridge Gazette* carried a good-humored "interview" with the "Enemy Commander, King Rat": "Having had more than we could stomach of Spam, ice cream, and cookies, we thought we would get back to a more normal diet," King Rat was quoted as saying. The *Gazette* ran a series of similar "interviews" through January and February, a progress report on the increasingly victorious "war" on the rats. After six years the newspaper was getting back to something like its old peacetime news diet, and the people to something resembling their former, "normal" lives.

The houses were cleaned up, the windows replaced, the rats were gradually fought off, the weeds chopped down. The farmers, that first season back, did what they could with their devastated fields and planted new crops. The creepers were cut back from the houses. Fruit trees and bushes and hedges were trimmed; flowers were planted. Mr. Moore doubtless got himself a new lawn mower and started to coax his overgrown lawn into shape again. But if he and others grumbled less than before, it was still too early, at the dawn of 1945, for the evacuees to set their sacrifice within the proper historical context.

The local authorities wanted, however, to evoke that context at once, as did the American authorities, doubtless to help smooth over an area where Allied relations had been unduly strained. On January 5, 1945, four months before the German surrender, the *Gazette* reported that "The American Memorial" was to be put up on the shore at Slapton: It was to be a diplomatic thank you to the people of the South Hams who had vacated the evacuated area. The design for the memorial that had been accepted—an eighteen-foot-high obelisk carved from Dartmoor granite—had been sent to the Americans for their approval. By April they had approved it and agreement on a site had been reached with Herbert Whiteley, owner of Slapton Sands and the surrounding land. The memorial was to be built on the beach roughly at the point that had divided the Red and White Beaches of Exercise Tiger. Councillors were worried about the stability of the site on the beach: They thought that the memorial might soon start to tilt.

But it went up, a granite obelisk with an inscription thanking the 3,000 evacuees "who generously left their homes and their lands to provide a battle practice area for the successful assault on Normandy."[36] It listed the villages by name but, confusing villages with parishes, omitted Sherford. The memorial was not, of course, to say thank you for Exercise Tiger, but, remembering Tiger, the clerical error is typical; it was not the first, nor would it be the last, one. Against the backdrop of Tiger, there is another feature of the inscription that strikes one as curious. Most memorials are to the dead, but this one was to the living, and its inscription claimed that the evacuation had "resulted in the saving of many hundreds of lives."[37] There was no mention of the fact that on the way to this beach hundreds of lives had been lost.

CHAPTER

13

If the memorial on Slapton Sands can be taken to symbolize an unusually close instance of Anglo-American cooperation and shared sacrifice, the postwar history of the Tiger disaster is for the greater part a story not of coming together, but of distance and dispersion. It is necessary to say something about this complex postwar background.

The great majority of those Americans who had survived Tiger, and D Day, and the whole war, were back in the United States, in their old homes or new ones, but anyway far from the English Channel and the South Hams. And the point must be made that the United States is a very large country: Survivors of the disaster were likely to be living far from one another, especially given the American policy by which servicemen had been allocated to their units and ships. The Americans had learned from the First World War, when individual communities had been devastated by the decimation or wiping out of a particular unit heavily manned by citizens drawn from a single place. Against that background, it was conscious policy in the Second World War to disperse men from particular towns or cities, even from the same state, as widely and distantly as possible in different units and ships. In a form of insurance policy, the postwar impact of potential bloodbaths— like Convoy T-4—was democratically budgeted against, so that any especially heavy burden of bloodshed and grief would be evenly distributed (a system that, in the case of Missouri and the 3206th Quartermaster Service Company, would appear to have broken down).

By the same logic, after the war it would be correspondingly unlikely that two mothers whose sons had died in the same incident would meet one another, or that one Tiger survivor would bump into another in a bar, say, and compare notes. Nor, of course, did the great majority of the survivors know the name of the exercise that they had survived. Many did not even know what had hit them that night: Some Tiger veterans would still think in the late Eighties that it had been a

German U-boat. There was no ready reference to identify what they had undergone. It wasn't only the American public who did not know about them; in a sense they themselves didn't know what they had lived through. In the words of one: "None of us survivors really knew what happened to us, and what part we were playing in this preinvasion exercise."[1] The survivors, and the next of kin of those who had not survived, lacked a retrieval system by which to pool memories of, and information about, a disaster that the American authorities were anyway not eager to publicize. It must be noted once more that because of the preinvasion need for secrecy the T-4 disaster had missed its historical moment. It would take many years before the moment came round again.

And there one touches upon another dimension to the distance: It wasn't only the physical distance of the Atlantic Ocean, and the wide open spaces of the United States; it was also, increasingly, a distance in time. Forgetting, and grief, and memory, have their own dynamics, which work themselves out in their own time.

One popular stereotype of the old soldier or sailor is of him buttonholing anyone who'll listen to his experiences. If there is truth in that stereotype at all, it tends to become true only many years afterward. It took an *ancient* mariner to stop the wedding guest; a young one would more probably have been silently sobbing inside himself.

More often the survivor of a bloody wartime encounter will irrationally but guiltily blame himself for having survived when so many perished. He has experienced something so horrifically far outside the normal pale as to be almost incommunicable, and communication of it is further hampered by his guiltily perceiving the fact of his own survival as something almost shameful, to be lived down in silence. Tom Clark's query in his letter to his father, as to why his life had been spared, is today seen as typical of posttraumatic stress disorder: in war terms, post-Vietnam or, in Britain, post-Falklands syndrome.

Survival is not, to the survivor, something to brag about. More than forty years later Tom Clark would still be more impressed not by his own survival, but by the fact that others did not survive:

I see their faces in their last moments as they look at me, their hands in mine pushing off backward into the cold water. Some of them in silence asking why did we perish? My heart says if I had an hour to give you, it is yours. You and I must go over the side and into the water. God bless you, my comrades.[2]

Nor was Angelo Crapanzano a braggart about his survival—very far from it. In November 1944 he finally got his postponed thirty days' survivors' leave, and returned to the States for it. He spent Thanksgiving with his family and went to his high school's football game traditionally played on Turkey Day morning. The band started to play the national anthem, the Stars and Stripes went up the flagpole: He saluted and "openly wept."

Openly—but he had not told his family about the details of his survival. Those he kept to himself. Nor did he tell his childhood sweetheart, Ida, whom he married in June 1947; nor his two daughters, when they were grown up. And the Bronze Star that he had been awarded for saving his shipmate's life, that was kept in a shut drawer: "I wanted to forget, I just couldn't talk about what happened. The words wouldn't come out without me filling up. I just kept the memory of the nightmare bottled up inside—and it smoldered."[3]

The posttraumatic disorder of the T-4 disaster was made no easier to deal with by the deafening official silence after the war. Never mind the flags and the bugles, where were the journalists and the historians to bring knowledge of this disaster to the American consciousness, to give it its place in history?

There was a silence, but it should be set in perspective. It was by no means as comprehensive as has been suggested. On April 29, 1944, the day after the disaster, newspapers in England and the U.S. services paper *Stars and Stripes* had carried German news-agency reports of the E-boat attack. On August 7, Associated Press issued a report from SHAEF in London. And there were other, isolated, and locally generated stories in the American press before the war was over: for example, a story of January 1945 in the *Y Tribune* in Johnstown, Pennsylvania, about local boy Private John A. Perry "Home for Furlough after Terrifying War Experience in English Channel." These stories are sketchy in the extreme and none of them mentions Tiger or T-4 by name, but they contradict claims that there was a total American and Allied news blackout on the disaster even after D Day.

Exercise Tiger was mentioned by its code-name in Ralph Ingersoll's *Top Secret* and in the selection of Harry Butcher's diaries, both published in 1946; both books contain outline accounts of the E-boat attack. A disaster in the course of the April exercise was mentioned in passing in Kay Summersby's *Eisenhower Was My Boss,* published in 1949.

There were mentions of the Tiger disaster in two books published in the United States in 1951. *Cross-Channel Attack,* a volume of the official history, *The United States Army in World War II,* mentioned

Tiger by name and gave a few details of the E-boat attack, calling it "a serious note of war . . . amid all the simulation." More importantly that year, Omar Bradley published *A Soldier's Story,* in which he called the Tiger disaster "one of the major tragedies of the European war." Here was a book likely to be picked up and understood by the general reader, and here, at last, was a chance to air the Tiger disaster and put it on the popular record.

One avid reader of *A Soldier's Story* was Eugene Caffey, former commander of the First Engineer Special Brigade. He noted Bradley's suggestion to Collins at Slapton Sands that he "assign a new commander to the Utah Beach engineer brigade"—exactly what had happened with Caffey's sacking a few days after the disaster. Caffey noted also Bradley's admission that "not until four years after the war did I learn that these engineer troubles during the Utah rehearsal had been caused not by a breakdown in command but rather by the S-boat [*Schnellboot*] attack." Seven years later, Caffey had at last been supplied with the background to his sacking.

They had, for Caffey, been "seven miserable years," and he sat down to write a letter to the American adjutant general to put the record straight. He had, he wrote,

> always felt shamed and discredited because . . . at a crucial time I was relieved from command of an organization destined to play an important part in one of the great undertakings of all warfare. To make the disgrace more unbearable . . . there was a complete unawareness on my part of anything I had done or failed to do to deserve it.[4]

Caffey commented, with Bradley's published remarks in mind, that "it is ironic that I was relieved for a reason which it is stated did not exist," and that he would have been spared his seven years of "shame" and "disgrace" if the fact "had been known and evaluated then instead of later."[5]

According to Howard DeVoe, a Tiger veteran and later the company historian of units of the First Engineers, Caffey also wrote to Bradley, saying that in his view the misunderstanding lay behind his failure to achieve the rank of Brigadier General; his military career had been blighted by a disaster for which he had not been in the slightest to blame. But Caffey's son, Lochlin Caffey, told DeVoe that his father had not worried about his lack of promotion so much as "the cloud over his unit"; the Tiger disaster, said his son, had until his death been "one of his greatest sorrows."[6] Eugene Caffey, too, was a victim of Tiger.

In a later volume of the U.S. Army Second World War official history, *Logistical Support of the Armies,* published in 1953, the Tiger disaster was again mentioned with the exercise's code-name, and called "a tragic encounter." But none of these published references, not even Bradley's, amounted to anything like shouting the story of T-4 from the rooftops. In a way, as with the American memorial on Slapton Sands, it is the omissions in places where one would expect to find references that are more striking.

Perhaps the most eloquent omission is from *Turn To,* an in-house history of *LST 511* published in December 1945. *Turn To* has a history of the ship from her launch in Seneca in December 1943 to her decommissioning in Norfolk, Virginia, in November 1945. But there is no mention of the most traumatic and destructive episode in that history, the night that the *511* was fired upon by a sister ship. That episode was still being "hidden," as it were, even from those to whom it had happened.

Publications intended for general consumption were almost as taciturn. Intriguing is the absence of any reference in George C. Marshall's *Biennial Report of the Chief of Staff of the United States Army, July 1, 1943 to June 30, 1945.* This detailed document was, despite its dry-as-dust title, a bestseller of its day, as the general public rushed to catch up on wartime matters thitherto classified and surrounded by hearsay. The war in Europe had ended, and one would have expected a mention of Tiger, and T-4; we know, from Eisenhower's letter to him, that Marshall knew of the disaster. Nor is there any mention in Fleet Admiral King's report covering the period, but that was published while the war in Europe was still being waged. King's final report, published in October 1945, gives, as part of a general list of ships lost, the date on which LSTs 507 and *531* were sunk, and where they were sunk, but nothing else. (But nor did King's first report, published in 1944, make any mention of the destruction of Convoy PQ-17.)

The omission of the disaster from Eisenhower's *Crusade in Europe* (1948) is the most interesting. If anyone possessed the knowledge, and the popular clout, to put the story of Convoy T-4 on the historical map, it was Eisenhower. His failure to do so should be set not only against his "virtually sacred" relationship with the GI, and his postwar reverence for, and consistent honoring of, America's war dead, but against Winston Churchill's discreet reference to the disaster in *Closing the Ring,* volume 5 of *The Second World War,* published in 1952. Churchill's is a more exhaustive work than Eisenhower's, but it still seems strange that a British leader should mention an American wartime disaster, and an American leader make no mention of it at all.

This is not to exaggerate the importance of T-4. The attack on it was, as Churchill described it, only "a minor success" for the enemy (although a major one for the E-boats), and to the Allies the chief strategic implications of the attack lay in the loss of two vitally necessary LSTs and in the possibility that the Germans may have learned something from it of intelligence value. But a great many men died, and one would have thought—expected, even—that after the war some effort might have been made by those in the know to honor them. It was a suitable time for mourning and yet, in public at least, there was none, only a few passing references in a few books.

On the whole, the record, or the absence of one, justifies Angelo Crapanzano's complaint that the disaster "didn't even make the history books. They remembered Pearl Harbor, Iwo Jima, Okinawa, Midway, but Tiger faded into the past, unknown."[8] It is indeed a curious neglect on the part of a nation that has so consistently honored its war dead; but the dead of Tiger did not, of course, die successfully in the pursuit of a victory. They perhaps appeared to the United States, and still appear, too much like losers, the "noble six hundred" whom *Liberty* magazine had predicted no one would need to sing when the war was over.

Their memories of horror bottled up inside them, wanting perhaps, like Angelo Crapanzano, to forget, but unable to, the survivors faced up to the peace they had fought for, and got on with their lives. And in the former South Hams evacuation area, too, life slowly returned to "normal." Time passed and, gradually, year by year, the face of its landscape was once more the familiar, fussily informal face of England.

Under the peaceful English exterior, however, the memory of the American wartime "occupation" remained. It was as though, despite the distances in space and time, there had been a bonding between this corner of England and men thousands of miles away over the Atlantic whom the war had brought together and the peace had dispersed.

The old soldier now working for the gas company in Topeka, Kansas, say, and the LST vet who was now a roofing contractor in Chicago may never have met and may have landed on different Normandy beaches; but both had "rehearsed" on Slapton Sands. The name of Tiger as yet meant nothing to them; the name of the beach recalled a period of their lives.

The T-4 disaster was and is an American story, but its unity and common ground lay in southwest England and the South Hams. And if the American survivors had not forgotten Convoy T-4, neither had the people of the evacuation area and its environs forgotten the Americans. Here was potential for a retrieval system, the key that would, when the time came, open the memories locked up in the United States, in individual minds, and still classified files. And this is what, eventually, would happen, in an Anglo-American collaboration of the unconscious, an information explosion that would fill this hole in the American collective memory. But not yet; not for years. Only when the time came.

In the former evacuation area, memories of the Americans were buried everywhere. Buried both figuratively—in people's minds, and local place-names like Million Dollar Point—and physically, in the sea and under the soil. They were even buried under paintwork, in designations like Sergeants' Mess, or Cookhouse, painted on doors of houses in the evacuated villages and later painted over.[9]

They were buried in the Slapton lake—or Ley—behind the beach. In 1956 live land mines were found where the Americans had dumped them, in rushes at the Ley's edge.[10] In the dry summer of 1976 the lake's level sank, to reveal stakes that the Americans had driven into its bed as practice for the bridge they were to build at Utah.[11] There were memories physically embedded in the trees. Grace Bradbeer recalled the story of an old woman one night after the war sitting before a wood fire that suddenly exploded, filling her legs with shrapnel.[12] To this day sawmills will turn down trees from the area, lest shrapnel buried inside them ruin the saws.

There were things that the Americans had intentionally buried, things that they had not needed in Normandy and that it had not been economical to take back with them to the United States when the war was over. At Stover near Newton Abbot, for example, the former site of the 316th Station Hospital, now a home for old Polish refugees, the Americans buried large quantities of drugs and surgical ware before taking their leave from Britain. They filled in two swimming pools—the land dips slightly to this day. In the trees of Stover, Americans carved their names, their units, the names of the women they loved.

One tiny but telling example of South Devon holding the key to an American memory. All the more telling, really, for being so tiny. Geraldine James and her family live in a 1930s house called Windfall, about a hundred yards from Slapton Sands. One day in the early 1980s she was having trouble with her television set and called the repairman. He climbed out of her bedroom window on to a lead-covered roof. Examining the aerial, he noticed, scratched into the roof, an inscription: "Austin Chestnut, March 30, 1924, February 20, 1944, Hillsboro, Ohio, aged 20." Mrs. James found it "eerie."[13]

In 1987, while working on a radio program about Tiger, I thought I would try to find out what became of Austin Chestnut, an American Midwest surname that could easily have named someone in the South Hams. There is one Chestnut in the Hillsboro directory; I rang the number. Gilbert Chestnut was doing his chores, his wife said, but she called him to the phone and in a slow drawl he told me that his cousin Austin had "died in the war." But Austin had a brother Cecil—he pronounced it *Sea-sill*—in Cincinnati.

I rang Cecil, who, amazed, told me that Austin had worked on their parents' sixty-five-acre corn and tobacco farm near Hillsboro before being drafted into the army and trained as a tank driver. He had been in England and had died in the first two weeks of the Normandy invasion.

I rang Cecil Chestnut again with another inquiry but his line was busy. When at last I got through, he told me he'd been telling his and Austin's brother in Florida about my call—"the darndest thing since the war." And that was when he started crying. I said sorry; he said it was good to cry.[14]

After forty-three years, an Ohio boy's homesick inscription on a South Hams rooftop overlooking the English Channel had returned home and become grief. The farm boy Austin Chestnut did not die in Tiger, but his story is in part the postwar story of the Tiger disaster, the long, retreating tide of forgetting, the quick incoming flood tide of memory; time coming full circle, the improbable linking of this or that American big city or small town, or Ohio farmstead, with a South Devon beach.

But why Slapton Sands as a focus for memory? The disaster did not, after all, occur on land, but at sea. Nor was the nearest landfall Slapton Sands, or anywhere in South Devon. It was Chesil Beach, in South Dorset.

From the Dorset coast it had actually been possible to witness the attack as it unfolded some twelve miles out to sea. It had been quiet that night at the Cove Inn, and Doris Saunders, the landlady, remembered that she and her husband had turned in fairly early: "Then the gunfire woke us. . . . I remember thinking that this was it . . . a full-scale invasion. . . . In the morning we found out it had been an exercise, and we stood outside again, watching the medical men scramble up over the pebbles carrying stretchers."

The Cove Inn was high enough up to provide "a grandstand seat."

So was Blacknor Fort, 200 feet up on the cliffs on the west coast of Portland Isle.

In 1902 a battery of two big guns had been installed at Blacknor for the defense of the western approach to the Channel.

Their caliber was 9.2 inches, and their range, from their cliff-top aerie, was sixteen miles. The guns were on traversing mountings, for easy maneuverability, and in 1944 they were targeted by radar. Manned by the Royal Coastal Artillery, their crews regularly won prizes for long-range gunnery and were by repute the most accurate gunners in Britain.

On that night, according to one source, the men of the Blacknor battery "watched the distant killing—fretting. They had orders not to fire, for their shells would cause as much damage to the Americans as the Nazis in such a close fight."[15] According to another story still current in the Portland area, the Blacknor battery did fire at the E-boats.

A local story also has the Blacknor battery firing—not at the German E-boats, but at the American LSTs. I tell the story here in outline and without much comment, although to some it may appear typical of the folktales upon which Thomas Hardy drew for his "Wessex" novels set in Dorset.

According to this story, there were either very few E-boats or none at all. Certainly not the nine that are given in the Germans' own logs. The existence of those logs, together with the reminiscences of surviving E-boat commanders, is the biggest barrier that an apologist for this version of that night's events has to get around. In other respects, however, the story is highly plausible.

In April 1944 Barbara Bruford was a member of the Women's Royal Navy serving in a secret radio listening post on Portland Bill. The post was for "Y" intercepts: tactical interception of operational messages between enemy ships. It specialized in monitoring E-boat messages. Mrs. Bruford was on duty that night in the watch room, and heard nothing. Normally, she said, the Germans on the E-boats "shouted their heads off" during an action, as they did not know that the British could intercept their VHF transmissions.

She looked out from the listening post and "saw three ships burning like mad." Thereupon, she says, "we redoubled our efforts to find anything coming through on the radio but there was nothing. There were no E-boats there." Mrs. Bruford suggested that the heavy losses that night had been sustained by the Americans firing upon one another.[16]

Others, however, recruited Mrs. Bruford's story (which she told in January 1988) as evidence for a long-standing tale that the Americans had been fired upon by the Blacknor battery. According to this tale, while there may have been a couple of E-boats mixed up in the fray, they had been in the vicinity for the purpose of intelligence-gathering, not attack. Nine E-boats would never have ventured under the guns of a convoy of LSTs, and if E-boats really had managed to torpedo no fewer than three of the shallow-draft LSTs, then they had, statistically, enjoyed a phenomenal hit rate that night.

Another thing: The men on the E-boats, so this story went, had spoken in terms not of seeing the E-boats, but of hearing them (the American reports do, in fact, give sightings of the boats, but none of the sightings is in detail). And what had the men said they sounded like? "Express trains," a description that could equally, or more fittingly, be applied to the sound of incoming high-caliber shells, like, for example, those of the Blacknor battery.

And there was a story from Blacknor Fort itself to back up this interpretation of events. There had, apparently, been another communications breakdown. Blacknor, tracking the LSTs on radar, had asked them to identify themselves and, failing to get a reply, the guns had been loaded and given ranges of 16,000 yards (in this version, the ships were closer to shore than indicated in official records). The guns had then opened fire with a total of six 9.2-inch shells. Then, abruptly, cease-fire was ordered. An officer came hurrying by, and a bombardier asked him, "What is happening, sir?" To this the officer had replied, "We've hit an American troopship. There are hundreds in the water."

In the immediate aftermath of this fiasco the battalion manning the battery had been hurriedly dispersed—to Nairn in Scotland and to batteries in Cornwall. The authorities had arranged a cover-up and concocted the story of an E-boat attack. The alleged German news agency report of the attack, datelined Berlin, had, in fact, been faked by the allies; thus the peculiar description of the attack's location (it is indeed peculiar) as having been "west of the Isle of Wight." And on May 19, in a direct response to the communications confusion, new and harmonious recognition signals for British home waters had come into effect.[17]

Occurring as the Tiger disaster did at a time of secrecy, it has been especially vulnerable to subsequent myth making. The story above, like another story that the LSTs were mistakenly bombed by the RAF, is perhaps an example of that. But the story also illustrates that there is a Dorset dimension to popular knowledge and myth surrounding the

Tiger disaster. John Hockaday, a Dorset man, writes that Slapton Sands were "merely the venue," and criticizes commentary on the Tiger disaster that nevertheless "orients itself," from there. "The story makers," he said, "cannot get away from Slapton in their own minds."[18]

He has a point. The disaster occurred neither in Devon nor Dorset, but at sea: to be precise, at reference 50°25′ 2°52′W. That, however, is only twelve miles from the Dorset coast; it is more than thirty miles from Slapton Sands.

The psychology of memory and remembrance requires, however, a place and a name for the mind to lock on to; imagination can no more warm to a set of map coordinates than to the initials and numbers of LSTs crewed by "the forgotten men of the fleet."

Tiger was an amphibious exercise. The story of the Tiger disaster is likewise amphibious. It insists on relocating itself from the sea to the beach for which the men had been bound when they met the E-boats, to Slapton Sands. It had, after all, been the apron of the dress rehearsal stage; before D Day a lot of props had been dropped, laid and mislaid there. . . .

The American memorial, with its error of omission, stands on a beach whose name is a misnomer. Slapton Sands is not sand at all, but shingle. It sounds a firmer foundation than sand, but it isn't; the councillors were right to worry about it as the memorial's site. Slapton Sands is far from static. In a slow-motion version of the sea itself it responds to the winds and storms that come in off the English Channel, heaving and sinking in crests and troughs, changing shape like a living, organic thing.

The constantly shifting shingle made nonsense of the neat maps of minefields prepared, first, by the British, who in 1940 had sown the beach with mines against the Germans, then by the Americans, who had mined Slapton Sands to augment the rehearsal "realism." In 1943, with the evacuation, U.S. engineers had swept the beach to remove the British mines, but by then the mines had had three years in which to get lost and, anyway, the mine detectors of the time really worked only down to a depth of eighteen inches. Then the Americans had laid their own mines.

At the end of June 1944, after the Americans had left the evacuation area for Normandy, the U.S. army in London stated that it hoped to have cleared the area of all military ordnance by the end of August, which was, in fact, about when the first evacuees returned to the inland villages. But the Americans had been unable to grant Slapton Sands a

Type II certificate confirming that every mine had been accounted for, and when, on July 30, 1945, a certificate was at last issued, it was only a IIA, indicating incomplete clearance.[19]

The problem of unexploded wartime ordnance was, of course, legion throughout much of Britain: To this day wartime bombs and mines continue to turn up. But on Slapton Sands much of the ordnance was American; its periodic reemergence from the shingle over the postwar years would serve as prompts to keep alive in the local memory a story that seemed to have dried in the telling.

There would, over the years, be many visits to Slapton Sands by the Royal Navy bomb disposal squad from Devonport Dockyard. The local council would still be worrying about the beach in 1980; in 1983 live shells were found both on the shore and in the sea. Almost certainly Slapton Sands has still not given up the last of its wartime secrets. There has been a pattern to the bomb squad's visits, which have tended to follow periods of storm and high seas that have unsettled the beach.

In early 1950, for example, Maurice Lawson of Torcross post office reported that "recent storms have moved quite a large quantity of shingle." Mr. Lawson, apparently a keen walker on the beach, said that it "has been gradually flattening out of recent times . . . uncovering old pieces of metal defense works." In March that year he found one, a live "aerial torpedo," which was, in fact, a British-made rocket of the type the Americans had tested on their exercises, including exercise Tiger: it weighted fifty pounds, twenty-nine of them high explosive.[20]

In May, four American antitank mines turned up on the beach, bringing that year's total of mines to nine. A visiting officer discovered several more by visual search alone. An area of the beach five hundred yards by thirty was roped off and warning notices were put up. A meeting of the Kingsbridge Council heard that "there were still numerous explosives of various kinds on Slapton Sands." But, the councillor said, "there was no need for alarm. . . . These mines have not been fused and are in no way dangerous, but we are taking precautions."

Reswept, the area yielded an arsenal of rusty ordnance: 128 antitank mines, 44 grenades, a bazooka, and another rocket. At the same time nearby Blackpool Sands—the "Green Beach" of Exercise Tiger—was reswept. On May 22 the roped-off area was declared clear of ordnance[21]; it may have been, but, as we shall see, the beach as a whole was far from clear. This would be important in the gradual postwar uncovering of the Tiger story.

An important development in that uncovering occurred in 1954, ten years after Tiger and D Day. In July, General Alfred M. Gruenther, the Supreme Commander, Allied Forces in Europe, flew in to RAF Merryfield from Paris. From Merryfield, with his wife and members of his staff, he flew by helicopter to Dawlish, the home of Ralph Rayner, now a brigadier but still the local MP. Gruenther was in South Devon for the commemoration, at last, of the American memorial on Slapton Sands, a ceremony to which "as many as possible" of the 3,000 evacuees had been invited. The commemoration was on July 25. The Plymouth newspaper, the *Western Morning News,* reported that General Gruenther stood at the foot of the stone obelisk as the British and American flags were broken at their mastheads: "American artillery men, wearing parachute troops' helmets and scarlet necker-chiefs, British sailors with gleaming bayonets, Devon Regiment men in battledress, American airmen in their own shade of blue, and American sailors in their now familiar uniform stood motionless as the flags blew out toward France." Whether because of the cloudy, drizzling weather or "the rather bitter memory of the evacuation days,"[22] only a thin scattering of local folk turned up.

In his address General Gruenther mentioned, although not by its code-name, the Tiger disaster. According to the *Dartmouth Chronicle,* he "lifted the veil . . . on a well-kept secret of the training of the U.S. troops." It had indeed been well kept. "The facts," said the *South Devon Times,* "were known to quite a number of local people, but they loyally and discreetly kept their mouths shut on the subject." The Lord Lieutenant of Devon, Lord Fortescue, who had told the people of the South Hams about the evacuation, said that the story of the "tragic happening" had come as "complete news" to him. "Astonishment was expressed," said the paper, "even in official circles" when General Gruenther's speech was published: "[T]he War Office knew nothing and U.S. Navy headquarters professed ignorance."

The *Western Morning News* quoted General Gruenther as saying that at the time of the disaster he had been in Italy, "and a staff officer came to me to see if we had any landing ships to replace those which had been sunk. . . . The reserve of these ships had been reduced by this mishap to zero." On Slapton Sands the general also took the opportunity to extol NATO and the postwar Anglo-American alliance based on the cooperative closeness exemplified by the wartime sacrifice of the South Hams.[23] Thirty years later, in 1984, the defense attaché at the U.S. embassy in London would stand at the same spot and speak of "the price of freedom."[24]

Slapton Sands is indeed a good place to go to wonder at the enduring closeness of the Anglo-American "special relationship." Most people who visit the beach, however, do so for less pretentious reasons; to swim, to fish at the surfline, or simply to walk and take the sea air. The Slapton Ley and the surrounding acres are also visited by naturalists and nature lovers, who come to study the many species of birds, plants, and insects, some of them rare. Most of Devon's coot breed on the Ley, which is also the water in Devon most frequented by freshwater ducks; it was these that drew the wildfowlers to the Royal Sands Hotel before the war. Botanists come to study the strapwort— Slapton is the one place in Britain where it still grows. Other unusual plants in the area are the bird's-foot trefoil, the pennyroyal mint, thorn apple, bogbean, sea radish, sea spurge and the yellow-horned poppy. Of Britain's forty-plus species of dragonfly, seventeen have been counted on the Ley.[25]

The Ley and the surrounding land once formed part of the large Stokely estate, whose last owner, Herbert Whitley, died in 1955. For a time there was a possibility that the Ley would be drained and a row of houses built along the beach; but the Whitley Trust stepped in and bought the Ley and the land, turning the entire area into a protected nature reserve. In 1959 it was leased to the Field Studies Council, and in that year a field center was set up in Slapton village.[26]

Today the three-mile crescent of Slapton Sands, and the hinterland immediately behind it, are part of Britain's Heritage Coastline. Where young Americans trained for war, all is now peaceful. Tanks and half-tracks once tore up the grass verges and meadowland; now warning notices and stakes driven into the verges prevent Sunday drivers from parking their cars, perhaps on a precious colony of strapwort. And it is forbidden to pick wildflowers or other plants.

For those who know something of its wartime history, however, Slapton Sands can still produce hallucinatory images of violence and death. For more than twenty years a regular annual visitor to the beach has been the former signalman of the *496*, Manny Rubin. An American who has gone the full historical circle, he lives today in Plymouth, where the Pilgrim fathers started from and where he has his own company, Pilgrim Textiles.

One September afternoon in 1987, I stood with Manny Rubin on Slapton Sands. Behind us, on the beach road known locally as "the Torcross line," tourists were savoring the drive along the coast; in the sea a line of white buoys marked off an area barred to the water-skiers.

A peaceful scene. But on Manny Rubin's forehead was the scar left there when the piece of galley stovepipe had hit him on the night of

Tiger; and in Manny Rubin's mind was his memory of the morning after Tiger, the sea floating with bodies "bobbing up and down."

Past and present came together as he told me how he had been on Slapton Sands one postwar November day, after a storm. On the stretch of the beach where it curves toward Berry Head there had been "thousands upon thousands of dead starfish, piled up three or four feet high." Start Bay had been floating with great clumps of seaweed torn by the storm from the seabed.

And that's just what it looked like that day. But every lump of seaweed was a man. A dead GI, a dead sailor, as far as the eye could see. Some of them were black. Covered with oil or burnt black. The rest didn't have a mark on them. They were almost angelic, just bobbing up and down, full pack. And some of them floated in to shore in a sitting position, and the next wave would take them out, or in a kneeling position, and the next wave would knock them flat. . . .

After Exercise Tiger, the *496*, his ship, had "buried herself in Cornwall." It was there that a mezzanine deck was installed and the *496* converted into a ship that could be used for hospital purposes, to bring wounded men back from France. But the *496* had also buried herself with shame, the shame her men felt for having fired on their sister ship, the *511*.

On D Day the *496* went into Omaha Beach, returned to England with wounded, and loaded up again with men and vehicles. The ship was making the Channel crossing once more when on June 11, off France, she was torpedoed and sunk.

The crew of the *496* included four black galley boys who cooked steaks for the officers and waited on them. There were lots of Southerners on the ship and, said Manny Rubin, "they called every colored boy contemptuously 'Henry.' " The torpedo that hit the *496* hit the galley section, and the four blacks went down with the ship off France. "And if you asked me who they were," says Manny Rubin today, "I'd say four guys called Henry. Isn't that terrible?"

Manny Rubin came up on deck to find the ship on fire, the metal deck plates curling upwards "like a banana skin" in the intense heat. His captain, Stanley Koch, lay dead in a pool of blood. Hurriedly before he abandoned ship, Rubin wrapped his signal flags around Koch and pushed him overboard, a makeshift sea burial.

The flags were an appropriate touch. Manny Rubin came from a Jewish high-fashion tailoring family in the Bronx. He had known the rag trade since childhood, and in his time in the navy he was called upon whenever its know-how was needed—a canvas shroud for a gun, a repair to a flag, "everything from bell-bottoms to body bags."

After he was discharged from the navy in April 1946, he decided to go back to the garment business. With his Cornish sweetheart, Alexandra, whom he had met while recuperating in the hospital after the *496* was sunk, he went to Chicago, where they were married. He found himself a job with Jensen swimwear and happily settled down to married life.

Practically every night, though, he would wake up from a nightmare. It wasn't the sinking of the *496* or the burial of his captain at sea. Always in his nightmare it was the night of Tiger, the green tracer coming at him as he ducked and called out "Momma!" The recurrent nightmare stopped only in 1948, when his son was born. "When I had a family I didn't give a shit about the past."

In 1951 he paid a visit to England for Jensen swimwear. He took the train to Cambridge and the American military cemetery there, where he placed flowers on his captain's grave; Stanley Koch's body had been recovered from the sea. In 1959 Jensen appointed him its representative in Europe. He was based in London until 1962, when Jensen, in a freakish coincidence, moved its British operation to Plymouth, the port where he had embarked for Tiger and for D Day, within driving distance of Slapton Sands across the headland.

> I was back in my nightmare area, but no one would believe my story of the tragedy off Slapton. People in America believed me, but not people here. My wife finally convinced me to keep quiet about it. People thought I was a loudmouthed American schnook because the story sounded so farfetched.

No matter: If others didn't believe him, his wife did, and he *knew*. Manny Rubin is a man of ritual. Every Fourth of July he flies, from his house in Plymouth, a Stars and Stripes that came from a wartime destroyer.

And every April 28 since 1962 he has picked flowers from his garden and driven to Slapton Sands. There, in a silent act of memory and homage to the dead, he has floated his flowers out upon the sea.[27]

For more than forty years Manny Rubin's flowers would be the only memorial to the forgotten dead of Exercise Tiger.

CHAPTER
14

Weather conditions were freakish in the South Hams in 1974. The sea behaved strangely. In August there was the lowest tide that anyone could remember—reputedly the lowest for seventy years. The local papers carried photographs of people walking over rocks and sand usually covered by sea.

But if the sea was unusually timid and retreating in August, it had in the early months of that year been lashed by storms and high winds into an unusual ferocity. In February "enormous seas battered Torcross. Further along the Line the tide went over the road and into the Ley. So big were the waves that the spray reached the top of the cliffs."[1] In April there would be a "tidy up campaign" to clear away the aftermath of the storms.[2]

It was thirty years since Exercise Tiger, and twenty-four since Maurice Lawson of Torcross post office had found the "aerial torpedo" on Slapton Sands. Now the beach had a new beachcomber, Kenneth Small, the proprietor of a local guest house. A student of the beach, he saw that those easterly February storms had "completely rearranged it," gouging out "a huge valley" in the beach near the American memorial.

To Ken Small that valley that had appeared overnight would come to seem providential; the same providence, perhaps, that had brought him to Torcross. That had been in 1968, when, with his wife, Ann, he had come to South Devon for a two-week touring holiday. But they hadn't toured. Torcross had been their first stop; and, said Ken Small, "something held me there for the full fortnight."

At that time Ken Small was, and had been for twelve years, a hairdresser working in Lincolnshire. Before that he had spent, successively, five years in the RAF and five in the police force; the career change from policeman to hairdresser is about as extreme as one can imagine, but in 1968 Ken Small was looking for another change in his life. Soon after returning to Lincolnshire he was telephoned from Torcross and told that the Cove Guest House there was up for sale. He traveled down to Devon and bought it, in a transaction he described as "extremely strange. I didn't even know how many rooms there were."

By September 1987, when I met him, Ken Small had become fascinated by Exercise Tiger. At the root of his fascination seemed to lie the "pretty nasty nervous breakdown" that he told me about on our first encounter at Slapton Sands. He had come to Torcross "for an idyllic life, to get away from it all"; the breakdown had come a year later. He never did "sort out the reason" for it: that mystery would become lost in his sense of the greater mystery of Tiger. Treatment for the breakdown had involved electroshock therapy and an intensive course of Valium tablets; but he had also helped to cure himself, with persistent beachcombing along Slapton Sands. Before Torcross he had never beachcombed; he soon found that he had a talent for it and that, as well as benefiting his mental recovery, it could be lucrative. Over the years, he told me, he had found in the shingle perhaps £10,000 worth of valuables: gold rings, and other lost jewelry, including, if I remember correctly, the circle of brass with a piece of cloudy white glass or semiprecious stone at its center that he wears on a chain around his neck. A hairdresser, or former hairdresser, might wear just such a pendant, but Ken Small attaches to his a special, talismatic significance.

He has other talismans. At the time of his breakdown he asked a friend who was a painter to put down on canvas some of the strange images that were floating in his mind. The four surrealistic paintings that his friend produced hang on the living room wall of Ken Small's guest house, oblique, dreamlike premonitions of the part that he was to play in the postwar uncovering of Tiger. I took, from memory, notes on the four paintings:

1. Figure (Ken Small?) in foreground, writing—Gothic ruined trees or arches in background—bearded God-the-Fatherish figure in clouds, with jutting head.
2. Pendant-sun or pendant-moon in sky. The Cove Guest House? Figure—Ken Small?—on terrace pointing at sun, moon.
3. Seascape. Lighthouse. (Start Point?) Faces, a man's and a woman's, in the dark swell of a wave. Faces in the clouds.
4. Adoration, worship scene—Cove House in background? Pendant on the ground, flat, its chain trailing over some rocks.

If his painter friend helped Ken Small in his recovery, so did a local boat owner and fisherman, Tony Steer, whom he met on the beach.

Tony Steer befriended him and encouraged his beachcombing, and also in 1971 told him of an object about a mile out to sea, in sixty feet of water, on which he and the other fishermen kept snagging their nets.[3]

Fishermen know the patches of sea that they habitually fish, and the seabed beneath them, much as a farmer knows his land. The sea between Start Point and Berry Head has been regularly fished for centuries, and on the Skerries, the shoal about a mile off Slapton Sands, are ancient mussel and scallop beds. The seabed of this area was well known to fishermen, flat shingle and mud, no rocky outcrops.

Now, however, in Start Bay and Lyme Bay, there were outcrops. Under the impartial surface of the sea, as under that of the land, were foreign bodies to snag nets and to jog the memory of Tiger into life again. For years one of them had been known through echo sounding. The echoes had picked up a wreck lying in forty-two meters of water in Lyme Bay, several miles west of Portland Bill. It was more than 200 feet long and, in one place only, twenty-seven feet high, and was thought from its shape to be the wreck of a submarine. Later, divers went down and found the wreck to be that of the *LST 507*.

A diving magazine reported that

> *LST 507* is . . . sitting upright with many of her vehicles still aboard. Most of these are not tanks, but half-tracks belonging to the 478th Amphibian Truck Company and the 557th Quartermaster Railhead Company. The seabed on which she sits is of gravel and shingle, and the water of this deep dive is often extremely dark, so great care must be taken in exploring the wreck.[4]

One wonders what a diver, if he explored closely, would find on the *507*'s tank deck.

The diving magazine advised that a boat that occasionally visited the wreck of the *507* was the *Barracuda* out of Exmouth. The *Barracuda*'s skipper, Paul Streeton, had often dived the *507* and knew of another landing ship in the same general area, deeper and upside down. "There can be little doubt," said the magazine, "that this is the *LST 531*."[5]

The diving fraternity had even pinpointed the whereabouts on the seabed of an LCVP that had been irreparably damaged in the attack on *LST 289*, and which the *289*'s captain, Harry Mettler, had ordered to be ditched overboard. The LCVP's number had been C23569, and the magazine asked divers to try to find its number plate.

The wreck that Tony Steer had told Ken Small about, however, was none of these, but the DD Sherman "swimming" tank that Eisenhow-

er's naval aide, Harry Butcher, had seen and recorded in his diary as
sinking on April 27, 1944, when it was launched as part of Tiger's
initial shock wave. In fact, two of the DDs had sunk that day, but the
army had been able to salvage one of them. This one was abandoned
where it had come to rest on the seabed, its cannon pointing toward
Slapton Sands. It, too, was known to the divers. In the 1960s diver
and diving writer Kendall McDonald had seen the underwater
Sherman, its hatch open "as if the crew had just popped out for a
smoke."[6] But it wasn't men now who popped in and out of the hatch,
but the conger eels that haunted the tank's interior. Thoroughly
"marinized," the underwater tank was an image that might have been
dreamed up by a surrealist painter, and Ken Small, when he came to
dive it, perhaps saw a family resemblance to his own images of faces
in the waves. The evidence is that in his private gallery of images,
that of the drowned tank began, from 1971 onward, to assume pride
of place.

On October 29, 1973, he wrote to Her Majesty's Customs and
Excise in Dartmouth in an effort to establish who owned the tank and
whom he might approach with a view to salvaging it. Referred to the
U.S. embassy in London, the embassy referred him in turn to the
Defense Supply Agency in Alexandria, Virginia, which wrote to him
toward the end of January 1974, telling him that the legal status of the
Sherman was being established. In February he received a letter from
a Lieutenant Colonel Busweld, which stated that although the tank had
effectively been demilitarized by its immersion in salt water for thirty
years, it could still not be considered as abandoned. It would,
however, be possible to sell the tank through the Defense Property
Disposal Service in Wiesbaden, West Germany.[7]

It was in that month, February, that Slapton Sands was battered by
enormous seas and the freak easterly storms. Ken Small already knew
that the beach hid wartime ordnance. In 1971 a mine had been
discovered during the building of a parking lot on the site of the old
Royal Sands Hotel; detonated by the bomb disposal men, it had left a
crater fifteen feet wide. Ken Small had witnessed that controlled
explosion; on Slapton Sands he had told me about, half acted out for
me, the explosion, first the column of shingle and gravel thrown high
into the air, then the loud report rumbling across the beach.

By this time, too, Ken Small knew local stories of the American
wartime presence. A farmer, Gordon Luscombe, who had been a boy
at the time of his return to the evacuation area, had told him of finding
bloodstains on the floor of an outbuilding, and a wooden cross with an

American helmet on it. He also knew stories dating from the American General Gruenther's visit of 1954, and earlier, of a disaster during the American exercises of 1944, with costly loss of life. His knowledge was incomplete, but he already knew enough to have been powerfully impressed by the apparently magical coincidence that the lettering on his car's license plate was UTA. In Ken Small, someone had come along who could make these unconscious connections; at some point the seed was sown of an obsession with images of an underwater tank, a wartime disaster, the sea and the land and Slapton Sands, South Devon, and the States. It struck him as "rather strange," even "incredible," and also rather suspicious that the American memorial on Slapton Sands made no mention of the men who had died.

Those men, in the words of the sister of one of them, "haunt the seacoast"[8]; by a sort of sympathetic magic they haunted Ken Small, too, as they did Tom Clark in faraway Texas, Angelo Crapanzano in New Jersey, Manny Rubin in Plymouth, and all the veterans and survivors. Ken Small had dived and seen the tank, but it was on that February day of beachcombing that he seems first to have felt really close to these forgotten men of the war. He entered the single hollow that the sea had delved out of Slapton Sands to find that the sands had pried from the beach secrets it had kept for thirty years; "3.03 bullets, .22 bullets, actual live shells; live land mines; military buttons." He also found signet rings and wondered whether they had belonged to the Americans who had died. "Could they have come from these men? I don't know." It struck him as "uncanny" that his beachcombing had brought him into such close sympathetic contact with these ghosts of the seacoast. These dead men were as alive to him as the ammunition he had found.

Inspired by his finds, it was now that his idea of salvaging the underwater Sherman began to gain momentum. It wasn't simply a dramatic seaward extension of his beachcombing; he wanted the tank to be an informal memorial to the men. In March 1974 he took up Lieutenant Colonel Busweld's suggestion and wrote to the Defense Property Disposal Service in Wiesbaden. In reply, Wiesbaden sent him an informal draft agreement asking him to make an offer for the tank. Over the telephone, he offered one pound. Finally, to cover administrative costs, a charge of fifty dollars was agreed upon.

Meanwhile a host of bureaucratic difficulties had arisen from the offices of Her Majesty's Receiver of Wrecks and from American Defense Property Disposal in England. It was objected that no private individual would be permitted to buy the tank, which had anyway to be demilitarized and whose nationality and ownership had yet to be established. There could be bodies in the tank, which could make it a grave. Bomb disposal, Devonport, would have to be at hand—an expensive inconvenience for which Ken Small would have to pay. The Receiver of Wrecks would have to decide the tank's potential liability to duty and Value Added Tax.

Throughout these and later difficulties in salvaging the tank Ken Small continued to believe that "somebody, or something, was urging me to carry on."[9] He wrote back to Wiesbaden and received a letter from Sally Nagata of Defense Property Disposal stating: "I have said I will sell it to you on behalf of the Government of the United States and that is that." In August he signed the draft agreement and sent it to Wiesbaden with a money order for fifty dollars; in November Sally Nagata returned a countersigned copy of the agreement. Ken Small of Torcross was now officially the owner of a Second World War Sherman tank, a mile out to sea, maybe, and deep underwater, but *his*. Over the next few years he made several dives down to it, and brought up some brass fittings, including its twin propellers. One went to a fellow diver; one he kept for himself. It was cleaned, its brass brought to a high shine, and installed in his guest house living room, an obvious conversation piece for any passing visitor. Meanwhile, Ken Small wrestled with the larger problem of how to bring up the whole tank.

The decade from 1974 was to be an apparently quiet but, in fact, highly significant period in postwar unearthing of the Tiger disaster. During it the British thirty-year rule came into effect and the Freedom of Information Act was introduced in the United States. Now it became possible for anyone wishing to research the disaster, always assuming he knew of it, to dig up wartime files. They would refresh memories, fill in some gaps where memory had lapsed and give a framework in which to assemble memories into a mosaic, an overall picture. The files provided the beginnings of a memory retrieval system, but it still took fairly specialized knowledge to know what to look for, and, of course, there were many relevant files in many different locations, all over the United States as well as in London.

Perhaps the first person to consult a Tiger file in any detail, or at any rate to publish and make widely available information based on it, was the Washington-based British writer Anthony Cave Brown, author of the encyclopedic compilation of Second World War secrets, *Bodyguard of Lies*. It was published in 1975, and the few pages on

Tiger, a skeletal sketch of the disaster, were largely based on File NRS 601 from the Washington Navy Yard. Cave Brown's book did a little to build up an informal "survivors" file on the disaster. For example, Wendall Hoppler, then working as a mailman in Waukegan, Illinois, chanced to pick up a copy of the book at his small local library. Interested, and knowing the reality behind Cave Brown's few pages, he inquired further and managed to obtain via the library system copies of the battle logs of the LSTs *507* and *531*. He wasn't supposed to copy them, but did anyway, and was perhaps the first veteran of Tiger to obtain any archival material on the disaster.[10]

Cave Brown's book carried the billing: "Enough material here for twenty espionage novels." An independent researcher could, in theory, in 1975, have used his few pages on the disaster as a platform on which to build up a complete documentary account of it. The next development was not documentary, however, but fictional, a novel that was neither espionage nor prompted by Cave Brown's cue, but a "faction" set on the ambiguous borderline between fact and fiction.

Best-selling British novelist Leslie Thomas had long had an idea of setting a book "in a place at the edge of the war." He had himself spent time in such a place. In September 1943, as a twelve-year-old Barnardo's boy, he had been evacuated to Kingsbridge in South Devon. In the late Seventies he was back in South Devon to research a travel article. The visit stirred his childhood memories of the vast American presence in the area. More specific memories, too. The two boys killed while playing with an American grenade (see p. 154) had been classmates of his.

These personal memories were supplemented by a visit to Washington. Now he had the makings of his novel, *The Magic Army,* published in 1981. Most of the book is about the Americans in Devon and their impact on the local life there. The book's culmination, about a ninth of its total wordage, is an account of the Tiger disaster.

Its merits as a novel aside, however, *The Magic Army* did not, despite its wide readership, carry the full impact of a factual exposé. It was received as a fiction "widely based on fact." In it, Exercise Tiger was fictionalized as Exercise Lion, and when Leslie Thomas did a short television piece in the wake of the book's publication and said that there really had been an E-boat attack, "a furious ex-commander in naval intelligence telephoned to say it never happened." Other people did pick up on the factual basis to his account: Thomas received letters from the United States inquiring about men who might have died in the disaster.[11] But almost forty years on the story of Tiger, true to its old form, was still falling into the gap between realism and reality where "faction" is set, and getting lost there.

An instance of the extraordinary ignorance that continued to enshroud the story was in a book by Eisenhower's son, John Sheldon Doud Eisenhower, published in 1982. "Happily," it said, "no enemy air or submarine attacks had attacked the ships involved in the exercise—which had happened before."[12] Literally, that statement was correct: but when such misinformation continued to surround the true story, it is little wonder if some survivors suspected a concerted cover-up.

One person who knew something of what had really happened was Dr. Ralph Greene of Chicago. In the early Eighties he was in the U.S. National Archives in Washington looking into another story of the war—a malaria and hepatitis outbreak among American troops, which had complicated the buildup to D Day. In consulting the records of the 228th Station Hospital where he had served, Dr. Greene found papers referring to the mysterious influx, in late April 1944, of wounded men whom he and the other doctors had been required to treat in silence, "like veterinarians." The incident had puzzled him at the time; now he had some documentation of it, as well as the few pages in *Bodyguard of Lies* and the other books. A retired pathologist, he also had time at his disposal. He started to try to find out about the disaster. . . .

Meanwhile, however, a much bigger force than any single individual was beginning to build up in the background. The English Channel is notorious for its powerful tides and the crosscurrents and tide races around headlands like Start Point, Berry Head, and Portland Bill. After the same fashion, a tide race of remembrance was beginning to gather with the imminence of June 6, 1984. On the fortieth anniversary of D Day the media spotlight would turn upon Utah, Omaha, and the other beaches of Normandy. Her Majesty the Queen, President Reagan, President Mitterand, Mrs. Thatcher and Chancellor Kohl of West Germany would stand on those beaches, remembering the men who had fallen in the liberation of Europe. The television companies would soon be starting to fix their schedules, to cast about for original angles on the D Day story, to plan as in a military campaign how they intended to cover it. The South Hams, too, had legitimate reasons for remembrance. Why shouldn't at least some of the spotlight fall upon South Devon and Slapton Sands?

As it happened, 1983 saw a vivid illustration of just how strongly the wartime American presence lived on in South Devon's memory. In 1981 former Royal Navy sailor Harry Unsworth had taken a job in a food factory at Stover, site of the wartime 316th Station Hospital. He had seen the Americans' names carved in the trees and inquired locally about the wartime past of the camp, only to discover that people knew little about what had gone on there. He wrote letters and met a former member of the 316th who had married an Englishwoman and settled locally. Out of this contact grew a plan to hold the fortieth anniversary of the 316th on their wartime territory of South Devon.

In September 1983 fifty veterans of the 316th and their wives crossed the Atlantic and gathered in Newton Abbot. There was a parade through town, in which the Americans traveled in wartime jeeps driven by Englishmen dressed as GIs. A crowd of several thousand strong lined the streets. Shopkeepers hung out signs like "Yanks Go Home—with our best wishes." In the streets, records of "Over There" and other 1940s favorites were played. There was a visit to Slapton Sands, and to the Duke and Duchess of Devon at their home, Powderham Castle. American flags were everywhere. "I never thought I'd see the day," said one veteran, "when the English would open their hearts to the Yanks like that."[13]

Also that September the South Hams District Council was preoccupied with the forthcoming D Day anniversary. It was necessary to plan early. The Council's then-chairman, Percy Moysey, told a meeting that a special committee had been set up. "We hope," said the Council's secretary, "to stage an exhibition of artifacts and want people who were connected with the landings and evacuation to be involved." He added that there would, the following June, be "a dignified ceremony of remembrance and commemoration"[14]—this would be the grand reunion of former evacuees of June 2, 1984.

Against the same background, on October 27 the Council told Ken Small, in response to his inquiry, that it would be prepared to assist in proposals to display the tank at Torcross, always assuming, of course, that it could be salvaged; in November, Dolphin Diving Supplies of Dartmouth carried out a feasibility study.

Small, local matters, the stuff of provincial journalism; but out of such local particulars would be generated the publicity that would eventually enable the scattered Tiger survivors and veterans across the United States to pool their memories and to know, at last, what they had experienced and lived through. The key to their retrieval system would be television. In Plymouth the local commercial station, TVS, had been looking for a strong local angle on the topical D Day story.

Since 1982 a proposal had been kicking around TVS for a program looking back at the period of wartime American "occupation" of the area. This idea was now taken by the station's small documentary department. Frank Wintle, the producer, would make "a program about the sociological impact of the American presence in what was then a very isolated part of Britain."[15]

They did a week's trial filming, then sat back to view the rushes and see how the idea was shaping up. Frank Wintle was struck by "the ferocity of the contents"—in one interview, for example, a farmer pointing out his battle-scarred barn. Also over that week "various older people" had referred to the disaster on the night of April 28, 1944. Frank Wintle realized that there had been an underlying violence to the American presence and that the war games on Slapton Sands had been very tough indeed; the program's focus began to shift away from the original "sociological" idea to the disaster of Exercise Tiger.

It was ambitious stuff for a local television station. "We did a trawl of the records," said Frank Wintle, "but found absolutely nothing." How, then, was the story to be pursued? Of course, in the United States. "We thought we would have to activate the American side of things." But how? The program had a limited budget. At last, through a complicated sequence beginning with an American woman who worked in the press office of TVS, Frank Wintle got the break he needed and made contact with Ralph Greene in Chicago. Greene (like Leslie Thomas at his home in Hampshire) had copies of American records and thus a factual framework for the indispensable American side of the story. Filming went ahead, and on January 12, 1984, TVS screened its documentary, *Sands of Silence*. A sketchy account of the disaster, it was still the most comprehensive thus far. The sands of the title were the nonexistent sands of Slapton, "half revealing," in the words of the commentary, "half concealing."

With the TVS program, the story of the Tiger disaster had, as it were, entered the public domain in South Devon; the program further stirred wartime memories, which were anyway being encouraged to come out into the open with the imminence of the D Day anniversary. The disaster was forty years old, but the story of it was still brand new, and in the program's wake it now acquired an unexpected and extraordinary dimension.

A Plymouth-based free-lance journalist, Alma Taft, was driving down a Cornish country road. Her car radio was on and a woman was speaking on BBC Plymouth with a Devon accent as rich as clotted cream. She was telling a story that had never been told before. Slapton Sands had been only "half concealing"—this was a wartime secret that the woman had kept to herself for forty years.

If Mrs. Dorothy Seekings—and never was a woman more aptly surnamed—had maintained her elected silence all that time, she would certainly make up for it over the next four years, when her macabre and haunting tale would be carried by television, radio, and newspapers all over the world.

It is always, in every detail, the same tale. Mrs. Seekings was the daughter of Mr. Trowt, the baker of Stoke Fleming who throughout the wartime evacuation period had been the Ministry of Food's bread supplier to the village Blackawton. But Mr. Trowt had also baked doughnuts, of which the American soldiers—or doughboys—had taken delivery in large quantities. His daughter, Dorothy, then twenty-three, her husband away fighting the Japanese, sometimes did the doughnut delivering. One day in April 1944 she had been walking along the Totnes road, a basket of doughnuts in her hand, when an army truck pulled up and an American soldier she knew offered her a lift. After a time, the driver pulled up his truck again, saying he had to "unload." She thought that he meant ammunition boxes, until she, too, got out of the truck and went to its tailgate:

. . . and I seen all these dead men laying one on top o'nother in the back of the truck. Opposite field was the dark Americans, which was the hospital field for the darks.

INTERVIEWER: Colored? Black?

SEEKINGS: Black. Well, I didn't like to say black. But dark ones. And they were digging and I could see the earth mounted up in the field. And they came out and they carried the men into the field.

INTERVIEWER: When you say men, I mean, were they soldiers?

SEEKINGS: Oh soldiers, yes, in their uniforms. And they were in dark green, which was wet. But they were not blasted or anything. But I didn't know at the time, they were drowned.

INTERVIEWER: Just let me be quite clear. You went to the back of the lorry, and you saw . . .

SEEKINGS: All these men . . .

INTERVIEWER: Stacks and stacks . . .

SEEKINGS: Stacks, laid in a big lorry on top of each other.

INTERVIEWER: Right. And what happened then?

SEEKINGS: Well, then they were taken out and put into the field.

INTERVIEWER: Mm.

SEEKINGS: And I've always known it as the American burial ground.[16]

Mrs. Seekings insisted that the field she had in mind was *still* the American burial ground. The bodies had not been disinterred. There they still were, in unconsecrated English soil, the forgotten American dead of a forgotten episode of the Second World War. But not forgotten by her. "The parents of these boys," she said, "should know where they're lying. They're somebody's boys. And the Americans say they took 'em back, but they did not take them back. They're still in the fields."

Here was a burial of more than live land mines or shrapnel, or the sea burial of a Sherman tank: a burial of men. And here, too, was one hell of a story. Hearing it, Alma Taft turned her car around and drove at once from Cornwall to Stoke Fleming. Dorothy Seekings still lived there, opposite the church, in the house that had been her father's bakery. In her living room she repeated her story of the burial ground to Alma Taft, who the next day telephoned Leslie Thomas (he had appeared in *Sands of Silence*). Thomas was interested in this new and topical twist in the Tiger story and made the long journey down to the South Hams to hear it for himself; meeting Mrs. Seekings, he was inclined, as Alma Taft had been, to believe her.[17]

While Ken Small was preoccupied with salvaging his undersea Sherman tank, former chef and treasure hunter Dave Kimberley had set his sights on digging up an underground submarine. It was, he believed, buried in Coronation Park, a waterside recreation area in Dartmouth. Formerly known as the Coombe Mud, the area had been filled in and turned into the park. Kimberley believed that the submarine was, like the other buried things of South Devon that he had looked for, American. Parents of a friend of his, he said, had seen it buried when Coronation Park was extended at the end of the war.

In this subplot of the postwar Tiger story, Dave Kimberley, with his passion for buried machinery, is the rude mechanical. His interest in buried American wartime treasure seems to have begun in 1981, when a Harley Davidson military motorcycle was dug up on the site of a planned housing estate at Heathfield, near Newton Abbot. Of early 1940s vintage, it had been unearthed in perfect condition, greased and still in its original packing case. It was worth a good deal of money, and there were thought, or rumored, to be many more Harley Davidsons buried on the same site, perfectly preserved in the peat soil.

And that wasn't all. In 1944 Heathfield had been a supply depot for the Americans. Harry Unsworth of Newton Abbot had taken an interest in the site and told a newspaper he had found "40-gallon drums packed with servicemen's clothing" buried there. He also believed there to be

Dodge command cars, personnel carriers, "and an endless amount of spares from the motor pool."

With other local people, Dave Kimberley formed a consortium with a Dutch company called Osiris-Cesco to recover this "vast treasure trove." It was perhaps at this time that Mr. Kimberley acquired his proton-magnometer—a giant metal detector—with which, perhaps, Osiris-Cesco's confidential magnetic survey of the Heathfield site was drawn up. The survey showed three main dumps, one of them only yards from the first phase of the proposed housing development. The consortium got to work, but "folded after only a few shallow digs."

The idea of excavating the dumps would be revived over the following years, but, frustrated for the time being, Dave Kimberley now turned his attention to the Coronation Park submarine. In January 1983 he approached the South Hams District Council for permission to survey the park, and at the same time asked Osiris-Cesco to send a survey team. Meanwhile, local people in Dartmouth had begun to cast doubt on his idea that it was a Second World War American submarine. No, they said, the Coombe Mud had become Coronation Park in the 1920s; the submarine buried there was a German one of the First World War. Others said it was an old British submarine.

By July 1983 Dave Kimberley had got his permission and swept Coronation Park with his proton-magnometer, to discover that the submarine, whatever its identity, was not alone: The park was "a graveyard of ships," with a total of seven vessels buried beneath its lawns and flower beds. "My next aim," he said, "is to get permission from the South Hams Council to carry out an excavation."

While still awaiting permission, however, he was diverted by Dorothy Seekings's announcement in February 1984 of "the American burial ground." He told Harry Unsworth that he intended to use his proton-magnometer to trace the buried soldiers by the metal studs on their boots; Unsworth told him that it would never work—the studs were of an artificial, nonmetallic material. Dave Kimberley persisted, however. Only days after Dorothy Seekings broke her silence, he was in Blackawton, inside the old evacuation area. He told a newspaper that he hoped to locate the buried men by using his detector to pick up the presence of their uniform buttons, much as he had located the dumps at Heathfield, or the ship's graveyard in Coronation Park.[18]

With the intervention of Dorothy Seekings, the Tiger story had grown the kind of wings that could take it across the Atlantic to the United

States. Any television piece requires a minimum number of people with something to say who are prepared to say it to the camera. Now the name of Dorothy Seekings could be added to the list of potential interviewees, like Leslie Thomas and Ralph Greene.

So, too, now, could the name of Manny Rubin. A keen supporter of Plymouth Argyle football club, he had once or twice told the story of Tiger in the Argyle clubroom. No one had believed him. But when *Sands of Silence* was televised, a sports journalist who had heard him in the clubroom realized that he had not, after all, been telling "tall stories to keep up with the boys," but the truth. He told a fellow journalist on the local paper, who, in turn, telephoned Alma Taft. She visited Manny Rubin at his home in Plymouth, astonished to find a veteran of Tiger on her, and South Devon's, own doorstep. Manny Rubin, too, was astonished. Alma Taft "was the first person to believe my story."[19]

Here was the seed corn of what would turn out to be a great granary of information on the Tiger disaster. In February Alma Taft got on the telephone and contacted the American networks: NBC, CBS, and ABC. In the meantime, however, a British television reporter had become interested. On a visit to her parents in the Devon village of Shaldon, near Teignmouth, Jane Corbyn of Channel 4 News heard from her mother about the *Sands of Silence*. The story, so little known outside Devon, caught her imagination, and on March 1 Alma Taft told ABC in New York that they had better hurry: Other people were interested. On March 3 Nola Safro of ABC's weekly feature program *20/20* left the United States for South Devon. There she did some preliminary filming, including an interview with Dorothy Seekings, before deciding that the story was too big to simply "throw on TV." She felt that more research must be done and more interviewees tracked down, and returned to the United States. There on March 12, in Chicago, *20/20* interviewed Ralph Greene, who also gave the program "complete access to everything he had, all the files he had accumulated." In the first week of April 1984 *20/20* would be back in South Devon to do more interviews.[20]

By then, though, Jane Corbyn had already begun to compile her report. It was to her that Manny Rubin, one day on Slapton Sands in early April, gave his first interview about Tiger. He had been upset by Dorothy Seekings's story of the American burial ground, the idea that the bodies of his comrades had been disposed of like so much war waste; but it upset him, too, to be in that place, on Slapton Sands, "the surf breaking only at the shoreline." He remembered the sea as it had been on the dawn following the disaster, the seaweed torn up by the November storm, his nightmare of the German tracer coming at him out of the night. Most upsetting of all, he was believed at last, he was telling his story. Overcome, he burst into tears.[21]

Tiger's time had come round again.

CHAPTER
15

The Tragic Secret of Slapton Sands, ABC television's *20/20* special on the Tiger disaster, was the single most important postwar development in the story. One could go so far as to say that without it the story would probably never have come fully out into the open, because until the ABC program there wasn't the necessary retrieval system. With it, the tide of forgetting turned; memory came flooding back.

Other American networks covered the story, too, but none with the prominence given it by *20/20.* For the first time the United States at large learned of this inexplicably neglected episode of its wartime history. For the first time, too, the program held up the mirror of public attention to those who had actually *been there* or who had otherwise suffered over the years as a result of Exercise Tiger. Among those millions of viewers were some who had survived the attack on T-4, others who had sailed on the convoy, others who were next of kin of men who had died, as well as men who had been on the other Tiger convoys or on other ships in the area—a massive jigsaw, whose pieces were scattered in memories across the United States, and which, when put together, would make up the big picture of which each individual experience was part.

The Tragic Secret went out across the nation on May 3, 1984. Among those watching television that night was Stella Rouggley, of St. Louis, Missouri. During the war her brother, Howard Wagner, had wanted to join the navy but because of color blindness had instead been drafted into the army. With him was his best friend, Delmar Allen. "They went all through school together," Stella Rouggley told me, "and all through service, and"—as a member of the doomed 3206th Quartermaster Service Company—"they died together in Exercise Tiger."

The body of neither man had been recovered and, said Stella,

"When you don't have a grave it's kind of hard." Back in 1944, her mother had tried to find out more about the circumstances of Howard's death, but "Nobody told us anything. All we found out we found out ourselves."

They hadn't found out much. In 1956, for example, when the Wall of the Missing was commemorated at the American Military Cemetery in Cambridge, England, the names of both Howard Wagner and Delmar Allen were listed there. But she hadn't found that out until 1961, and then only by accident, when Howard's name on the wall was spotted by a friend visiting England. Already unhappy with the U.S. government's handling of the affair, she was now watching *20/20* and listening to Dorothy Seekings tell her story of American soldiers killed in Exercise Tiger and buried in a mass grave in an English sheep field. It seemed the final outrage. Was this why her brother's body had never been recovered? Was this why he had no known grave?

By making public acknowledgment of the forty-year-old "tragic secret," the program gave the go-ahead for grief. It also made the Tiger disaster a legitimate subject of conversation. To survivors, the broadcast came as a profound relief. Angelo Crapanzano saw it at his home in New Jersey. What had most puzzled Stella Rouggley was that her brother had died on April 28—before the invasion of Europe. To her it had meant that "something pretty shady was going on."[1] Angelo Crapanzano knew that he had been on an exercise, but he, too, was puzzled and had lived much of his life under the shadow of Tiger.

Denied his survivor's leave, his ship had been among the first LSTs to go into Utah Beach on D Day. Up to October 1944 he made the Channel crossing twenty times: "My nerves were shot. I never slept on the ship while we were under way." Then he got his leave. It was just afterward that he had his first nervous collapse: "I knew I could never go down an engine room again." A psychiatrist at the Amphibious Base in Solomons, Maryland, told him his experience of Tiger lay at the root of his collapse, and suggested a medical discharge. But he fought off that idea and received an honorable discharge in November 1945. He got a job in a die making plant, earned a living, and raised a family. "But under the surface of contentment I was a guy that just wasn't into the simple, ordinary pleasures of life. I became very sensitive and bitter about war."

The wars continued: Korea in 1950, Vietnam in 1960. In 1961 he suffered a serious bout of depression; there would be four more bouts over the following years. Sometimes there would be reasons for depression, as when, in 1982, his company was sold and "after

thirty-six years of faithful service,'' he lost his job. But always the
same underlying cause—Tiger.

Tiger had still been there even with the ''inner peace'' he had begun
to win for himself in his new job as a school custodian, but now he was
watching *The Tragic Secret of Slapton Sands*. Back during the
Vietnam War he couldn't bear ''to see the terrible roll of fine young
men, every night on the news programs.'' To him, then,

> television had seemed a curse; now it seemed a cure. The truth was finally
> told. The dark curtains were rolled back, and it was as if someone had
> opened a relief valve in my body. Now I could open up and attempt to talk
> about it—that's what I needed. Like the man said, ''Just what the doctor
> ordered.''[2]

Tiger had been discovered for a postwar public. Extraordinarily, it
was to be discovered a second time, in an even bigger welter of
publicity.

The publicity had not escaped people living in the Slapton Sands
area. For a month or so the unusual fauna of this stretch of Heritage
Coastline had been supplemented with repeated sightings of reporters
and television crews walking the beach. The Slapton Ley had
seventeen kinds of dragonfly, but over Slapton Sands helicopters hired
by the American networks swooped and hovered, taking aerial shots.
Quite a stir had been created by the revival of the Tiger story that had
interested Ken Small for several years.

One April day Alma Taft was on Slapton Sands with a television
reporter when Ken Small approached her. He told her about his
underwater Sherman tank, for which, by this time, he had an official
site on land near the beach. If, that is, he recovered it. He asked Alma
Taft whether, if he did so, would she get the recovery on to television.[3]

Now, a matter of days after ABC's broadcast, he was poised to
salvage his tank from the sea. After last-minute hitches, everything
was ready. A diving tender and navy divers had checked the tank for
explosives and human remains, and found none. (Manny Rubin in
Plymouth, hearing of the plan to recover the tank and fearing it might
be a sea grave, had offered £1,000 *not* to salvage it.) The divers had
evicted the conger eels and used a suction hose to clear silt from the
tank's interior. South West Recovery of Saltash, Cornwall, had offered
the use of powerful winch vehicles free of charge. The underwater
work was to be done by eight students from the Fort Bovisand Diving
School as part of their course.

By May 17 they had attached four ten-ton flotation bags to the

Sherman, suspending it above the seabed. South West Recovery began to winch it in for its forty-year overdue amphibious landing on Slapton Sands. When its turret and most of its superstructure were out of the water Ken Small climbed aboard and, as hundreds of sightseers watched from the Torcross Line, broke a bottle of champagne over the Sherman to launch it onto the land.

Meanwhile, a friend of Ken Small's was making a video film of the recovery. I saw it on one occasion at his guest house. The video caught the moment when the tank, the beach behind it, reached firm concrete.

> At 4:20 P.M., with a considerable creaking and breaking up of encrusted barnacles, the entire running gear came to life and ran as freely as the day it boarded the LST. Grease could be seen oozing from various nipples and the vertical volute spring suspension worked a treat as the tank came over the crest of the slipway.[4]

At the same time, seawater poured and trickled down the tank's sides and tracks. Watching the video, Ken Small said that it was "weeping." Against the musical soundtrack—the theme from *Bilitis*—that didn't sound unreasonable.

Another video records the next development in the story: the Slapton Sands commemorative ceremony of June 2, 1984. It was a virtual rerun of the 1954 one, but with a much bigger local attendance despite the distance in time—or because of it; perhaps the edges of painful memories had been softened. The by-now customary functionaries were there: the Lord Lieutenant of Devon, a bishop, a British Vice Admiral, the defense attaché from the U.S. embassy in London. Once again, Church and State and the armed forces of both countries joined in celebrating the Anglo-American "special relationship" and in honoring the sacrifices that are "the price of freedom." There were British and American guards of honor and, off Slapton Sands, a British and an American warship. The ex-evacuees and other guests around the obelisk sang the hymns "All People That on Earth Do Dwell" and "Now Thank We All Our God." Then one of the ships fired a salute and a single plane flew past. "What a memorable day it was," the video's voice-over enthused, "despite a near gale-force wind."

At a reception held afterward in a big marquee the video camera settled briefly on Ken Small. By now his tank was in place on its Torcross site, hard by Slapton Sands, painted with black preservative, its cannon pointing seaward, one Englishman's informal memorial to the American dead of Tiger. The South Hams District Council had put up a plaque there:

> This American Sherman tank took part in the D Day Practice Landings at Slapton Beach in 1944 when it was lost at sea and there remained until its recovery in 1984. It stands as a memorial to those American lives lost during the course of the D Day practice landings at Slapton Beach in 1944. Their sacrifice was not in vain. Be they ever at peace.

There were short interviews with ex-evacuees and with the American defense attaché, Colonel A. B. Renshaw of the U.S. air force. Describing the Slapton Sands area as "unspoiled . . . a very rare piece of real estate," the Colonel added that it was "an area of special interest for American families." But there wasn't, he said, enough publicity about Slapton Sands: "More Americans would come if they knew about the tragic accident. . . ."[5]

In Everett, Washington, Joseph McCann, formerly of the *515*, had seen *The Tragic Secret of Slapton Sands*. After the war he had become a policeman until invalided out of the force because of injuries suffered in the line of duty: Some hoodlums had run him over in their car. Joseph McCann had been told in the war never to talk about Tiger, and he hadn't, not even to his wife. Now he did.

Tom Clark, formerly of the *507*, had also seen the program at his home in Texas. He contacted Nola Safro of *20/20*. She put him in touch with Angelo Crapanzano, Manny Rubin, and John Doyle, the taciturn former skipper of the *515* whom ABC had traced and interviewed for the program. On June 4 Angelo Crapanzano wrote to Manny Rubin in Plymouth, telling his story. "I would like to hear from you," his letter ended. "Please write me."

As yet Dr. Eugene Eckstam of Monroe, Wisconsin, had not been "found," as he would put it, by Tom Clark. That would happen in the autumn of 1984, and would come as "about as much of an emotional shock as the torpedo was a physical shock." Dr. Eckstam had been in touch over the years with his former shipmate Ed Panter, so one more name was added to the snowballing list of survivors.

For forty years Dr. Eckstam had "tried in vain" to forget Exercise Tiger; now, reminded of it, he threw himself into trying to understand what it was that he had experienced as a young man, using his personal computer to compile lists of survivors, finding new ones, putting them in touch with one another. By December 1987 his local paper would be able to report that he "spends much of his time trying to uncover the whole story and locate others who share both his nightmares and his quest for the truth."[6]

The world's press descended on Normandy for the D Day anniversary of June 6. One focal point of interest was the American military cemetery at St. Laurent, overlooking Omaha Beach. Twenty years before, Eisenhower had gone there for a television special called *D Day Plus 20*. The interviewer, Walter Cronkite, asked him what went through his mind when he returned to Normandy. Eisenhower said that it wasn't the tanks, the guns, the planes, the ships, or the victory. It was the families of the men buried in the American cemetery. He could never come to this spot, he said, without thinking of how blessed he and his wife were to have grandchildren, and of the couples in America who had never had that blessing, because their only son was buried in France. . . .[7]

In a story that abounds in Anglo-American coincidences, the next development is one of the more improbable. That August, Alma Taft visited the United States for a family reunion. In the 1680s, a branch of her family had emigrated to the United States and settled in Mendon, Massachusetts, where the reunion was being held. Alma Taft took her video recordings of the *20/20* and Channel 4 News pieces about the disaster.

It was her first family reunion. At it she met an uncle, Seth Taft, who was then running for the governorship of Ohio. He saw her recordings and told her, "Well, of course, you know that we have someone in the government at the moment." He meant William Howard Taft, Deputy Secretary of Defense of the United States. The No. 2 man in the Pentagon was Alma Taft's cousin.

Later, from Philadelphia, Alma Taft telephoned William Taft's office. An appointment was arranged, and she went to see him. She told him the story of the *20/20* special, and about Dorothy Seekings's story of the bodies of Americans buried and abandoned in a South Devon field. She told him about Ken Small's Sherman tank, and that she thought it important there should be a memorial on Slapton Sands.

A few weeks later, back in England, she was telephoned by the then assistant army attaché at the U.S. embassy in London, Lieutenant Colonel Tom Haase. Ken Small had been in touch with him, and he told her that the Embassy was planning a dedication ceremony for that November, a religious service to be held at the Torcross tank.

One "teeming, rainy" November day, a chauffeur-driven embassy car, Stars and Stripes pennant fluttering, followed Alma Taft's small sedan down the narrow South Devon lanes. At Slapton Sands Ken Small and a crowd of local people waited in the drizzle around the Sherman tank. Also there were members of the South Hams District Council, which had organized the ceremony and announced it in the local press. Tom Haase arrived. He was wearing his army dress uniform. "A churchman gave a lovely little service," then Tom Haase and others snapped to attention as a U.S. marine played "taps," the American equivalent of the British last post.[8]

It was the second open-air service on Slapton Sands within six months, but the June 2 reunion, like the American memorial of 1945 around which it was held, had been in honor of the evacuees. At the reception afterward, asked about the dead of Tiger, Lieutenant Colonel Renshaw had replied, "I was going to say more about that, but I thought that that's not the reason we're here today."

Now American officialdom had repaired that omission. The ghosts of the seacoast had been laid to rest at last. Or had they?

Not to Ken Small's way of thinking.

Two people whose brothers had died in the T-4 disaster would be inspired by the *20/20* special to come to England to try to find out more for themselves. One of them was Edward Kaska of Emmaus, Pennsylvania. On April 28, 1944, when he had been a midshipman at the U.S. Naval Academy, his brother, Albert, had been a crewman on *LST 531*, plodding through the waters of Lyme Bay. He and his family had experienced the same puzzled hurt suffered by all the next of kin who received the official telegram. With the *20/20* program at least some of the puzzlement had been cleared up. But he wanted to know more, and in late 1984 he went with his wife to South Devon and Slapton Sands.

He questioned British officials; a British naval officer took him by boat to the area of sea where the E-boat attack had happened. There he laid a wreath on the water in memory of his brother.

Edward Kaska was to be an important cross-pollinator of contacts. By this time he was already in touch with Douglas Harlander, senior surviving officer of his brother's ship, the *531*, and now a dentist in Frederic, Wisconsin.

Wisconsin, he discovered, had also been the home of another crewman who had died aboard the *531*. He had obtained, from U.S. records, a list of the dead and missing of *LST 531*, and on it the name of a sailor called Melvin Jansen was just below that of his brother. Both were listed as missing. He found out that Melvin had hailed from Appleton, Wisconsin. In the Appleton telephone book 156 Jansens were listed. Edward Kaska began ringing them up and made contact at last with David and Stanley Jansen, Melvin's brothers.

A local newspaper in Wisconsin picked up the story. "Now," the headline ran, "they know how Melvin Jansen died. . . ."[9]

In Red Bluff, California, Floyd Hicks, formerly of *LST 515*, had seen *20/20* and made contact with his old skipper, John Doyle. Floyd Hicks would be another important agent in the coming together of the Tiger story. Soon he was in contact with his former shipmate Joseph McCann, in Washington State. From John Doyle he learned of the existence of Angelo Crapanzano, and in his turn put Crapanzano in touch with McCann.

"That *20/20* show," said Angelo Crapanzano, "opened up a whole new world for me." Now the darkest corner of his memory was about to be opened up. On March 30, 1985, he wrote to Joseph McCann. After identifying himself, he asked "the big question": "The odds are 3 to 1 that you picked me up. Can you remember that much about who or what you saw and picked up? I was hanging on a burnt-out raft. . . ."

One Sunday evening soon afterwards, Joseph McCann telephoned. Angelo Crapanzano told the story in a letter to Manny Rubin. McCann told him "I did pick you up," and Crapanzano asked, "How did you know it was me?" McCann explained how on the first run past Crapanzano's raft he thought the three men on it were dead. On his way back, though, he noticed movement and dragged the men aboard his LCVP. One of the men rescued, whom he knew now to be Angelo Crapanzano, had been mumbling about his legs.

Crapanzano told Manny Rubin:

> When our conversation ended and I hung up, I sobbed uncontrollably for about ten minutes. My wife was startled and couldn't understand why I was so upset. When I told her, she sighed, "My God, that was close!" Fate had given me a second chance and made me wait forty years to hear the unbelievable truth.[10]

In early April, Angelo Crapanzano's new world opened up even more with a visit from his fellow survivor, Tom Clark. From the same ship, they had not set eyes on one another since its sinking and had plenty of notes to compare. They looked at photographs and Angelo got his Bronze Star out of its drawer.

Already there was talk of a Tiger reunion. Floyd Hicks was trying to arrange one for August and had placed an advertisement in the American Legion magazine. At his home in Lakeland, Florida, former *515* crewman and retired mailman Wendell Hoppler saw the advertisement and was "overjoyed." So Hoppler's name was added to the list of known Tiger veterans and survivors, rescuers and rescued.

Wendell Hoppler, in contacting Floyd Hicks, was able to give him the whereabouts of another former *515* crewman. One of his regular stops as a mailman had been a woodworking shop in Skokie, Illinois. Delivering mail there one day, as he had been for five years, he overheard a customer telling the man behind the counter that her son, who was in the modern American navy, had been assigned to an LST. The man behind the counter told her that he had been on one in the war, the *LST 515*. Wendell Hoppler, standing there all the years later with his sack of mail, could hardly believe his ears.

The woodworking shop belonged to Hermann "Buddie" Grosse. Hoppler and he had both been on the *515* but hadn't known one another. They had compared notes, but hadn't been able to agree on memories until Hoppler mentioned Exercise Tiger and the fat man who had been the last person the *515* had picked out of the water. Then it had all come tumbling out: "Oh, What a Beautiful Morning," Beachhead, all their memories.[11]

Wendell Hoppler would be at the reunion. So would Buddie Grosse. It was for men of the *515*, but, of course, Angelo Crapanzano and Tom Clark of the *507* would be able to attend it too. "I'm afraid to fly," said Crapanzano, "but I'll take the train."[12]

April 28 came round again, and now it was time for Manny Rubin to make his annual visit to Slapton Sands. He turned up there as usual, with his flowers, but this time, instead of floating them out upon the sea, he thought he would place them on the Sherman tank, in a cut-glass vase he had brought for the purpose. He did so, and went for something to eat. When he came back to the tank, someone had stolen the vase.

By now, news of the Sherman tank had crossed the Atlantic and letters from veterans scattered throughout the United States had begun to arrive at Ken Small's guest house. Among them was one from Atlee Wampler, Jr., a former major in the Seventieth Tank Battalion to which the Sherman had belonged, inviting Small to a reunion of the Seventieth to be held in Harrisburg, Pennsylvania, in September.

Another letter was from Charles J. Myers, secretary and treasurer of the Seventieth Tank Battalion Association. Mr. Myers had a matter of deep concern to raise, a matter, he said, that "still bothers us all." "Do you think," he asked Ken Small, "our comrades received a proper burial, or do you think they are still buried in an unmarked grave?"

Ken Small was asking about locally to try to discover the answer to that question. "Things are becoming quite interesting," he told a reporter, "but I'm not saying anything more than that now."[13]

Stella Rouggley of St. Louis was also very concerned about the burial story. In the first week of June 1985 she and her husband visited the South Hams in an attempt to explore the story more deeply. A local newspaper described her as "distraught," and it was her husband, himself a former soldier, who did most of the asking and talking.

"We were never told," he said, speaking of his wife's brother, "where he was buried, or whether the body was recovered or anything. Put yourself in that position and how would you react?"

He said they had met mixed reactions when making their inquiries among residents of the South Hams. "Some talk freely and some turn and walk away. I can understand why—some don't want their peace and serenity disturbed." But Dorothy Seekings, with whom they were staying, had spoken to them, and they believed her when she said that the bodies were still there. An exhumation "would have been the talk of the town. You can't tell me otherwise," he said. "There is a doubt there," he added, and while that doubt remained they would go on digging for the facts.[14]

In making their inquiries, the Rouggleys heard of Ken Small and went to visit him at his guest house. In the dining room he showed them a list he had received from the United States: eight pages of names of men of the First Engineer Special Brigade who had died on the night of Tiger.

On page eight Stella Rouggley saw the name of her brother, Howard W. Wagner, Pvt., 3206th QM Sv Co. So far as the Tiger affair was concerned, it seemed that the Cove Guest House, Torcross, had begun to assume some of the functions of a U.S. diplomatic mission.

*   *   *

The reunion arranged by Floyd Hicks took place a little later than originally planned, in the first week of September 1985, at Chicago's Continental Hotel. About seventy veterans and survivors of Tiger and Convoy T-4 were present. "We started with nothing in getting this together," said Floyd Hicks, "so this is a pretty good turnout. But we do want to have contact with more of the survivors."

There were men from the *507* there, like Tom Clark and Eugene Eckstam, but most were from the *515*, men who had learned, from John Doyle's repeated playing of it as the ship's reveille, to loathe "Oh, What a Beautiful Morning." Now, with Doyle in their midst, the old and aging men put *Oklahoma!* on a record player and played the song they had learned by heart in the morning of their lives.

Wendell Hoppler had heard "Oh, What a Beautiful Morning" down the Illinois and Mississippi rivers, in the Gulf of Mexico, on the Atlantic crossing to Europe, in the English Channel. For forty-one years he had been unable to hear the song without a smile coming to his face, and now he and all of them smiled to hear it again.

Another thing all the old *515* crew members had in common was a memory of the fat man they had plucked from the water in the aftermath of the Tiger attack, the last man they rescued. No one knew or could remember his name, but they all remembered him. They called him simply "the fat man."

At the 1985 reunion a story went the rounds that the sailor who had actually picked "the fat man" out of the sea had run a small business after the war and that one day a man had come in looking for a job. He was "the fat man." He was hired, and worked with his rescuer until his death in the early 1980s.

More mysterious was a story that *didn't* do the rounds at the reunion. It came from two army men, strangers, who arrived late at this mainly navy gathering. One of them let fall that he had buried the dead of Exercise Tiger in a South Devon field. But it was late, with a lot of drink taken, and no one, anyway, seemed to know who the men were. Eugene Eckstam did a double take and asked the one who had spoken up whether what he had said was true. The man said it was. But somehow his remark wasn't picked up and the story he had to tell wasn't told. The man himself wasn't sure whether it wasn't too secret to tell, even at this late date, and he had, after all, made his remark in the company of men who were used to being disbelieved and whose own credulity was already strained simply by being there, after forty-one years, talking and drinking together.[15]

*   *   *

By now Ken Small's sense of mission was complete. It was the duty of the U.S. authorities to honor their thitherto forgotten dead, and it was his duty to persuade them to do just that, by putting up a memorial to the men on Slapton Sands. By a chain of events that he saw in a mystical, providential light, he was to succeed triumphantly in his unusual ambition.

At the Harrisburg reunion Atlee Wampler arranged that Ken Small should meet his Congresswoman. Beverley B. Byron of Maryland's Sixth District was an old friend of Wampler's. At their meeting, Ken Small showed her—and she admired—some of the jewelry he had picked up in his beachcombing on Slapton Sands. He told her about his ten-year struggle to salvage the Sherman tank, his informal memorial and his hope that the Americans would now see fit to put up a formal memorial of their own. Toward the close of their conversation Mrs. Byron opened her desk drawer and took out a book. "Is it a coincidence? I don't know," said Ken Small, but the book was *My Three Years with Eisenhower*. Its author, Harry Butcher, Eisenhower's naval aide, had been Beverley Byron's father.

Now Ken Small of Torcross was in contact with someone in the government of the United States who had, as it were, family connections with the story of Exercise Tiger. Beverley Byron gave him "her assurance" that she would introduce a bill in Congress in order to try to raise the necessary funds for a memorial. Meanwhile on September 11, 1985, she introduced in Congress a motion of thanks to Ken Small for having salvaged the Sherman tank.[16]

A year later Manny Rubin was telephoned by a reporter from BBC Television in Plymouth. By now his story of Convoy T-4 was known and accepted not only in the Plymouth Argyle clubroom, but also further afield, and the reporter thought he might be interested to know that there was an E-boat in Plymouth harbor.

It was one of the Cherbourg flotilla that had attacked T-4, perhaps the very one that had sunk the *531* or *507*, or fired the yellowish green tracer of Manny Rubin's recurrent nightmare. Renamed *The Baltic Surveyor,* it had been converted into a six-berth pleasure cruiser, but, as the TV reporter would note, it still looked sinister enough. Painted black, a flag flew from its masthead showing the iron cross in black against a red ground. The boat's owner and skipper, Mike Watkiss, later told the TV reporter that he had thought of mounting a dummy cannon at the bow, "but I already get stopped enough."

The TV report showed Manny Rubin standing on the dock, arms

akimbo, staring at the E-boat in total disbelief. "It's like seeing a ghost," he said. "It's scary. I wish we could have hit it once, just once, but we never touched the son-of-a-gun."

The pleasure cruiser did not please him at all. He strode over to it, and in camera, gave it a hard kick on its hull. A man appeared from below—Mike Watkiss. He wore a black shirt and had a drink in his hand. "Steady on," he said, "what do you think you're doing?"

Manny Rubin's reply was edited out.

"I'm trying," he said, "to kick the sides in on this fucking thing!"

On January 6, 1987, Beverley Byron introduced her bill in Congress. "Be it enacted," began House Resolution 314, "that the Secretary of Defense shall prepare a plaque honoring all American servicemen who lost their lives at Slapton Sands, England, during 'Operation Tiger,' a secret exercise which served as a rehearsal for the invasion of Normandy, and shall make arrangements for the placement of such a plaque at the Operation Tiger Memorial in Torcross."

The thing was done: There would be a memorial. It was perhaps to make assurance doubly sure, though, that Ken Small now sought to go still higher in the machinery of American government. Alma Taft had told him that Caspar Weinberger's Deputy Secretary of Defense, William Taft, was her cousin, and had given him the telephone number of Taft's secretary. From Torcross he telephoned the Pentagon, and telephoned again, until his persistence won the day and a meeting was agreed to. Ken Small flew to the United States, where, on May 18, he spent an hour and more with William Taft at the Pentagon. He was given a guided tour of the building, and someone told him that President Reagan was to send him a personal thank-you letter "for campaigning for so long."

A photograph of Slapton Sands would be hung on the wall of William Taft's Pentagon office. A similar photograph is in the defense attaché's office at the U.S. embassy in London. The story of the Tiger disaster was one that the American authorities were beginning to know rather well. For more than forty years, apparently, no one had heard of it; now it seemed that the story would not go away. No amount of exorcism seemed to do the trick; but perhaps, finally, the ghosts of the seacoast would be happy with their memorial.

If visiting the Pentagon had been a little like walking on air, earthier matters awaited Ken Small on his return to Torcross. The plaque for the memorial would be cast in Colorado, and flown from there to Europe for the journey to Slapton Sands, but the stone would come from the English West Country. The council suggested Cornwall, but Ken Small wanted a chunk of Devon granite, and at last a piece was chosen from Merivale quarry, on Dartmoor, about an hour's drive from Torcross. Describing him as "dazed," a local newspaper quoted Ken Small as saying "It's like a dream come true. I would never have given up—it's something which is too important to me."[18]

Back in 1984 the South Hams Council had taken note of the hundreds of American veterans who had visited Normandy for the D Day anniversary. Were the South Hams sufficiently publicizing their own connection with D Day and the invasion of Europe? In August it was announced that the council had completed purchase of the Old Rocket House in Torcross, with a view to turning it into a museum. "We are planning," said Frank Palmer of the council, "to open it as an interpretative center based on the use of this part of the South Hams as a secret battle practice zone."[19]

At the same time, Frank Palmer praised Ken Small. "We're delighted," he said, "that there has been a successful conclusion to Mr. Small's campaign. He has worked tremendously hard, and will be very relieved that we are on the last lap now."

In London one of the local press reports on the forthcoming Torcross memorial was seen by James Dalrymple, a journalist on *The Independent*. Earlier in his career he had worked in the West County, where he had heard rumors of the Tiger disaster. He thought he would ring up Ken Small and find out more.

But, of course, there were *two* stories of potential national and international interest to be found within a matter of miles of one another in the South Hams: not only Ken Small in Torcross, with his memorial, but Dorothy Seekings in Stoke Fleming, with her story of bodies in the fields. This was a story that Ken Small also wanted to explore. In mid-September he "hinted" to a local newspaper that he, too, thought that the bodies of Tiger's victims may still lie buried in Devon.

His suggested site, though, was in another field, not the one near the Sportsman's pub, just outside Blackawton, which Dorothy Seekings had pointed out. He would not say where "his" field was, but it was quite clearly somewhere else, because this field was "close to the site of the U.S. landings." Someone had taken him there and told him that in the war two brick and concrete bunkers had been in the field. The bodies of the Americans had been placed in the bunkers; then the steps down to them had been blown up, sealing off the bunkers and turning them into tombs.[20]

Here was a variation upon the darker note that Dorothy Seekings had already introduced into the Tiger story. It was a note of paganism.

James Dalrymple's article was published in *The Independent* on September 16, turning Ken Small into an overnight celebrity. From now on, the telephone at his Torcross guest house would ring with increasing frequency and letters would arrive every day, as other newspapers, television and radio stations, and private individuals all over the world pursued the story, added to it the little that they knew, or made inquiries. From September 16 onward Ken Small was in what he once described to me as "the jungle of journalism."

On the same day the bronze plaque cast in Colorado was flown to the U.S. army base in Heidelberg. A few days later Alma Taft was in the U.S. embassay in London. In the defense attaché's office she saw the plaque, *en route* for Torcross.

Now everything was coming together. In late October 500 members of the United States LST Association gathered together for a grand reunion in Newport News, the shipbuilding yard of Norfolk, Virginia, the world's biggest naval base. The association had been formed only in 1985, but it already had many members, and the former "forgotten men of the fleet" were already considered important enough for Vice President George Bush to attend their convention.

A Baptist minister from the Deep South, who had once been a crewman on an LST, gave a "speaking-in-tongues" style sermon. A congressman, in a speech, said that LSTs "were a big part of why the Allies won World War II" (and it was at Newport News, in 1942, that the first American LST had been built). Veterans of the wartime LSTs were taken on tour of a modern one—a highly sophisticated ship, but still the same old design at heart. A lot of the men shed a tear as a wreath from a coast guard vessel was laid on the surface of one of the dockyard's channels. There was a gun salute and "taps" was sounded by a bugler.

There was a lot of talk, too, about Exercise Tiger, and about the memorial plaque to be unveiled in Torcross the following month. "It's long overdue," said a former crewman of the *496*. "This has meant a lot of sadness and tragedy for a lot of people."[21]

CHAPTER
16

S tella Rouggley had consoled herself with the thought that her
brother was buried in such "a beautiful part of England." But the
idea that the bodies of American soldiers had been left in some
temporary and unmarked corner of a foreign field was still a shocking
one and, if untrue, an insult to the United States.

In September, with the memorial in the offing, Ken Small said:

> No useful purpose would be served by digging up the question of the
> bodies. I didn't want this bodies business brought up. What would be the
> point if they were found and dug up? All it would do would be to cause
> sensationalism and upset a lot of people.[1]

By late October he had backed off still further from the "bodies
business." What seems to have decided him was a letter from a retired
U.S. navy captain, Henry Durham. His letter to the Cove Guest House
said that the bodies of an estimated 700 to 800 soldiers and sailors,
most of them drowned, had been carried to Portland on the decks of
ships that had combed the area. If they had gone to Portland, in Dorset,
then they had not washed up on Slapton Sands almost fifty miles
distant across Lyme Bay. Accordingly, Ken Small revised downward
his earlier estimate of the men he thought to have been buried in the
area. He added that he now believed that such locally buried bodies as
there had been were no longer in their local resting places: the U.S.
authorities had, after all, exhumed them.[2]

But as Ken Small was backing off, Dorothy Seekings was wading
in. In late September, five days after making Ken Small famous, *The
Independent* reported on the story that she had to tell. It had either
grown since she first broke her silence in 1984, or she hadn't then told
all that she knew. Now she elaborated a little upon what had caused her
to hold her tongue for forty years. "I really believed that I would be

punished if I talked about it. I never stopped thinking about that day, and what I had seen, but I never told anybody.''

She had seen a fair amount, the baker's daughter with her basket of doughnuts, that spring day of 1944. There hadn't been only the lorry in which she had traveled, but other lorries, too, all similarly loaded with bodies. The burial had gone on ''for hours.'' There had been no religious formalities and no honor guards. Two days later another lorry had pulled up outside her father's bakery and a soldier had lifted the tarpaulin at its tailgate to show her more bodies, soaking wet as the others had been and none apparently wounded.

And that was not all. James Dalrymple had spread out a large-scale map of the locality, on which Mrs. Seekings had pinpointed what she believed to be a ''vast graveyard,'' with bodies buried in locations ''over an eight-mile radius.'' ''I never saw any more actual burials,'' she said, ''but my friends among the soldiers told me that they were burying them in fields all over the area, and it was going on all the time.''

Among the grave sites that she located was the one in which Ken Small had earlier believed. ''The farmer who lived there,'' she said, ''told me about it, but he would never admit it to anybody else.'' She added that other bodies had been buried in shallow graves in fields around Strete church, and others still in a mass grave on the landward side of Slapton Ley.[3]

Three thousand miles away in North Carolina a retired tax collector named Emmett Bailey heard about the ''bodies business'' and was appalled. The story, or stories, seemed to him a slur upon the United States, the United States Army and, ultimately, himself. In 1944 Emmett Bailey had been a corporal in the Sixty-fifth Quartermaster Registration Company, responsible for telling soldiers what to do with casualities. He and his outfit had been ''closely involved in the clearing-up operation after Exercise Tiger.'' He had ''no personal knowledge of any of the deceased being buried locally,'' and was ''very disturbed indeed to hear these stories of mass graves in the South Hams.''[4]

Emmett Bailey made up his mind to visit Torcross, and on Sunday, November 15, was among the four hundred or so people there to attend the dedication of the memorial. The weather was cold and drizzling. Manny Rubin thought it appropriately somber weather for the somber occasion.[5] He was the one veteran of Convoy T-4 who was present, and in Alma Taft's view ''that day really belonged to Manny Rubin.''[6]

It was Ken Small's day, too, of course. He felt overwhelmed, but perhaps a little overshadowed, too. At any rate, a newspaper reported that he "was left on the sidelines clutching his wreath of poppies."[7] On his wreath was a handwritten card: "I gave sixteen years. These men gave their lives. May they forever rest in peace."[8] Stella Rouggley was one of the "personal mourners" who, said the newspaper, found that "the media ballyhoo from more than ten international TV companies stripped the occasion of privacy and deep meaning."[9]

It was just after the Enniskillen bomb outrage in Northern Ireland, and sniffer dogs had "swept" the Sherman tank and the entire site for explosives. Important people were expected on Slapton Sands that day. William Taft would not, after all, be there, as had been rumored, but the U.S. defense attaché and a lieutenant general would represent him and the American army, some of whose men had been flown in from Ludwigsburg, West Germany, to make a color guard. The British Minister of Defense, George Younger, likewise wasn't there, but through his representative, General Sir Peter Whiteley, he had sent his "sincere good wishes."[10]

Congresswoman Beverley Byron was in Torcross. With Peggy Verniquet, the then chairwoman of the South Hams Council, she would unveil the memorial. The removal of the Stars and Stripes from the chunk of Dartmoor granite would be the central event of the ceremony, which would be conducted by the vicar of Stokenham.

In all the protocol Manny Rubin was quite lost. To him the ceremony was "like a family funeral,"[11] but, as the drizzle turned into driving rain, he found himself at the back of the crowd. General Sir Peter Whiteley, after inspecting the color guard, made what Manny Rubin thought was "a proper speech"; of Beverley Byron's response, he thought, by contrast, that "it was as though she was running for reelection."[12]

The speeches were made and, after prayers, the memorial was unveiled and dedicated. A hymn was sung. There was a blessing, and the Kingsbridge Silver Band played the two national anthems. The ceremony ended with "a haunting and faultless 'taps' " played by an American army bugler, "perched on a sandy mound between the crashing sea and the peaceful freshwater lake."[13]

Ken Small stepped forward and placed his wreath of poppies before the memorial. His eyes were "brimming with tears" and he was "unable to speak."[14] Others felt the same. "At the time," said Emmett Bailey, "I never shed a tear but I can hardly keep my eyes dry today."[15] At the back of the crowd Stella Rouggley was in tears and

Manny Rubin close to them. "I feel," he said, "peace of mind at last."[16]

Speaking of the memorial, and paying tribute to Ken Small, Joseph McCann far away in Washington State spoke for all the veterans and survivors of Convoy T-4 when he said that "it kind of eases all that bitterness to know that it was a British citizen who led this. I'm really happy to see that it was a British citizen that really led the drive."[17] McCann meant that in Ken Small's persistent lobbying for a memorial Britain had helped to pay off the debt incurred by the failure of T-4's Royal Navy escort back in 1944.

There was another side to the memorial ceremony, however, which the *Torquay Herald-Express* touched upon in its report. Although it called the ceremony "a touching service on the beachhead," it added that "attempts by military chiefs, ambassadorial staff, and local councillors to maintain a dignified air of reverence on a sad occasion were only partly successful."[18] Despite the passage of years Tiger had lost none of its ferocity, and if the service around the new memorial was bittersweet, it was also simply bitter.

Stella Rouggley, noted the *Western Morning News*, "still felt some bitterness at the long delay in recognition."[19] More trenchantly, there was, said the *Herald-Express,* "smouldering anger among the veterans."[20] Part of the anger was occasioned, like Stella Rouggley's lingering bitterness, by the long delay. Others, believing the stories of bodies in mass graves, were angry on that account. Others still, disbelieving the stories, were furious at the worldwide publicity that they had been given.

Emmett Bailey's anger had brought him 3,000 miles to Torcross. "I came," he said, "to put to rest these stories about mass graves."[21] Before the service, he and Dorothy Seekings, the chief promulgator of the stories, had come face to face and there had been "a sharp confrontation."[22] Bailey said that if the bodies of American soldiers were still buried near Slapton Sands, he would pay for their disinterment and repatriation to the United States. "On the other hand," he added, "if someone does do any excavating, the cost of damage to property should be borne by these people who are making all these claims about mass graves."[23]

"God our help in ages past," the congregation had sung at the service following that "sharp confrontation," "our hope in years to come." The chunk of Dartmoor granite with its plaque cast in Colorado had been unveiled and blessed by a priest, to become a formal, Christian memorial. Still the unconscious would be held by a sense that the reality was, or might be, not the granite and bronze, but a brick and concrete shambles, or a field by the Sportsman's pub, in which men had been hastily entombed. The pagan image of a mass burial predated the God of "ages past" and would continue in years to come to subvert the hope that the men memorialized might now "rest in peace."

Frustratingly, the "bodies business" could apparently neither be proved nor disproved. Whether you believed the stories or not was a matter of faith, not in God but in the U.S. authorities or Dorothy Seekings and the other local people who thought like her.

Nor did the plaque on the memorial lay the ghosts of the seacoast. There is a permanence to words in bronze, but these words were, by and large, so misleading, open to dispute, or just plain wrong that they might equally have been writ in water. According to the *Herald-Express,* another cause for anger among the veterans was that "the navy personnel on the support craft who also perished have been virtually forgotten."[24] Certainly the privately funded plaque had a strong military bias. The United States Navy got a mention on it at all only thanks to William Kuntz, formerly of the *289,* who saw in the States a report of the proposed inscription. "It was," said Ken Small when contacted by Kuntz, "a sheer oversight on my part."[25] He told the Pentagon, which added the navy to the inscription, in a clause, however, which misleadingly suggests that men from all eight LSTs of T-4 had died in the attack.

Atlee Wampler, Jr., who was at the Torcross ceremony, said that the inscription was "written with love and honor for the guys of my generation that were lost in this disaster called Exercise Tiger."[26] It would be a mistake to lose sight of the memorial's central significance as an act of love and honor, but at the same time it must be pointed out that the inscription is riddled both with errors of omission—like the American obelisk farther down Slapton Sands—and of commission. True to its tradition of clerical error, Exercise Tiger has been erroneously remembered. And mistaken identity is no way to set about laying ghosts.

Errors of omission: The First Engineer Special Brigade is nowhere mentioned on the plaque, nor are the initials and numbers of the four LSTs that came under attack (*LST 511* by her own side). Perhaps the oddest error of commission is the mention of the 279th Engineer Combat Battalion. Historian Howard DeVoe has established that at the time of Exercise Tiger this unit was still in training in Texas.[27] Almost as odd is the mention of the Seventieth Tank Battalion, of which Ken

Small's Sherman had once been part. The Seventieth had indeed taken part in Exercise Tiger, but, according to the secretary of the Seventieth Association, "we were on shore nearly twenty hours prior to the E-boat attack. . . . The 70th lost no personnel during the exercise, and we had no people on the convoy."[28] Why, then, does the Torcross inscription give members of the Seventieth as having "perished off the coast of Slapton Sands"?

Two days after the memorial was dedicated, former Pentagon official historian Charles MacDonald, who attended the Torcross ceremony, wrote, "I deeply regret that I was not called in on this project soon enough to have corrected the errors on the plaque."[29] Those errors alone assure that Exercise Tiger will not yet be forgotten. One day in the future there is likely to be yet another ceremony on Slapton Sands, commemorating a corrected memorial. William Kuntz is one of those determined to get the plaque recast: "I'll keep fighting until it gets done."[30] Howard DeVoe wrote of his belief that "we definitely have enough proof to convince others that the 1st Eng. Spec. Bgde. and the U.S. navy should be at the top of any of the memorials built or to be built. These men deserve it and then some."[31] Dale Rodman wrote that "Mr. Ken Small and I have begun a campaign to have a new plaque which is historically correct made to replace the one now in place. We hope to have this done on the forty-fifth anniversary of the disaster."[32]

That was written on December 17, 1987, just over a month after the Torcross ceremony. That same week, in the United States, another campaign had been initiated. On December 10 Congressman Douglas Applegate of Ohio's Eighteenth District had introduced a joint resolution: "Now, therefore, be it Resolved by the Senate and House of Representatives of the United States of America in Congress assembled, That April 28, 1988, is designated as 'National Day of Remembrance of the 749 American Victims of Operation Tiger.' "[33]

That figure—749—is to be found on the Torcross memorial, whose plaque also makes mention of the Fourth Infantry Division. While other statements in the inscription are wrong or right, these two are open to dispute. Almost fifty years after Exercise Tiger they remain matters of contention and conjecture: not only how many men died, but also who they were.

IV

"THE FIELD
WHERE THE
SOLDIERS ARE..."

CHAPTER

17

There has never been a definitive death toll for the attack on Convoy T-4. Until there is one—if there ever is—the memory of Tiger's victims is likely to haunt the seacoast. Ghosts thrive on mystery, and here there prevail conditions that, whether or not there is a mystery, are at least encouraging to the mystery-minded. Exploring this real or possible mystery, I was often reminded of one of the notes to *The Waste Land*, about an Antarctic expedition. "It was related," wrote T. S. Eliot, "that the party of explorers, at the extremity of their strength, had the constant delusion that there was *one more member* than could actually be counted."

Delusory or not, the counting for Convoy T-4 is complex and, because of the grim reality behind the numbers (and the possible hidden reality *behind the numbers*), intensely depressing for the person counting. I hope to spare the reader both the depression and most, at least, of the mind-numbing number crunching. But some of the complexities cannot be ducked in exploring the problem to its source or sources.

The counting abounds in incidental pitfalls. There are numerical illusions. For example, the number of one of the army units, the 531st Engineer Shore Regiment, is also the number of one of the ships that went down, *LST 531*. And the LSTs, as well as their own initials and navy numbers, had, for security reasons, army serial numbers. The army serial number of *LST 507*, for example, was *496*, which was, confusingly, the *navy* serial number of another of the LSTs.

There are other traps for the unwary. Donald S. Bryant, a private in the 531st Engineer Shore Regiment, did die in Tiger; not on Convoy T-4, however, but in an unrelated incident on the day before April 27.[1] William P. O'Connell, a first lieutenant in the 385th Fighter Squadron, died on April 28 and is buried in the American military cemetery in Cambridge, but there is no reason to suppose that he therefore died in Tiger.

Much of the primary source material is missing. Douglas Harlander's report of the sinking of *LST 531* states that "no publications, records, or accounts were saved."[2] James Murdoch, of *LST 507*, before his ship was sunk, "turned over the key of the ship's office to the ship's yeoman to enable the yeoman to save the ship's records." He adds in his report that "one of the storekeepers took the records over the side with him," and that the senior quartermaster, just before abandoning ship, had the ship quartermaster's notebook. But "the yeoman and senior quartermaster were not rescued, and the records they carried have not been recovered; the records carried by the storekeeper were lost at sea."

Later in his report, Murdoch writes of "a water-soaked and much pen-deleted army roster" that he himself had carried overboard. But the (possibly definitive) roster of army personnel aboard the *507* had been left behind ashore, and that roster had not been traced.[3]

Other records were lost not in water but in a fire that gutted the four-story national personnel records center in St. Louis, Missouri, in 1972. It is possible that the *507*'s shore roster was burned in that fire, together with other records from which an authoritative picture could be built up. But St. Louis fire or not, a U.S. Department of Defense public information series on Exercise Tiger (prepared in 1988 in response to hostile media coverage and a flood of "citizen mail") admits that "personnel rosters and ships' manifests for the troop carriers in Exercise Tiger had been inadequate."[4]

So there is not a full documentary basis for the compilation of a death toll of one hundred percent accuracy, and perhaps would not have been even had rosters and manifests survived. This admitted inadequacy is uncharacteristic. Historian Howard DeVoe writes of those who claim, as several of the survivors do, that the death toll was 1,000 or more, that they "just don't know the system very well. In the army, even for landings, heads are counted, checked off on landing lists, locations noted in files, etc., so much so that it would be almost impossible to have a stowaway."[5] For Convoy T-4, apparently, that rigorous system broke down; even the U.S. authorities implicitly admit that it did.

Their admitted inability to give a definitive death toll for the disaster is not a matter of a death or two (how cold that sounds, but how unforgiving it would be not to allow statisticians and compilers of lists at least a small margin of error); disagreements over the death toll involve differences of hundreds of deaths. And yet the record of the United States in this area over the years is generally so excellent that it does not seem unreasonable, in context, to expect a death toll of 100 percent accuracy.

The American army of the Second World War had graves registration units, whose job it was to account for the dead, their possessions and their whereabouts, and the identities of the missing. The United States has a long tradition (longer than Britain's) of repatriating its dead from foreign wars. In June 1988, to give one vivid example, the bodies of twenty-eight unidentified Americans killed in the War of 1812 against Britain were repatriated from Canada in coffins draped with the Stars and Stripes. The U.S. ambassador to Canada said that the repatriation showed his government's respect for American citizens killed in battle. ''Today in the U.S.,'' he said, ''we are concerned about returning the missing in action in Southeast Asia, and we show the same respect to those who died 174 years before.''[6]

The American Department of Defense leaflet on Exercise Tiger states that ''honoring those who gave their lives in defense of their country is a tradition in the United States.'' Former official U.S. army historian Charles MacDonald, who came out of retirement to look into Tiger for the Defense Department, has written that

> soon after World War I, Congress created an independent agency, the American Battle Monuments Commission, to construct overseas U.S. military cemeteries. . . . Anybody who has seen any of these cemeteries, either those of World War I or of World War II, recognizes that no nation honors its war dead more appropriately than does the United States.[7]

All of which is perfectly true, and should give pause to cavalier suggestions that the United States army and government in this instance dishonorably forgot and abandoned not only the bodily remains but also the very identities of American servicemen. At the same time, though, the very strength of the American tradition in this area makes it all the odder that, as the above-mentioned Defense Department leaflet states, ''no official list of names of the casualties of Exercise Tiger has ever been compiled, nor can one be derived from the information available to the Department of Defense.''

Appropriate honoring of the dead is one thing; however, it must first be known, not necessarily *where* they are, but *who* they are. And knowing who means knowing how many.

This confusion cannot be ascribed to the customary chaos of war. The graves registration units were trained to function in battle conditions, and did so very well. But Tiger was not a battle—it was an exercise, and the six weeks before D Day allowed plenty of time for the compilation of an accurate death toll. It was, after all, the first real training that many men of the graves registration units had had, "the first major test they were put to," as a history of the Graves Registration Command describes their perspective on the disaster.[8] For them, too, rehearsal realism had turned abruptly into reality. They had even lost, by their own reckoning, sixteen of their own men in the attack. Are we to suppose that they fell down badly on this "first major test"?

I should stress that I have in mind not the physical burial of bodily remains but the documentation, name by individual name, of the dead and missing. The available evidence is that this was meticulously done. James W. Chandler, a crewman on *LST 289*, is a case in point. He was at first classified MIA. On July 8, 1944, as though upon the expiry of a deadline, or a lifeline, the status of all the men previously declared MIA would be officially altered to KIA. But James Chandler's status had already been altered to KIA on a list prepared *before* July 8.

This was puzzling and even slightly suspect until I discovered that James Chandler had been the rear gunner on the *289* who had stayed at his post and kept the bridge informed about the torpedo that would hit the ship's stern. He had, brutally stated, been blown to pieces, and the graves registration men (or their navy equivalent) had not known how to classify him, MIA or KIA. Eventually he was classified on the bias of his dental records.[9]

The army documentation was, or should have been, equally meticulous. In the United States Army it is the practice for every unit to prepare daily "morning reports"; taken together, they make, in effect, a diary of the unit. The morning reports—those that survived the 1972 fire—are stored in the St. Louis records center. A summary of them for the 531st Engineering Shore Regiment, a unit of the First Engineer Special Brigade, from April 28 to May 3, carefully lists men by companies, and details whether they were KIA, MIA, or rescued.[10]

That is the degree of pinpoint precision still possible more than forty years on. And yet, apparently, there is a lingering uncertainty as to whether or not one hundred or more men died (possibly several hundred more), who they were, what ship or ships they were on, what units they belonged to. Soldiers, and sailors, of course, live on rumor, but usually, when the time comes, there are the hard facts to lay the rumors to rest. Here there aren't. By a sort of paradox, it is the habitual meticulousness of the American record keeping that enhances the sense that there is something exceptional here requiring an explanation.

At his home in Carmichael, California, Tiger survivor Dale Rodman sought that explanation. Eventually, after intensive study of three separate lists, he prepared an overall list comprising all the known, named men who died on Exercise Tiger, some who almost certainly died on the exercise, and others who may have died on it. As he studied, he must often have reflected how easily his own name might have been on one of those three lists.

In London I have pored over the same lists, night after night, the names of hundreds of men, dead nearly fifty years ago, swimming before my eyes. Howard DeVoe studied the lists in Syracuse, New York. And always each of us, after repeated recounts, barring disagreement over this name or that which raises or lowers the tally, has come to a figure somewhere in the 637 to 641 region, not far off Tennyson's round figure of the ``noble six hundred'' who were in the charge of the Light Brigade.

The three lists are those of the United States Navy, the First Engineer Special Brigade, and the Cambridge cemetery list of those Americans buried there, or whose names appear on the Wall of the Missing, who died on April 28, 1944.

It is the consensus of those who have gone into this carefully that the navy list of navy losses—198 men—is definitive. Certainly the only numerological problem it has ever presented is that because one of the wounded navy men died later in the hospital it was originally given as 197.

The First Engineer Special Brigade list naming 413 men* is a little more problematical. It may or may not be definitive. The problem arises from the Cambridge cemetery list.

On the Cambridge list are some of the same men who appear on the First Engineer list, but under different units. That difficulty sorted out, however, the Cambridge list gives a number of names of men who died on April 28, who may or may not have been temporarily or otherwise attached to the First Engineers but whose names and units do not appear on the First Engineer list.

The American presence in Britain just before D Day was huge, however, and people were dying of other things as well. There is no firm evidence that these men played any part in Convoy T-4 of Exercise Tiger, although in several cases it seems plausible that they did.

There is one unit listed at Cambridge, however, that was part of Convoy T-4 and not part of the First Engineers. These men's names

---

* 414 including Donald Bryant.

appear on no other known list and would not have been known to have been on the convoy but for the independent research outlined above. The 3891st Quartermaster Truck Company, attached to the Seventh Corps, was given in a SHAEF message of May 6, 1944, as having been aboard *LST 507*. Two of its men who died on April 28 are buried at Cambridge.

The same May 6 message gave the first platoon of the 440th Engineer Company as having been on the same ship. The company affiliations of this platoon haven't been traced, and names of its men appear on no known list of the dead, but if it lost no one that night, it was very lucky.

Most dramatically, the Cambridge list gives nineteen men of the Thirty-fifth Signal Construction Battalion as having died on April 28. The men's names are not on the First Engineer list, which also does not name the unit. At the time of writing no one has been able to trace records of this battalion and again there is no paperwork evidence to link its deaths to Convoy T-4 or, indeed, to Exercise Tiger at all. But they were engineers; it is hard to imagine what other cataclysm they died in that day and—as we shall see—there is numerical evidence, exact if circumstantial, that suggests that they did die on T-4. If so, this makes their absence from other lists somewhat puzzling. If they did not die on Tiger, then these are men whose deaths have as yet no history; if they did die on Tiger, then their deaths have had no history until now.

Adding the named men of the Thirty-fifth Signal Construction Battalion and the 3891st Quartermaster Truck Company produces a death toll of 632, just short of the lowest "official" toll of 639. But this is not yet to go to the heart of the problem, because against that 639 reckoning has to be set the other one, also "official," of 749, the figure that appears on the Slapton Sands memorial.

In the little that has been published on the Tiger disaster over the years these two figures, 639 and 749, crop up again and again in different texts or, on at least one occasion, in the same one. In *The Invasion Before Normandy,* published in 1987, Edwin P. Hoyt remarks, "In the end, 749 were buried . . ." only to give, fifty pages farther on and without comment, a table in which the dead add up to 639.[11]

It cannot be that *both* of those figures are "about right"; it may be that neither of them is. They are too far apart to be approximations of the same figure, and yet both have pedigrees going back to American documents drawn up within days of the disaster. These are the figures, and the pedigrees, and the papers, that have to be reckoned with in trying to arrive at a picture of the true situation. Behind the conflicting figures lie conflicting traditions of the death toll.

The earliest published source I have found that gives the 639 figure as an unequivocal fact is Samuel Eliot Morison's *The Invasion of France and Germany, 1944–1945*, an official American navy history that came out in 1957.[12] Morison's sources were the after-action reports of Harry Mettler (skipper of *LST 289*), Douglas Harlander and James Murdoch (senior surviving officers of the *531* and the *507* respectively), reports that were gathered by Bernard Skahill and, with his own report, presented by him to Rear Admiral Moon, whence they landed on the desks of admirals Kirk, Stark, and, eventually, King. The after-action reports were drawn up on May 2, four days after the disaster.

The naval after-action figures for navy and army deaths drawn up just after the disaster approximate, therefore, the calculations of Dale Rodman and others carried out using detailed, if disparate, lists more than forty years later. That the 639 figure is a navy one is a point made by historian Gordon Harrison in a footnote to his *Cross-Channel Attack*, published in 1951. In the same footnote, however, he reported that "Jones, historian for engineer units that were chiefly involved in the disaster, gives 749 killed."

What Harrison says next about Jones should be quoted separately. It is that he "bases his calculations on after-action reports of the units and detailed casualty breakdowns. Even so, he feels his figures may be incomplete."[13] The point is that whereas Morison based his figure on *navy* after-action reports, Jones, according to Harrison, based his figure on *army* ones.

In his main text, Harrison fudges the issue (and who can blame him?) with "about 700 men lost their lives." This is perhaps the point at which to mention that the commander of Seventh Corps, General Collins, stated in his autobiography that the E-boat attack cost "over 700 lives,"[14] a figure from an army man that matches Jones's army-based figure of 749. But, of course, the overall commander of Collins's army, General Bradley, evidently thought, or was left with the impression, that the whole "major tragedy" was only "a minor brush with the enemy."

The army's after-action reports and detailed casualty breakdowns were possibly lost in the 1972 St. Louis fire. Certainly no one has ever reported seeing any such detailed material, after many attempts to unearth it. It is even open to question (we have only Morison's authority for it) whether detailed primary army material was consulted by the source whom Harrison cites, Clifford Jones, author of a wartime study called *Neptune: Training, Mounting, The Artificial Ports.* It is necessary to take a close look at this source.

Jones was one of the "rolling" historians of the war whose job it was to gather raw material for later, more leisurely, official histories. He wrote *Neptune* at some time after D Day, and his pages on Exercise Tiger are the first known to have been written by someone who was not in some way involved. They are, therefore, particularly important, although not thereby especially authoritative, and it is important to gauge how much credence should be attached to them.

Jones begins with a brief account of the E-boat attack and its immediate aftermath, and follows with a brief survey of the casualties sustained. In his text he refers three times to the use of army records. It is not clear what the records he studied were, nor how detailed they were. One of them, for internal evidence, was a memorandum of May 10, 1944.

Jones, then, had access to army records that were subsequently misplaced, lost, or burned—no one would appear to have retrieved them from an archive since. He stresses that his is an entirely army-based account, and that "the final account of this incident must take into account naval records not available in the European Theater."

He meant not available to him at the time of writing. Ironically, it is the army records that he saw, not the navy records that were inaccessible to him at the time, that historians now need in order to produce "the final account." But the army and navy records cannot be so starkly separated. The navy figures, as has been noted, include army casualties, and the army figures include navy casualties; both sets of figures are, as it were, amphibious, as Tiger was. Jones gives his figures in terms of ships: "Most of the casualties were from *LST 531.* There were only 290 survivors of 744 soldiers and 282 sailors. Aboard *LST 507* there were 13 dead."[15]

Add up those figures and the death toll is 749. But Jones has confused *LST 289*—which had 13 dead, all sailors—with *LST 507*—which had many more dead. Perhaps the confusion arose from a mix-up over the army serial numbers of the ships. More than forty years later Dale Rodman and I would experience a similar mix-up.

Does Jones's confusion over ships, then, invalidate the calculation that he gives? Not necessarily, because exactly the same calculation exists in an earlier text. From this text, which gives the *right* ships, it is clear that while Jones confused the identities of ships, he did not confuse the numbers of survivors, soldiers, and sailors, which are the same in his text as in the earlier one.

On April 30, two days after the disaster, Rear Admiral Moon sent a message whose recipients included Kirk, Ramsay, Collins, and Bradley (the message makes it difficult to understand Bradley's assertion that he only learned of ''this major tragedy of the European war'' four years after the war had ended). Moon's message said: ''regret to report LSTs *507, 531* loaded with estimated 744 army and 282* navy personnel sunk by torpedoes.'' The message gave losses aboard *LST* 289 as thirteen. Its figure for ''total known'' survivors—''ambulatory survivors, 257; litter cases, 33''—adds up to Jones's 290.[16]

Rear Admiral Moon, then, was working on April 30, 1944, with figures that were later consulted by Clifford Jones. He was, in turn, consulted by Gordon Harrison, whence, by a variety of routine republications, the 749 figure gained general acceptance, to the point where it is to be found cast in bronze on Slapton Sands.

On April 30 the documentation for the navy's assessment of an overall death toll of 639 had not yet reached report form. The senior officers or surviving officers would present their papers two days later, on May 2. It was on April 30 that Douglas Harlander of the *LST 531* recalls encountering Rear Admiral Moon in Plymouth. It was then, apparently, that Moon asked him to do his ship's after-action report, after which he ''expressed hope that there would be more survivors than accounted for.''[17]

When Moon sent his message he didn't yet have the slight measure of solace that the navy after-action reports would indeed give. For numbers of army men aboard the ships, he was apparently relying on army records, which Jones also later saw. It might be noted that Jones's text lets the figures stand without qualification, although one would judge that they were, as Moon's message states, ''estimated.'' On the other hand, Jones states that the records he consulted were ''possibly not complete,'' which, if anything, suggests that a revised estimate of the death toll should tend upward from 749.

The two conflicting ''traditions'' of death tolls clearly derive from differing army and navy assessments of army dead. But why—and especially in view of the inadequate rosters and manifests—should one trust the navy's assessment of army dead more than the army's own, if earlier, assessment? We have the navy's assessment of the navy's death toll, and can be satisfied with it. But for the identifiable army death toll we have only the list of the First Engineers. It falls well short

---

* 307 according to the navy's after-action reports; the difference of twenty-five is accounted for by the twenty-five medical corpsmen—Arthur Victor *et al*—aboard *LST 507*.

of the overall army assessment, or estimate, and slightly short, even, of the navy's assessment.

The picture is so blurred that former Pentagon historian Charles MacDonald, in a press conference on the eve of the dedication of the 1987 Slapton Sands memorial, suggested that the way to add up the overall toll was to add the army figure of 749 to the known navy dead of 198 to make a total of 947. Later persuaded that the army figure included navy losses, he revised his assessment to 749.[18]

That is still the higher "traditional" figure, however, and to attach credence to it is still to believe in the authority of army records that no one now living appears to have seen. What if those authoritative-sounding "army records" were, in fact, hurried estimates rushed out between April 28 and April 30, as unreliable as such estimates in the immediate wake of a disaster often are?

The second week of May 1944 was not the immediate wake, however. The evidence is strong that the responsible U.S. authorities had by then compiled complete lists of the dead and missing, army and navy, of Convoy T-4.

Harry Butcher, Eisenhower's naval aide, was in a position to know what the picture was at that period, and in his diary entry for May 9, calling the disaster "an unfortunate mix-up of signals and a sad fate for many fine lads," he wrote that "casualties were much higher than first stated; between 750 and 800."[19]

It was on the following day that the telegrams of death, army and navy, started to go out across the United States. May 10 was also the date of a memorandum that appears to have been one of Clifford Jones's sources. By this stage, however unclear the overall death toll may be now, it must have been clear to the U.S. authorities.

By August 1944 it was, or should have been, still clearer. On August 7 the Associated Press issued an agency report from SHAEF that 442 soldiers had died in the disaster—312 MIA and 130 KIA. It was shortly after this—around August 10—that the second wave of telegrams went out, stating that those previously classified MIA were now deemed to have been killed in action.

Over the months since April 28 the military bureaucracy had apparently been ticking away and had come up with a figure of 442 soldiers, one more than the navy's assessment of May 2, only four days after the disaster. And that one extra can be accounted for by Donald Bryant, who died on April 27. His inclusion in the reckoning is a clue to suggest that by August the authorities were working from army figures, including the list, on which Bryant also appears, compiled by the First Engineers. But no researcher has come up with a document giving an overall army rationale, complete with names and units, for that figure of 442. That would be left to Dale Rodman and others to attempt many years later.

Now we tread on dangerous ground. If that figure of 442 released in August was comprehensive and correct, as it should have been, then there is no puzzle about the death toll of Convoy T-4: it was 639. Although there is evidence that a figure of around 749 was in circulation in the second week of May 1944, it must, on the above assumption, be discounted.

On the same assumption, one has to marvel at the efficiency and pinpoint accuracy of the navy assessment of army losses, made so soon after the event and made apparently without reference to ships' manifests. Not only was it more accurate than the army's own earlier assessment of its own losses, it was, because of the inclusion of Donald Bryant, more accurate than the army's later assessment, too.

One has to conclude also that Eisenhower's naval aide, Harry Butcher, was evidently not as well informed as one might reasonably have supposed that he was, and that Clifford Jones, as an army historian, was not all that he might have been. Finally, the compilers of the army's ''morning reports'' from April 29 to 30, or the people who added up their figures, were, evidently, singularly inefficient.

Alternatively, considering all the above, the army losses on Convoy T-4 were greater than 442, and in releasing that figure in August SHAEF was, for reasons of its own, consciously massaging the statistics in order to bring them into line with the navy figures and to make the army losses appear less than they really were. That is an extraordinary suggestion. Unless it can be substantiated, the evidence, despite its puzzling nature and the gaps in it, is that the definitive death toll of Convoy T-4 was 639 and that the ''tradition'' of 749 leading from Rear Admiral Moon's message of April 30, 1944, through Jones, Harrison, and Ruppenthal* to the Slapton Sands memorial, is a false one and must be discounted.

Still, however, as we shall see, the uneasy sense persists that *there are more men than can actually be counted*. If this is not a delusion, then there had to have been more army men on the ships than are given in the navy's after-action reports of May 2. If the navy figures are correct, so is the 639 death toll. But if there were more men aboard, more men died. If there were many more men, there were many more deaths.

How were the figures prepared for each of the different ships that

---

* ''Army records list 749 fatalities and more than 300 injured.''[20]

came under attack? *LST 289* can be eliminated from the reckoning. Although army men were wounded, no army man was killed. So can *LST 511*: Men were wounded, but no one was killed.

For *LST 531*, Douglas Harlander received his figures from the convoy's commander, Bernard Skahill.[21] They gave a total of 354 soldiers aboard; with 44 army survivors, the army death toll on *LST 531* was therefore 310. The bulk of that figure is accounted for by the dead of the 3206th Quartermaster Service Company (195 men).

Adding, from the First Engineer list, the dead of other units known to have been aboard *LST 531*, the figure swells to 291. Turning to the Cambridge cemetery list, and adding the 19 men of the Thirty-fifth Signal Construction Battalion, the grand total is 310. Forty-five years later, those extra 19 men slot into the statistics as neatly as the final piece in a jigsaw puzzle.

An LST can carry only so many vehicles and men, and that limit sets a limit on fantasy too. Aboard *LST 531* that night there were a reported 496 men, including 142 sailors. That is a respectable complement and, taking the navy's detailed calculation of its own losses together with the calculation above, every one of them can be accounted for. The evidence is that the figures that Bernard Skahill gave Douglas Harlander were perfectly correct. There is not a shred of evidence that *LST 531* had statistical stowaways aboard.

If there are to be extra army men in the reckoning, then they must have been on *LST 507*, *and there can have been only so many of them.* What is the evidence that there were any at all?

In the *507*'s after-action report there is an element of admitted doubt as to how many army men were aboard. James Murdoch, the ship's executive officer and the report's compiler, based his figure of 282 on what he was told by Captain Ray Seibert, the senior army officer aboard the *507*. But a check of the "water-soaked and much pen-deleted army roster" that he himself carried overboard gave a figure of 294 Army personnel. Captain Seibert died in the water and James Murdoch died after the war, so they cannot be asked about these figures, although Murdoch, at the time, thought Seibert's figure of 282 to be "the correct one." And Tom Clark, who knew James Murdoch and shared a raft with him, found him to be a "dedicated officer" who "paid attention to detail."[22]

The difference between Seibert's figure and the figure given in the "pen-deleted roster" is too small to be significant to this argument. Other evidence, however, bafflingly suggests a much greater number of soldiers aboard *LST 507* that night.

An anomaly that has haunted Dale Rodman, himself a former army man, is his distinct recollection of up to 600 soldiers aboard. ''It has always puzzled me,'' he writes, ''how Lieutenant Murdoch placed the number of army personnel aboard . . . at only 282. An LST has troop quarters for about 300. These sleeping areas were full, and men were sleeping on deck, in vehicles and on the tank deck.''[23] Medical corpsman Arthur Victor, who was also on the *507*, recalls that it was ''packed,'' and gives a figure of ''about 500 soldiers.''[24]

Neither Rodman nor Victor conducted a formal count, however. Perhaps it only *felt* to them, especially after the years that had passed, as if there were hundreds more soldiers aboard. More substantially, however, both men remember that there were, as well as engineers, infantrymen aboard.

Dale Rodman recalled that ''about one-half'' of the soldiers were infantrymen, and, himself an engineer, he was well placed to draw the distinction. It was clear enough. The engineers wore pocket patches and their trouser legs were tucked into their paratroopers' boots. The men of the Fourth Infantry Division wore green ivy-leaf shoulder insignia. The engineers carried M1 carbines, while the infantrymen had larger, and larger caliber, M1 rifles. Dale Rodman is positive that the soldier who at his suggestion fired a shot to set an LCVP free was an infantryman and used an M1 rifle to do so.

Arthur Victor, too, specified that the soldiers aboard *LST 507* were ''infantrymen and combat engineers.'' On *LST 496* Manny Rubin recalled seeing soldiers with the ivy-leaf shoulder insignia—he thought that most of the army men on his ship were infantry. Eugene Carney, an infantryman of the Fourth Division, was aboard *LST 515*. Joseph McCann of the same ship is certain that soldiers of the Fourth Infantry Division were among the men he picked out of the water.[25] Finally, there is the typewritten evidence of Clifford Jones and his ''army records'' for the presence of the Fourth Infantry aboard Convoy T-4. Its ships, he wrote, ''were loaded with troops of the 1st Engr Sp Brig., the 4th Div, and VII Corps.''

Things get murkier still when we consider that there is evidence from James Murdoch himself that throws the figure of 282, vouched for by him, into doubt. On August 16, 1944, he was interviewed at the Pentagon about the sinking of *LST 507*. From questions asked in the interview, it emerges that the U.S. authorities, even after the Associated Press release of August 6, were apparently still uncertain as to who exactly had been aboard the ship.

''Those army troops you had aboard,'' the interviewer asked

Murdoch, "were they a hospital unit?" Murdoch replied, "No, sir, the army personnel aboard were men of the 4th Army assault troops."[26]

Murdoch presumably meant soldiers of the Fourth Infantry Division, but what matters is that he specified, in answer to that highly specific question, not engineers but "assault troops." That implicitly contradicts his after-action report of early May, because the figure of 282 (which he repeated in his Pentagon interview) could only have covered engineers. The implication of his statement of August 16 is that many, if not most, of the troops aboard were, on the contrary, infantrymen. With Tom Clark, one begins to wonder, "Could there have been two lists? Engineers *and* infantry."[27]

According to the after-action reports, the *507* was carrying 72 fewer soldiers than the *531*. Perhaps more significantly, the ship had fewer soldiers aboard for Exercise Tiger than she had been scheduled to have.

An army loading list—what the soldiers called a ship sheet—has survived for *LST 507* for Exercise Tiger. Dated April 18, 1944, it shows that 352 soldiers were originally allotted to the ship, only two fewer than the army complement that traveled aboard *LST 531*.[28] It is possible, of course, that the number of soldiers to travel on *LST 507* was revised downward before she sailed. Other evidence, however, suggests that if there was any revision, it was more likely to have been upward rather than down, because as well as ghostly soldiers who are apparently present but who cannot be counted, his tangled story involves a ghostly ship.

I had been puzzled even before learning of this ship by a reference in the Royal Navy's file on the Tiger disaster to the corvette *Azalea* "steaming with nine ships in line ahead."[29] Not nine ships *including* the corvette, but nine ships *with* her. But there were only eight LSTs on Convoy T-4.

On April 15, eleven days before troops were due to be loaded aboard T-4, the *LST 508* was sailing in heavy fog from Southampton to Plymouth. In a collision with a British freighter, her port side anchor was ripped off and her bow doors were damaged, making her temporarily inoperable as a landing ship. In Plymouth she was put into dry dock and, the story still goes among her surviving former crew members, "Lady Luck was with us, because a few days later we found out that *LST 507* replaced us."[30]

Documents of the time tell a slightly different story. A list drawn up on April 18 shows that a total of thirty LSTs were to take part in Exercise Tiger. In a message of May 1 Rear Admiral Moon said that over the night of April 27–8, while Convoy T-4 was still at sea, there were twenty-one LSTs under the protection of his Force U in Lyme Bay. Twenty-one from thirty is nine, the nine LSTs, the last on the list of April 18, which were to have made up T-4, the last LST convoy of Exercise Tiger. Conclusively, a landing table of April 14 shows that *LST 508* had been scheduled to load up with men and vehicles on the third tide, with LSTs *507, 289,* and *499.* It was on the following day that *LST 508* collided with the British freighter.[31]

No sooner is the ghost ship identified, however, than another specter presents itself. According to *LST 508*'s ship sheet, 345 soldiers were to have made the amphibious journey to Slapton Sands aboard her. How, without the *508,* would they participate in Exercise Tiger?

The obvious answer is the one that must have seemed obvious at the time. On an LST, space for vehicles was strictly limited—a tank deck, for example, would take only twenty-two Dukws—but room could be made for men aboard other LSTs. According to Bernard Skahill's communications officer, Moses Hallett, Exercise Tiger was ''short two or three LSTs'' and ''doubling up of troops on LSTs occurred.''[32]

One of those missing LSTs was the *508,* although it would appear that it was only at a very late hour that the exercise's planners realized that it was unavailable in dry dock. The *508*'s ship sheet for Tiger is dated April 24, the eve of the exercise, by which time the *508* had been out of action for nine days. And according to the ship sheet, forty of the soldiers who were to have traveled aboard her were from the Fourth Quartermaster Company, while the remainder—305 men—were from the Eighth and Twenty-second Regiments of the Fourth Infantry Division.

It is clear, then, that up until almost the last minute the people responsible for ''marrying'' soldiers and ships were either unaware that the *508* was unavailable or were still counting on her to make it. Was the resulting surfeit of men of the Fourth Infantry Division dealt with by informally reallocating them, or some of them, to the *LST 507*?

The informality of such a last minute reallocation would explain the absence of these men from the navy's later, formal reckoning of how many soldiers there were. It would explain why the U.S. Department of Defense considers the personnel rosters and ships' manifests to have been ''inadequate.'' It would explain the perceived presence of infantrymen aboard *LST 507,* and the question that Murdoch was asked in the Pentagon. Finally, it would explain the continuing confusion over the death toll.

If there were infantrymen aboard *LST 507,* then infantrymen died.

Equally, however, infantrymen would surely have survived. Why did no infantryman come forward during the media blitzes of 1984 and 1987? Why has none come forward since? Why have no papers been unearthed from archives, or memories from minds, to establish definitively that there were indeed other men aboard *LST 507* that night, some of whom did indeed die?

Or did they all die, in Tiger, in the invasion of Europe, or over the forty and more years that have passed since the war? One ends where one began: with questions, doubts, and a possible mystery.

In July 1988 Dale Rodman wrote:

> It is obvious to me that high command of the army and navy were not aware of any change [in the LST loading plans]. Since they were not aware of the presence of the infantry aboard *LST 507*, necessary documents were not requested or received at SHAEF Headquarters. The handling of the dead, wounded, and survivors was by the 4th Infantry Division Headquarters without ever reaching high command. The recovered dead were buried, according to accepted procedure, in the area, and families were notified. Until proven otherwise I will believe the recovered dead from the infantry are still where they were buried 44 years ago.

In July 1988 Howard DeVoe wrote that he stood "100 percent" by the death toll of 639,

> since there is no proof of the 749 figure, and since there are no records indicating any deaths or losses for the 4th Division units. In the U.S. services they never fail to list men, whether dead, missing, wounded, captured, or what. You can be sure men will have their names on a list somewhere. This is why I am certain none of the 4th Division units had any losses.

On the face of it the two positions outlined above are irreconcilable. There is, however, an unexpected explanation that finds common ground between them.

CHAPTER

18

In 1957 former Royal Navy sailor Julian Perkin became manager of Stokeley Barton, a farm whose fields ran down to the edge of Slapton Ley, the lake just to the back of Slapton Sands. *Barton* is Old English for the threshing floor of a farmyard. But the Oxford dictionary defines it also as "a demesne farm," and nowadays it tends to mean simply a farm of more than 500 acres or the largest farm in a given parish. Stokeley Barton was the largest farm in the parish of Stokenham, one of the villages that had been evacuated in 1943 to make way for "The American Battle School." In 1957 its fields were still pitted with shell craters and littered with shrapnel. They were fields of Mars. Thirteen years had passed, but the farmland still testified to the war rehearsals of the Americans. Julian Perkin was daily reminded not only of the role this area had played during the war, but of the role that *he* had played.

"In all my daily tasks," he said, "the husbandry of animals, etc., I would walk past the American memorial to the evacuation. Arriving at a particular place, one would think back. . . ."[1]

In April 1944 Julian Perkin had been a commission warrant candidate on the Royal Navy destroyer HMS *Obedient*. One of the ships that went belatedly to the rescue of Convoy T-4, *Obedient* had participated the day before, April 27, in the softening-up naval bombardment just prior to Tiger's "D Day" landing. From two miles out to sea, the destroyer on which he served had shelled the farmland that he now managed. This or that crater could have been caused by a shell from the four-inch gun that he had manned.

In the four years that he would spend at Stokeley Barton, he would impart this fact to no one, and not because he felt bound by wartime secrecy. There were local and diplomatic reasons for discretion. There was still bitterness. Memories of the evacuation and the damage that "The American Battle School" had caused were still fairly fresh. So when local people told their tales of the evacuation area, Julian Perkin kept his peace. He didn't want it to get around that a fraction at least of the damage could be laid at the door of the manager of Stokeley Barton.

Tales of Americans who had been killed, their bodies hastily buried in local fields, were among those he heard. The stories were current well before Dorothy Seekings chose to break her silence in 1984. By then they had been legion in the South Hams for forty years. On July 14, 1944, the evacuees had not even returned to their homes when the Reverend H. Stone told a meeting of the Kingsbridge Rural District Council, "I have heard from several people that the Americans buried their dead in a field at Slapton." Lieutenant Colonel F. A. Ibert replied that an American officer had informed him that "such a statement as that was definitely false."[2]

But the denial had not stamped out the stories. Nor have official American denials since 1984 stamped them out. They are still current, and in the South Hams one will find few people, of whatever degree of sophistication, who do not attach credence to them.

If the bodies of American soldiers really had been interred in the South Hams evacuation area, where had they come from? It has already been noted that the attack on Convoy T-4 occurred off the coast of Dorset rather than Devon. From the point of attack, Slapton Sands was more than thirty miles away across Lyme Bay, a steaming time, at the convoy's five knots per hour, of about six hours.

A ship, however, moves under its own power: a dead body in the sea is at the mercy of the tides. LSTs *507* and *531* were sunk in some of the most complex tidal water in Europe, so complex that the sea around Portland Bill is the smallest area of British coastal waters to merit a chart to itself in the Admiralty series covering the coast.[3] Whether the tide is incoming or outgoing, the tidal patterns of these waters are distorted by the massive press of water draining into the main body of the Channel from either side of Portland Bill. A further complicating factor is the Portland Ledge, an underwater shelf off the tip of the Bill that creates a tremendous tide race, to west or east depending on the tide's direction.

The configuration of these waters, according to Dorset sailor John Hockaday, is such that "for anyone to suggest that bodies could go to Slapton from Portland waters, even in days, shows no knowledge of the sea or the local tides and currents." Hockaday calls the tide races "great circling eddies, opposing each tide flow. You go in one. You go around and just drifting you reach a point where the flow changes, and you start all over again."[4]

On the morning of April 28, 1944, the tide was running not westward, toward Start Point and Slapton Sands, but eastward across "Dead Man's Bay" toward Chesil Beach, Portland Bill, and around Portland Bill further east toward St. Alban's Head. The tide was building toward the spring tides of May 1–3 when the tidal variation between maximum high and minimum low is at its most extreme. Then the tide rip would have been at its most powerful and the bodies might have gone anywhere. Until then, the indications are that if bodies washed up anywhere, it was on beaches to the east, away from Slapton Sands.[5]

Were the bodies of the dead, then, gathered together and moved overland to the South Hams evacuation area? Common sense echoes John Hockaday's objection: "Why send the dead many miles over narrow country roads, crowded with convoys, etc., all the way to Slapton. . . . ?"

Why indeed? In fact, we can reconstruct from documents what actually did happen. A message of April 29 from Southern Base Section stated "248 dead sent to Brookwood." This was Brookwood Cemetery in Surrey. In the words of "Passing in Review," a history of the American Graves Registration Command, Brookwood "took care of everything [i.e., all American forces' deaths] south of London"; Cambridge "took care" of the north.

"Passing in Review,"giving a figure of "some 260 casualties," goes into more detail:

> Colonel Hutchins, the Q.M. of Southern Base Section, was prepared to bury these in the standby plot which had been reserved near Portsmouth but on orders of Major Whitney, Captain Barfield proceeded to the Southern Base and moved all of these casualties to Brookwood Cemetery. Colonel Horner of a nearby depot provided the necessary labor and transportation.[6]

That is clear enough. The recovered dead of Convoy T-4 were moved, not westward to Slapton and the evacuation area, but eastward, to Brookwood. From there, when the war was over, they were repatriated to the United States or, when Brookwood ceased to be an American war cemetery in 1956, they were disinterred (the bodies had been embalmed) and moved north, to Cambridge, where some of them lie today.

The Associated Press report of August 7, 1944, defined the army missing as those whose bodies were not recovered. If this was true of the navy as well, then the majority of the missing—almost 400 men, according to the 639 death toll—apparently went down with LSTs *507* and *531*, and lie today at the bottom of "Dead Man's Bay."

If one adds together the 130 reported army dead (as distinct from missing) and the 118 navy, one has a total of 248, precisely the number of men whom the message of April 29 gives as having been "sent to Brookwood."

Still greater precision is possible. The list of men of the First Engineer Special Brigade who died on T-4 runs to eight pages. After the war a page-by-page breakdown was prepared of the dead and the whereabouts of their bodies. It shows that only 153 bodies of brigade members were recovered. Eighty-seven of them were repatriated to the United States; sixty-five are buried in Cambridge cemetery. Total so far: 152. The last one, Robert Motley of the 557 Railhead Company, is buried in Normandy. It is not known how Robert Motley—killed twelve miles off the Dorset coast and six weeks before the Normandy invasion—comes to lie now in Normandy.[7]

The breakdown of navy deaths indicates that 117 bodies were recovered. Add that to the figure for the First Engineers and the figure is 270. The mathematics suggest therefore that a further 22 bodies were reclaimed from the sea after April 29 and the body count figure of "248 dead."

According to available records, then, there were some 270 dead men floating in the sea off Dorset in the dawn of April 28, 1944. However many hundreds of bodies those who saw them thought they saw, or later thought that they had seen, there were about 270 of them.

Nor, whatever the local stories suggest, is it likely that any of them were buried hastily in a mass grave, or graves, in the South Hams. The 248/270 figure tends to confirm the overall 639 death toll. It would be invidious to invoke those phantom infantrymen about whose presence on Convoy T-4 we speculated in the last chapter simply in order that they should act as reinforcements for the bodies in the water and authenticate what may or may not be a fantasy of those bodies hurriedly buried in a mass grave forgotten since the war.

Central to this confusion is the identification of the bodies in the water with the idea of the bodies in the fields. In 1984, for example, the *New York Times* said that the bodies in the water "were surely the bodies Mrs. Seekings, then 23, remembers seeing."[8] Reprinted in the *International Herald Tribune,* that identification has since been more or less automatically accepted by those who have looked into or at the matter, whether or not they have been believers in the "bodies in the fields" stories. It is partly on the basis of this identification, for example, that Stella Rouggley, for one, believes or believed her brother to have been buried in the South Hams.

But we *know* what the U.S. authorities did. The thirteen navy dead of *LST 289* provide the smallest sample for closer analysis. The remains of James Chandler, as noted earlier, were not recovered. Four of the remaining twelve are buried at Cambridge. The remaining eight were repatriated to the United States, where they were reburied in cemeteries in Illinois, Missouri, Virginia, Connecticut, North Carolina, and Wisconsin.

There is no reason to believe that there would be a different result if one went to the office of the army's memorial affairs division in Washington and inquired one by one after all the named and reported dead of LSTs *507* and *531*. Certainly the authorities were behaving most eccentrically if they suddenly decided, if and when more bodies were reclaimed from the sea, to break with the precedent they had already set and to move them sixty miles westward for burial in a mass, unmarked grave.

Why should they have done so? To believe that they did or might have done so requires one to believe beforehand that there *were* other men aboard Convoy T-4, a number of whom died, and that for some reason, even though other deaths hadn't been concealed, it was decided to conceal *theirs,* or at any rate their bodily remains; therefore their bodies were separated from the rest, buried separately and forgotten. There is no firm ground for any of these beliefs. To try to hold to them all would strain the credulity of the most determined conspiracy theorist.

What then of the stories of ``bodies in fields''?

One freezing day in February I visited Dorothy Seekings at her house, once her father's bakery, in Stoke Fleming opposite the church and the churchyard. In her entrance hall were some cages containing birds: a cockatoo, a green parrot, a dove that had belonged to her daughter. She had told me she would say nothing; she was saving what she knew for a book she would be writing with someone from the United States. But she showed me into her living room and took out the old photograph album she used as her file. It held news clippings, letters from the U.S. battle monuments commission and the department of the army, and a few photographs, among them one of ``Eddy,'' the American army man who, she said, had given her the lift that spring day in 1944.

After her disclosure of 1984, she said, an American had come from the United States especially to see her, a tall, white-haired ``policeman sort of man" called (she thought) Arthur White. He had seen her on ABC television's *20/20* special. In the war he had been an officer stationed at Wadstay House, near Blackawton. He had asked her: "What sort of doughnuts did your father make?"

"Round ones with jam in the middle."

"Not one with holes?"

"No."

"You're right, Mrs. Seekings. And were there any black men among the bodies? Any injuries?"

"No."

"You're right. I wanted to look you in the eyes. Every word you're saying is true."

Hearing of "Mr. White," I thought of the "dark ones," the black soldiers who, Dorothy Seekings had said, had dug the mass grave. Here, apparently, was someone who could corroborate her story. But Mrs. Seekings was well named; she set one seeking. She could not, or would not, give me an address or telephone number whereby I might contact her mysterious visitor. She wasn't even too sure what he was called.

Who else then? She told me about Fred, and Cyril, and Sandy, all regulars at the London Inn in Stoke Fleming. Oh, and there was Wally, a retired Royal Navy man living in Dartmouth. I had seen his name on a wreath at the Torcross memorial, "from Wally," the British Legion poppies washed pale by three months of rain.

A man had seen her on television in Australia. (The likeness of Dorothy Seekings had appeared on TV screens and in newspapers all over the world. "My name's gone everywhere," she told me.) He had, she said, contacted her and confirmed her story. When the bodies had been unloaded from "her" truck, which Eddy was driving, he had been on the road behind her, in another truck belonging to the Royal Navy College in Dartmouth; he, too, had seen the bodies unloaded.

Later I found out who this man was: John Bowden, born and bred in the South Hams but later resident in Bombala, New South Wales. His sister-in-law, Nancy Bowden, of Torquay, told me that he knew about the "bodies business" but "didn't like to talk about it." And sure enough, when I wrote to him, I received no reply.[9]

Mr. Bowden would in his way prove as elusive as the mysterious Mr. White, about whose tenuous existence as a witness Mrs. Seekings appeared quite unconcerned. With me, she stuck to her story as firmly as she had with everyone since 1984. Pointing out of her window she said, ''The bodies washed up on Blackpool Sands. I saw them. The sea was black with bodies.''[10]

It was getting late. Sooner than go down to the London Inn and accost strangers with my grisly questions, I thought I would go inland, to Blackawton. There I booked a room at the Normandy Arms, a fifteenth-century inn that had been renamed by a landlord whose son had died in the invasion of France. There were bars called The Dug-Out and The Beaches Bar. Paintings of Eisenhower, Admiral Andrew Cunningham, Montgomery, Bradley, and de Gaulle hung on the walls alongside helmets and gas masks and a copy of the poster proclaiming the evacuation of Blackawton and the other South Hams villages.

The next morning I walked down the road to Blackawton church. In late 1944 it had been littered with broken bottles and stained glass, the remains of what appeared to be a large and rowdy party. Now all was in order. I saw the chancel screen with its faded paintings of pomegranates, Catharine of Aragon's emblem, and the Norman font with its ''honeysuckle cable adornment.''

Farther down the road in Blackawton I knocked at the door of Kathleen Langford, whose name Dorothy Seekings had given me as that of someone who could confirm her story. As it turned out, she could do nothing of the sort, although she did say that Mrs. Seekings ''wouldn't deliberately lie. That I do know.'' Otherwise there was nothing about the story that she definitely ''knew.'' In 1944, aged thirteen, she had lived in Dartmouth. She remembered that she had been forbidden by the authorities to ride her bicycle any farther than the Sportsman's Arms public house, at the edge of the evacuation area and slightly short of the field where Dorothy Seekings had seen the bodies buried.

For herself, she had seen nothing. Her ''knowledge'' of the field was not only postwar, but post-1948. She had known Dorothy Seekings since the 1950s, but the first time she had heard her story had been when Mrs. Seekings went public with it that year. On the one hand Mrs. Langford was impressed by the story. On the other, she doubted it and found it morbid. ''That field,'' she told me, ''always gave me the willies. There's something there, something evil, like floating spirits. If only the field was blessed, that was all. Just a sprinkling and say a small prayer. If it was blessed, it would stop. I wouldn't want them dug up, as Dorothy does. I don't think that's a Christian attitude. I think it's sick. They don't like her talking about it in the pub. It puts people off. Not everyone likes talking about death.''

She found both Blackawton and Stokenham "weird." In Stokenham, she said, lived "Reefer," a regular of the Church House Inn, who had told a story of digging up bones. But for all her sense of the local "weirdness," she recognized that there was no concrete proof of a cause for disquiet dating from 1944:

> I've asked people who've ploughed that field if they've found anything, and they haven't. That field's been ploughed and ploughed. They'd have found something. And why didn't Dorothy mention her story before? I think it's when they brought that tank up. That bloody black tank. It looks more German than American. I'd rather have swans about. It's a nature environment, isn't it?[11]

My next stop was Stone Farm, in one of whose fields, according to Dorothy Seekings, the American soldiers had been buried. The field was across the road from Wadstay House, where "Mr. White" had been based. Behind the field the track to Stone Farm overlooked a steep, wild valley. By now a sleet storm had blown up, and in the high wind the sleet lashed my face as I undid the hurdle gate to the farmyard. I looked into the valley. It was a plausible backdrop for a mass grave, although I knew that the farmer, Nolan Tope, poured scorn on the idea that there was any such horror on his land.

He was not in when I called. Doubtless, though, he would have told me what he had told others: that he had no time for ghouls who came to his land looking for nonexistent graves, and would see the trespassers off; that in 1944 his elder brother had walked to work every morning along the field's edge, and had seen nothing; that, some years before, the local authority had dug a trench across the field, for a drain or mains and nothing had been unearthed.[12]

South Hams councillor Percy Moysey had advised me to visit another local farmer called Mr. Buckpitt, a surname that I had seen on an old gravestone in Blackawton churchyard. "He knows a lot about the bodies question," Mr. Moysey had told me, "genuine stuff." By the time I arrived at his farmhouse the sleet had abated. A few damp flakes floated down to land among the crocuses in the grass verges.

It was as if Mr. Buckpitt had known I was coming. He came out of his house and stood there, truculently, in slippers and green overalls, a couple of Border terriers at his heels. It was clear that I wasn't going to be invited in. Mr. Buckpitt had had about enough of people with notebooks and television cameras.

"It's all rubbish," he almost shouted at me, "I'm fed up with it! There are no bodies there. People make up these stories for money. I was farming those fields in 1944. There were British military police around here, and I can tell you that there were no bodies. But the media don't print what I say. They interview me, but they don't show the interviews. No, you don't get round me. I won't say anything. It's all people making money. Why should you be any different? *These men died for our freedom.*''[13]

From Blackawton and its surrounding farmland I returned to the coast. In the village of Strete I knocked on the door of Manor Farm. Mrs. Ethel Pratt came to the door and told me her husband, Edward, was out. She let me into her kitchen. Manor Farm, she said, was ''very, very old.'' She and her husband had taken over its tenancy in December 1944, ''when the Americans moved out.'' That winter ''it snowed and snowed. The place was filthy. There was no electricity and it was freezing cold. This room was part of the woodhouse-cum-workshop. Down there was a butcher's-cum-dairy. We've converted it into our lounge. Next door was the granary. We've turned it into part of the house.'' That winter, she said, gypsies would come to their door trying to sell them linoleum. ''We've lived here in Strete ever since.''

I told Mrs. Pratt I had come to ask her husband about the field where he had said the Americans were buried. She looked at me. ''I see. Did someone tell you about that?''

Little by little, asking my questions, the name of Edward Pratt had filtered into the story. Ken Small had told me that he had promised not to tell who had taken him to the field where underground bunkers had been blown up to make a tomb for the Americans. Anyway, he had added, the man was not well and did not want to be disturbed by questioners. Then I had learned that Edward Pratt suffered from arthritis of the hip. It was on the basis of that clue that I had made my remark to Mrs. Pratt. She said, ''Well, that you must find out from him. Whether there are bodies buried there.'' She told me I could find her husband up the road in the Dutch barn where they kept their hens.

The weather was changeable that day, alternating periods of sleet and sun. Now it was sleeting again. In a small anteroom inside the barn an electric heater took the edge off the cold. On a table, eggs were heaped in cardboard trays. Old farming implements hung from the ceiling—a rusty heart-shaped shovel, a tool that I imagined would be useful for cutting up turnips and mangles. Outside, the wind howled.

I called out Mr. Pratt's name. No answer. I looked through a second door into the main interior of the barn. In the half-light, hay was strewn everywhere. Hens were clucking behind a wooden partition at the far end of the barn. Edward Pratt limped out from behind the partition, supporting himself on a rubber-tipped walking stick. In his free hand he held a red plastic bucket full of eggs. He turned down my offer of help and limped to the outer anteroom.

He wore a waxed jacket and flat cap. His eyes twinkled shrewdly. He set down the bucket of eggs and leaned on the heater. I told him why I had come and, echoing Mr. Buckpitt, he said, "I won't do anything where someone's making money out of it." He added, though, that "when the time comes" he would "get on" to me.

At the mention of Mrs. Seekings he laughed quietly. The one thing she had "got right," he said, was the iron hurdle gate that newspaper pictures had shown "her" field as having. So Mr. Pratt's own, different field had a hurdle gate, too, and it was in "his" field, he was convinced, that the Americans had buried their dead.

"I know where they are," he said, "if they are still there, which I think they are. You're within half a mile of them now."

He emphasized this. *"You are. Half a mile, now!"*

He told me that the British "Air Ministry" also knew where the bodies were. This was a new one. I asked whether the underground bunkers in "his" field had been British-built. "The RAF was stationed at this place," he said. "They had to get out in a hurry. That's how I know. That's why I say Air Ministry."

But Edward Pratt and his wife had come to Manor Farm only in early 1945, after the Americans had gone. How could he know all this?

"Because," he said, "of a man called Denis Emus."

Denis Emus had had a meat-packing business with stalls at London's Smithfield Market. Back in the Fifties or Sixties Edward Pratt had sold lambs to him. During the war Denis Emus had been in the RAF, stationed in Devon.

Now I had a name and, possibly, corroboration. But for the moment Edward Pratt in his Dutch barn, the sleet storm raging outside, was oblique and oracular. Before the bodies of the Americans had been entombed, he said, "they were put into pits, shallow graves, then moved to a special place." How had he known about the pits? Because back in 1945 "in one instance there was a cross on top of one with a helmet with a bullet hole in it. In the field we found dog tags and life belts. We excavated some of the pits, but there was nothing."[14]

This was extraordinary, and against all known American practice. Was I to believe that the American authorities had discarded the dog tags of the men as if they were not men at all, but dogs indeed? And had Edward Pratt kept any of the dog tags? They alone would amount to sort of proof. No, he had not kept them.

Later, when I was back in London, I explored the avenue of inquiry that Edward Pratt had opened up for me. Denis Emus had given up his meat-packing business, but I was able to trace him through the records of Smithfield Market to his home in Beckenham, Kent. In April 1944 he had, as he remembered, been second in command of an air-sea rescue squadron based at Bolt Head, near Salcombe in South Devon.

''I have got a vague recollection,'' he said, ''which you have stirred for me, that the Americans did have some sort of disaster.'' But he knew no more than that:

> I haven't seen Eddy Pratt or heard of him since the Fifties or Sixties, and for him to say that I told him anything to do with bodies is not true. I think he's mixing up. He must be thinking of someone else. But what you're saying is news to me.[15]

His wartime commanding officer, Eric Seabourne, lived in Frogmore, a village near Kingsbridge. All he knew of the ''bodies in the fields'' story was what he had picked up from press reports since 1984.[16]

I contacted Edward Pratt again. Calmly, he told me that Denis Emus would not have known, and that he had not told me that Denis Emus had known. So, I said, Denis Emus said something to you that, added to what you already knew or guessed, completed the picture?

''Perfectly correct.''

''He didn't realize the implications of what he told you?''

''Correct.''

''But Denis Emus was based at Bolt Head, near Salcombe. That's a way away from here.''

''Ah yes, but he's forgotten where he was based next. There were two airstrips here, on my farm. There, that should tell you all you need to know. But you're not going to pump anything else out of me.''[17]

The next time I talked to Denis Emus he turned up his wartime log. He took me through it, date by date and posting by posting, and we found out that his memory had indeed played a trick on him. The reality did not support Edward Pratt's story, however. In April 1944 Denis Emus had not been at Bolt Head, but even further afield, either at Drem, near Edinburgh, or at Warmwell, near Dorchester. He hadn't flown from Bolt Head until September 1944. Bolt Head had been ''a bleak place, very much a couple of fields on top of a cliff. We didn't mix with the locals down there all that much. We had our own little mob.''[18]

I rang Edward Pratt. ''I understood,'' he said, ''that Denis Emus was stationed here in Strete. But it could have been his salesman. The only thing I understood from one of them was that they had to get out of a certain situation for this reason.''

Over the telephone, he added more detail to the story he had told in the Dutch barn:

> When we came down here there were three buildings in that field. They were knocking them down and bricking it up [the tomb]. There's only one building now. A kind of monument, that's how it seems to me. And there's a house built within twenty-five yards of it. I'm pretty sure that they [i.e., the bodies] are there. They took away some, but I'm 99 percent sure there are some there now.

And he added: ''The one thing that beat me was that we found so many dog tags cut off.''[19]

But these investigations came late, after my day in the South Hams. On the evening of that day I was asking myself what lay behind the stories I had gathered. Dorothy Seekings and Edward Pratt differed in their identification of the burial place, but were agreed that there had been, and still was, a mass grave of Americans. Neither of them appeared able to come up with independent corroboration for their stories; but neither could their stories be categorically denied, and after a little reflection this began to seem the most impressive fact about them.

When Dorothy Seekings broke her silence in 1984 she could not have known that American archives lacked the paperwork to prove her wrong. She had not seen the Defense Department leaflet issued only in 1988 stating that ''personnel rosters and ships' manifests for the troop carriers in Exercise Tiger were inadequate.'' Without that sketchiness in the United States, these sketchy stories in the South Hams could not have survived. Certainly they could not have survived retelling in the wider world outside the South Hams, in newspapers and on television. The sheer weight of documentation would have crushed them at the source. How could Dorothy Seekings have known this? How could Edward Pratt have known? It was, at the very least, a remarkable coincidence.

I had begun my day at the Normandy Arms in Blackawton; I finished it at the Tower Inn, Slapton. Leaving my luggage in my room, I went down to the bar for a drink, which I felt to be well deserved after so much sleet and strangeness. A wood fire was blazing. At the bar beside me a man was giving directions to another man. ''Go down the hill,'' he said, ''then turn right.'' And then, when the other man wasn't sure where he meant: "You *know,* the field at the corner there, the field where the soldiers are. . . . ''

The name of the man giving directions was Connor Turley. He was Irish and had lived for years in the South Hams, where he worked for a local dairy company and was a regular at the Tower Inn. Not only had I said nothing about the purpose of my visit to the South Hams, I had only just arrived in Slapton and at the Tower Inn. Yet here was a stranger overheard in a pub talking of a field full of soldiers as if it were a well-known local landmark.

It evidently wasn't well known, however, because the other man had to ask Connor Turley what he meant. Connor Turley explained. A little later, still marveling at his explanation, I leaned down the bar, introduced myself, and asked why he had described a wheat field, an ordinary field full of winter wheat, as "the field where the soldiers are."

He stared at me. "Why," he said, "because of the green wheat just poking through the soil. It looks like spears or bayonets, and it's all in line, like soldiers."

"Is that what you would usually call them? Soldiers?"

"Why not?"[20]

Tope, Pratt, Buckpitt, Seekings. All day I had felt as if I had strayed into a macabre version of *Cold Comfort Farm.* Here, though, was something closer to *The Golden Bough.*

Bread and wheat had run in a steady refrain through this story of soldiers. The farmers of the South Hams had been urged, in the middle years of the war, to grow wheat. It had been a crime then to waste bread. Dorothy Seekings was a baker's daughter and the delivery of doughnuts figured in her story.

It was in his diary entry for the day of the Tiger disaster that Harry Butcher had made his celebrated remark about the American soldiery being as "green as growing corn." In the First World War, and earlier, American soldiers had been nicknamed "doughboys"; in the Second World War Omar Bradley had been "the doughboys' general." In one explanation the word derived from the American war with Mexico in 1848, when infantry marching along the Rio Grande would be whitened by the dust of the adobe earth—doughboy being a corruption of adobe. In another derivation, it was a British navy term for soldiers, whose large brass buttons were said to resemble the dough dumplings that the sailors baked.[21]

"Doughboy" sounded substantial, but in war a soldier was at the evanescent borderline of life.

Where have all the soldiers gone?
Gone to flowers, every one.

Flowers or corn, or tares (T-4's call signal had been TARE-4). A doughboy was a sort of premature ghost, his uniform whitened with adobe dust, like flour. What had the sister of a soldier written to me? "They haunt the seacoast, and do not want to be forgotten."

The roots of these associations went deeper. In my teens, in Robert Graves's collection of the Greek myths, I had read the story of the serpent's teeth. Cadmus had killed the serpent—or dragon—guarding the Castalian Spring. The goddess Athene had appeared and ordered Cadmus to sow the serpent's teeth, like seed corn, in the soil.

"When he obeyed her," in the Graves version, "armed Sparti, or Sown Men, at once sprang up, clashing their weapons together." Athene gave some of the serpent's teeth to Jason. "All day he ploughed, and at nightfall sowed the teeth, from which armed men immediately sprouted."[22] Jason's field, like Connor Turley's, or the fields of Dorothy Seekings and Edward Pratt, had been full of "soldiers."

Back in London I thought I would try some sortilege and took down my abridged *Golden Bough*. The index gave one entry under Devonshire ("harvest customs in"). It referred me to a couple of pages about the myth of the god Osiris.

"If I am right," wrote Sir James Frazer, "the key to the mysteries of Osiris is furnished by the melancholy cry of the Egyptian reapers, which down to Roman times could be heard year after year sounding across the fields, announcing the death of the corn-spirit, the rustic prototype of Osiris. . . . Down to recent times Devonshire reapers uttered cries of the same sort, and performed on the field a ceremony exactly analogous to that in which, if I am not mistaken, the rites of Osiris originated."

Frazer added:

> The story that the fragments of Osiris's body were scattered up and down the land, and buried by Isis on the spot where they lay, may very well be a reminiscence of a custom . . . of dividing the human victim in pieces and burying the pieces, often at intervals of many miles from each other, in the fields."[23]

I thought of the picture that Dorothy Seekings had painted of "a vast graveyard, with bodies buried in locations over an eight-mile radius." Was this the explanation for the stories of the South Hams? Over forty years, had the folk memory of the violently slain Americans mutated into a modern version of an ancient myth? ''The fragments of Osiris's body''—were they *their* bodies, ''scattered up and down the land''?

By this reading the American soldiers, whether or not they were with the Christian God, were themselves folk gods of a kind, haunting this corner of Devonshire.

POSTSCRIPT

If the sacrificial fertility myth of Osiris helps to explain the wartime evacuation area's abiding fascination with "the bodies in the fields," it still does not go to the heart of the problem. If the stories are rooted in psychology and anthropology, are they, or were they once, also rooted in fact? If the Americans were the "Sown Men" of the South Hams, had they also *really* been sown in its soil?

While on-the-spot excavation could conceivably prove that there is substance to the stories, it could never completely disprove them. The suggested locations, or some of them, are too large and if nothing were found, other locations would doubtless soon suggest themselves.

This gives the storytellers of the South Hams an unfair advantage over the U.S. authorities, who would wish to stamp out the stories. Without the physical evidence, the storytellers cannot prove their case. But their stories remain effective despite the absence of positive proof, and there is a sense in which they do not need proof in order to be effective. Without firm documentary evidence, however, the U.S. authorities cannot positively *disprove* them.

So far this story has exhibited two areas of research that are especially resistant to verification. The matter of how many men were aboard Convoy T-4, and how many died, was looked into in the last chapter. If that chapter were presented as evidence in a legal sense, I believe that the likely finding would be in favor of a death toll of 639. And yet the American authorities have never thrown their weight behind this as being the correct figure. On the contrary, they confess that the documentation for Exercise Tiger was "inadequate."

The second difficult area involves the stories of bodies in fields. Here the official American position is clearer. Typical of it is a letter of October 1987 from Deputy Assistant Defense Secretary William E. Hart to Senator Robert Dole. It said that "rumors that the victims of the German E-boat attack are buried anonymously under concrete in a mass grave in a sheep pasture are unfounded."

At the same time, however, the letter stated that "the 749 American victims were *temporarily* interred at Slapton Sands" (underlining in original).[1] I hope that the extreme improbability, to state it no more strongly, of a burial of T-4 victims in the Slapton Sands area has been established in my last chapter. According to this letter, however, the current South Hams "rumors" did once have a basis in fact. That, coming from the U.S. Department of Defense, is an extraordinary enough admission.

The two areas of difficulty become more problematic when they are perceived to be interrelated. The implication is that a supposed surplus of deaths above the 639 figure accounts for the mass burial or burials in the South Hams. And those South Hams stories, on the no-smoke-without-fire principle, encourage the idea that there must have been a surplus. Otherwise, how could American soldiers have been buried in the Slapton Sands area, as the U.S. Defense Department apparently confirms they were?

Where Convoy T-4 is concerned, the evidence for a surplus is not solid enough. Nor is there any *necessary* connection between the two areas of difficulty. If one abandons the casual assumption that bodies on the water after the attack on Convoy T-4 later became bodies in South Devon fields, the difficulties look less challenging. One then finds oneself drawn to the conclusion that the figure on the Slapton Sands memorial is wrong and that the true death toll was 639. At the same time, the South Hams stories start to look like expressions of folk myth.

Or . . . *other* bodies were buried.

There is evidence to suggest that the South Hams stories, if they do have an undertow of folk myth, might also be manifestations of folk memory. Here we move into an area of darkness still deeper than that that has surrounded the story told in this book so far.

One steps into the darkness simply by stepping back one day, from April 28, 1944, to April 27. Tiger's "D Day" on Slapton Sands. It will be recalled that on April 27 Rear Admiral Moon postponed Exercise Tiger's "H Hour" by one hour, from 7:30 A.M. British Double Summer Time, to 8:30.

Ships of the gunfire support group were due to start bombarding the shore with their preliminary softening-up fire fifty minutes before H Hour. The ships were deployed in eight "fire support" groups out in Start Bay and Lyme Bay, some of them up to twelve miles off the coast.

Under the old schedule the bombardment would have begun at 6:40

A.M. Under the new, hastily revised schedule, the first shells would have been fired at 7:40 A.M., ten minutes after the old H Hour. But what if soldiers failed to get the message about H Hour's postponement, and landed at their previously appointed times? They would have been on the beach when the ships offshore opened up with their preliminary fire for the revised H Hour.

There is documentary evidence that there were soldiers who did fail to learn of the postponement and did land at their old appointed time. According to the Force U War Diary, "because some of the units and ships failed to receive the signal, Wave # 2 landed on Green Beach at the original time."[2]

John Moreno recalled that "some troops were under fire from the army amphibious tanks firing as they approached the beach. The landing craft were pitching in the seas and the tank guns were not gyro-stabilized, so some of their rounds went wild." Moreno could not, however, recall "anything about U.S. troops being hit by friendly gunfire."[3]

But there is evidence of death on Slapton Sands on Exercise Tiger's D Day. Edwin Hoyt records that two bodies were washed up at the surfline, where they were seen by Sergeant Barnett Hoffner of the 203rd Engineer Combat Battalion. When he and some fellow engineers went to look at them, an officer yelled at them, "Christ, haven't you ever seen a dead man before? Break it up!"[4]

The Force U diary specifically states, though, that "scheduled gunfire had to be canceled for the safety of own troops. After, however, adjustment had been made to the new H Hour, the landing proceeded as planned and with fair precision."

"Fair precision" was not the impression of some men who were responsible for the "scheduled gunfire." John Towner was a sublieutenant on HMS *Hawkins,* one of the gunfire support ships. He understood that there were "heavy casualties amongst the American lads who went ashore," and that the cause of the casualties was a mix-up after the postponement of H Hour. "The captain and others on our bridge," he said, "were considerably shaken when they realized the enormity of the tragedy that was going on ashore."[5]

According to Towner it was an American ship inshore from the *Hawkins* that caused all the damage. But Bill Hiscock, who was also on the *Hawkins,* believed at the time that his own ship was responsible for heavy casualties. The log of the *Hawkins* is certainly suggestive of some chaos caused by H Hour's postponement. According to it, the *Hawkins* "commenced approach to bombardment target" at 6:00 A.M.

At 6:55 she "commenced tactical 7.5′ and 4′ bombardment shoot," and continued firing until 7:05, when orders were received to "retard zero hour 1 hour."

At 7:40 the log records that "504th Tactical U.S. Army started seaward landings." At this time, said Bill Hiscock, the *Hawkins* fired some 120 shells at the beach, and "we heard that there'd been casualties ashore. The 'buzz' went through the ship that we hit some on the beach."[6]

The picture offered by John Towner of an "enormity" corresponds with another "buzz" that Bill Hiscock heard in the immediate aftermath of Tiger—that on the exercise as a whole, Convoy T-4 included, up to 1,100 American lives were lost.

That "buzz" in its turn corresponds with the evidence of Julian Perkin of HMS *Obedient,* another of the gunfire support ships. The former commission warrant candidate and manager of Stokeley Barton is today a council member for the South Devon district of Teignbridge. He told me that on April 27 *Obedient* was "within good visual range" of Slapton Sands, "probably two miles offshore. There were ships bombarding from further out. There were ships ashore from us."[7]

"It was felt at the time that men were dying," he said. "I heard that there were hits on particular buildings. The story that got to us was that quite a number of men were killed in the bombardment. Ongoing opinion and intelligence reports suggested that the Americans lost a total of 1,200 men on Exercise Tiger [including Convoy T-4]."

No official papers have come to light to suggest heavy casualties on Slapton Sands on the 27th. Either the three former Royal Navy men—who live in different places in Britain and are unknown to one another—are reporting inaccurate, forty-five-year-old hearsay, or there were heavy casualties and the fact has been covered up.

A few points in passing. Here is a rationale for the U.S. Defense Department's admissions that documentation—which, according to Howard DeVoe, the U.S. forces "never fail" to give—was "inadequate" and that bodies were "temporarily interred" at Slapton Sands. It provides a rationale, too, for the South Hams stories. Men who were killed on or near Slapton Sands were buried nearby: Here is an explanation that at last makes sense.

More evidence for it is provided by a U.S. army veteran called Harold McAulley. He is the old soldier who turned up at the *LST 515*'s reunion in Chicago with a story of having buried victims of Exercise Tiger.

From England I telephoned Harold McAulley at his 256-acre farm outside Hollandale, Wisconsin. "It's hill country here in Wisconsin," he told me. "Kind of puts you in mind of Ireland, when it's green. But it's not green now."

It was June 1988 and Wisconsin was one of the Midwest states in the grip of drought. "The hills," said Harold McAulley, "are burnt just like Africa. Corn—we used to have 150 bushels per acre. This year we won't have fifty. This is the worst in history."[8]

By April 1944 Harold McAulley was an experienced veteran of the European war. His unit was the 479th Amphibious Truck Company, part of the First Engineer Special Brigade. It had participated in the North African, Sicilian, and Italian mainland campaigns before its transfer to England in the run-up period to the Normandy invasion. A check against the Exercise Tiger ship sheets reveals that the 479th landed on Slapton Sands very early on the morning of the 28th, just after midnight. The Army serial number of the LST that carried the company was the last in the list before the LSTs of Convoy T-4.

Another veteran of the 479th, Lester Limbaugh of Tennessee, confirmed that from Slapton Sands the company had witnessed the attack on Convoy T-4 some thirty miles away across Lyme Bay. "We saw fire and heard explosions," he said, "but we didn't know what it was."[9]

McAulley said that on Exercise Tiger he had been in charge of four Dukws. After daybreak that morning he had been detailed to pick up bodies from the water and the beach and to take them inland to where a mass grave was being dug. In my conversations with him he consistently identified these bodies with the victims of the nighttime attack that he and his company had distantly witnessed.

In the pursuit of rehearsal realism Exercise Tiger had even made provision for fake wounded to be treated by the medics and fake dead to be "buried" by the Graves Registration Command in a fake temporary cemetery.[10] But this had been no fake burial in which Harold McAulley had found himself caught up, but a real burial of real men.

"The 479th did the burying," he told me. "A guy from the 531st Shore Regiment drove the bulldozer." Remembering Dorothy Seekings, I asked whether black soldiers had been involved in the burial. "Black men digging the grave?" he said. "I don't think there was a black man there."

He continued: "They were mass graves, I can tell you that." I asked how many men, 100, 200? "I would say more than that by the time it was all done. How long were we there? Cripes, I'd say two or three days."[11]

I tried to pinpoint the place where the burial had been. It was, he said, no more than a few hundred yards inland, a description that fitted Edward Pratt's suggested grave site, but not that of Dorothy Seekings.

"You know that beach," he said, "there were dunes. . . ."[12] This worried me a little. Slapton Sands is not sand, and has no sand dunes. But forty years had passed and by April 1944, Harold McAulley had seen a lot of beaches.

After the burial, a chaplain had said a service over the grave, while a ranking officer stood to attention, saluting.

This was the outline of the story that Harold McAulley told to me in mid-1988 and that he had told in part in Chicago in 1985. Nervously, he asked me whether this thing was still classified and whether he would get into trouble.

He repeated that question the third time I telephoned him, in July 1988. By then there had been a little rain in Wisconsin. "It's starting to green up a bit, but the corn got so hurt I don't think we'll get much." He had bought some subsidized government hay for cattle feed. "I feel pretty good about it."[13]

But there was more to Harold McAulley's story. Coupled with the accounts of the three former Royal Navy men, it begged a very big question: *Who* were the men whom he and others had buried? I had not asked that question when Harold McAulley, in our first telephone conversation and with no prompting from me, supplied a name. We have his word for it that one of the men he buried near Slapton Sands was an American soldier called Joseph Trainor.

Harold McAulley had known Joseph Trainor in Wisconsin before the war. Trainor had also hailed from Wisconsin. He had worked for a man called Albert Reeves, who ran a milking-machine company. "I knew Joe Trainor fairly well before I went into the war," Harold McAulley told me, "I knew who he was. His cousin worked for my dad on the farm here. We'd meet at dances and stuff."

It wasn't McAulley who had found Joseph Trainor's body—"He came in on a weapons carrier"—but it was McAulley who had recognized his prewar acquaintance from the Wisconsin farms and buried him. "I buried him a bit special," he said. Later I rang and asked if he could be absolutely sure about this. "Gosh, if I was wrong, I was wrong," he said, "but that was Joe Trainor."[14]

By the summer of 1988, before my first contact with Harold McAulley, McAulley's story was known to the surviving members of Joseph Trainor's family. His sister, Eileen, lived a few miles from Hollandale at Barneveld, Wisconsin. As soon as I had spoken to

Harold McAulley I telephoned her (she was in the barn when I rang) and asked if she had the telegram and follow-up letters from the War Department, which, after the usual pattern, would have followed in the wake of her brother's death.

She wasn't too sure if they were still extant. Her brother, Peter Trainor, had given them to the local representative of the American Legion. In 1984 a tornado had hit Barneveld: "It took out the Legion Hall," she told me. And in 1986 Peter Trainor had died in a tractor accident.[15]

Barneveld's local legion representative, Jerry Williams, told me the papers had survived the tornado.[16] He sent me copies. The standard telegram wasn't among them, but there was the standard follow-up letter from Major General Ulio, the United States Adjutant General.

> It is with regret that I am writing to confirm the recent telegram informing you of the death of your son, Private First Class Joseph R. Trainor, 36,227,819 Infantry. . . .[17]

There was only one problem with the Adjutant General's letter: Dated June 27, it stated that Joseph Trainor had been "killed in action on June 6, 1944, in France."

Jerry Williams had told me that he knew there was "some dispute" over when and where Joseph Trainor had died. But this was more than "some dispute." The Adjutant General said that Joseph Trainor had been killed on D Day, in France, while Harold McAulley claimed to have "buried him a bit special" six weeks before, in South Devon.

"I fully understand your desire," the Adjutant General's letter went on, "to learn as much as possible regarding the circumstances leading to his death and I wish that there were more information available to give you. Unfortunately, reports of this nature contain only the briefest details, as they are prepared under battle conditions and the means of transmission are limited."[18]

Fair enough. But we have seen that the bureaucratic machine of the U.S. forces was capable in time of disgorging details of a man's death. With Joseph Trainor no details were ever forthcoming. His family was not even sent his identity tag.[19]

The Adjutant General's letter ended: "It is my hope that in time the knowledge of his heroic service to his country, even unto death, may be of sustaining comfort to you."[20]

Harold McAulley's story from Wisconsin strikingly endorses similar stories of an anonymous mass burial that have been current in the South Hams since 1944. A problem with his story, however, is that, like those of Dorothy Seekings and Edward Pratt, it lacks independent corroboration.

Other veterans of the 479th Amphibious Truck Company cannot confirm that men of the company were responsible for any mass burial.[21] Harold McAulley had not said, however, that the *entire* company participated in the burial.

Other veterans are also unable to confirm that Harold McAulley had told his story to them *before* 1984, when Dorothy Seekings told hers. The first confirmation of his telling it dates from the Chicago reunion of 1985. He had also told it to American Legion representative Jerry Williams before I contacted him.

The first that McAulley's fellow veteran Lester Limbaugh ever heard of the story was when McAulley, in the immediate wake of my first conversation with him, telephoned Tennessee and told it to him. And Lester Limbaugh has known "Mac" since the war. "Mac is a bit of a dreamer," he told me. "I have come up with a couple of things he had dressed up a little. On the other hand, there was a story about him delivering a baby in Italy, which I didn't believe at first, but which turned out to be true." Lester Limbaugh added that "some people who were in the war, they do dream up things."[22]

From my research for this book I can confirm that observation, with which many of the survivors would also agree. It would be surprising if, after more than forty years, personal experiences that were extreme at the time had not acquired a dreamlike quality. But in no case have I come up with the wholesale manufacture of experiences that did not occur, and from my contacts with survivors of Convoy T-4 I can confirm that accounts that at first seemed a little unreal turned out, when corroborated by others, to have been true.

From this perspective, Harold McAulley's possible error over sand dunes on Slapton Sands, for example, falls within an acceptable margin of error; the assertion that he buried a named individual near Slapton Sands, if untrue, falls outside that margin. But Harold McAulley sticks to the assertion. "I've known this story since the war," he told me. "One night in town about thirty years ago I was drinking, and I told a guy about it. But I never mentioned it to Joe Trainor's brothers."[23]

It is possible that Harold McAulley had continued to be impressed by wartime injunctions about secrecy, as Dorothy Seekings said that she had been impressed, but had been emboldened by the belated publicity surrounding Exercise Tiger to tell what he knew at last, as she had been emboldened. Certainly he worries, even so many years after the war, that he might be construed as having broken a wartime secret.

Since the Chicago reunion of 1985 he has stuck to his story. When I telephoned him again in September 1988, three months after our original conversation, he had by chance just come back from a reunion of the 479th Amphibious Truck Company at Christney, Indiana. There had been twenty-four men at the reunion. He had told them his story of the mass burial and Joseph Trainor, and had been advised to keep it to himself. "I don't want to end up in a court having to prove this," he told me. He was worried, too, that Joseph Trainor's family might be upset, and his old comrades had advised him "not to mess with it."

At the same time he stuck firmly to his story and, when I asked him bluntly if he was making it up, emphatically denied that he was. "Not unless there were two Joseph Trainors," he said.

Just after the Christney reunion he had tried to trace a veteran of the 479th, Junior A. Bunting, who had been with him on Slapton Sands that day, only to discover that Bunting had died in 1951.[24] This is behavior more reminiscent of a man marooned with a memory than of someone who has dreamed up a tall tale. It may yet be proved that McAulley's improbable story of having buried Joseph Trainor, like his improbable story of having delivered a baby in Italy, is true.

A later letter to Joseph Trainor's family from the U.S. authorities, dated July 8, 1946, stated that Trainor's remains were "interred in the U.S. Military Cemetery, St. Laurent, plot D, row 9, grave 167. . . . The War Department has now been authorized to comply, at Government expense, with your feasible wishes regarding final interment, here or abroad, of the remains of your loved one."[25]

The superintendent of the St. Laurent cemetery,* Joseph Rivers, told me that the "D" designation was for a burial site in a temporary cemetery closed at the end of the 1940s, after which the remains buried there "were either reburied or moved to another cemetery."[26]

Joseph Trainor had been reburied in plot 1, where Robert Motley, who definitely died in Exercise Tiger, was also buried. According to Harold McAulley, however, that was Joseph Trainor's second reburial, because McAulley had buried him "a bit special" in a mass grave across the English Channel, in England, six weeks before D Day.

The St. Laurent cemetery confirmed what Eileen Trainor in Wisconsin had already told me—that Joseph Trainor had been in the U.S. Rangers. The Second Ranger Battalion to which he belonged had suffered heavy casualties on D Day, scaling the Pointe du Hoc between

---

* Now officially the Normandy American Military Cemetery and Memorial, Colleville-Sur-Mer.

Utah and Omaha beaches. According to Cornelius Ryan in *The Longest Day,* "By the end of the day there would be only ninety of the original 225 still able to bear arms."[27] Other rangers of the Second Battalion died on Omaha Beach, four miles away. But in the European theater of war the rangers "specialized in spearheading amphibious operations,"[28] and if they spearheaded the D Day assault, it is reasonable to suppose that they were also in the D Day rehearsal Exercise Tiger.

Where did Joseph Trainor die, at Omaha Beach, the Pointe du Hoc, or on Slapton Sands? When did he die, at the end of April 1944 or on D Day? If Harold McAulley is correct, then the books were cooked in the case of Joseph Trainor. And if they were cooked for him, they were cooked for others, too.

"I have heard," wrote Howard DeVoe, "that no fighting unit men would be buried in Cambridge but they would be buried in France. Sure, but when Tiger happened there was no France."[29]

McAulley's story, however, suggests that official dates of death were bureaucratically postponed *to make it appear* as if men who died in England had died in France. Thus a temporary mass grave in South Devon. And if "when Tiger happened there was no France," the Allies had been in France for two months when SHAEF in London announced the figure of 442 army dead in Tiger.

It is interesting, too, to note that the figure was expressed as part of the total Allied casualties of 116,148 suffered in the invasion of France up to July 20, 1944. Total American casualties were given as 70,009, of whom 11,156 were killed and 6,143 were missing. The stories of McAulley and the former Royal Navy men cast doubt on whether all those men really did die in France.[30]

The Pointe du Hoc assault was itself futile enough. Staged in order to knock out big guns believed to be on the clifftop, it was discovered that there were no big guns there. That futility at least took place in a context of battle. It pales in comparison with the futility of the attack on Convoy T-4, which, in its turn, pales in comparison with the futility of a naval and military mix-up on an exercise, resulting in the heavy bombardment of one's own "spearhead" fighting men.

If there was such a mix-up, it is not difficult to imagine why the authorities should have chosen to cover it up, not only in the extremely tense and secretive period just preceding D Day, but ever since. A deeply hidden story like this could explain the puzzling postwar neglect of the story of Convoy T-4: it got caught up, perhaps, in a greater secrecy.

It could also explain the "snapping" of Rear Admiral Moon's mind and his subsequent suicide. Moon could not be held directly to blame for the mix-ups surrounding T-4, but if soldiers were shelled on the beach, it was as a consequence of his decision to postpone H Hour.

The blunderers would have wanted their blunders hidden, and there would have been the need at this crucial period to maintain confidence in the high command. There may, just before D Day, have been security implications in sending throughout the United States telegrams announcing the deaths of "spearhead" troops. It would have been of more "sustaining comfort" to a family to believe that a man had died in "heroic service to his country, even unto death."

And if there were such a cover-up, how else would it be revealed, unless by just such an accident of chance as Harold McAulley, one of the buriers, having known Joseph Trainor, one of the buried, before the war?

But if Joseph Trainor did die in South Devon, where are his remains now? If it seems melodramatic to suppose that a cross bearing his name stands now upon empty ground in Normandy, almost as melodramatic is the notion that his body was disinterred and shipped across the Channel (although one wonders how Robert Motley's remains come to lie in Normandy, not far away in the same cemetery plot). However, the U.S. authorities did offer to repatriate Joseph Trainor's remains, which suggests that they are where the authorities have said they are, in Normandy.

On balance it appears unlikely that "the field where the soldiers are" is in South Devon. The soldiers are in Cambridge cemetery in England, or in cemeteries across the United States; they are in Normandy, where so many of them "died for our freedom."

Another possibility emerges, however. It depends upon the name of one man and upon the word and memory of another. It is the possibility that an undisclosed number of the Normandy gravestones commemorate men who did not die there on D Day or afterwards, but across the English Channel in England six weeks earlier, on a windswept South Devon beach called Slapton Sands.

NOTES AND REFERENCES

Where an abbreviated source is given below, full details of the work referred to will be found in the Bibliography.

All interviews and telephone conversations are with, and all personal letters are to, the author unless stated otherwise.

PART ONE: BOLERO

CHAPTER ONE

1. Quoted in Katherine Tupper Marshall, p. 147.
2. *Time,* May 1, 1944.
3. *Newsweek,* Jan. 31, 1944.
4. *Life,* June 5, 1944.
5. Bradley, *A General's Life,* p. 241.
6. Gunther, p. 175, and in other books; probably originally from "virtually sacred" in Butcher, p. 456.
7. Patton, p. 336.
8. Bradley, *A Soldier's Story,* p. 249.

CHAPTER TWO

1. Ralph Rayner, letter to a constituent, Mr. Soper of Slapton, July 18, 1944.
2. Ralph Rayner in a broadcast on CBS and NBC, 1944, quoted in *Torquay Herald-Express,* D Day supplement, June 2, 1984.
3. *Kingsbridge Gazette and South Devon Advertiser,* Jan. 15, 1943.
4. *Kingsbridge Gazette,* Jan 29, 1943.
5. *Kingsbridge Gazette,* April 9, 1943.

6. *Kingsbridge Gazette,* May 7, 1943.
7. *Kingsbridge Gazette,* June 25, 1943.
8. *Kingsbridge Gazette,* Sept. 10, 1943.
9. *Kingsbridge Gazette,* June 18, 1943.
10. *Kingsbridge Gazette,* Aug. 20, 1943.
11. *Kingsbridge Gazette,* Sept. 24, 1943.
12. Bradbeer, p. 45.
13. Ibid., p. 49.
14. This and all subsequent material attributed to Nancy Hare compiled from reports in the *Western Morning News* (Plymouth), Feb 11, March 24, March 31, April 18, 1984.
15. Bradbeer, p. 53.
16. Ibid., p. 57.
17. *Dartmouth Chronicle,* Dec, 23, 1983.
18. Unnamed evacuee speaking in video of reunion produced by South Hams District Council, 1984.
19. *Dartmouth Chronicle,* Dec. 23, 1983.
20. Bradbeer, p. 61.
21. Leaflet in the possession of Mrs. Dorothy Seekings, Stoke Fleming, South Hams.
22. *Dartmouth Chronicle,* Dec. 23, 1983.
23. Bradbeer, p. 68.
24. Ibid.
25. Rayner, in his broadcast; see note 2.
26. *Hansard,* Nov. 25, 1943, col. 109.
27. Bradbeer, p. 71.
28. Dwight D. Eisenhower, p. 262.
29. These stories were given to the author by Harry Unsworth of Newton Abbot.
30. Bradbeer, pp. 72–3.
31. Belfield and Essame, p. 18.
32. Bradley, *A General's Life,* p. 234.
33. Dwight D. Eisenhower, p. 263.
34. Collins, p. 180.

CHAPTER THREE

1. Quoted in Bradley, *A General's Life,* p. 228.
2. Emanuel ("Manny") Rubin, interview, Jan. 16–19, 1988.
3. Churchill, p. 226.
4. Rubin, see note 2.
5. Ibid.
6. M. C. McMahon, former UDT (Underwater Demolition Team), interview with Ralph Greene, March 6, 1984.

7. Emanuel Rubin, interview with Ralph Greene, May 31, 1984.
8. Churchill, p. 226.
9. Bradley, *A General's Life*, p. 228.
10. As quoted by Emanuel Rubin in interview; see note 2.
11. Howard Buhl, of *LST 494*, personal letter to Ralph Greene, Aug. 20, 1983.
12. Wendell Hoppler in interview with Ralph Greene, May 11, 1985.
13. Elwin Hendrick, personal letter, July 27, 1988.
14. Chapter 2 of Tom Clark's manuscript enclosed with personal letter.
15. Ibid.
16. Ibid.
17. Ibid.
18. Ibid.
19. Ibid.
20. Ingersoll, p. 101.
21. Morgan, p. 178.
22. Ibid., p. 180.
23. Selection from diary published in *Torquay Herald-Express,* D Day supplement, June 2, 1984.
24. Captain Power, R.N., quoted in Churchill, p. 383.
25. Ingersoll, p. 101.
26. Bradley, *A General's Life,* p. 248.
27. Confirmed by Ingersoll, p. 101; and Hatch, p. 136.
28. Hermann "Buddie" Grosse in interview with Ralph Greene, May 11, 1985.
29. Elwin Hendrick. (R.G.)*
30. Wendell Hoppler. (R.G.)
31. "Beachhead had quite a life," according to Floyd Hicks of the *515* (personal letter, June 27, 1988, enclosing a short article, "A Dog's Life" by David Roop, the *515*'s engineering officer, who died in October 1986). "Beachhead was bought by the crew in New Orleans in January 1944," said Floyd Hicks, and David Roop's article (date and place of publication unknown) takes up the story:

He must have been smuggled aboard the ship after midnight when the ship's crew was asleep and the OD [officer of the day] was off somewhere having a cup of coffee. On D Day he was first off the ship at Utah Beach, and after that he was always first on the beach. Where he wandered it is hard to tell, but he had enough time between tides that he accomplished his missions and always got back to the ship before the ramp went up and the bow doors closed. One day he was found hanging over the side by his forepaws. Another time he broke a leg falling down a ladder, and the ship's doctor (George Hawley) fixed him by putting on a full plaster cast. In our

---

* For further information on references marked (R.G.), see Appendix II.

35 trips from England to the Normandy beaches he was at the bow doors
greeting the GIs coming aboard, and I saw serious-faced soldiers break into
grins and laughter.

David Roop believed that Beachhead got lost on the *515*'s return to the United
States (Boston, Massachusetts) in August 1945. But according to Floyd
Hicks, "Beachhead was sold to the mayor of Boston after we got back to the
States and had a beautiful home for the rest of his life."

32. Ingersoll, p. 106.
33. Dwight D. Eisenhower, p. 273.
34. Ingersoll, pp. 106–8.
35. Ibid.
36. Ibid.
37. Ibid.
38. Wendell Hoppler. (R.G.)

PART TWO: TIGER

CHAPTER FOUR

1. Collins, pp. 185–93.
2. Ibid.
3. Ibid.
4. Ibid.
5. Thomas Glennon, Comdr. USNR (Ret.), interview with Ralph Greene,
   Oct. 19, 1984.
6. King, p. 621.
7. "The Other D Days," p. 10.
8. John A. Moreno, Capt. USN (Ret.). (R.G.)
9. Rear Admiral Sir Ralph Leatham, quoted in "The Other D Days," p. 7.
10. Rear Admiral E. J. P. Brind CBE, Assistant Chief of Naval Staff
    (Home), letter of Aug. 7, 1944: Tiger file, MOD.
11. Leatham, Tiger file, MOD.
12. Hill, pp. 44–51.
13. Ibid.
14. Ibid.
15. Ibid.
16. Ibid.
17. Roger Hill, personal letter, Feb. 5, 1988.
18. Gunther, p. 81.
19. Ibid.
20. Burch, pp. 19–20.
21. Ibid.
22. Ralph Greene, from his wartime experience as a censor of letters.

23. Opinions expressed in personal letter to Ralph Greene, Feb. 11, 1984; the letter writer, perhaps unsurprisingly, wishes his name withheld.
24. Quoted in Ralph Greene, "Tiger Burning."
25. Morgan, p. 286.
26. James E. Arnold, NOIC, Utah, U.S. Naval Institute Proceedings, 73: 671, 1947. (R.G.)
27. John Moreno. (R.G.)
28. Collins, p. 193.
29. Operating Order No. 2–44, April 18, 1944, reproduced in "The Other D Days," p. 14.

CHAPTER FIVE

1. Operating Order No. 2–44, April 18, 1944, reproduced in "The Other D Days," p. 14.
2. Woodward, p. 148.
3. Hoyt, p. 99.
4. Thomas Glennon. (R.G.) Glennon apparently remembers the briefing as having been on April 26. The British officer's semiprophecy is quoted in Walter Karig and Earl Buxton, *Battle Report on the Atlantic War,* New York, Farrer Rhinehart Inc., 1946, p. 293. (R.G.)
5. Moses D. Hallett, personal letter to Ralph Greene, Sept. 7/8, 1983; copy enclosed in personal letter, Hallett to author, June 28, 1988.
6. Ralph Leatham, letter to Rear Admiral John Hall, USN, May 5, 1944, reproduced in "The Other D Days," p. 23.
7. Rear Admiral Llewellyn V. Morgan, letter of July 17, 1944; Tiger file, MOD.
8. Quoted by Chalmers, p.108.
9. Chalmers, p. 108.
10. "Report by Naval C-in-C on Operation Neptune, 1944," vol. I, Appendix 2, pp. 32–3.
11. Ibid.
12. Morison, p. 65.
13. Ibid., p. 67.
14. Ibid., p. 66.
15. Chalmers, p. 198.
16. Report by Naval C-in-C; see note 10.
17. Hawley, George, M.D. (R.G.)
18. Ex-RN Communications Officer, who wishes to remain anonymous, interview with Ralph Greene, June 4, 1984.

CHAPTER SIX

1. Or, perhaps, the contrary. The First ESB tucked in their trouser legs *because* they wore paratroop "jump" boots. But why did they wear the

boots? A former brigade member says that it was because of the suspiciously high incidence of broken ankles during the African and Italian landings, causing men to be invalided out of action. Thus the "jump" boots—to give support to the soldiers when they jumped from their landing craft. Harold McAulley, telephone conversation, June 24, 1988.

2. Bradley, *A Soldier's Story,* p. 248.
3. Hoyt, p. 83.
4. Dale Rodman, enclosure in personal letter, Feb 17, 1988. Dale Rodman also provided information on the First Engineer Special Brigade.
5. Theodore S. Liska, formerly Fourth Infantry Division, personal letter Feb. (undated) 1988.
6. M. C. McMahon interview with Ralph Greene, March 6, 1984.
7. Wendell Hoppler, personal letter, July 14, 1988.
8. Eugene Eckstam, personal letter to Ralph Greene, Aug. 25, 1984; copy enclosed in personal letter, Eckstam to author, June 23, 1988.
9. Robin Power, RN, report on LSTs quoted by Churchill, p. 383.
10. Angelo Crapanzano, personal letter to Ralph Greene, Aug. 1, 1984; copy enclosed in personal letter, Eckstam to author, June 23, 1988.
11. Tom Clark, personal letter to his father, July 4/5, 1944; copy enclosed in personal letter, Clark to author, March 14, 1988.
12. Douglas Harlander to Ralph Greene, June 30, 1985; copy enclosed in personal letter, Harlander to author, June 4, 1988.
13. Henry Schrawder, personal log. Enclosed in personal letter, Feb. 20, 1988.
14. Eugene Carney, personal communication with Ralph Greene, April 16, 1984.
15. Arthur Victor, personal log of late 1970s/early 1980s.
16. Eugene Eckstam; see note 8.
17. Tiger file, MOD.

CHAPTER SEVEN

1. David Roop. (R.G.)
2. Hermann Grosse. (R.G.)
3. Wendell Hoppler. (R.G.)
4. George Hawley. (R.G.)
5. Moses Hallett, personal letters to Ralph Greene, Sept. 7, 8, 1983; copies enclosed in personal letter, Hallett to author, June 28, 1988.
6. George Geddes, transcript of interview with CTF 125 (Moon) April 29, 1944. U.S. Navy NRS 601. Other information from Jean Geddes, his widow, in conversation Jan. 30, Feb. 1, 1988.
7. Elwin Hendrick, personal letter, July 27, 1988.

8. Eugene Eckstam, personal letter to Ralph Greene, Aug. 25, 1984; copy enclosed in personal letter, Eckstam to author, June 14, 1988.
9. Naval message, HMS *Scimitar* to C-in-C, Plymouth, 270752; Tiger file, MOD.
10. Interview between Moon and CO, HMS *Scimitar,* April 29, 1944; US Navy file NRS 601.
11. Quoted in "The Other D Days," p. 15.
12. Eugene Carney. (R.G.)
13. Joseph Kennedy. (R.G.)
14. Moon to Eisenhower, message of May 1, 1944, 1150B; Eisenhower Library.
15. Summersby, p. 130.
16. Lord Terence Lewin in conversation, April 19, 1988.
17. John Moreno. (R.G.)
18. Capt. St. John Cronyn, writing on behalf of Director of Tactical, Torpedo, and Staff Duties Division, memorandum of July 3, 1944; Tiger file, MOD.
19. Henry Cooke, Deputy Director of Operations Department, June 7, 1944; Tiger file, MOD.
20. Cronyn, see note 18.
21. Ibid.
22. Ibid.

CHAPTER EIGHT

This chapter is largely based on the materials listed in Appendix I, and on U.S. Navy file NRS 601, with some additional materials from Appendix II, and the Royal Navy file on Tiger (MOD). Additional sources are listed below:

1. German logs on the E-boat attack: Ninth E-Boat flotilla log entry for 0134, April 27, 1944; enclosed in personal letter from Eugene Eckstam.
2. James Murdoch, interview at the Pentagon, Aug. 16, 1944; Library of Naval Training Center, Great Lakes, Illinois.
3. David D. Moore, Capt. Infantry, Commanding: report of May 1, 1944, from HQ, 478th Amphibian Truck Company to Commanding General, First Engineer Special Brigade, APO 230, U.S. Army.
4. Schrawder's commendation: dated December 9, 1946, Admiral R. L. Conolly to Schrawder. Enclosed in personal letter, Schrawder to author, Feb. 20, 1988.
5. Stanley Stout, personal letter to Tom Clark (who received letter March 24, 1988). Quoted in personal letter to author, April 8, 1988.
6. "Soldiers making the D Day landings still wore the CO_2-inflatable belt": information given by John Moreno to Ralph Greene.
7. The "is the presence . . . water," Glaister, p. 155.

CHAPTER NINE

1. Murphy, p. 240.
2. Twecwyn Cole Morgan, letter to *Dorset Evening Echo,* March 12, 1988; confirmed in conversation, July 26, 1988.
3. Fred Beattie, open letter to his former shipmates, Sept. 7, 1987.
4. Message of 291640B, Southern Base Section to SHAEF, Ref. No.: 13592; Eisenhower Library.
5. Lt. Col. B. H. Grundborg, CO, HQ, Sub Area V, to CO, HQ D Marshaling Area. HQ, APO 155, U.S. Army, April 30, 1944.
6. Senior surviving officer, USS *LST 531*, to Commander, LST, Flotilla 11, July 22, 1944, enclosure in personal letter, Henry Schrawder to author, Feb. 20, 1988.
7. Greene and Allen, p. 27. Additional detail in Ralph Greene, "Tiger Burning."
8. Joseph Sandor, quoted in *The Stuart News,* Dec. 7, 1987.
9. Bradley, *A Soldier's Story,* pp. 248–9.
10. F. H. Hinsley *et al.,* pp. 56–7.
11. Ibid.
12. Ibid.
13. Harry Butcher, Diary, p. 1230; Eisenhower Library.
14. Walter Bedell Smith, message addressed "For Combined Chiefs of Staff," signed "Eisenhower," message of 291111B; Eisenhower Library.
15. ANCXF to Eisenhower, 291000B; Eisenhower Library.
16. Eisenhower to Marshall, April 29, 1944; Eisenhower Library.
17. John Fletcher. (R.G.)
18. George Geddes, interview with Rear Admiral Moon; see note 6, Chapter Seven.
19. Capt. St. John Cronyn, memorandum of July 3, 1944; see note 18, Chapter Seven.
20. Admiral Sir Ralph Leatham, Report of Proceedings—Night of April 27/28, May 23, 1944; Tiger file, MOD.
21. Henry Cooke, DDOD (C), June 7, 1944; Tiger file, MOD.
22. George Geddes, interview with Rear Admiral Moon; see note 6, Chapter Seven.
23. John Moreno. (R.G.)
24. Jean Geddes, telephone conversations, Jan. 30, Feb. 1, 1988.
25. Eugene Caffey, letter to The Adjutant General, Dept. of the Army, Washington, July 19, 1951. Letter traced by Howard DeVoe.
26. Butcher, p. 456.
27. Ibid.
28. E-boat log, message from *S-138* on behalf of *S-136*, 0035 (their time), p. 7. Translated by Dr. William Fletcher, U.S. Naval Academy; copy enclosed in personal letter, Eugene Eckstam, July 23, 1988. This passage

was later misunderstood to mean that sailors *had* been captured ("The Other D Days").
29. Ingersoll, p. 105.
30. F. H. Hinsley *et al.*, pp. 56–7.
31. Bennett, p. 50.
32. Moses Hallett, personal letter, June 28, 1988, enclosing "slightly corrected copy" of letter to Ralph Greene, July 5, 1983.
33. Bernard Skahill; U.S. Navy file NRS 601.
34. Rear Admiral Don P. Moon, U.S. Navy file NRS 601.
35. Ibid.
36. Butcher, pp. 458–9.

CHAPTER TEN

1. All information on Conrad Schwechheimer, Pfc. 557th QM Railhead Company, in personal letter (with enclosures), Helen Metel (née Schwechheimer), March 2, May 24, 1988.
2. Cpl. Joseph Ciccio to Rose Ciccio, April 17, 1944; in personal letter enclosed, Rose Ciccio, July 12, 1988.
3. David Mare to Howard DeVoe, Jan. 14, 1988.
4. William Reckord, personal memoir.

CHAPTER ELEVEN

1. George Cronin, telephone conversation, Jan. 21,1988.
2. Woodward, p. 133.
3. Ibid.
4. Chalmers, pp. 211–12.
5. Ibid.
6. Woodward, pp. 139–40.
7. Ibid.
8. Ibid.
9. Ibid., footnote p. 135.
10. "Report by Naval C-in-C on Operation Neptune, 1944," vol. I, Appendix 2, p. 33.
11. Chalmers, p. 211.
12. Ibid.
13. Ibid.
14. Woodward, p. 148.
15. Chalmers, p. 210.
16. Ibid., p. 211.
17. Henry Schrawder, personal letter, Feb. 20, 1988.

18. Marvin Wohlbach. (R.G.)
19. Eugene Eckstam, personal letter to Ralph Greene, Aug. 25, 1984; copy enclosed in personal letter, Eckstam to author, June 23, 1988.
20. Angelo Crapanzano, personal letter to Ralph Greene, Aug. 1, 1984; copy enclosed in personal letter, Eugene Eckstam to author, June 23, 1988.
21. Eisenhower, p. 270.
22. Bradley, *A General's Life,* p. 27.
23. Eisenhower, p. 270.
24. Collins, p. 201.
25. Ibid., p. 207.
26. Ibid., p. 187.
27. History of the First Engineer Special Brigade, p. 29; Department of the Army, Washington.
28. Bradley, *A General's Life,* p. 249.
29. Ryan, p. 167.
30. Information from Jean Geddes, conversation, Feb. 1, 1988.
31. Rear Admiral Llewellyn V. Morgan, Director of Signal Division, July 17, 1944; Tiger file, MOD.
32. Weighley, p. 226.
33. Buell, pp. 457–8.
34. Adm. H. K. Hewitt, "Preparations for Anvil-Dragoon," Proceedings, U.S. Naval Institute, July 1954. (R.G.)
35. John P. Fletcher, conversation with Ralph Greene, Sept. 20, 1986.
36. Weighley, p. 226. See also *The Evening Star,* Washington D.C., Aug. 9, 1944: "Combat fatigue, Secretary of the Navy Forrestal said yesterday, apparently caused one of the Navy's youngest rear-admirals to take his own life after participating in the invasion of Europe."
37. John Moreno, personal letter, Sept. 11, 1988.
38. Moses Hallett, personal letter to Ralph Greene, Sept. 7, 1983; copy enclosed in personal letter, Hallett to author, June 28, 1988.
39. Rear Admiral E. J. P. Brind, CBE, ACN (H) (Assistant Chief of Naval Staff [Home]), letter of Aug. 7, 1944; Tiger file, MOD.
40. Ibid.
41. Ibid.
42. Hoyt, p. 134.
43. John Doyle, personal letter, May 28, 1988.
44. Adm. H. R. Stark, USN, letter to C-in-C, U.S. Fleet [Admiral King], May 19, 1944; NRS 601.
45. Elwin Hendrick. (R.G.)
46. Elwin Hendrick, personal letter, July 27, 1988.
47. David Moore, personal letter to Howard DeVoe, Jan. 14, 1988.
48. Jones, p. 254; see Archival material, p. 292.
49. Papers of Jeanne Porado, sister of William H. Schreiber, Seaman 2c, USNR, *LST 507.*
50. Eugene Eckstam, newsletter of April 20, 1988.

PART THREE: THE BURIAL GROUND

CHAPTER TWELVE

Note: All *Kingsbridge Gazette* references are to the front page unless stated otherwise.

1. *Kingsbridge Gazette and South Devon Advertiser,* Nov. 19, 1943, p. 4.
2. Their names were John Auger (aged 8) and John Lethbridge (11). Report in the *Kingsbridge Gazette,* May 19, 1944.
3. *Dartmouth Chronicle,* Dec. 23, 1983. (R.G.)
4. Ralph Rayner, letter to his constituent Mr. Soper of Slapton, July 18, 1944.
5. *Kingsbridge Gazette,* Nov. 19, 1943, p. 5.
6. Ibid., p. 4.
7. Ralph Rayner to Mr. Soper; see note 4.
8. *Daily Express,* May 8, 1944.
9. *Kingsbridge Gazette,* July 21, 1944.
10. Ibid.
11. *Kingsbridge Gazette,* Aug. 4, 1944.
12. *Kingsbridge Gazette,* July 21, 1944, p. 3.
13. *Kingsbridge Gazette,* Aug. 4, 1944, p. 8.
14. Ibid.
15. *Kingsbridge Gazette,* July 21, 1944.
16. John Hannaford, interview, Sept. 24, 1987.
17. *Kingsbridge Gazette,* July 21, 1944.
18. *Kingsbridge Gazette,* Aug. 4, 1944.
19. *Kingsbridge Gazette,* July 21, 1944.
20. Ibid., p. 3.
21. Ibid.
22. G. C. N. Mackarness, Regional Information Officer, SW Region; *Kingsbridge Gazette,* Aug. 4, 1944.
23. Bradbeer, p. 94.
24. Letter in the *Kingsbridge Gazette,* Sept. 1, 1944.
25. Farmer (name not known) speaking in the South Hams District Council video of the ceremony of June 2, 1984.
26. *Kingsbridge Gazette,* editorial of Aug. 18, 1944.
27. Ibid.
28. *Kingsbridge Gazette,* Aug. 25, 1944.
29. Bradbeer, p. 122.
30. *Kingsbridge Gazette,* Aug. 4, 1944. Mr. Mackarness again.
31. Letter in the *Kingsbridge Gazette,* Aug. 25, 1944.
32. *Kingsbridge Gazette,* Sept. 1, 1944.
33. Ibid.
34. Bradbeer, p. 113.
35. *Kingsbridge Gazette,* Jan. 12, 1945.

36. Inscription on the American memorial, Slapton Sands. The complete inscription reads:

This memorial was presented by the United States Army authorities to the people of the South Hams who generously left their homes and their lands to provide a battle practice area for the successful assault on Normandy in June 1944. Their action resulted in the saving of many hundreds of lives and contributed in no small measure to the success of the operation. The area included the villages of Blackawton, Chillington, East Allinton, Slapton, Stokenham, Strete, and Torcross together with many outlying farms and houses.

37. The inscription; see note 36.

CHAPTER THIRTEEN

1. Angelo Crapanzano, personal letter, May 11, 1988.
2. Tom Clark, personal letter, March 14, 1988.
3. Angelo Crapanzano, personal letter, May 11.
4. Col. Eugene Caffey, letter to the Adjutant General, Dept. of the Army, Washington D.C., July 19, 1951.
5. Ibid.
6. Howard DeVoe, letter to Executive Director, General of the Army Omar Bradley Foundation, Carlisle Barracks, Penn., Jan 21, 1985.
7. Churchill, p. 546.
8. Angelo Crapanzano, personal letter, Feb. 8, 1988.
9. Information from Harry Unsworth of Newton Abbot.
10. "The Other D Days," p. 29.
11. Information from Pierre Verniquet, Totnes.
12. Bradbeer, pp. 137–8.
13. Geraldine James, on *Large Slow Target*, BBC Radio 4, Nov. 13, 1987.
14. Gilbert and Cecil Chestnut, telephone conversation, Oct. 15, 1987.
15. *Dorset At War*, p. 241.
16. *Dorset Evening Echo*, Jan. 29, 1988.
17. John Hockaday, telephone conversation, July 27, 1988, and personal letter (undated), 1988.
18. John Hockaday; see note 16.
19. "The Other D Days," p. 29.
20. *Kingsbridge Gazette*, March 24, 1950.
21. "The Other D Days," p. 29.
22. Arthur L. Clamp, *Exercises Tiger and Fabius: an illustrated account of the American Forces assault exercises held at Slapton Sands in 1944 as a rehearsal for part of the D Day landings in France*, booklet, Plymouth, Westway Publications, 1986.

23. *Western Morning News* (Plymouth), July 26, 1954.
24. Slapton Sands reunion, June 2, 1984; "A Commemoration of the Evacuation of the Area and Exercises Tiger and Fabius"; video produced by South Hams District Council.
25. Bradbeer, pp. 134–5.
26. *Kingsbridge Gazette,* June 21, 1974.
27. Emanuel Rubin, interview, Slapton Sands, Sept. 23, 1987.

CHAPTER FOURTEEN

1. *Kingsbridge Gazette,* Feb. 15, 1974.
2. *Kingsbridge Gazette,* April 19, 1970.
3. Ken Small, interview for CBC, Sept. 24, 1987; telephone conversations, Sept.–Nov. 1987; conversation, Cove Guest House, Feb. 10, 1988.
4. Kendall McDonald, "Victims of Devon's D Day," *Diver,* Jan. 1987.
5. Ibid.
6. Kendall McDonald, telephone conversation, Jan.7, 1988.
7. All details of Ken Small's buying and salvaging the tank from Casely.
8. Mrs. Helen Metel, personal letter, March 2, 1988.
9. Ken Small, interview for CBC, Sept. 24, 1987.
10. Wendell Hoppler, telephone conversation, July 10, 1988, and personal letter, July 14, 1988.
11. *Daily Mail,* Oct. 1, 1987. Other information from Leslie Thomas in telephone conversation, Sept. 1987, and during work on *Large Slow Target,* Nov. 1987. Also: *The Sunday Telegraph,* Oct. 11, Oct. 18, 1981.
12. John Sheldon Doud Eisenhower, p. 458.
13. Information from Harry Unsworth, Newton Abbot, in the form of undated articles from newspapers in Devon (identity of newspapers not known) and one in the United States (*Daily News,* Ohio).
14. *Torquay Herald-Express,* Sept. 19, 1983.
15. Frank Wintle, telephone conversation, July 11, 1988.
16. Transcript of tape-recorded BBC interview acquired from BBC Plymouth for *Large Slow Target.* Further details not at hand.
17. Alma Taft, telephone conversation, July 10, 1988; *Daily Mail,* Oct. 1, 1987.
18. Kenneth David Kimberley's story is told in the *Torquay Herald-Express,* Jan. 24, Feb. 14, March 31, May 4, July 9, and Sept. 19, 1983; and in the *Dartmouth Chronicle,* Feb. 17, 1984. I first learned of Mr. Kimberley from Harry Unsworth of Newton Abbot on Feb. 10, 1988. I am also indebted to Mr. Unsworth for a copy of an article in the *Sunday Independent* (Devon), Sept. 6, 1987, about the Heathfield site.
19. Emanuel Rubin, telephone conversation.

20. Nola Safro, telephone conversation, July 12, 1988.
21. Alma Taft, July 10, 1988; Jane Corbyn, July 13, 1988.

CHAPTER FIFTEEN

1. Stella Rouggley, interviewed by the author on Oct. 27, 1987, for *Large Slow Target,* BBC Radio Nov. 4, 13, 1987.
2. Angelo Crapanzano, personal letter, May 11, 1988.
3. Alma Taft, telephone conversation, July 10, Aug. 4, 1988.
4. Casely.
5. Video prepared by the South Hams District Council.
6. *Monroe Evening Times* (Wisconsin), Dec. 28, 1987.
7. Ambrose, p. 293.
8. Alma Taft, telephone conversations, July 10, Aug. 4, Sept. 23, 1988.
9. *Sunday Post-Crescent,* Appleton-Neenah-Menasha, Wisconsin, Dec. 6, 1987.
10. Angelo Crapanzano, personal letter to Joseph McCann, March 30, 1985, and to Emanuel Rubin, Jan. 25, 1988.
11. Wendell Hoppler, personal letter, July 14, 1988.
12. *The Dispatch,* Hudson/Bergen Counties, N.J., April 12, 1985.
13. *Kingsbridge Gazette,* May 17, 1985.
14. *Kingsbridge Gazette,* June 14, 1985.
15. Information on Chicago reunion from *Chicago Sun-Times,* Sept. 8, 1985; Wendell Hoppler personal letter, July 14, 1988; and Eugene Eckstam personal letter, June 23, 1988.
16. Ken Small interview, Sept. 24, 1987; and press reports.
17. BBC local television report, Sept. 1987; copy in possession of Emanuel Rubin, Plymouth.
18. *Torquay Herald-Express,* June 1, 1987; and interview with author, Sept. 24, 1987. There is some confusion about the date of Ken Small's meeting with William Taft. According to Ken Small in an interview it was Tuesday, May 18. But according to the Seventieth Tank Battalion Association newsletter, *The Peckerwood Reporter* (no. 120, Summer 1988), it was in 1986; May 18 was a Tuesday in 1987 but not in 1986.
19. *Torquay Herald-Express,* Aug. 21, 1987; story by Liz Phillips.
20. *Torquay Herald-Express,* Sept. 14, 1987.
21. LST reunion, Oct. 22–5, 1987, Newport News, Norfolk, Virginia. Video film of the reunion (not broadcast) in possession of Emanuel Rubin, Plymouth.

CHAPTER SIXTEEN

1. *Kingsbridge Gazette,* Sept. 11, 1987; article by Steve Peacock.
2. *The Times,* Nov. 13, 1987.

3. *The Independent,* Sept. 21, 1987, p. 2.
4. *Torquay Herald-Express,* Nov. 16, 1987; report by Liz Phillips.
5. Emanuel Rubin, interview, Jan. 16–17, 1988.
6. Alma Taft, telephone conversation, July 10, 1988.
7. *Torquay Herald-Express,* Nov. 16, 1987.
8. *Kingsbridge Gazette,* Nov. 20, 1987, p. 32.
9. *Torquay Herald-Express,* Nov. 16, 1987.
10. *Torquay Herald-Express,* Nov. 16, 1987; *Kingsbridge Gazette,* Nov. 16, 1987.
11. Emanuel Rubin, Associated Press report, Nov. 15, 1987.
12. Emanuel Rubin, interview, Jan. 17, 1988.
13. *Torquay Herald-Express,* Nov. 16, 1987.
14. Associated Press report, *Denver Post,* Nov. 16,1987.
15. *Western Morning News,* Nov. 16, 1987; article by Sue Morgan.
16. Associated Press report, *Denver Post,* Nov. 16, 1987.
17. Quoted in *Everett Herald* (Washington State), Nov. 11, 1987, pp. 1–11A.
18. *Torquay Herald-Express,* Nov. 16, 1987.
19. *Western Morning News,* Nov. 16, 1987.
20. *Torquay Herald-Express,* Nov. 16, 1987.
21. *Western Morning News,* Nov. 16, 1987.
22. *Torquay Herald-Express,* Nov. 16, 1987.
23. Ibid.
24. Ibid.
25. Quote from Ken Small in *Springfield News-Sun* (Ohio) ("Local Living," p. 1B), Nov. 15, 1987.
26. Atlee Wampler, personal letter, Feb. 29, 1988.
27. Howard DeVoe, newsletter, "Operation Tiger Update," July 8, 1988:

   This writer received a letter a week ago from Carl Effler, reunion chairman for the 279th Eng. Com. Battalion. He tells me he can prove they were in Texas taking basic training on April 28, 1944, and were only in England the night of September 30, 1944, when they trans-shipped to Omaha Beach for European service. This can be attested to by their former C. O., Harry Loving, and their Exec. Major E. Hunter Smith. This eliminates them from the operation.

28. Charles J. Myers, secretary and treasurer, Seventieth Tank Battalion Association, personal letter to Dale Rodman, July 30, 1988.
29. Charles MacDonald, personal letter to Dale Rodman, Nov. 17, 1987.
30. Quoted in *Springfield News-Sun* (Ohio), Nov. 15, 1987.
31. Howard DeVoe, newsletter, "Operation Tiger Update," July 8, 1988.
32. Dale Rodman, personal letter, Dec. 17, 1987.
33. House Joint Resolution 418 in the House of Representatives, Dec. 10, 1987, "To Designate April 28, 1988, as 'National Day of Remembrance of the 749 American Victims of Operation Tiger.' "

PART FOUR: "THE FIELD WHERE THE
SOLDIERS ARE . . ."

CHAPTER SEVENTEEN

1. Dale Rodman, personal letter, Aug. 12, 1988:

Donald S. Bryant appears on the Brigade list but not on the 531st ESR
morning reports (Apr. 28–May 4). These reports list 18 dead and missing
(all killed Apr. 28, '44). The loading tables show 12 trucks and 24 men
aboard *LST 531*. The survivors list (*#531*) lists 6 men from the 531st ESR.
If Bryant is included the total becomes 25. If Bryant was killed during Tiger
it was before the 28th and the only other day was the 27th.

A good example of Dale Rodman's detailed research into casualty figures.

2. Harlander's report, U.S. Navy file NRS 601.
3. Murdoch's report, U.S. Navy file NRS 601.
4. U.S. Department of Defense, Public Affairs, Public Information Series
   (numbered PC 36).
5. Howard DeVoe, personal letter to Eugene Eckstam, Apr. 26, 1988.
6. *The Times*, July 2, 1988.
7. Article in *Army*, June 1988.
8. L. R. Talbot, "Passing in Review: the Story of American
   Graves Registration Command in Europe and Africa," Document
   D769.75. L55, Chapter 26, p. 2.
9. Information from William Kuntz, personal letter, Jan. 21, 1988; and
   Gerald Frederick, telephone conversation, May 14, 1988. Mr. Frederick
   is under the impression that Chandler's wife was expecting a child, and
   that he took a bet with another expectant father on the same ship as to
   whose child would be born first.
10. Morning report summary prepared by Dale Rodman from documents
    obtained from National Personnel Records Center, St. Louis, Mo.,
    March 11, 1988.
11. Hoyt, pp. 118, 155.
12. Houson.
13. Harrison, p. 270.
14. Collins, p. 188.
15. See archive material, p. 286.
16. Moon, message of April 30; Eisenhower Library.
17. Douglas Harlander, personal letter, July 7, 1988.
18. Charles MacDonald, Associated Press agency report, Nov. 15, 1988;
    telephone conversation, Feb. 4, 1988; correspondence, March 1988;
    interview with author for *Large Slow Target*, BBC Radio 4, Nov. 13,
    1987.
19. Butcher, pp. 458–9.

20. Ruppenthal, p. 352.
21. Harlander, July 22, 1988.
22. Tom Clark, personal letter, Oct. 11, 1988.
23. Dale Rodman, personal letter, Aug. 26, 1988.
24. Arthur Victor, "log" of late Seventies/early Eighties, p. 2.
25. Joseph McCann, statement obtained by Dale Rodman, *515* reunion, Reno, Nevada, Sept. 23, 1988.
26. James Murdoch, Pentagon interview recorded Aug. 16, 1944. Declassified Sept. 27, 1958. Library of Naval Training Center, Great Lakes, Illinois. Copy provided on loan by Angelo Crapanzano.
27. Tom Clark, personal letter, Oct. 11, 1988.
28. Ship sheet for *507* obtained by Dale Rodman; see Archival sources.
29. St. John Cronyn, letter, July 3, 1944; Tiger file, MOD.
30. Information in personal letter from Angelo Crapanzano, May 30, 1988, quoting Stephen Horvath and Andrew Yakim, former crew members of the *508*, from *Large Slow Target* (LST Association history publication, 1986), vol. II.
31. Landing table of April 14; obtained by Dale Rodman from Carlisle Barracks (Microfilm Box 2127).
32. Moses Hallett, quoted by Dale Rodman in personal letter, Sept. 27, 1988.

CHAPTER EIGHTEEN

1. Julian Perkin, in conversation, Aug. 4, 1988.
2. *Kingsbridge Gazette and South Devon Advertiser,* July 21, 1944, p. 1.
3. *Approaches to Portland,* Admiralty Tidal Stream Atlas, No. 257, Taunton Hydrographic Dept., 1973.
4. John Hockaday, personal letter (undated), 1988.
5. Information from Geoffrey Page, Rowing Correspondent of the *Daily Telegraph* and *Sunday Telegraph.*
6. L. R. Talbot, "Passing in Review: the Story of American Graves Registration Command in Europe and Africa." Document D769.75.L55, Chapter 26, pp. 2–3.
7. Jean Marie Ward, Directorate for Public Correspondence, Office of the Assistant Secretary of Defense (Public Affairs), letter to Dale Rodman, April 20, 1988:

Only two individuals are listed in the Normandy American Cemetery and Memorial as having died on April 28, 1944. The memorial, which commemorates those whose remains were not recovered, lists EM-3 Sylvester M. Burns (USN), Serial No. 8212720. He received a Purple Heart. Another apparent Exercise Tiger victim, Private Robert P. Motley (USA, Serial No. 33042113), is buried in Plot I, Row 25, Grave 22. He also received the Purple Heart. EM-3 Burns and Private Motley were from Pennsylvania and Virginia, respectively.

8. Article by Jon Nordheimer, *New York Times Service,* reprinted in the *International Herald Tribune,* April 28–9, 1964, p. 2.
9. Letter to John Bowden, July 5, 1988. The *Dartmouth Chronicle,* Feb. 17, 1984, reported that Mrs. Nancy Bowden of Torquay "revealed that her brother-in-law rang her after seeing reports of the mass grave on Australian TV—and told her he, too, had seen dead U.S. soldiers being unloaded from lorries for burial in the South Hams."
10. Dorothy Seekings, interview, Feb. 8, 1988.
11. Kathleen Langford, interview, Feb. 9, 1988.
12. Marcus Davidson, BBC TV, conversation, Feb. 11, 1988. Based on Mr. Davidson's conversations with Nolan Tope. Also, the *Dartmouth Chronicle,* Feb. 17, 1984: "Mr. Tope declared that there was no evidence to show that bodies are buried in his field and he was adamant that no one would be allowed on his land to carry out investigations or excavations."
13. Mr. Buckpitt, Feb. 9, 1988.
14. Edward Pratt, Feb. 9, 1988.
15. Denis Emus, telephone conversation, Feb. 11, 988.
16. Eric W. Seabourne, DFC, telephone conversation, Feb. 11, 1988.
17. Edward Pratt, telephone conversation, June 26, 1988.
18. Denis Emus, telephone conversation, June 26, 1988.
19. Edward Pratt, telephone conversation, June 28, 1988.
20. Connor Turley, conversation in The Tower Inn, Slapton, Feb. 9, 1988.
21. See Stallings for the *adobe* explanation. The alternative explanation is in *Brewer.* Information from Billy Balch, London.
22. Graves, pp. 195, 230.
23. Frazer, pp. 444–5.

POSTSCRIPT

1. William E. Hart, Deputy Assistant Defense Secretary, to Senator Robert Dole, Oct. 21, 1987.
2. Quoted in personal letter, John Moreno, Sept. 11, 1988.
3. John Moreno, personal letter, Nov. 15, 1988.
4. Hoyt, p. 116.
5. John Towner, letter to *The Guardian,* April 1981, and conversation with the author, Aug. 4, 1988.
6. Bill Hiscock, conversation, Jan. 27 and Aug. 22, 1988. Extract from the log of the *Hawkins* and enclosed personal letter, Hiscock to author, 1988 (undated).
7. Julian Perkin, telephone conversation, Aug. 4, 1988.

8. Harold McAulley, telephone conversation, June 24, 1988.
9. Lester Limbaugh, telephone conversation, Aug. 30, 1988.
10. Hoyt, p. 88.
11. Harold McAulley, telephone conversation, June 24, 1988.
12. Harold McAulley, telephone conversation, Sept. 13, 1988.
13. Harold McAulley, telephone conversation, July 21, 1988.
14. Harold McAulley, telephone conversation, June 24, 1988.
15. Eileen Trainor, telephone conversation, June 25, 1988.
16. Jerry Williams, Past State Commander, Madison V. A. Hosp. Rep., Eveland-Trainor Post No. 433, Barneveld, Wisconsin; telephone conversation, June 25, 1988.
17. Letter to Mrs. Amelia Trainor (Joseph Trainor's mother), from Major General J. A. Ulio, the Adjutant General's Office, Washington D.C., June 27, 1944; enclosed in personal letter, Jerry Williams to author, July 6, 1988.
18. Ibid.
19. Eileen Trainor, telephone conversation, Aug. 22, 1988.
20. See note 17.
21. Letters from Laurence McDaniel (July 25, 1988) and John DiBello (undated). John DiBello's letter states: "I did not help in removing men from the water or in the burial detail."
22. Lester Limbaugh, telephone conversation, Aug. 30, 1988.
23. Harold McAulley, telephone conversation, Sept. 13, 1988.
24. Harold McAulley, telephone conversation, June 24, 1988.
25. Letter to Mr. Louis Trainor (Joseph Trainor's father), from Major General T. B. Larkin. The Quartermaster General, War Department, Washington D.C., July 8, 1944; enclosed in personal letter Jerry Williams to author, July 6, 1988.
26. Joseph Rivers, letters, Aug. 8, Aug. 16, 1988; telephone conversation, Aug. 15, 1988.
27. Ryan, pp. 172–4.
28. Information in *Encyclopedia Americana*.
29. Howard DeVoe, personal letter, July 10, 1988.
30. *Stars and Stripes*, 1944. Collection of Dale Rodman.

BIBLIOGRAPHY

PUBLISHED SOURCES

Ambrose, Stephen E. *Eisenhower*. London: Allen & Unwin, 1984, vol. 1.

Belfield, Eversley and H. Essame. *Battle for Normandy*. London: Batsford, 1965.

Bennett, Ralph. *Ultra in the West: The Normandy Campaign 1944–1945*. London: Hutchinson, 1979.

Bradbeer, Grace. *The Land Changed Its Face*. Dartmouth: Harbour Books, 1984.

Bradley, Omar N. and Clive Blair. *A Soldier's Story*. New York: Holt, 1951.

Bradley, Omar N. *A General's Life*. London: Sidgwick & Jackson, 1983.

Buell, Thomas. *Master of Sea Power: A Biography of Fleet Admiral Ernest J. King*. Boston, Mass.: Little, Brown, 1980.

Burch, Stanley. "Eisenhower," *News Chronicle Book Profile*. N.C., 1952.

Butcher, Harry C. *My Three Years with Eisenhower*. London: Heinemann, 1946. (Complete original manuscript in Dwight D. Eisenhower Library, Abilene.)

Casely, Steve. "Wreck Recovery, the Tank That Missed D Day," *After the Battle*. No. 45., 1985, pp. 19–32.

Cave Brown, Anthony. *Bodyguard of Lies*. London: W. H. Allen, 1976.

Chalmers, W. S. *Rear-Admiral, Full Cycle: the Biography of Admiral Sir Bertram Home Ramsay KCB, KBE, MVO*. London: Hodder & Stoughton, 1959.

Churchill, Winston S. *Closing the Ring. The Second World War*, Vol. 5. London: Cassell & Co. Ltd, 1952.

Collins, James Lawton. *Lightning Joe, An Autobiography*. New Orleans: Louisiana State University Press, 1979.

Eisenhower, Dwight D. *Crusade in Europe*. London: Heinemann, 1948.

Eisenhower, John Sheldon Doud. *Allies: Pearl Habor to D Day*. New York: Doubleday, 1982.

Frazer, James George. *The Golden Bough: A Study in Magic and Religion*, abbr. ed. London: Macmillan, 1932.

Glaister, John. *Glaister's Medical Jurisprudence and Toxicology*. Ed. Edgar Rentoul and Hamilton Smith. Edinburgh and London: Churchill Livingstone, 1973.

Graves, Robert. *The Greek Myths*. Vol. 1. London: Pelican, 1955.

Greene, Ralph C., and Oliver E. Allen. "What Happened off Devon." *American Heritage*, Vol. 36, No. 2, February/March 1985.

Gunther, John. *Eisenhower, the Man and the Symbol*. London: Hamish Hamilton, 1952.

Harrison, Gordon. *Cross-Channel Attack: United States Army in World War II, The European Theater of Operations*. Washington, D.C.: Office of the Chief of Military History, Department of the Army, 1951.

Hatch, Alden. *General Eisenhower*. N.C.: Skeffington and Co. Ltd, 1946.

Heavey, William F. *Brigadier General, Down Ramp! The Story of the Army Amphibian Engineers*. Washington, D.C.: Infantry Journal Press.

Hill, Roger. *Destroyer Captain*. Wellingborough, Northants: William Kimber, 1975.

Hinsley, F. H. et al. *British Intelligence in the Second World War*. London: HMSO, 1988.

Hoyt, Edwin P. *The Invasion Before Normandy: The Secret Battle of Slapton Sands*. London: Robert Hale, 1987.

Ingersoll, Ralph. *Top Secret*. New York: Harcourt Brace, 1946.

Irving, David. *The Destruction of P.Q. 17*. Wellingborough, Northants: William Kimber, 1980.

King, Ernest. J. *Fleet Admiral*, "Second Official Report to the Secretary of the Navy, March 1, 1944 to March 1, 1945" in *The War Reports of Marshall (Army), Arnold (Air Force), and King (C-in-C, U.S. Fleet, and Chief of Naval Operations)*, Philadelphia and New York, Lippincott, 1947.

Legg, Rodney. *Dorset's War 1939–45*. Wincanton, Somerset: Wincanton Press, 1986.

Marshall, George. *Biennial Report of the Chief of Staff of the United States Army, July 1, 1943 to June 30, 1945*.

Marshall, Katherine Tupper. *Together*. London: Blandford, 1947.

Morgan, Frederick, KCB (COSSAC). *Overture to Overlord*. London: Hodder & Stoughton, 1950.

Morison, Samuel Eliot. *The Invasion of France and Germany. History of United States Naval Operation in World War II*, vol XI., Boston, Mass.: Little, Brown, 1962.

Murphy, John. *Dorset at War*. Wincanton, Somerset: Dorset Publishing Company, 1979.

Patton, George S. *War As I Knew It*. Boston, Mass.: Houghton Mifflin, 1947.

Ramsay, Winston. "The Other D Days," *After the Battle*, No. 44, 1984, pp. 1–31.

Ruppenthal, Roland. *Logistical Support of the Armies: United States Army in*

World War II, the European Theater of Operations. Washington, D.C.: Office of the Chief of Military History, Department of the Army, 1953, vol. 1, *May 1942–September 1944*, p. 352.

Ryan, Cornelius. *The Longest Day: June 6, 1944*. London: Gollancz, 1960.

Stallings, Lawrence. *The Doughboys*. New York: Harper & Row, 1963.

Summersby, Kay. *Eisenhower Was My Boss*. N.C.: Werner Laurie, 1949.

Weighley, Russell F. *Eisenhower's Lieutenants*. London: Sidgwick & Jackson, 1981.

Woodward, David. *Ramsay at War*. Wellinborough, Northants: William Kimber, 1957.

ARCHIVAL MATERIAL

Archival material came to me both directly from the archives themselves, and indirectly from people who had consulted them, usually Dr. Eugene Eckstam and Dale Rodman. The chief archival source was U.S. Navy file NRS 601 from Washington Navy Yard, "Tiger Exercise: E-Boat Attack, April 28, 1944, in English Channel Area." With great generosity, Dr. Eckstam copied this file in its entirety and sent it to me. With equal generosity, J. R. Cranny of Dorset sent me a microfilm of it. A number of people provided me with after-action reports from NRS 601, available from the Library of the Naval Training Center, Great Lakes, Illinois. From the same source Angelo Crapanzano obtained and sent to me a transcript of James Murdoch's Pentagon Interview of August 1944. Another document in the possession of many survivors is the Navy list of casualties, "Dead, wounded, and missing of LSTs engaged in action with enemy E-boats, April 28, 1944 (LSTs *507, 531, 289, 511*)." Other archival material and sources are listed below.

BRITAIN

Ministry of Defence (MOD), London

Archive of Empress State Building, Fulham, Royal Navy inquiry into the attack on Convoy T-4, BSR 576. Also in Public Records Office, Kew.

Histories of HMS *Azalea*, HMS *Scimitar*.

UNITED STATES

Department of the Army, Washington

History, the First Engineer Special Brigade.

Short paper on Exercise Tiger by Howard G. DeVoe, historian of the 531st Engineer Shore Regiment.

Whereabouts of the dead of *LST 289*, obtained by Winston Ramsay, March 27, 1984 (Memorial Affairs Division).

Dwight D. Eisenhower Library, Abilene, Kansas

Butcher, Harry C., diary.
Correspondence: Eisenhower, Marshall.
Messages: Moon, SHAEF, ANCXF.
SHAEF Staff Message Control: messages, Exercise Tiger.

Military Field Branch, Military Archives Branch, National Archives, Suitland, Maryland

Company History, Thirty-third Chemical Decontamination Company, U.S. Army.
First Engineer Special Brigade historical report, Record Grp. 407, Box 19038, En. Br. 1-1-01. Including list of troops aboard LSTs *507* and *531*.
Jones, Clifford, "Neptune: Training, Mounting, the Artificial Ports." A number of copies of the relevant pages of this were in circulation among a variety of Tiger survivors. The most complete copy I found, incorporating a vital page missing from all the others, was loaned to me by Emanuel Rubin, who had been given it by a journalist from, of all places, *Le Figaro* in Paris.

National Personnel Records Center, St. Louis, Missouri

Morning reports, the 531st Engineer Shore Regiment, 33rd Chemical Decontamination Co., 478th Amphibious Truck Co., 557th Quartermaster Railhead Co. Obtained, compiled, and interpreted by Dale Rodman.

Pentagon, War Department Records Branch

Microfilm, Items Nos. 2216, 2217: Boat Assignment Tables (ship sheets) LST loading and landing tables, troop lists, etc., for Exercise Tiger (2216) and D Day (2217).

U.S. Army Military History Institute, Carlisle Barracks, Pennsylvania

Fourth Infantry Division, Item 2216, FO No. 1, Exercise Tiger field orders, April 18, 1944. (See also Pentagon, War Department, Records Branch.)
Samuel Forgy Papers, Philip C. Gowdy Collection. "Personnel Killed in Action April 28, 1944 During Invasion Exercise Tiger." Enclosure 4c of "History of the First Engineer Special Brigade," including page-by-page breakdown of men missing, buried in Cambridge, England, and repatriated to the United States.
Talbot, L. R. "Passing in Review: The Story of American Graves Registration

Command in Europe and Africa." n.p., 1955. D769.75.L55, Chapter 26.

U.S. Battle Monuments Commission

Army survivor list of *LST 531*.
Lists of graves and commemorations of the missing, Cambridge, Normandy, and the United States.

U.S. Department of Defense (Public Affairs)

Public Information Series leaflet *Exercise Tiger*, PC 36 (1988).

U.S. Naval Academy, Annapolis, Maryland

Material on Rear Admiral Don Pardee Moon.

Washington Navy Yard

A couple of "status record cards" dealing with *LST 531* obtained by Eugene Eckstam in pursuit of his conviction (proved correct) that the bow of *LST 531* remained floating for some while after the E-boat attack.

Informal Histories

"World War II History of the 479th Amphibian Truck Co." from Harold McAulley *via* Dr. Eckstam.
Turn To, a history of *LST 511*, from Robert Briggs; no other information available.

APPENDIX I

SURVIVORS, PARTICIPANTS, RESCUERS, AND
RESCUED:
MATERIAL IN THE POSSESSION OF NIGEL LEWIS

All interviews and telephone conversations are with, and all letters are to, the author unless stated otherwise.

BRITAIN

HMS *Saladin*

Perkin, Julian: Telephone conversation, Aug. 4, 1988; article in *Western Morning News*, March 21, 1984.

HMS *Sutton*

Johnson, Leslie: Letter, Feb. 23, 1988; telephone conversation, March 3, 1988.

UNITED STATES

LST 58

Irwin, Howard: Telephone conversation, Jan 15, 1988; letter, January 18, 1988; telephone conversation, March 8, 1988.

LST 289

Frederick, Gerald: Telephone conversation, May 14, 1988. Letter May 19, 1988.

Kuntz, William: Letter, Jan. 21, 1988. Interview, *Springfield* [Ohio] *News-Sun*, Nov. 15, 1987.

Moore, David: Company Commander, 478th Amphibian Truck Company and senior army officer aboard *LST 289*. Letter to Howard DeVoe, Jan. 14, 1988; letter to Dale Rodman, March 22, 1988.

Rubin, Emanuel ("Manny"): Interviewed on Slapton Sands, Sept. 23, 1987, and in Plymouth, Jan. 16/17, 1988. Also numerous telephone conversations. *Western Evening Herald* (Plymouth), interview May 28, 1984.

Sandor, Joseph: Interview in *The Stuart News*, Dec. 7, 1987.

LST 499

Dunn, Vincent: Letter, March 20, 1988.

LST 507

Bartholomay, Raymond: Memoir dated Dec. 9, 1987. Copies with Eugene Eckstam and Dale Rodman. A further memoir (undated) in possession of Eugene Eckstam.

Beattie, Fred: "Dear Gene and fellow shipmates." Letter of Sept. 7, 1988, ("Log") to Eugene Eckstam and others.

Clark, Tom: Letters, Feb. 15, March 14, April 8, April 12, July 17, 1988; letter to Senator John Melcher, recommending recognition of John Doyle's gallantry, May 13, 1986; letter to his father, July 4/5, 1944; part of Chapter 11 of an unfinished novel set aboard *LST 507* (fictionalized as *LST 503*) and written in the 1950s. Interviewed (with Angelo Crapanzano) in *The Dispatch*, Hudson Bergen Counties, N.J., April 12, 1985.

Crapanzano, Angelo: Letters, Feb. 8, May 11, May 23, May 30, 1988; letters to Manny Rubin, June 4, 1984, Jan. 25, 1988; personal memoir in possession of Eugene Eckstam, Aug. 1, 1984; letter to Joseph McCann, March 30, 1985. Interview in *The Dispatch* (see Tom Clark, above).

Eckstam, Eugene: Newsletters to Tiger survivors and veterans, Oct. 1987, April 20, 1988. Letters, June 14, June 23, July 1, July 27, Aug. 23, 1988. Several telephone conversations. Interviewed in *Monroe Evening Times*, Dec. 28, 1987, and in *Wisconsin State Journal*, June 5, 1988. Numerous enclosures in letters, including personal memoirs, computer printouts of lists of survivors, veterans, etc.

Fedyszyn, John: Letters to Dale Rodman, Aug, 5, 1987, March 28, April 8, 1988.

Gifford, Stanley: Letter, June 7, 1988; letter to Dale Rodman, March 17, 1988.

Greene, Richard: Letters (two) to Eugene Eckstam, 1987 (undated). Letter to Eugene Eckstam, July 3, 1988.

Menzies, John: Letter to Dale Rodman, April 20, 1988.

Morse, Leslie: Letters to Eugene Eckstam, Dec. 19, 1987, July 5, 1988; letter to Dale Rodman, March 20, 1988; letter to author, June 5, 1988.

Myers, Allan: "Dear Survivor from 507" letter of April 11, 1988. Copy in possession of Eugene Eckstam.

Nickson, Albert: Personal memoir ("Log"), six pages. In possession of Eugene Eckstam.

Reckord, William: Personal memoir in possession of Dale Rodman and Eugene Eckstam.

Redieske, William: Personal memoir in possession of Dale Rodman and Eugene Eckstam.

Rodman, E. Dale: Extensive correspondence dating from Dec. 17, 1987. Personal memoir. Numerous enclosures, including U.S. archival material, memoirs, tables, figures, etc.

Victor, Arthur: Telephone conversations with NL, June 21, July 10, 1988. Personal memoir written May/June 1944 and checked with Adelbert Sickley. Later memoir of late 1970s/early 1980s (undated). Letter to NL, July 13, 1988.

LST 511

Briggs, Robert: Letter (undated). Enclosure: *Turn To,* a history of USS *LST 511*, Dec. 1945.

LST 515

Carney, Eugene: Quoted in *American Heritage* magazine, Feb.–March 1985.

Doyle, John: Letter, May 28, 1988.

Hallett, Moses: Telephone conversation, June 24, 1988. Letters, June 29, July 16, 1988.

Hendrick, Elwin: Letter, July 27, 1988.

Hicks, Floyd: Letter, June 27, 1988.

Hoppler, Wendell: Telephone conversation, July 10, 1988. Letter, July 14, 1988. Personal memoir enclosed.

Imhof, Donald: Letter, June 10, 1988.

McCann, Joseph: Letter, July 10, 1988. Interview in *The Herald,* Everett, Washington, Nov. 11, 1987.

LST 531

Gosselin, Raymond: Note in answer to questionnaire issued by Eugene Eckstam.

Harlander, Douglas: Letters, June 4, July 22, July 28, 1988. Letter to Howard DeVoe, Dec. 31, 1987; letter to Edward Kaska, Jan. 2, 1985.

Holland, William: Letter to Eugene Eckstam (undated).

Perry, John: Letter, June 1, 1988. Enclosed: interview printed in *The Tribune-Democrat* (undated) and a newspaper article (newspaper not known) of Jan. 25, 1945, about his survival.

Schrawder, Henry: Letter, Feb. 20, 1988, with enclosures.

Secreti, Louis: Note (undated) to Eugene Eckstam, about the floating bow of *LST 531*.

USS *Bayfield*

Morens, John: Letters, Sept. 11, 1988, Nov. 25, 1988.

USS Tide-Am-125

Modeste, Charles: Letter to Sylvia Chase, ABC TV, May 16, 1984. Letters, Feb. 12, April 25, May 30, 1988.

APPENDIX II

SOURCE NOTES FOR ADDITIONAL RESEARCH MATERIAL PROVIDED BY
RALPH GREENE (R.G.)

Breher, Charles, in conversation, April 6, 1984.

Buhl, Howard (*LST 494*), personal letter, Aug. 20, 1983.

Carney, Eugene (Fourth Infantry Division), in conversation, April 16, 1984.

Deniero, Louis (*LST 511*), personal letters, May 20, Aug. 21, 1983.

Fletcher, John, personal letter, Sept. 6, 1986; in conversation, Sept. 20, 1986.

Glennon, Thomas, personal letter, July 13, 1984; interview, Oct. 19, 20, 1984.

Grosse, Hermann "Buddie" (*LST 515*), interview, May 11, 985.

Hawley, Dr. George (Lt. s.g. MC, USNR, *LST 515*), personal letters, June 28, Aug. 24, 1983; in conversation, Feb. 5, 1984; interview, June 19, 1984.

Haywood, William (*LST 289*), personal letters, June 6, 1983, March 4, 1984. William Haywood is the source for the story of Joseph Griffin.

Hendrick, Elwin (*LST 515*), personal letters, June 10, 29, 1985; interview Sept. 6, 1985.

Hicks, Floyd (*LST 515*), interview, Jan. 20, 1985; personal letter, July 18, 1985.

Hoppler, Wendell (*LST 515*), interview, May 11, 1985.

Kennedy, Joseph (*LST 289*), personal letters, May 24, July 14, 1983.

McMahon, Martin (Underwater Demolition, USN; aboard *LST 289*), interview, March 6, 1984.

Moreno, John A., personal letters, July 7, Oct. 6, 1984; interview, Feb. 7, 1985.

Roop, David A. (*LST 515* LCdr, USN Ret.), personal letters, June 1, July 15, 1983; in conversation, April 30, 1984.

Sickley, Adelbert (*LST 507*), personal letter, June 16, 1985; interview, Sept. 5, 1985.

Victor, Arthur (*LST 507*), personal letter, July 7, July 19, 1985.
Wilson Dr. J. B., personal letter, April 27, 1984.
Wohlbach, Marvin (*LST 511*), personal letter, June 19, 1985; interview, Sept. 5, 1985.

INDEX

ABC Television. *See 20/20*
Admiral Hipper (German battleship), 46
Airborne Division, 82nd, 54
Airborne Division, 101st, 34, 54
Airborne landing, behind Utah Beach, 143–144
Allen, Delmar, 196–197
Allied relations. *See* British-American cooperation
American Army Battle School, 9, 15, 153
  see also Slapton Sands; South Hams
American Naval Task Force, 43, 44
Amphibious forces, uniform of, 24–25
Amphibious Truck Company, 478th, 183
Amphibious Truck Company, 479th, 255, 258
  reunion, 259
Anvil/Dragoon invasion, 146
Applegate, Douglas, 216
Arlington, East, 161
Arnold, James, 48–49
Azalea, HMS, 68–69
  commander questioned by Don Moon, 128
  Convoy T-4 and, 71, 129–130
  failure to acknowledge E-boat danger, 76, 79, 128–129

Bailey, Emmett, 212, 213, 214
Balloons, as ship protection, 62
Baltic Surveyor, The (converted E-boat), 207

Bartholomay, Raymond, 87, 98
Barton, Raymond O., 61
Battle inoculation, 32
Bayfield, USS, 41, 73, 126
Beattie, Fred
  abandons USS *LST 507*, 88, 89, 90
  aboard USS *LST 507*, 80, 83, 85
  Convoy T-4 survivors and, 101, 104, 110
Biennial Report of the Chief of Staff of the United States Army (Marshall), 169
Bieri, Bernhard, 141
Bigot (security rating), 48
Blackawton church, and South Hams evacuation, 14
Black men
  first seen by South Hams residents, 17
  known only as Henry, 179
Blacknor Fort, 173, 174
Black soldiers, 99, 240
  return of South Hams to civilians, 156
  in construction battalions, 153
Blimp, signaling USS *LST 496*, 28
Bocage, 20
Bodyguard of Lies (Cave Brown), 186–187, 188
Body recovery, 111–112, 113–114, 115–117
Bolero (D Day buildup), 3, 16, 25, 37, 153
  see also Exercise Tiger; Slapton Sands; South Hams

Bombardment rehearsal, for D Day
 landing, 33–34, 252–253, 260–261
Bomb disposal, at Slapton Sands,
 175–176, 184
Bowden, John, 240
Bowles, Eddie, 11–12
Bradbeer, Grace, 19, 159, 163
Bradley, Omar, 60, 62
 on amphibious tank, 34–35
 annoyed at delay of Convoy T-4,
  125
 author of *A Soldier's Story*, 168
 on necessity Utah Beach landing,
  41
 on no needless loss of life, 4
 on Operation Tiger, 5
 on shortage of LSTs, 25–26
Bread
 supply to South Hams during evac-
  uation, 13
 wastage decried, 8
Breher, Charles, 112
Brind, E. J. P., on responsibility for
 Convoy T-4 losses, 147
Britannia Royal Naval Hospital, 122
British-American cooperation for D
 Day, 139–141, 142–143, 165
 Dwight D. Eisenhower on, 47–48
British attitudes toward American soldiers, 48
Brown, Jerry, 88, 101
Bruford, Barbara, 173–174
Bryant, Donald S., 219, 228
Bunting, Junior A., 259
Burial, mass, of Convoy T-4
 victims, 191–192, 193, 201, 206
 dug by Harold McAulley, 255–256,
  257–258
 mapped by Dorothy Seekings, 212
 persistence of rumors, 251–252
 with possible shore bombardment
  victims, 253–261
 pursued by Ken Small, 209–210
 unlikely, 238
Bush, George, 210
Butcher, Harry C.
 on American soldiers as "green as
  growing corn," 247

on amphibious tank, 184
anticipates German opposition to
 Exercise Fabius, 130–131
author of *My Three Years with Eisenhower*, 207
on Convoy T-4 death toll, 228, 229
on Exercise Tiger, 16
on LST losses, 125
Byron, Beverly, Exercise Tiger memorial and, 207, 208, 213

Caffrey, Eugene, 60–61
 relieved of command, 130, 168
Cambridge cemetery, list of Exercise
 Tiger victims, 223, 230
Cannon, Herbert, 17
Carney, Eugene, 65, 94, 105
 on Convoy T-4 drills, 72
 on late casualties, 110–111
Carpenter, Charles, 18
Casualty letters to families, 134–138
Cave Brown, Anthony, 186–187
Chandler, James W., 222
Chemical Decontamination Company,
 Thirty-third, 61, 78, 79
Cherbourg
 E-boat home port, 52
 naval bombardment considered, 142
Chesil Beach, 118–119, 172
Chestnut, Austin, 172
Churches in South Hams evacuation
 area, 13–15, 161–162
Churchill, Winston
 author of *Closing the Ring*, 169–
  170
 on bombing French roads and rail-
  ways, 126
 on LSTs, 23, 25
Ciccio, Joe, 137–138
Clark, Jim, 30
Clark, Tim, vii, 64, 65
 at Exercise Tiger reunion, 206
 on Convoy T-4
  departure of, 70, 71
  losses, 148–149, 166
  shelling of, 80
 Convoy T-4 survivors and, 100–
  102, 104, 123

on James Murdoch, 230
sees *20/20* coverage of Exercise
   Tiger, 200
USS *LST 507* and, 29, 30, 79, 80,
   85–86, 88, 89, 90–91
Closing the Ring (Churchill), 169–
   170
Codebook destruction on USS *LST
   507,* 86
Coles, Frank, 17
Collins, James Lawton
   on Cotentin peninsula assault, 22
   on delay of Convoy T-4, 125
   with Don P. Moon, 41–42, 144
   relieves Eugene Caffrey of com-
      mand, 130
Command organization for Exercise
   Tiger, 44–49
Communications failure, 70, 128
   and Blacknor battery, 174
Communications systems, not pre-
      pared for Exercise Tiger, 56–57,
      58–59
Compensation Act of 1939, 155
Convoy PQ 17 destruction, 45–46,
   129, 169
Convoy T-4
   attack on
      aftermath, 97, 118, 129
      alternative theories, 173–175
      location of, 174, 175
      shelled by E-boats, 80–83
      ships torpedoed, 83, 84, 86, 92–
         93
      significance of, 170
      witnessed from Slapton Sands,
         255
   blame for destruction not assign-
      able, 129, 147–148
   body recovery, 111–112
   call signal TARE-4, 248
   command structure, 67
   composition and loading of, 62,
      63–65, 232–233
   drifting bodies of victims, 237–239
   effect of debacle on officers, 139–
      143
   escort, 69, 70, 71

evasive actions, 95
ignorance of attack
   circumstances among survivors,
      165–166
   lack of escort discovered, 75
   losses of, 125–126, 134, 145, 167–
      168, 169–170
   silence imposed, 119–124, 138,
      148–150, 167
   see also Burial, mass, of Convoy
      T-4 victims; Exercise Tiger; ships
      by name
Cooke, Henry, 129
Corbyn, Jane, 194
Crapanzano, Angelo, 64, 65, 120
   aboard USS *LST 507*, 78, 79–80
   at abandonment of USS *LST 507*,
      88, 89
   Convoy T-4 survivors and, 200
   on dying soldiers, 102
   effect of Exercise Tiger on, 167,
      197–198
   on escort for Convoy T-4, 71
   on lack of recognition of Convoy
      T-4 disaster, 170
   reassigned to USS *LST 294*, 143
   rescue by Joseph McCann, 107–
      108, 110, 203
   on torpedoing of USS *LST 507*, 84,
      86
Cronin, George, on possible British-
      American rift, 139
Cronyn, John, 128–129
Cross-Channel Attack (Harrison),
   167, 225
Crusade in Europe (Eisenhower), 169

Dailey, Carl, 87, 90
Daimler-Benz engines, 52, 94
Dalrymple, James mass burial and,
   209, 210, 212
D Day
   air attack feared on fleet in British
      harbors, 62
   bombardment preceding, 33
   buildup (Bolero), 3, 16, 25, 37,
      153
   casualties, 260

D Day (*cont.*)
  date predictable from South Hams
    evacuation, 19
  exercises. *See* Landing exercises by
    name
  fortieth anniversary commemora-
    tion, 188, 201
  importance of tides, 53–54
  invasion perceived as imminent by
    Germans, 131
  invasion scale unique in military
    experience, 42
  landing plan, 32
  location and campaign of deception,
    20
  need to fix date, 141
  postponed for LST production, 26
  secrets threatened, 131–132
  see also British-American coopera-
    tion for D Day; Neptune, Opera-
    tion; Overlord, Operation
DD tank. *See* Tank, amphibious
Death, causes of, in Exercise Tiger,
  114–115
Dempsey, Jack, 17
Deniero, Louis, 96
DeVoe, Howard, 168, 216, 234, 260
Doughboy, for American soldiers,
  247–248
Doyle, John
  at Exercise Tiger reunion, 206
  as commanding officer of USS *LST*
    515, 28–29, 36, 67, 68, 71
  commended, 133
  contacted by Floyd Hicks, 203
  deserving decoration, x
  imposed silence on Convoy T-4
    losses, 120
  mistakes shelling of Convoy T-4 for
    false alarm, 82
  on rescuing Convoy T-4 survivors,
    104–105
  on responsibility of Bernard Skahill
    for Convoy T-4 losses, 148
Dragoon/Anvil invasion, 46
Drowning, as cause of death for Convoy T-4 victims, 114–115
Duck. *See* Dukw

Dukw
  Duplex Drive, 34
  name derivation, 30
  operation on beach, 33
Dunn, Victor, 83

E-boat (German torpedo boat)
  Convoy T-4 attack and, 79–82,
    173–174
  Convoy T-4 survivors and, 131–
    132
  Convoy T-4 threat, 105, 108
  danger to Exercise Tiger, 52–55, 63
  design, 52
  detected by USS *LST 496* and USS
    LST 58, 94
  dispatch decoded too late, 125
  effect on D Day invasion, 142
  mistaken for friendly craft, 92
  need to attack bases of, 141–142
  operations, 53–54
  penetration of patrol lines by, 75
  in Plymouth Harbor, 207–208
  reports of, 74–75
  and HMS *Azalea,* 128
Eckstam, Eugene, 81, 120–121
  at Exercise Tiger reunion, 206
  compiles list of Convoy T-4 survi-
    vors, viii, 200–201
  reassigned to USS *LST 391*, 143
  on USS *LST 507*, 65, 84–85, 86,
    87–88, 89, 90
Eggs (American soldier encamp-
    ments), 37
Eisenhower, Dwight D., 62, 141
  on airborne Utah Beach landing,
    143–144
  on amphibious tank, 34
  author of *Crusade in Europe*, 169
  on Bertram Ramsay, 140
  on Convoy T-4 losses, 125, 126
  decides on D Day landing area,
    32
  on families of D Day victims, 201
  on necessity of British-American
    cooperation, 47–48, 142–143
  on necessity of Utah Beach landing,
    41

plans assault on Cotentin peninsula, 21–22
as Supreme Commander, 4
Eisenhower, John Sheldon Doud, 188
Elles, Hugh, 10
Ellis, Clarence, 99
Emus, Denis, 244–246
Engineer Combat Battalion, 203rd, 253
Engineer Combat Battalion, 279th, erroneously cited on Exercise Tiger memorial, 215
Engineer Company, 440th, aboard USS *LST 507*, 224
Engineer Shore Regiment, 531st, 255
number confused with USS *LST 531*, 219
records available, 222
Equipment buildup, prior to D Day, 18
Escort recommendation for convoys, 133
Exercise Beaver, 31, 42, 53, 60
paratroop drop tested, 54
Exercise Fabius
casualties, 133
Exercise Tiger and, 56–57, 126
German opposition expected, 130–131
Exercise Fox, 31, 33, 53
Exercise Duck, i, ii, iii, 31, 51, 60
Exercise Tiger
bombardment plan, 33–34, 252–253
contributory causes to disaster, 43–49, 56–58, 65–66, 132–133
death toll, 216, 219–234, 251–252
from shore bombardment, 252–254, 260–261
and Exercise Fabius, 126
H Hour postponement for, 74, 144
history publicized, 186–191, 193–195, 226
information about, 119–124, 138, 148–150, 167, 186
landing craft use in, 33
memorial, 207, 208–210
inscription errors, 215–216
memorial ceremonies, 199, 200, 202, 213
mixed command, 43–49
number of ships participating, 73, 232–233
order in D Day exercise series, 31
overlap with Exercise Fabius, 56–58
planning for, 43–50, 54–56
possible E-boat attack on, 53
reunion, 204, 206
20/20 coverage of, 196–197, 198, 200, 203
victims included in D Day casualty toll, 260
see also Convoy T-4; ships by name

Falklands War, 53
Fedyszyn, John, 121
Fighter Squadron, 385th, 219
Fire hazard from gasoline and oil, 87, 91, 133
First Engineer Special Brigade, 60–62, 168, 255
Caffrey relieved of command of, 130
death toll, 145, 230
not on Exercise Tiger memorial, 215, 216
uniform of, 60
victims of, 205, 223, 238
Fletcher, John, 127
Force U, 126, 233
War Diary, 253
Fortescue, Lord, 10–11
Fortitude (deception campaign for D Day), 20, 35
Fourth Infantry Division, 34, 43, 73
presence at Exercise Tiger questioned, 216, 231
role to play in D Day invasion, 61
Frederick Gerald, 95, 122
Freedom of Information Act, 186
Funnies (specially altered tanks), 34, 35

Garton, Charles, 96
Geddes, George C.
    responsibility for Convoy, T-4
        losses, 128–130, 145, 147
    on U-boat and E-boat danger, 68,
        76
German intelligence, and D Day,
    131–132
Gerow, Leonard T., 62
Gill, Franklin "Scotty," 79, 80
Glennon, Thomas, 55
Gold Star Mother, 4
Graves registration units, 221–222,
    255
Greene, Ralph, x, 124, 188, 190, 194
Griffin, Joseph, 96
Grosse, Hermann "Buddie," 36, 67,
    204
Gruenther, Alfred M., 177

Haase, Tom, 201–202
Halifax, Nova Scotia, as last, North
    American Port of LST convoys,
    28
Hallett, Moses D., 55, 92, 94
    aboard USS *LST 507*, 81
    on Bernard Skahill, 67
    on extra troops aboard Convoy T-4,
        233
    possible court-martial, 132, 147
    on radio frequency for Exercise Ti-
        ger, 56, 58
    radios report of attack on Convoy
        T-4, 97
    on rescue of Convoy T-4 survivors,
        110
Hannaford, John, 157
Hardenbergh, Selby, 33
Hare, Nancy, assisting with South
    Hams evacuation, 11, 13, 18, 19
Harlander, Douglas, 64, 65
    after-action report for USS *LST
        531*, 227
    as chief surviving officer of USS
        LST 531, 133
    during torpedoing of USS *LST 531*,
        92
    on Exercise Tiger death toll, 230

hospitalization of, 121
reports loss of USS *LST 531*
    records, 220
rescue of, 112
in touch with Edward Kaska, 202
Harley Davidson motorcycle found
    buried at Heathfield, 192
Harrison, Gordon, 225
Hart, William E., on mass burial ru-
    mors, 251–252
Hawkins, HMS, Exercise Tiger shore
    bombardment by, 253–254
Hawley, George, 67
Hendrick, Elwin, 28, 69, 111, 123
    on reported quarantine of Convoy
        T-4 survivors, 123
    on responsibility for Convoy T-4
        losses, 148
Heroism disdained, 4
Herring boxes (LCTs), 24
Hewitt, Kent, 146
H Hour postponement, for Exercise
    Tiger, 74
Hicks, Floyd, viii, 107, 112, 120
    arranges Exercise Tiger reunion,
        204, 206
    sees *20/20* show on Exercise Tiger,
        203
Hiscock, Bill, 253, 254
Hoch, Eugene, 121
Hockaday, John, 236
Hoffmann, Bruce, 80, 83, 101
    drowned, 106–107
Hoffner, Barnett, 253
Holcombe, Thomas, 93, 97
Holland, William
    at abandonment of USS *LST 531*,
        93–94
    with dead man in life raft, 104
Homes, condition of, following South
    Hams occupation, 162–163
Hoppler, Wendell, 28, 78, 94
    on approaching danger of war, 38
    at Exercise Tiger reunion, 204, 206
    obtains battle logs of LSTs, 187
    on Skahill, 67, 119
Hospitalization of survivors, 121–124
Hoyt, Edwin, 253

Hypothermia
    deaths from, 98, 114
    symptoms, 102

Independent, The, 209, 210
    reports Dorothy Seekings' story,
        211
Infantrymen, training needed, 31–32
Ingersoll, Ralph, 31, 37, 167
    on Convoy T-4 survivors, 131–132
Intelligence function of landing exer-
    cises, 35–36
*Invasion of France and Germany,
    1944–1945, The* (Morison), 225
Irwin, Howard, 95

James, Geraldine, 171
Jansen, Melvin, 203
Jensen, "Swede," 107
Johnson, Leslie, 115–117
Jones, Clifford, 225–226, 227

Kaska, Albert, 202
Kaska, Edward, 202
Kennedy, Joseph, 73, 95
Kimberley, Dave, buried submarine
    and, 192–193
King, Ernest, 42, 46–47, 140
    war report, 169
Kingsbridge Gazette, 16
    on occupation of South Hams, 154,
        155–156
    on return of South Hams to civil-
        ians, 160–161, 163
Kirk, Rear Admiral, 139
    on need to attack E-boat bases, 141
    tension with Bertam Ramsay, 140,
        142
Knox, William Franklin, 117
Koch, Stanley, 179
Kown, Marvin, 103
Kuntz, William
    on Exercise Tiger memorial inscrip-
        tion, 215, 216
    on torpedoing of USS *LDT 289*, 96

Landing craft use in Exercise Tiger,
    33

Landing exercises
    deterioration in, 37–38
    intelligence function of, 35–36
    purposes, 32–33
    see also exercises by specific
        names
Landing strategy, for D Day, 32
Langford, Kathleen, mass burial story
    and, 241–242
Large Slow Target (BBC Radio
    show), ix
Large Slow Target (LST), 23
Lawson, Maurice, 176
LCT (Landing Craft, Tanks), 24
LCVP C23569, from USS *LST 289*,
    193
LXVP (Landing Craft, Vehicles and
    Personnel), 28, 86
    deployed to steer USS *LST 289*, 96
    rescuing survivors of Convoy T-4,
        103–104
Leatham, Ralph
    on British-American cooperation,
        44, 45
    on danger of E-boat attack, 53
    orders naval cover, 63, 74
    responsibility for Convoy T-4 disas-
        ter, 128, 129
    on *Scimitar*, 69
Leigh-Mallory, Trafford, 143–144
Lewin, Terence, 74
Lewis, Raban, 94, 104
Liberty magazine, 3–5
Life belts
    inflatable, as cause of death, 64,
        114
    lights, 91
Lifeboats, attempt to launch aboard
    USS *LST 507*, 86
Life rafts, 87, 89, 90, 93
    with concentric rings of survivors,
        102
Limbaugh, Lester, 258
    on witnessing attack on Convoy
        T-4, 255
Logistical Support of the Armies, 169
Longest Day, The (Ryan), 145, 260
Loom of the moon, 84

Loss of life
Exercise Tiger vs. Utah Beach assault, 145
needless, 3–5
Louis, Joe, 17
LST (Landing Ship, Tanks)
crew training needed, 33
design and function, 23–25, 29
named by initials and numbers, 24
production, 26
shortage of, 22, 25–26
transfer from Mediterranean, 141
LST 58, USS, 63, 68
abandons pantoons, 97
during shelling of Convoy T-4, 82
hunts for E-boats, 95
refuge at Chesil Beach, 118
LST 289, USS, 63, 70
crew observes burning of USS *LST 507*, 91
discipline aboard, 72
ditched LCVP, 183
no army fatalities aboard, 230
returned to port, 113, 122
survivors after war, 149, 215
torpedoed, 95–96
LST 496, USS, 63, 68, 82
conversion to hospital ship, and sinking, 179
launch and maiden jouney, 26–28, 38
refuge at Chesil Beach, 118
serial number confused with USS *LST 507*, 219, 226
survivors after war, 178–179
LST 499, USS, 63, 70, 82, 95
evading torpedo, 83
refuge at Chesil Beach, 118
LST 507, USS, 63–64, 70, 136–137, 169
abandoned, 91
death toll, 230–231
during shelling of Convoy T-4, 79–81, 82–83
number of soldiers aboard, 232, 233–234
records lost at sea, 220

serial number confused with USS *LST 496*, 219, 226
service aboard, 29–30
sinking, 98, 101
survivors of, 105, 143, 200
torpedoed, 84–85
wreck discovered, 183
LST 508, USS, misses Convoy T-4, 232–233
LST 511, 63, 68, 124–125
discipline aboard, 72
during shelling of Convoy T-4, 82
history in *Turn To*, 169
mistakenly attacked by USS *LST 496*, 97
no fatalities aboard, 230
refuge at Chesil Beach, 118
survivors after war, 143, 203
torpedoed, 96–97
LST 515, USS
as Convoy T-4 command ship, 67
crew of, 28
discipline aboard, 71–72
during shelling of Convoy T-4, 81–82
launch, 29
maiden voyage, 36–37, 38
rescue of survivors, 105, 106–107, 113, 119
veterans after war, 148, 200, 202, 204
LST 531, USS, 63, 68, 82, 169, 202
death toll, 230
number confused with 531st Engineer Shore Regiment, 219
records lost at sea, 220
survivors, 202
3206th Quartermaster Service Company aboard, 134, 230
torpedoed, 92–93
wreck discovered, 183
Luftwaffe, decline of, 52
Luscombe, Gordon, 184

McAulley, Harold, on mass burials, 206, 254–256, 257–259
McCann, Joseph, 119, 200

in contact with Angelo Crapanzano, 203
on presence of Fourth Infantry on Convoy T-4, 231
rescuing survivors of Convoy T-4, 107–109, 111
MacDonald, Charles, 221, 228
McDonald, Kendall, 184
McGarigal, John, 89, 107
McMahon, Martin, 63, 70–71, 95, 123
aboard USS *LST 289*, 70–71
Mae West (life jacket), 80
Magic Army, The (Thomas), 187
Map
of Convoy T-4 attack site, 77
of South Hams evacuation area, 7
Marshall, George C.
author of *Biennial Report of the Chief of Staff*, 169
on loss of life, 3–4
Mass burial. *See* Burial, mass, of Convoy T-4 victims
Memorial at Slapton Sands, to South Hams evacuees, 164–165, 175, 177, 185, 207
see also Exercise Tiger, memorial
Menzies, John, 79
Mettler, Harry, 96, 113, 122
commended, 133
declines to rescue USS *LST 507* survivors, 91
evading E-boat torpedos, 95
shelling of Convoy T-4 and, 81
MGBs (motor gunboats), 63
Minesweeping
of Slapton Sands, 175–176
see also Bomb disposal
Mississippi River, LST route down, 27, 30
Modeste, Charles E., 113
Montgomery, Bernard Law, 21, 22, 131–132
Moon, Don P., 84, 126
with Arthur Struble, 43–44
Exercise Tiger and, 233
breakdown over losses, 127–128, 130, 261

danger of E-boat attack, 55
distributes orders, 56
flaws in command chain, 45, 47
H Hour postponement, 74, 144, 252–253
on protection of flotilla, 73
report on losses, 133, 227
experiments with landing craft use, 33
personality and military experience, 42, 74, 144, 145, 146
proposes suspending Normandy invasion, 144
suicide, 146–147
Moore, C. L. G., 162–163
Moore, David, 91, 138, 149
Moreno, John, 74–75, 127, 147
on early troop landings at Exercise Tiger, 253
on HMS *Scimitar* mix-up, 130
Morgan, Frederick, 22
on battle inoculation of Private Snodgrass, 31
on British-American cooperation, 48
Morgan, Llewellyn V., 56, 145
Morgen, Tecwyn, 118–119
Morison, Samuel Eliot, 225
Morse, Leslie, 79, 104, 121
Motley, Robert, 238, 261
Motor gunboat (MGB), 63
Motor torpedo boat (MTB), 63, 119
Moysey, Percy, 242
Murdoch, James, 87
on Fourth Infantry Division aboard USS *LST 507*, 231–232
USS *LST 507* and, 133
death toll, 230
Mustard gas, feared for Normandy invasion, 61
Myers, Charles J., 205

Nagata, Sally, 186
Neptune: Training, Mounting, The Artificial Ports, 226
Neptune, Operation, 35–36, 37
need for ships, 142
planning for, 143

Neptune, Operation (*cont.*)
  see also D Day; Overlord, Operation
Newport News, first American LST constructed at, 210
News blackout. *See* Silence imposed about Convoy T-4 losses
Nickson, Albert, 110, 121
  with Convoy T-4 survivors in sea, 101
  USS *LST 507* and, 80, 85, 86
Normandy
  beach composition 33
  similarity to South Hams, 19–20
Normandy American Military Cemetery and Memorial, 259
Normandy invasion. *See* D Day; Neptune, Operation; Overlord, Operation
Northern Reward, HMS, 68

Obedient, HMS, 111
  shore bombardment by, 235, 254
Observers, at Exercise Tiger, 62
O'Connell, William P., 219
Omaha Beach landing rehearsal, 31
Onslow, HMS, 112, 121
Overlord, Operation, 35, 37, 126
  command structure, 44
  naval operational orders, 57
  see also D Day; Neptune, Operation

Panter, Ed, 85, 86
Patton, George S., 4
Perkin, Julian
  on rescuing survivors of Convoy T-4, 111
  service aboard HMS *Obedient*, 235–236, 254
  on shore bombardment casualties, 254
Perry, John A., 94, 167
Plymouth War Order, 45
Pointe du Hoc assault, 259–260
Pontoons, to bridge Slapton Ley, 63, 97
Porado, Jeanne, vii
Posttraumatic stress disorder, 166, 167

Pratt, Edward, 243–246
Premonition of doom, by Convoy T-4 participant, 72–73
Propaganda scheme, and Exercise Fabius, 131
Proton-magnetometer, 193

Quartermaster Railhead Company, 557th, 183
Quartermaster Registration Company, 65th, 212
Quartermaster Service Company, 3206th, 134, 137
Quartermaster Truck Company, 3891st, aboard USS *LST 507*, 224

Radio frequencies, for Convoy T-4, 56, 58–59, 129, 132
Ragusa, Paul, 100
Ramsey, Bertram, 62
  on Convoy T-4 losses, 126
  on E-boat bases, 141–142
  on E-boat danger, 55, 63
  Operation Overlord and, 57
  and planning for D Day, 57–58, 140–141
  planning for invasion operations, 57, 58
Ranger Battalion, Second, 259–260
Rats, in South Hams, 157, 163
Rayner, Ralph, 177
  South Hams evacuation and, 6 9–10, 15, 155–156
Reckord, William, 87, 138
Red Cross, 10
Renshaw, A. B., 200
Rescue delay, as cause of deaths for Convoy T-4, 114
Rhino (method of digging through coastal brush), 20–21
Richardson, M. T., 74
Rodman, E. Dale, vii, 61, 63, 79
  aboard USS *LST 507*, 78–79, 81
  compiles list of Exercise Tiger victims, 222–223
  with Convoy T-4 survivors on LCVP, 103

during fire aboard USS *LST 507*, 85
  on errors on Exercise Tiger memorial, 216
  on Exercise Tiger death toll, 225, 229
  on number of soldiers aboard USS *LST 507*, 231, 234
  rescue, 112
Roop, David, 108
Roosevelt, Franklin D, faces LST shortage, 26
Rosiek, Joseph, 79, 88, 112
Rouggley, Stella, 196–197
  at Exercise Tiger memorial dedication, 213–214
  on mass burial, 205, 211
Royal Sands Hotel, 34, 184
Royal Society for the Prevention of Cruelty of Animals, 10, 12
Rubin, Emanuel "Manny"
  at Slapton Sands memorial Sherman tank, 204
  concern over Sherman tank salvage, 198
  effects of Exercise Tiger on, 178–180
  on presence of infantry on USS *LST 496*, 231
  reveals story of Exercise Tiger, 194–195
  as signalman, 26
  views E-boat in Plymouth Harbor, 207–208
  witnesses burning of USS *LST 531*, 91, 92
  wounded aboard USS *LST 496*, 97
Rutherford, William
  at abandonment of USS *LST 507*, 86, 87, 88, 89
  with survivors in sea, 98, 100
Ryan, Cornelius, 260

Safro, Nola, 194, 200
Saladin, HMS, 66, 75, 79
  not present at E-boat attack, 76
  rescue of survivors, 105–106
Sandor, Joseph, on bodies in water, 125

Sands of Silence (documentary), 190, 194
Saucier, Henry Q., 109
Saunders, Doris, 172
Sausages (staging areas), 37
Schnellboote. See E-boat
Schrawder, Henry, 64, 92, 93, 143
Schwechheimer, Conrad, 135–136
Scimitar, HMS
  as Convoy T-4 escort, 60–70, 75, 76, 130
  rammed, 66
Scott, Kenneth, 100
Sea temperature, 73
Seekings, Dorothy (Dorothy Trowt), 13, 193–194, 197, 205, 209
  mass burial story, 191–192, 211–212, 239–241
  military injunctions on secrecy and, 258
SHAEF (Supreme Headquarters Allied Expeditionary Force), 25, 122
  forbids questioning of Convoy T-4 survivors, 124
Shea, John, 63, 69
Sherman tank. *See* Tank, amphibious
Shipyards, in American Midwest, 26, 28
Sickley, Adelbert, 103, 105–106, 121–122
Siebert, Ray, 230
Signal Construction Battalion, Thirty-fifth, 224
  death toll, 230
Silence imposed about Convoy T-4 losses, 119–124, 138, 148–150, 167
Skahill, Bernard Joesph, 97
  as commander of Convoy T-4, 67–68, 70, 81
  on death toll from USS *LST 531*, 230
  failure to make escort liaison for Convoy T-4, 55
  possible court-martial, 132
  on rescuing survivors, 104–105, 110
  resentment against, 119

Skahill, Bernard Joesph (*cont.*)
  responsibility for Convoy T-4
    losses, 147–148
  USS *LST 507* and, 92, 133
Skate, HMS, 66
Slapton Assault Training Area, 30
Slapton Sands, 60
  as bombardment target, 34
  Convoy T-4 attack site and, 236
  division into Red Beach and White
    Beach, 33
  ecology and environment, 178
  freak tides, 181
  memorial at. *See* Exercise Tiger,
    memorial; Memorial at Slapton
    Sands
  minesweeping of, 175–176
  prepared for Operation Tiger, 43
  reporters at, 198
  similarity to Utah beach, 21–22
  see also Burial, mass, of Convoy
    T-4 victims; South Hams
Small, Kenneth, 181–183
  Exercise Tiger memorial and, 212–
    213, 215, 216
  on mass burial of Convoy T-4 vic-
    tims, 205, 207, 208–209, 209,
    211
  promotes salvage of sunken tank,
    184, 185–186, 189, 198–199
  tribute to, by Joseph McCann, 214
Smith, Bedell, 126
Soldier's Story, A (Bradley), 168
South Hams
  American soldiers at, 14–15, 16–
    17, 18, 30
  bitterness among residents, 235
  compensation for evacuated resi-
    dents, 155–156
  evacuation, 10–16, 19, 30
  geography and economy, 6–8
  requisitioned for training area, 9
  return to civilians, 156–164
  reunion of evacuees, 189, 199–200
  similarity to Normandy, 19–20
  traces remaining of American pres-
    ence, 171
  see also American Army Battle

School; Exercise Tiger, memo-
    rial; Slapton Sands
Spam, 163
Staging areas, for Operations Neptune
    and Overlord, 37
Star, Alan, 87, 100
Stark, H. R., responsibility for Con-
    voy T-4 losses, 148
Station Hospital, 228th, 188
  receives Convoy T-4 survivors,
    124
Station Hospital, 316th, 123, 189
Steer, Tony, 182–183
Stokely Barton, 235–236
Stout, Stanley, 103–104
Strete, 157–158
Struble, Arthur, 43–44, 127
Submarine danger in Atlantic, 38
Suesse, Ralph A., 112
Survivors
  clinging to life rafts, 102
  conflicts among, 99
  rescue of, 91, 130
    by E-boats, possible, 131–132
    by HMS *Saladin,* 105–106
    by LCVPs, 103–104
    by USS *LST 515,* 106–111
    and convoy policy, 104–105
Survivor's leave denied, 120, 143
Sutton, HMS, 115–116
Swarts, Lieutenant, 83, 85
  with Convoy T-4 survivors in wa-
    ter, 101
  dead of hypothermia, 109–110

Taft, Alma, 190, 192, 194, 198
  promotes Exercise Tiger memorial,
    201
Taft, William Howard, 201, 208, 213
Tanatside, HMS, 75
Tank, amphibious, 34–35, 144–145
  landing and loss at Exercise Tiger,
    74
  salvage of, 184, 185–186, 189,
    198–199
  waterproofing, 35
  wreck off Slapton Sands, 183
Tank Battalion, 70th, 204–205

mistakenly included on Exercise Tiger memorial, 215–216

Tank Destroyer Battalion, 893rd, 17

Tank, Sherman, as Exercise Tiger memorial, 199–200, 201, 203, 204, 213

Tedder, Arthur, 62

Thomas, Leslie, 187, 192

Tide-AM-125, USS, 112, 113

Tides
  at Slapton Sands, 181
  importance in D Day invasion, 53–54
  and possible transport of bodies from Convoy T-4, 236

Tirpitz (German battleship), 46

Tope, Nolan, 242

Torpedo boat, German. *See* E-boat

Towner, John, on deaths from shore bombardment, 253–254

Tracer coloring, 52, 81

Tragic Secret of Slapton Sands, The. *See* 20/20

Trainor, Joseph, burial of, 256–257, 259, 261

Trombold, Walter, ix

Troop buildup, prior to D Day, 3, 17, 18

Trowt, Dorothy. *See* Seekings, Dorothy

Turn To, 169

TVS television station, 189–190

20/20, Exercise Tiger story, x, 194, 196–197, 198, 200, 203

U-boat fleet decline, 52

Ultra (intercept and decoding operation), on E-boat
  intelligence from Convoy T-4 attack, 132

United States Army in World WAr II, The, 167–168

United States LST Association, 210

Unsworth, Harry, 188–189, 192–193, 193

U.S. Seventh Corps, 22, 41

Utah beach, similarity in Slapton Sands, 21–22

Utah Beach landing
  command of, 41
  loss of life in, 145
  planned by Eisenhower, 54, 143–144
  rehearsal. *See* Exercise Tiger
  use of amphibious tanks at, 144–145
  vital to Normandy invasion, 41, 143–144

Victor, Arthur, viii, 120, 121
  attempts to free life raft, 86
  burning of USS *LST 531*, 85, 93
  on Convoy T-4 survivors, 123
  with Convoy T-4 survivors in sea, 98, 99–100, 104
  during shellling of Convoy T-4, 81, 82
  rescued, 106, 109
  USS *LST 507* and, 65, 72, 231
    abandonment of, 87, 88–89, 90, 91
    torpedoing of, 84

Wachter, John, 95, 97

Wagner, Howard, 196–197, 205

Wahlberg, Brent, 94

Walters-Symons, Tom, 160

Wampler, Atlee, Jr., 204–205, 207
  on Exercise Tiger memorial, 215

War Powers Act, 1939 (British), 10

Weinberger, Caspar, 208

Western Naval Task Force (American Naval Task Force), 43, 44

Wheat, referred to as soldiers, 246–247

Whiteley, Peter, 213

Whitely, Herbert, 164, 178

Wills, Godfrey, 12, 13

Wilson, J. B., 105

Wintle, Frank, 190

Wohlbach, Marvin, 124, 143

Women's Voluntary Service, 10, 12

Younger, George, 213